# THE LIFE AND WORKS OF MENCIUS

## By MENCIUS

## Translated by JAMES LEGGE

The Life and Works of Mencius
By Mencius
Translated by James Legge

Print ISBN 13: 978-1-4209-7891-9
eBook ISBN 13: 978-1-4209-8026-4

Cover Image: a detail of "Mencius preaching revolution", European School, c. 19th century (chromolitho) / © Look and Learn / Bridgeman Images.

Please visit *www.digireads.com*

# CONTENTS

## PROLEGOMENA.

## THE WORKS OF MENCIUS.

*Prolegomena.*

## CHAPTER I. OF THE WORKS OF MENCIUS.

### SECTION I. THEIR RECOGNITION UNDER THE HAN DYNASTY, AND BEFORE IT.

1. IN the third of the catalogues of Lĕw Hin,[1] containing a list of the Works of Scholars which had been collected up to his time (about A.D. 1), and in the first subdivision, devoted to authors of the classical or orthodox School, we have the entry—"The Works of Mencius, in eleven Books." At that date, therefore, Mencius' writings were known and registered as a part of the literature of China.

2. A hundred years before Hin, we have the testimony of the historian Sze-ma Ts'ëen. In the seventy-fourth Book of his "Historical Records," there is a brief memoir of Mencius, where he says that the philosopher, having withdrawn into private life, "with his disciples, Wan Chang and others, prefaced the *She* and the *Shoo,* unfolded the views of Confucius, and made 'The Works of Mencius, in seven Books.'"

The discrepancy that appears between these testimonies, in regard to the number of the Books which went by the common name of Mencius, will be considered in the sequel. In the mean while it is shown that the writings of Mencius were recognized by scholars a hundred years before the Christian era, which takes us back to little more than a century and a half from the date assigned to his death.

3. Among writers of the Han dynasty earlier than Sze-ma Ts'ëen, there were Han Ying, and Tung Chung-shoo, contemporaries, in the reigns of the emperors Wăn, King, and Woo, (B.C. 178-86). Portions of their Works remain, and in them are found quotations from Mencius. Later than these there were Yang Hëung (B.C. 53-A.D. 18), who wrote a commentary on Mencius, which was existing under the Sung dynasty, and Wang Ch'ung (died about A.D. 100), who left a chapter of animadversions on our philosopher, which still exists.

4. But we find references to Mencius and his Works anterior to the dynasty of Han. Between him and the rise of the Ts'in dynasty flourished the philosopher Seun K'ing. of whose writings enough is still preserved to form a large volume. By many he is regarded as the ablest of all the followers of Confucius. He several times makes mention of Mencius, and one of his most important chapters,—"That Human Nature is Evil," seems to have been written expressly against Mencius' doctrine of its goodness. He quotes his arguments, and

---

[1] See Vol. I., Proleg., pp. 4, 5.

endeavours to set them aside.

5. I have used the term *recognition* in the heading of this section, because the scholars of the Han dynasty do not seem to have had any trouble in forming or settling the text of Mencius such as we have seen they had with the Confucian Analects.

And here a statement made by Chaou K'e, whose labors upon our philosopher I shall notice in the next section, deserves to be considered. He says:—"When Ts'in sought by its fires to destroy the classical books, and put the scholars to death in pits, there was an end of the School of Mencius. His Works, however, were included under the common name of 'Philosophical,' and so the tablets containing them escaped destruction." Ma Twan-lin does not hesitate to say that the statement is incorrect;[2] and it seems strange that Mencius should have been exempted from the sweep of a measure intended to extinguish the memory of the most ancient and illustrious sovereigns of China and of their principles. But the same thing is affirmed in regard to the writings of at least one other author of antiquity, the philosopher Yuh; and the frequent quotations of Mencius by Han Ying and Tung Chung-shoo, indicating that his Works were a complete collection in their times, give some confirmation to K'e's account.

On the whole, the evidence seems rather to preponderate in its favor. Mencius did not obtain his place as "a classic" till long after the time of the Ts'in dynasty; and though the infuriate emperor would doubtless have given special orders to destroy his writings, if his attention had been called to them, we can easily conceive their being overlooked, and escaping with a mass of others which were not considered dangerous to the new rule.

6. Another statement of Chaou K'e shows that the Works of Mencius, once recognized under the Han dynasty, were for a time at least kept with a watchful care. He says that, in the reign of the emperor Hëaou-wăn (B.C. 178-154), "the Lun-yu, the Hëaou-king, Mencius, and the Urh-ya were all put under the care of a Board of 'Great Scholars,' which was subsequently done away with, only, 'The Five King' being left under such guardianship." Choo He has observed that the Books of the Han dynasty supply no evidence of such a Board; but its existence may be inferred from a letter of Lëw Hin, complaining of the supineness with which the scholars seconded his quest of the scattered monuments of literature. He says:—"Under the emperor Hëaou-wăn, the Shoo-king reappeared, and the She-king began to sprout and bud afresh. Throughout the empire, a multitude of books were continually making their appearance, and among them the Records and Sayings of all the Philosophers, which likewise had their place assigned to them in the Courts of Learning, and a Board of Great Scholars appointed to

---

[2]She his great work, Bk clxxxiv., upon Mencius.

their charge."[3]

As the Board of Great Scholars in charge of the Five King was instituted B.C. 135, we may suppose that the previous arrangement hardly lasted half a century. That it did exist for a time, however, shows the value set upon the writings of Mencius, and confirms the point which I have sought to set forth in this section,—that there were Works of Mencius current in China before the Han dynasty, and which were eagerly recognized and cherished by the scholars under it, who had it in charge to collect the ancient literary productions of their country.

## SECTION II. CHAOU K'E AND HIS LABORS UPON MENCIUS.

1. IT has been shown that the Works of Mencius were sufficiently well known from nearly the beginning of the Han dynasty; but its more distinguished scholars do not seem to have devoted themselves to their study and elucidation. The classics proper claimed their first attention. There was much labor to be done in collecting and collating the fragments of them; and to unfold their meaning was the chief duty of every one who thought himself equal to the task. Mencius was but one of the literati, a scholar like themselves. He could wait. We must come down to the second century of the Christian era to find the first great commentary on his writings.

In the Prolegomena to the Confucian Analects, Section i. 7, I have spoken of Ch'ing Heuen or Ch'ing K'ang-shing, who died at the age of 74 some time between A.D. 190-220, after having commented on every ancient classical book. It is said by some[4] that he embraced the Works of Mencius in his labors. If he did so, which to me is very doubtful, the result has not come down to posterity. To give to our philosopher such a treatment as he deserved, and compose a commentary that should descend to the latest posterity, was the Work of Chaou K'e.

2. K'e was born A.D. 108. His father was a censor about the court of the emperor Hĕaou-gan, and gave him the name of Kĕa, which he afterwards changed into K'e for the purpose of concealment, changing also his original designation of T'ae-k'ing into Pin-k'ing. It was his boast that he could trace his descent from the emperor Chuen-hĕuh, B.C. 2510.

---

[3]See the same work, Bk clxxiv. pp. 9, 10.

[4] In the "Books of the Suy dynasty" (A.D. 589-617), Bk xxxix., we find that there were then in the national Repositories three Works on Mencius,—Chaou K'e's, one by Ch'ing Heuen, and one by Lĕw He also a scholar of Han, but probably not earlier than Chaou K'e. The same Works were existing under the T'ang dynasty (624-907);—see the "Books of T'ang," Bk. xlix. By the rise of the Sung dynasty (A.D. 975), however, the two last were both lost. The entries in the Records of Suy and T'ang would seem to prove that Ch'ing Heuen had written on Mencius, but in the sketches of his life which I have consulted,—and that in the "Books of the After Han dynasty" must be the basis of all the rest,—there is no mention made of his having done so.

In his youth K'e was distinguished for his intelligence and diligent study of the classics. He married a niece of the celebrated scholar and statesman Ma Yung, but bore himself proudly towards him and her other relatives. A stern independence and hatred of the sycophancy of the times were from the first characteristic of him, and proved the source of many troubles.

When he was over thirty, K'e was attacked with some severe and lingering illness, in consequence of which he lay upon his bed for seven years. At one time, thinking he was near his end, he addressed a nephew who was with him in the following terms:—"Born a man into the world, in retirement I have not displayed the principles exemplified on mount Ke,[5] nor in office achieved the merit of E and Leu.[6] Heaven has not granted me such distinction. What more shall I say? Set up a round stone before my grave, and engrave on it the inscription,—'Here lies a recluse of Han, by surname Chaou, and by name Kĕa. He had the will, but not the opportunity. Such was his fate. Alas!'"

Contrary to expectation, K'e recovered, and in A.D. 154 we find him again engaged in public life, but in four years he is flying into obscurity under a feigned name, to escape the resentment of T'ang Hang, one of the principal ministers, and of his partizans. He saved his life, but his family and relatives fell victims to the vengeance of his enemies, and for some time he wandered about the country of the Kĕang and Hwae, or among the mountains and by the seacoast on the north of the present Shan-tung. One day, as he was selling cakes in a market-place, his noble presence attracted the attention of Sun Ts'ung, a young gentleman of Gan-k'ĕw, who was passing by in a carriage, and to him, on being questioned, he made known his history. This proved a fortunate rencontre for him. Sun Ts'ung took him home, and kept him for several years concealed somewhere, "in the centre of a double wall." And now it was that he solaced his hard lot with literary studies. He wooed the muse in twenty-three poetical compositions, which he called "Songs of Adversity," and achieved his commentary on Mencius.

On the fall of the T'ang faction, when a political amnesty was proclaimed, K'e emerged from his friendly confinement, and was employed in important offices, but only to fall a victim again to the intrigues of the time. The first year of the emperor Ling, A.D. 168, was the commencement of an imprisonment which lasted more than ten years; but nothing could crush his elasticity, or daunt his perseverance. In 185, when he had nearly reached fourscore, he was active as ever in the field of political strife, and wrought loyally to sustain the fortunes

---

[5] It was to mount Ke that two ancient worthies are said to have withdrawn, when Yaou wished to promote them to honor.

[6] These are the well-known E Yin and T'ae-kung Wang, ancestor of the lords of Ts'e.

of the falling dynasty. He died at last in A.D. 201, in King-chow, whither he had gone on a mission in behalf of his imperial master. Before his death, he had a tomb prepared for himself, which was long shown, or pretended to be shown, in what is now the district city of Keang-ling in the department of King-chow in Hoo-pih.

3. From the above account of Chaou K'e it will be seen that his commentary on Mencius was prepared under great disadvantages. That he, a fugitive and in such close hiding, should have been able to produce a work such as it is shows the extent of his reading and acquirements in early days. I have said so much about him, because his name should be added to the long roll of illustrious men who have found comfort in sore adversity from the pursuits of literature and philosophy. As to his mode of dealing with his subject, it will be sufficient to give his own account:—

"I wished to set my mind on some literary work, by which I might be assisted to the government of my thoughts, and forget the approach of old age. But the six classics had all been explained and carefully elucidated by previous scholars. Of all the orthodox school there was only Mencius, wide and deep, minute and exquisite, yet obscure at times and hard to see through, who seemed to me to deserve to be properly ordered and digested. Upon this I brought forth whatever I had learned, collected testimonies from the classics and other books, and divided my author into chapters and sentences. My annotations are given along with the original text, and of every chapter I have separately indicated the scope. The Books I have divided into two Parts, the first and second, making in all fourteen sections.

"On the whole, with regard to my labor, I do not venture to think that it speaks the man of mark, but, as a gift to the learner, it may dispel some doubts and resolve perplexities. It is not for me, however, to pronounce on its excellencies or defects. Let men of discernment who come after me observe its errors and omissions and correct them;—that will be a good service."

## SECTION III. OTHER COMMENTATORS.

1. ALL the commentaries on Mencius made prior to the Sung dynasty (A.D. 975) having perished, excepting that of Chaou K'e, I will not therefore make an attempt to enumerate them particularly. Only three names deserve to be mentioned, as frequent reference is made to them in Critical Introductions to our philosopher. They were all of the T'ang dynasty, extending, if we embrace in it what is called "The after T'ang," from A.D. 624 to 936. The first is that of Luh Shen-king, who declined to adopt Chaou K'e's division of the text into fourteen sections, and many of whose interpretations, differing from those of the older authority, have been received into the now standard commentary

of Choo He. The other two names are those of Chang Yih and Ting Kung-choh, whose principal object was to determine the sounds and tones of characters about which there could be dispute. All that we know of their views is from the works of Sun Shih and Choo He, who have many references to them in their notes.

2. During the Sung dynasty, the commentators on Mencius were a multitude, but it is only necessary that I speak of two.

The most distinguished scholar of the early reigns was Sun Shih, who is now generally alluded to by his posthumous or honorary epithet of "The Illustrious Duke." We find him high in favor and reputation in the time of T'ae-tsung (977-997), Chin-tsung (998-1022), and Jin-tsung (1023-1063). By imperial command, in association with several other officers, he prepared a work in two parts under the title of "The Sounds and Meaning of Mencius," and presented it to the court. Occasion was taken from this for a strange imposture. In the edition of "The Thirteen King," Mencius always appears with "The Commentary of Chaou K'e" and "The Correct Meaning of Sun Shih." Under the Sung dynasty, what were called "correct meanings" were made for most of the classics. They are commentaries and annotations on the principal commentator, who is considered as the expounder of the classic, the author not hesitating, however, to indicate any peculiar views of his own. The genuineness of Shih's "Correct Meaning of Mencius" has been questioned by few, but there seems to be no doubt of its being really a forgery, at the same time that it contains the substance of the true Work of "the Illustrious Duke," so far as that embraced the meaning of Mencius and of Chaou K'e. The account of it given in the preface to "An Examination of the Text in the Commentary and Annotations on Mencius," by Yuen Yuen of the present dynasty, is—"Sun Shih himself made no 'Correct Meaning;' but some one—I know not who—supposing that his Work was really of that character, and that there were many things in the commentary which were not explained, and passages also of an unsatisfactory nature, he transcribed the whole of Shih's Work on 'The Sounds and Meaning;' and having interpolated some words of his own, published it under the title of 'The Annotations of Sun Shih.' He was the same person who is styled by Choo He 'A scholar of Shaou-woo.'"

In the 12th century Choo He appeared upon the stage, and entered into the labors of all his predecessors. He published one Work separately upon Mencius, and two upon Mencius and the Confucian Analects. The second of these,—"Collected Comments on the Analects and Mencius," is now the standard authority on the subject, and has been the test of orthodoxy and scholarship in the literary examinations since A.D. 1315.

3. Under the present dynasty two important contributions have been made to the study of Mencius. They are both published in the

"Explanations of the Classics under the Imperial dynasty of Ts'ing."[7]
The former, bearing the title of "An Examination of the Text in the
Commentary and Annotations on Mencius," forms the sections from
1039 to 1054. It is by Yuen Yuen, the Governor-general under whose
auspices that compilation was published. Its simple aim is to establish
the true reading by a collation of the oldest and best manuscripts and
editions, and of the remains of a series of stone tablets containing the
text of Mencius, which were prepared in the reign of Kaou-tsung (A.D.
1128-1162), and are now existing in the Examination Hall of Hang-
chow. The second Work, which is still more important, is embraced in
the sections 1117-1146. Its title is—"The Correct Meaning of Mencius,
by Tscaou Seun, a *Keujin* of Keang-too." It is intended to be such a
Work as Sun Shih would have produced, had he really made what has
been so long current in the world under his name; and is really
valuable.

SECTION IV. INTEGRITY; AUTHORSHIP; AND
RECEPTION AMONG THE CLASSICAL BOOKS.

1. WE have seen how the Works of Mencius were catalogued by
Lëw Hin as being in "eleven Books," while a century earlier Sze-ma
Ts'ëen referred to them as consisting only of "seven." The question has
very much vexed Chinese scholars whether there ever really were four
additional Books of Mencius which have been lost.

2. Chaou K'e says in his preface:—"There likewise are four
additional Books, entitled 'A Discussion of the Goodness of Man's
Nature,' 'An Explanation of Terms,' 'The Classic of Filial Piety,' and
'The Practice of Government.' But neither breadth nor depth marks
their composition. It is not like that of the seven acknowledged Books.
It may be judged they are not really the production of Mencius, but
have been palmed upon the world by some subsequent imitator of
him." As the four Books in question are lost, and only a very few
quotations from Mencius, that are not found in his Works which we
have, can be fished up from ancient authors, our best plan is to
acquiesce in the conclusion of Chaou K'e. The specification of "Seven
Books," by Sze-ma Ts'ëen is an important corroboration of it. In the
two centuries preceding our era the four Books whose titles are given
by him may have been made and published under the name of Mencius,
and Hin would only do his duty in including them in his catalogue,
unless their falsehood was generally acknowledged. K'e, devoting
himself to the study of our author, and satisfied from internal evidence
that they were not his, only did his duty in rejecting them. There is no
evidence that his decision was called in question by any scholar of the

---

[7] See Vol. I., Proleg., p. 21.

Han or the dynasties immediately following, when we may suppose that the Books were still in existence.

The author of "Supplemental Observations on the Four Books,"[8] says upon this subject:—"'It would be better to be without books than to give entire credit to them;'[9]—this is the rule for reading ancient books laid down by Mencius himself, and the rule for us after men in reading about what purport to be lost books of his. The seven Books we have 'comprehend [the doctrine] of heaven and earth, examine and set forth ten thousand topics, discuss the subjects of benevolence and righteousness, reason and virtue, the nature [of man] and the decrees [of Heaven], misery and happiness.'[10] Brilliantly are these things treated of, in a way far beyond what any disciple of Kung-sun Ch'ow or Wan Chang could have attained to. What is the use of disputing about other matters? Ho Sheh has his 'Expurgated Mencius,' but Mencius cannot be expurgated. Lin Kin-sze has his 'Continuation of Mencius,' but Mencius needs no continuation. I venture to say—*Besides the Seven Books there were no other Works of Mencius.*"

3. On the authorship of the Works of Mencius, Sze-ma Ts'ëen and Chaou K'e are agreed. They say that Mencius composed the seven Books himself, and yet that he did so along with certain of his disciples. The words of the latter are:—"He withdrew from public life, collected and digested the conversations which he had had with his distinguished disciples, Kung-sun Ch'ow, Wan Chang, and others, on the difficulties and doubts which they had expressed, and also compiled himself his deliverances as *ex cathedra* ;—and so published the Seven Books of his writings."

This view of the authorship seems to have been first called in question by Han Yu, commonly referred to as "Han, the Duke of Literature," a famous scholar of the eighth century (A.D. 768-824), under the T'ang dynasty, who expressed himself in the following terms:—"The books of Mencius were not published by himself. After his death, his disciples, Wan Chang and Kung-sun Ch'ow, in communication with each other, recorded the words of Mencius."

4. If we wish to adjudicate in the matter, we find that we have a difficult task in hand. One thing is plain,—the book is not the work of many hands like the Confucian Analects. "If we look at the style of the composition," says Choo He, "it is as if the whole were melted together, and not composed by joining piece to piece." This language is too strong, but there is a degree of truth and force in it. No principle of chronology guided the arrangement of the different parts, and a foreigner may be pardoned if now and then the "pearls" seem to him

---

[8] See Vol. I., Proleg., larger Work, p. 132.

[9] Mencius, VII. Pt II. iii.

[10] This is the language of Chaou K'e.

"at random strung;" yet the collection is characterized by a uniformity of style, and an endeavour in the separate Books to preserve a unity of matter. This consideration, however, is not enough to decide the question. Such as the work is, we can conceive it proceeding either from Mencius himself, or from the labors of a few of his disciples engaged on it in concert.

The author of the "Topography of the Four Books"[11] has this argument to show that the works of Mencius are by Mencius himself:—"The Confucian Analects," he says, "were made by the disciples, and therefore they record minutely the appearance and manners of the sage. But the seven Books were made by Mencius himself, and therefore we have nothing in them excepting the words and public movements of the philosopher." This peculiarity is certainly consonant with the hypothesis of Mencius' own authorship, and so far may dispose us to adopt it.

On the other hand, as the princes of Mencius' time to whom any reference is made are always mentioned by the honorary epithets conferred on them after their death, it is argued that those at least must have been introduced by his disciples. There are many passages, again, which savour more of a disciple or other narrator than of the philosopher himself. There is, for instance, the commencing sentences of Book III. Pt I.:—"When the Duke Wăn of T'ăng was crown-prince, having to go to Ts'oo, he went by way of Sung, and visited Mencius (lit., *the philosopher Măng*). Mencius discoursed to him how the nature of man is good, and when speaking, always made laudatory reference to Yaou and Shun. When the crown-prince was returning from Ts'oo, he again visited Mencius. Mencius said to him, 'Prince, do you doubt my words? The path is one, and only one.'"

5. Perhaps the truth after all is as the thing is stated by Sze-ma Ts'ĕen,—that Mencius, *along with some of his disciples,* compiled and composed the Work. It would be in their hands and under their guardianship after his death, and they may have made some slight alterations, to prepare it, as we should say, for the press. Yet allowing this, there is nothing to prevent us from accepting the sayings and doings as those of Mencius, guaranteed by himself.

6. It now only remains here that I refer to the reception of Mencius' Works among the Classics. We have seen how they were not admitted by Lĕw Hin into his catalogue of classical works. Mencius was then only one of the many scholars or philosophers of the orthodox school. The same classification obtains in the books of the Suy and T'ang dynasties; and in fact it was only under the dynasty of Sung that the works of Mencius and the Confucian Analects were authoritatively ranked together. The first explicitly to proclaim this honor as due to our

---

[11] See Vol. I., Proleg., larger Work, p. 132.

philosopher was Ch'in Chih-chae,[12] whose words are—"Since the time when Han, the Duke of Literature, delivered his eulogium, 'Confucius handed [the scheme of doctrine] to Mencius, on whose death the line of transmission was interrupted,'[13] the scholars of the empire have all associated Confucius and Mencius together. The Books of Mencius are certainly superior to those of Seun and Yang, and others who have followed them. Their productions are not to be spoken of in the same day with his." Choo He adopted the same estimate of Mencius, and by his "Collected Comments" on him and the Analects bound the two sages together in a union which the government of China, in the several dynasties which have succeeded, has with one temporary exception approved and confirmed.

## CHAPTER II. MENCIUS AND HIS OPINIONS.

### SECTION I. LIFE OF MENCIUS.

1. THE materials for a Memoir of Mencius are very scanty. The birth and principal incidents of Confucius' life are duly chronicled in the various annotated editions of the Ch'un Ts'ëw, and in Sze-ma Ts'ëen. It is not so in the case of Mencius. Ts'ëen's account of him is contained in half a dozen columns which are without a single date. That in the "Cyclopædia of Surnames" only covers half a page. Chaou K'e is more particular in regard to the early years of his subject, but he is equally indefinite. Our chief informants are K'ung Foo, and Lëw Hëang in his "Record of Note-worthy Women," but what we find in them has more the character of legend than history.

It is not till we come to the pages of Mencius himself that we are treading on any certain ground. They give the principal incidents of his public life, extending over about twenty-four years. We learn from them that in the course of that time he was in such and such places, and gave expression to such and such opinions; but where he went first and where he went last, it is next to impossible to determine. I have carefully examined three attempts, made by competent scholars of the present dynasty, to construct a Harmony that shall reconcile the

---

[12] The name and the account I take from the "Supplemental Observations on the Four Books," Art. L on Mencius. Chih, I apprehend, is a misprint for Che, the individual referred to being probably Ch'in Foo-leang, a great scholar and officer of the 12th century, known also by the designations of Keun-keu and Che-chae.

[13] This eulogy of Han Yu is to be found subjoined to the brief introduction in the common editions of Mencius. The whole of the passage there quoted is:—"Yaou handed [the scheme of doctrine] down to Shun: Shun handed it to Yu; Yu to T'ang; T'ang to Wăn, Woo, and the Duke of Chow; Wăn, Woo, and the Duke of Chow to Confucius; and Confucius to Mencius, on whose death there was no farther transmission of it. In Seun and Yang there are snatches of it, but without a nice discrimination: they talk about it, but without a definite particularity."

statements of the "Seven Books" with the current chronologies of the time, and do not see my way to adopt entirely the conclusions of any one of them.[14] The value of the Books lies in the record which they furnish of Mencius' sentiments, and the lessons which these supply for the regulation of individual conduct and national policy. It is of little importance that we should be able to lay them down in the strict order of time.

With Mencius' withdrawal from public life, all traces of him disappear. All that is said of him is that he spent his latter years along with his disciples in the preparation and publication of his Works.

From this paragraph it will be seen that there is not much to be said in this section. I shall relate, first, what is reported of the early years and training of our philosopher, and then look at him as he comes before us in his own pages, in the full maturity of his character and powers.

2. Mencius is the latinized form of Măng-tsze, "The philosopher Măng." His surname thus connects him with the Măng or Măng-sun family, one of the three great Houses of Loo, whose usurpations were such an offence to Confucius in his day. Their power was broken in the time of duke Gae (B.C. 493-467), and they thenceforth dwindle into comparative insignificance. Some branches remained in obscurity in Loo, and others went forth to the neighbouring States.

The branch from which Mencius sprang found a home in the small adjacent principality of Tsow, which in former times had been made known by the name of Choo. It was absorbed by Loo, and afterwards by Ts'oo, and its name is still retained in one of the districts of the department of Yen-chow in Shan-tung. Confucius was a native of a district of Loo having the same name, which many contend was also the birth-place of Mencius, making him a native of Loo and not of the

---

[14] The three attempts are—one by the author of "Supplemental Observations on the Four Books," an outline of which is given in his Notes on Mencius, Art III; one by the author of the "Topography of the Four Books," and forming the 24th section of the "Explanations of the Classics under the Ts'ing dynasty;" and one prefixed to the Works of Mencius, in "The Four Books, with the Relish of the Radical Meaning" (Vol. I., Proleg., larger Work, p. 131). These three critics display much ingenuity and research, but their conclusions are conflicting.—I may be pardoned in saying that their learned labors have affected me just as those of the Harmonizers of the Gospel Narratives used to do in former years,—bewildering more than edifying. Most cordially do I agree with Dean Alford (New Testament, Vol. 1., Proleg., I. vii. 5):—"If (? since) the Evangelists have delivered to us truly aud faithfully the Apostolic Narratives, and if (? since) the Apostles spoke as the Holy Spirit enabled them, and brought events and sayings to their recollection, then we may be sure that, *if we knew the real process of the transactions themselves, that knowledge would enable us to give an account of the diversities of narration and arrangement which the Gospels now present to us.* But *without such knowledge,* all attempts to accomplish this analysis in minute detail must be *merely conjectural,* and must tend to weaken the Evangelio testimony rather than to strengthen it."

State of Tsow. To my mind the evidence is decidedly against such a view.[15]

Mencius' name was K'o. His designation does not appear in his Works, nor is any given to him by Sze-ma Ts'ĕen or Chaou K'e. The latter says that he did not know how he had been styled; but the legends tell that he was called Tsze-keu, and Tsze-yu. The same authorities—if we can call them such—say that his father's name was Keih, and that he was styled Kung-e. They say also that his mother's maiden surname was Chang. Nothing is related of the former but that he died when his son was quite young, but the latter must have a paragraph to herself. "The mother of Mencius" is famous in China, and held up to the present time as a model of what a mother should be.

The year of Mencius' birth was probably the 4th of the emperor Lĕeh, B.C. 371. He lived to the age of 84, dying in the year B.C. 288, the 26th of the emperor Nan, with whom terminated the long sovereignty of the Chow dynasty. The first twenty-three years of his life thus synchronized with the last twenty-three of Plato's. Aristotle, Zeno, Epicurus, Demosthenes, and other great men of the West, were also his contemporaries. When we place Mencius among them, he can look them in the face. He does not need to hide a diminished head.

3. It was his misfortune, according to Chaou K'e, "to lose his father at an early period;[16] but in his youthful years he enjoyed the lessons of his kind mother, who thrice changed her residence on his account."

At first they lived near a cemetery, and Mencius amused himself with acting the various scenes which he witnessed at the tombs. "This," said the lady, "is no place for my son;"—and she removed to a house in the market-place. But the change was no improvement. The boy took to playing the part of a salesman, vaunting his wares, and chaffering with customers. His mother sought a new house, and found one at last close by a public school. There her child's attention was taken with the various exercises of politeness which the scholars were taught, and he

---

[15] Yen Joh-keu and Ts'aou Che-shing stoutly maintain the different sides of this question, the latter giving five arguments to show that the Tsow of Mencius was the Tsow of Loo. As Mencius went from Ts'e on the death of his mother to bury her in Loo (Bk II. Pt II. vii.), this appears to prove that he was a native of that State. But the conclusion is not necessary. Loo was the ancestral State of his family, and on that account he might wish to inter his parent there, according to the custom of the Chow dynasty (see the Le Ke, Bk II. Pt I. i. 26). The way in which Tsow always appears as the residence of Mencius, when he is what we should say "at home," appears to me decisive of the question, though neither of the disputants presses it into his service. Compare Bk III. Pt I ii.; Bk VI Pt II i. and v. The point is really of no importance, for the States of Tsow and Loo adjoined. "The rattle of the watchman in the one was heard in the other."

[16] The legend writers are more precise, and say that Mencius was only three years old when his father died. This statement, and K'e's as well, are difficult to reconcile with what we read in Bk I. Pt II. xvi., about the style in which Mencius buried his parents. If we accept the legend, we are reduced there to great straits.

endeavoured to imitate them. The mother was satisfied. "This," she said, "is the proper place for my son."

Han Ying relates another story of this period. Near their house was a pig-butcher's. One day Mencius asked his mother what they were killing the pigs for, and was told that it was to feed him. Her conscience immediately reproved her for the answer. She said to herself, "While I was carrying this boy in my womb, I would not sit down if the mat was not placed square, and I ate no meat which was not cut properly;—so I taught him when he was yet unborn.[17] And now when his intelligence is opening, I am deceiving him;—this is to teach him untruthfulness!" With this she went and bought a piece of pork in order to make good her words.

As Mencius grew up, he was sent to school. When he returned home one day, his mother looked up from the web which she was weaving, and asked him how far he had got on. He answered her with an air of indifference that he was doing well enough, on which she took a knife and cut the thread of her shuttle. The idler was alarmed, and asked what she meant, when she gave him a long lecture, showing that she had done what he was doing,—that her cutting her thread was like his neglecting his learning. The admonition, it is said, had its proper effect; the lecture did not need to be repeated.

There are two other narratives in which Chang-she figures, and though they belong to a later part of Mencius' life, it may be as well to embrace them in the present paragraph.

His wife was squatting down one day in her own room, when Mencius went in. He was so much offended at finding her in that position, that he told his mother, and expressed his intention to put her away, because of "her want of propriety" "It is you who have no propriety," said his mother, "and not your wife. Do not 'the Rules of Propriety' say, 'When you are about to ascend a hall, raise your voice; when you enter a door, keep your eyes low?' The reason of the rules is that people may not be taken unprepared; but you entered the door of your private apartment without raising your voice, and so caused your wife to be caught squatting on the ground. The impropriety is with you and not with her." On this Mencius fell to reproving himself, and did not dare to put away his wife.

One day, when he was living with his mother in Ts'e, she was struck with the sorrowfulness of his aspect, as he stood leaning against a pillar, and asked him the cause of it. He replied, "I have heard that the superior man occupies the place for which he is adapted, accepting no reward to which he does not feel entitled, and not covetous of honor

---

[17] See Choo He's "Education tor the Young," at the commencement of the chapter on "Instruction," which begins with the educational duties of the mother, while the child is yet unborn.

and emolument. Now my doctrines are not practiced in Ts'e:—I wish to leave it, but I think of your old age, and am anxious." His mother said, "It does not belong to a woman to determine anything of herself, but she is subject to the rule of the three obediences. When young, she has to obey her parents; when married, she has to obey her husband; when a widow, she has to obey her son. You are a man in your full maturity, and I am old. Do you act as your conviction of righteousness tells you you ought to do, and I will act according to the rule which belongs to me. Why should you be anxious about me?"

Such are the accounts which I have found of the mother of Mencius. Possibly some of them are inventions, but they are devoutly believed by the people of China;—and it must be to their profit. *We* may well believe that she was a woman of very superior character, and that her son's subsequent distinction was in a great degree owing to her influence and training.

4. From parents we advance to be under tutors and governors. The moulding hand that has wrought upon us in the pliant years of youth always leaves ineffaceable traces upon the character. Can anything be ascertained of the instructor or instructors of Mencius? The reply to this inquiry must be substantially in the negative, though many have affirmed that he sat as a pupil at the feet of Tsze-sze, the grandson of Confucius. We are told this by Chaou K'e, whose words are:—"As he grew up, he studied under Tsze-sze, acquired all the knowledge taught by 'The Learned' and became thoroughly acquainted with 'The Five King,' being more especially distinguished for his mastery of the *She* and the *Shoo.*" A reference to dates, however, shows that this must be incorrect. From the death of Confucius to the birth of Mencius there were 108 years, and supposing—what is by no means probable—that Tsze-sze was born in the year his father died, he must have been 112 years old when Mencius was born. The supposition of their having stood to each other in the relation of master and scholar is inconsistent, moreover, with the style in which Mencius refers to Tsze-sze. He mentions him seven times, showing an intimate acquaintance with his history, but never once in a manner which indicates that he had personal intercourse with him.

Sze-ma Ts'ëen's account is that "Mencius studied with the disciples of Tsze-sze." This may have been the case. There is nothing on the score of time to make it impossible, or even improbable; but this is all that can be said about it. No famous names from the school of Tsze-sze have been transmitted to posterity, and Mencius nowhere speaks as if he felt under special obligation to any instructor.

One short sentence contains all that he has said bearing on the point before us:—"Although I could not be a disciple of Confucius myself, I have endeavoured to cultivate [my virtue] by means of others [who were]."[18] The chapter to which this belongs is rather enigmatical. The other member of it says:—"The influence of a sovereign sage terminates in the fifth generation. The influence of one who is merely a sage does the same." By "one merely a sage" Mencius is understood to mean Confucius; and by extending his influence over five generations, he shows how it was possible for him to place himself under it by means of others who had been in direct communication with the Master.

We must leave the subject of Mencius' early instructors in the obscurity which rests upon it. The first forty years of his life are little more than a blank to us. Many of them, we may be sure, were spent in diligent study. He made himself familiar during them with all the literature of his country. Its classics, its histories, its great men, had received his careful attention. Confucius especially became to him the chief of mortal men, the object of his untiring admiration; and in his principles and doctrines he recognized the truth for want of an appreciation of which the bonds of society all round him were being relaxed, and the empire hastening to a general anarchy.

How he supported himself in Tsow, we cannot tell. Perhaps he was possessed of some patrimony; but when he first comes forth from his native State, we find him accompanied by his most eminent disciples. He probably imitated Confucius by assuming the office of a teacher,—not that of a school-master in our acceptation of the word, but that of a professor of morals and learning, encouraging the resort of inquiring minds, in order to resolve their doubts and inform them on the true principles of virtue and society. These disciples would minister to his wants, though we may presume that he sternly maintained his dignity among them, as he afterwards did towards the princes of the time, when he appeared among them as a *lecturer* in another sense of the term. In Book VII. Pt II. xliii., and Book VI. Pt II. ii., we have two instances of this, though we cannot be sure that they belonged to the earlier period of his life.

5. The state of China had waxed worse and worse during the interval that elapsed between Confucius and Mencius. The elements of disorganization which were rife in the times of the earlier sage had gone on to produce their natural results. One feeble sovereign had followed another on the throne, and the dynasty of Chow was ready to vanish away. Men were persuaded of its approaching extinction. The feeling of loyalty to it was no longer a cherished sentiment; and the anxiety and expectation were about what new rule would take its place.

Many of the smaller fiefs or principalities had been reduced to a helpless dependence on, or been absorbed by, the larger ones. Of Loo, Ch'ing, Wei, Woo, Ch'in, and Sung, conspicuous in the Analects, we

---

[18] See Book IV. Pt II. xxii.

read but little in Mencius. Tsin had been dismembered, and its fragments formed the nuclei of three new and vigorous kingdoms,—Wei, Chaou, and Han. Ts'e still maintained its ground, but was barely able to make head against the States of Ts'in in the West and Ts'oo in the South. The struggle for supremacy was between these two, the former, as it was ultimately successful, being the more ambitious and incessant in its aggressions on its neighbours.

The princes were thus at constant warfare with one another. Now two or more would form a league to resist the encroaching Ts'in, and hardly would that object be accomplished before they were at war among themselves. Ambitious statesmen were continually inflaming their quarrels. The recluses of Confucius' days who withdrew in disgust from the world and its turmoil, had given place to a class of men who came forth from their retirements provided with arts of war or schemes of policy which they recommended to the contending chiefs. They made no scruple of changing their allegiance, as they were moved by whim or interest. Kung-sun Yen and Chang E may be mentioned as a specimen of those characters. "Are they not really great men?" it was once asked of Mencius. "Let them once be angry, and all the princes are afraid. Let them live quietly, and the flames of trouble are extinguished throughout the kingdom."[19]

It is not wonderful that in such times the minds of men should have doubted of the soundness of the ancient principles of the acknowledged sages of the nation. Doctrines, strange and portentous in the view of Mencius, were openly professed. The authority of Confucius was disowned. The foundations of government were overthrown; the foundations of truth were assailed. Two or three paragraphs from our philosopher will verify and illustrate this representation of the character of his times.

"A host marches [in attendance on the ruler], and stores of provisions are consumed. The hungry are deprived of their food, and there is no rest for those who are called to toil. Maledictions are uttered by one to another with eyes askance, and the people proceed to the commission of wickedness. Thus the royal ordinances are violated, and the people are oppressed, and the supplies of food and drink flow away like water. The rulers yield themselves to the [bad] current, or they urge their [evil] way [against a good one]; they are wild; they are utterly lost."[20]

"The five chiefs of the princes were sinners against the three kings. The princes of the present day are sinners against the five chiefs. The great officers of the present day are sinners against the princes.... The

---

[19] Bk III. Pt II. ii.
[20] Bk I. Pt II. iv. 6.

crime of him who connives at and aids the wickedness of his prince is small, but the crime of him who anticipates and excites that, wickedness is great. The officers of the present day all go to meet their sovereigns' wickedness, and therefore I say that they are sinners against them."[21]

"Sage kings cease to arise, and the princes of the States give the reins to their lusts. Unemployed scholars indulge in unreasonable discussions. The words of Yang Choo and Mih Teih till the empire. If you listen to people's discourses, you will find that they have adopted the views either of Yang or of Mih. [Now,] Yang's principle is—'each one for himself,' which does not acknowledge [the claims of] the sovereign. Mih's principle is—'to love all equally,' which does not acknowledge [the peculiar affection due to] a father. But to acknowledge neither king nor father is to be in the state of a beast. Kung-ming E said, 'In their kitchens there is fat meat. In their stables there are fat horses. But their people have the look of hunger, and on the wilds there are those who have died of famine. This is leading on beasts to devour men.' If the principles of Yang and Mih are not stopped, and the principles of Confucius not set forth, those perverse speakings will delude the people and stop up [the path of] benevolence and righteousness. When benevolence and righteousness are stopped up, beasts will be led on to devour men, and men will devour one another."[22]

6. It is in Ts'e that we first meet with Mencius as a counselor of the princes,[23] and it was in this State that he spent much the greater part of his public life. His residence in it, however, appears to have been divided into two portions, and we know not to which of them to refer many of the chapters which describe his intercourse with the prince and his ministers; but, as I have already observed, this is to us of little moment. Our interest is in what he did and said. It matters little that we cannot assign to each saying and doing its particular date.

That he left Ts'e the first time before B.C. 323 is plausibly inferred from Bk II. Pt II. xiv. 4;[24] and assuming that the conversation in the

---

[21] Bk VI. Pt II. vii. 1,4.

[22] Book III. Pt II. ix. 9.

[23] In the "Annals of the Empire" (Vol. I., Proleg., larger Work, p. 134), Mencius' visit to king Hwuy of Lëang is set down as having occurred in B.C. 335, and under B.C. 318 it is said—"Mencius goes from Lëang to Ts'e." The visit to Lëang is placed too early, and that to Ts'e too late. The disasters of king Hwuy, mentioned Bk I. Pt I. v 1, had not all taken place in B.C. 318; and if Mencius remained 17 years in Lëang, it is strange we have only five conversations between him and king Hwuy. So far from his not going to Ts'e till B.C. 318, it will be seen from the next note that he was leaving Ts'e before B.C. 323.

[24] Mencius' words are—"From the commencement of the Chow dynasty till now more than 700 years have elapsed." It was to the purpose of his argument to make the

same Book, Pt I. ii., took place immediately before or after his arrival,[25] we can determine that he did not enter the State before B.C. 331, for he speaks of himself as having attained at forty years of age to "an unperturbed mind." The two chapters contain the most remarkable expressions indicative of Mencius' estimate of himself. In the first, while he glorifies Confucius as far before all other men who had ever lived, he declines having comparisons drawn between himself and any of the sage's most distinguished disciples. In the second, when going away sorrowful because he had not wrought the good which he desired, he observes:—"Heaven does not yet wish that the empire should enjoy tranquility and good order. If it wished this, who is there besides me to bring it about?"

We may be certain that Mencius did not go to Ts'e uninvited. His approach was waited for with curious expectation, and the king, spoken of always by his honorary epithet of Seuen, "The Illustrious," sent persons to spy out whether he was like other men.[26] They had their first interview at a place called Ts'ung, which was so little satisfactory to the philosopher that he resolved to make only a short stay in the State. Circumstances occurred to change this resolution, but though he remained, and even accepted office, yet it was only honorary;—he declined receiving any salary.[27]

From Ts'ung he appears to have retired to P'ing-luh, where Ch'oo, the prime minister, sent him a present, wishing, no doubt, to get into his good graces. I call attention to the circumstance, though trifling in itself, because it illustrates the way in which Mencius carried himself to the great men. He took the gift, but subsequently, when he went to the capital, he did not visit the minister to acknowledge it. His opinion was that Ch'oo might have come in person to P'ing-luh to see him. "There was a gift, but no corresponding respect."[28]

When Mencius presented himself at the capital of the State, he was honorably received by the king. Many of the conversations with the sovereign and officers which are scattered through the seven Books, though the first and second are richest in them, must be referred to this

---

time appear as long as possible. Had 800 years elapsed, he would surely have said so. But as the Chow dynasty commenced in B.C. 1121, the year B.C. 322 would be its 800th anniversary, and Mencius' departure from Ts'e did not take place later that the year before B.C. 323.

[25] This chapter and the one before it have very much the appearance of having taken place on the way from Tsow to Ts'e. Mencius has been invited to a powerful court. He is emerging from his obscurity. His disciples expect great things for him. Kung-sun Ch'ow sees him invested with the government of Ts'e, and in the elation of his heart makes his inquiries.

[26] Bk IV. Pt II. xxxii.

[27] Bk II. Pt II. xiv

[28] Bk VI. Pt II.v.

period. The one which is first in place,[29] and which contains the fullest exposition of the philosopher's views on government, was probably first likewise in time.[30] It sets forth the grand essential to the exercise of royal government,—a heart on the part of the sovereign impatient of the sufferings of the people, and eager to protect them and make them happy; it brings home to king Seuen the conviction that he was not without such a heart, and presses on him the truth that his not exercising it was from a want of will and not from any lack of ability; it exposes unsparingly the errors of the course he was pursuing; and concludes by an exhibition of the outlines and happy issues of a true royal sway.

Of this nature were all Mencius' communications with the sovereign; but he lays himself open in one thing to severe censure. Afraid apparently of repelling the prince from him by the severity of his lessons, he tries to lead him on by his very passions. "I am fond of beauty," says the king, "and that is in the way of my attaining to the royal government which you celebrate." "Not at all," replies the philosopher. "Gratify yourself, only do not let your doing so interfere with the people's getting similar enjoyment for themselves."[31] So the love of money, the love of war, and the love of music are dealt with. Mencius thought that if he could only get the good of the people to be recognized by Seuen as the great aim which he was to pursue, his tone of mind would be so elevated, that the selfish passions and gratifications of which he was the slave would be purified or altogether displaced. And so it would have been. Where he fails, is in putting his points as if benevolence and selfishness, covetousness and generosity, might exist together. Chinese moralists rightly find fault with him in this respect, and say that Confucius never condescended to such a style of argument.

Notwithstanding the apparent cordiality of the king's reception of him, and the freedom with which Mencius spoke his mind at their interviews, a certain suspiciousness appears to have been maintained between them. Neither of them would bend to the other. Mencius would not bow to the royal state; Seuen would not vail bonnet to the philosopher's cloak. We have one amusing instance of the struggles to which this sometimes gave rise. One day Mencius was preparing to go to court of his own free will, when a messenger arrived from the king, saying he had intended to come and see him, but was prevented by a

---

[29] Bk I. Pt I. vii.

[30] I judge that this was the first *set* conversation between king Seuen and Mencius, because of the inquiry with which the king opens it,—"May I be informed by you of the transactions of Hwan of Ta'e, and Win of Tsin?" A very brief acquaintance with our philosopher would have taught him that he was the last person to apply to about those characters.

[31] Bk I. Pt II. i. iii. v.; *et al.*

cold, and asking whether Mencius would not appear at the audience next morning. Mencius saw that this was a device on the part of the king to avoid stooping to visit him, and though he had been about to go to court, he replied at once that he was unwell. He did not hesitate to meet the king's falsehood with one of his own.

He did not wish, however, that the king should be ignorant of the truth, and went out next morning to pay a visit of condolence. He supposed that messengers would be sent from the court to inquire about his health, and that, when they took back word that he had gone out visiting, the king would understand how his sickness of the day before was only feigned.

It happened as he expected. The king sent a messenger, and his physician besides. Mencius being out, they were received by Măng Chung, either his son or cousin, who complicated the affair by an invention of his own. "To-day" he said, "he was a little better, and hastened to go to court. I don't know whether he has reached it by this time or not." No sooner were the visitors gone with this story, than he sent several persons to look for the philosopher, and urge him to go to the court before he returned home.

It was now necessary that a full account of the matter should reach the royal ears; and to accomplish this, Mencius neither went home nor to the court, but spent the night at the house of one of the high officers. They had an animated discussion. The officer accused Mencius of showing disrespect to the king. The philosopher replied that no man in Ts'e showed so much respect for the sovereign as he did, for it was only he who brought high and truly royal subjects under his notice.

"That," said the officer, "is not my meaning. The rule is—'When the prince's order calls, the carriage must not be waited for.' You were going to the court, but when you heard the king's message, you did not do so. This seems not in accordance with that rule." Mencius explained:—"There are three things universally acknowledged to be honorable,—nobility, age, and virtue. In courts, nobility holds the first place; in villages, age; and for helping one's generation and presiding over the people, the other two are not equal to virtue. The possession of one of the three does not authorize the despising of one who has the other two.

"A prince who is to accomplish great deeds will have ministers whom he does not call to go to see him. When he wishes to consult with them, he goes to them. The prince who does not honor the virtuous, and delight in their ways of doing, to this extent, is not worth having to do with.

"There was T'ang with E Yin:—he first learned of him, and then made him his minister; and so without difficulty he became sovereign. There was the duke Hwan with Kwan Chung:—he first learned of him, and then made him his minister; and so without difficulty he became chief of all the princes.

"So did T'ang behave to E Yin, and the duke Hwan to Kwan Chung, that they would not venture to call them to go to them. If Kwan Chung might not be called to him by his prince, how much less may I be called, who would not play the part of Kwan Chung!"[32]

We are to suppose that these sentiments were conveyed to the king by the officer with whom Mencius spent the night. It is a pity that the exposition of them could only be effected in such a roundabout manner, and was preceded by such acts of prevarication. But where the two parties were so suspicious of each other, we need not wonder that they separated before long. Mencius resigned his honorary appointment, and prepared to return to Tsow. On this occasion king Seuen visited him, and after some complimentary expressions asked whether he might expect to see him again. "I dare not request permission to visit you [at any particular time]," replied Mencius, "but, indeed, it is what I desire."[33]

The king made another attempt to detain him, and sent an officer, called She, to propose to him to remain in the State, on the understanding that he should have a house large enough to accommodate his disciples, and an allowance of ten thousand measures of grain to support them. All Mencius' efforts had not sufficed to make king Seuen and his ministers understand him. They thought he was really actuated like themselves by a desire for wealth. He indignantly rejected the proposal, and pointed out the folly of it, considering that he had already declined a hundred thousand measures in holding only an honorary appointment.

So Mencius turned his back on Ts'e; but he withdrew with a slow and lingering step, stopping three nights in one place, to afford the king an opportunity to recall him on a proper understanding. Some reproached him with his hesitancy, but he sufficiently explained himself. "The king," he said, "is, after all, one who may be made to do good. If he were to use me, would it be for the happiness of Ts'e only? It would be for the happiness of the people of the whole empire. I am hoping that the king will change; I am daily hoping for this.

"Am I like one of your little-minded people? They will remonstrate with their prince, and on their remonstrance not being accepted, they get angry, and, with their passion displayed in their countenance, they

---

[32] Bk II. Pt II. ii.

[33] Bk II. Pt II. x. I consider that this chapter, and others here referred to, belong to Mencius' first departure from Ts'e. I do so because we can hardly suppose that the king and his officers would not have understood him better by the end of his second residence. Moreover, while Mencius retires, his language in x. 2 and xi. 5, 6 is of such a nature that it leaves an opening for him to return again.

take their leave, and travel with all their strength for a whole day, before they will rest."[34]

7. After he left Ts'e, Mencius found a home for some time in the small principality of T'ăng, on the south of Ts'e, in the ruler of which he had a sincere admirer and docile pupil. He did not proceed thither immediately, however, but seems to have taken his way to Sung, which consisted mostly of the present department of Kwei-tih in Ho-nan.[35] There he was visited by the heirson of T'ăng, who made a long detour, while on a journey to Ts'oo, for the purpose of seeing him. The philosopher discoursed on the goodness of human nature, and the excellent ways of Yaou and Shun. His hearer admired, but doubted. He could not forget, however, and the lessons which he received produced fruit before long.

From Sung Mencius returned to Tsow, by way of Sëeh. In both Sung and Sëeh he accepted large gifts from the rulers, which help us in some measure to understand how he could maintain an expenditure which must have been great, and which gave occasion also for an ingenious exposition of the principles on which he guided his course among the princes.

"When you were in T'se," said one of his disciples, "you refused 100 *yih* of fine gold, which the king sent, while in Sung you accepted 70 *yih*, and in Sëeh 50. If you were right in refusing the gift in the first case, you did wrong in accepting it in the other two. If you were right in accepting it in those two cases, you were wrong in refusing it in Ts'e. You must accept one of these alternatives." "I did right in all the cases," replied Mencius. "When I was in Sung, I was about to undertake a long journey. Travellers must be provided with what is necessary for their expenses. The prince's message was—'a present against travelling-expenses;' why should I have declined the gift? In Sëeh I was under apprehensions for my safety, and taking measures for my protection. The message was—'I have heard you are taking measures to protect yourself, and send this to help you in procuring arms.' Why should I have declined the gift? But when I was in Ts'e, I had no occasion for money. To send a man a gift when he has no occasion for it is to bribe him. How is it possible that a superior man should be taken with a bribe?"[36]

---

[34] Bk II. Pt II. xii.

[35] This is gathered from Bk III. Pt I. i. 1, where the crown-prince of T'ăng visits Mencius, and from Bk II. Pt II. iii., where his accepting a gift in Sung appears to have been subsequent to his refusing one in Ts'e.

[36] Bk II. Pt II. iii.

Before Mencius had been long in Tsow, the crown-prince of T'ăng succeeded to the rule of the principality, and, calling to mind the lessons which he had heard in Sung, sent an officer to consult the philosopher on the manner in which he should perform the funeral and mourning services for his father.[37] Mencius of course advised him to carry out in the strictest manner the ancient regulations. The new prince's relatives and the officers, of the State opposed, but ineffectually. Mencius' counsel was followed, and the effect was great. Duke Wăn became an object of general admiration.

By and by Mencius proceeded himself to T'ăng. We may suppose that he was invited thither by the prince as soon as the rules of mourning would allow his holding free communication with him. The chapters which give an account of their conversations are really interesting. Mencius recommended that attention should be chiefly directed to the encouragement of agriculture and education. He would have nourishment secured both for the body and the mind of every subject.[38] When the duke was lamenting the danger to which he was exposed from his powerful and encroaching neighbours, Mencius told him he might adopt one of two courses;—either leave his State, and like king T'ae go and find a settlement elsewhere, or be prepared to die for his patrimony. "If you do good," said he, "among your descendants in after-generations there will be one who shall attain to the Royal dignity. But results are with Heaven. What is Ts'e to you, O prince? Be strong to do good. That is all your business."[39]

After all, nothing came of Mencius' residence in T'ăng. We should like to know what made him leave it. Confucius said that, if any of the princes were to employ him, he should achieve something considerable in twelve months, and in the course of three years the government would be perfected.[40] Mencius taught that, in his time, with half the merit of former days double the result might be accomplished.[41] Here in T'ăng a fair field seemed to be afforded him, but he was not able to make his promise good. Possibly the good purposes and docility of duke Wăn may not have held out, or Mencius may have found that it was easier to theorize about government, than actually to carry it on. Whatever may have been the cause, we find him in B.C. 319 at the court of king Hwuy of Lĕang.

Before he left T'ăng, Mencius had his reencounter with the

---

[37] Bk III. Pt I. ii. The note of time which is relied on as enabling us to follow Mencius here is the intimation, Bk I Pt II. xiv., that "Ts'e was about to fortify Sĕeh." This is referred to B.C. 320, when king Seuen appointed his brother T'ĕen Ying over the dependency of Sĕeh, and took measures to fortify it.

[38] Bk III. Pt I. iii.

[39] Bk I. Pt II. xiii. xiv. xv.

[40] Confucian Analects XIII. x.

[41] Bk II. Pt I. i. 13.

disciples of the "shrike-tongued barbarian of the south," one Heu Hing, who came to T'ăng on hearing of the reforms which were being made at Mencius' advice by the duke Wan. This was one of the dreamy speculators of the time, to whom I have already alluded. He pretended to follow the lessons of Shin-nung, one of the reputed founders of the empire and the father of husbandry, and came to T'ăng with his plough upon his shoulder, followed by scores of followers, all wearing the coarsest clothes, and supporting themselves by making mats and sandals. It was one of his maxims that "the magistrates should be laboring men." He would have the sovereign grow his own rice, and cook his own meals. Not a few of "The Learned" were led away by his doctrines, but Mencius girt up his loins to oppose the heresy, and ably vindicated the propriety of a division of labor, and of a lettered class conducting the government. It is just possible that the appearance of Heu Hing, and the countenance shown to him, may have had something to do with Mencius' leaving the State.

8. Lëang was another name for Wei, one of the States into which Tsin had been divided. King Hwuy, early in his reign, B.C. 364, had made the city of Tae-lëang, in the present department of K'ae-fung, his capital, and given its name to his whole principality. It was the year before his death, when Mencius visited him.[42] A long, stormy, and disastrous rule was about to terminate, but the king was as full of activity and warlike enterprise as ever he had been. At his first interview with Mencius, he addressed him in the well-known words, "Venerable Sir, since you have not counted it far to come here, a distance of a thousand *le,* may I presume that you are likewise provided with counsels to profit my kingdom?" Mencius in reply starts from the word *profit,* and expatiates eloquently on the evil consequences that must ensue from making a regard to profit the ground of conduct or the rule of policy. As for himself, his theme must be benevolence and righteousness. On these he would discourse, but on nothing else, and in following them a prince would obtain true and sure advantages.

Only five conversations are related between king Hwuy and the philosopher. They are all in the spirit of the first which has just been described, and of those which he had with king Seuen of Ts'e. There is the same freedom of expostulation, or, rather, boldness of reproof, and the same unhesitating assurance of the success that would follow the

---

[42] There are various difficulties about the reign of king Hwuy of Lëang. Sze-ma Ts'ëen makes it commence in 369 and terminate in 334. He is then succeeded by Sëang whose reign ends in 318; and he is followed by Gae till 295. What are called "The Bamboo Books" extend Hwuy's reign to B.C. 318, and the next 20 years are assigned to king Gae. "The Annals of the Empire" (which are compiled from "The General Mirror of History") follow the Bamboo Books in the length of king Hwuy's reign, but make him followed by Sëang; and take no note of a king Gae.—From Mencius we may be assured that Hwuy was succeeded by Sëang, and the view of his Life, which I have followed in this sketch, leads to the longer period assigned to his reign.

adoption of his principles. The most remarkable is the third, where we have a sounder doctrine than where he tells king Seuen that his love of beauty and money and valour need not interfere with his administration of royal government. Hwuy is boasting of his diligence in the government of his State, and sympathy with the sufferings of his people, as far beyond those of any of the neighbouring rulers, and wondering how he was not more prosperous than they. Mencius replies, "Your Majesty is fond of war;—let me take an illustration from it. The drums sound, and the weapons are crossed, when suddenly the soldiers on one side throw away their coats of mail, trail their weapons behind them, and run. Some of them run a hundred paces, and some run only fifty. What would you think if those who run fifty paces were to laugh at those who run a hundred paces?" "They may not do so," said the king; "they only did not run a hundred paces, but they also ran." "Since your Majesty knows this," was the reply, "you need not hope that your people will become more numerous than those of the neighbouring kingdoms." The king was thus taught that half measures would not do. Royal government, to be effectual, must be carried out faithfully and in its spirit.

King Hwuy died in B.C. 319, and was succeeded by his son, the king Sëang. Mencius appears to have had but one interview with him. When he came out from it, he observed to some of his friends:—"When I looked at him from a distance, he did not appear like a sovereign; when I drew near to him, I saw nothing venerable about him."[43]

It was of no use to remain any longer in Lëang; he left it, and we meet with him again in Ts'e.

9. Whether he returned immediately to Ts'e we cannot tell, but the probability is that he did, and remained in it till the year B.C. 311.[44] When he left it about seven years before, he had made provision for his return in case of a change of mind in king Seuen. The philosopher, I apprehend, was content with an insufficient assurance of such an alteration. Be that as it may, he went back, and took an appointment again as a high noble.

If he was contented with a smaller reformation on the part of the king than he must have desired, Mencius was not himself different from what he had been. In the court and among the high officers his deportment was equally unbending; he was the same stern mentor.

Among the officers was one Wang Hwan, called also Tsze-gaou, a favorite with the king, insolent and presuming. Him Mencius treated

---

[43] Bk 1. Pt I. vi.

[44] This conclusion is adopted because it was in 311 that Yen rebelled, when the king said that he was very much ashamed when he thought of Mencius, who had strongly condemned his policy towards the State of Yen.—This is another case in which the chronology is differently laid down by the authorities, Sze-ma Ts'een saying that Yen was taken by king Min the son and successor of Seuen.

with an indifference and even contempt which must have been very provoking. A large party were met one time at the house of an officer who had lost a son, for the purpose of expressing their condolences. Mencius was among them, when suddenly Wang Hwan made his appearance. One and another moved to do him honor and win from him a smile,—all indeed but Mencius, who paid no regard to him. The other complained of the rudeness, but the philosopher could show that his conduct was only in accordance with the rules of propriety.[45]

Now and then he became the object of unpleasant remark and censure. At his instigation, an officer, Ch'e Wa, remonstrated with the king on some abuse, and had in consequence to resign his office. The people were not pleased with Mencius, thus advising others to their harm, and yet continuing to retain his own position undisturbed. "In the course which he marked out for Ch'e Wa," they said, "he did well, but we do not know as to the course which he pursues for himself." The philosopher, however, was never at a loss in rendering a reason. He declared that, as his office was honorary, he could act "freely and without restraint either in going forward or retiring."[46] In this matter we have more sympathy with the condemnation than with the defence.

Some time during these years there occurred the death of Mencius' excellent mother. She had been with him in Ts'e, and he carried the coffin to Loo, to bury it near the dust of his father and ancestors. The funeral was a splendid one. Mencius perhaps erred in having it so from his dislike to the Mihists, who advocated a spare simplicity in all funeral matters.[47] His arrangements certainly excited the astonishment of some of his own disciples,[48] and were the occasion of general remark.[49] He defended himself on the ground that "the superior man will not for all the world be niggardly to his parents," and that, as he had the means, there was no reason why he should not give all the expression in his power to his natural feelings.

Having paid this last tribute of filial duty, Mencius returned to Ts'e, but he could not appear at court till the three years of his mourning were accomplished.[50] It could not be long after this when trouble and confusion arose in Yen, a large State to the north-west of Ts'e, in the present Chih-le. Its prince, who was a poor weakling, wished to go through the sham of resigning his throne to his prime minister, understanding that he would decline it, and that thus he would

---

[45] Bk IV. Pt II. xxvii.

[46] Bk II. Pt II. v.

[47] Bk III. Pt I. v. 2.

[48] Bk II. Pt II. vii.

[49] Bk I. Pt II. xvi.

[50] Some are of opinion that Mencius stopped all the period of mourning in Loo, but the more natural concluaion, Bk II. Pt II. vii. 1, seems to me that he returned to Ts'e, and stayed at Ying, without going to court.

have the credit of playing the part of the ancient Yaou, while at the same time he retained his kingdom. The minister, however, accepted the tender, and, as he proved a tyrannical ruler, great dissatisfaction arose. Shin T'ung, an officer of Ts'e, asked Mencius whether Yen might be smitten. He replied that it might, for its prince had no right to resign it to his minister, and the minister no right to receive it. "Suppose," said he, "there were an officer here with whom you were pleased, and that, without informing the king, you were privately to give him your salary and rank; and suppose that this officer, also without the king's orders, were privately to receive them from you:—would such a transaction be allowable? And where is the difference between the case of Yen and this?"[51]

Whether these sentiments were reported to king Seuen or not, he proceeded to attack Yen, and found it an easy prey. Mencius was charged with having advised the measure, but he ingeniously repudiated the accusation. "I answered Shin T'ung that Yen might be smitten. If he had asked me—'Who may smite it?' I would have answered him—'He who is the minister of Heaven may smite it.' Suppose the case of a murderer, and that one asks me—'May this man be put to death?' I will answer him—'He may.' If he ask me—'Who may put him to death?' I will answer him—'The chief criminal judge may put him to death.' But now with one Yen to smite another Yen:—how should I have advised this?" This reference to "The minister of Heaven" strikingly illustrates what was said about the state of China in Mencius' time. He tells us in one place that hostile States do not correct one another, and that only the supreme authority can punish its subjects by force of arms.[52] But there was now no supreme authority in China. He saw in the emperor but "the shadow of an empty name." His conception of a minister of Heaven was not unworthy. He was one who, by the distinction which he gave to talents and virtue, and by his encouragement of agriculture and commerce, attracted all people to him as a parent. He would have no enemy under heaven, and could not help attaining to the Royal dignity.[53]

King Seuen, after conquering and appropriating Yen, tried to get Mencius' sanction of the proceeding, alleging the ease and rapidity with which he had effected the conquest as an evidence of the favor of Heaven. But the philosopher was true to himself. The people of Yen, he said, had submitted, because they expected to find in the king a deliverer from the evils under which they groaned. If they were pleased, he might retain the State, but if he tried to keep it by force, there would simply be another revolution.[54]

---

[51] Bk II. Pt II. viii.
[52] Bk VII. Pt II. ii.
[53] Bk II. Pt I. v.
[54] Bk I. Pt II. x.

The king's love of power prevailed. He determined to keep his prey, and ere long a combination was formed among the neighbouring princes to wrest Yen from him. Full of alarm he again consulted Mencius, but got no comfort from him. "Let him restore his captives and spoils, consult with the people of Yen, and appoint them a ruler—so he might be able to avert the threatened attack."[55]

The result was as Mencius had predicted. The people of Yen rebelled. The king felt ashamed before the philosopher, whose second residence in Ts'e was thus brought to an unpleasant termination.

10. We do not know that Mencius visited any of the princes after this. On leaving Ts'e, he took his way again to Sung, the duke of which had taken the title of king in B.C. 317. A report also had gone abroad that he was setting about to practise the true royal government, but Mencius soon satisfied himself of its incorrectness?[56]

The last court at which we find him is that of Loo, B.C. 309. The duke P'ing had there called Yoh-ching, one of the philosopher's disciples, to his councils, and indeed committed to him the administration of the government. When Mencius heard of it, he was so overjoyed that he could not sleep.[57]

The first appearance (in point of time) of this Yoh-ching in the Seven Books is not much to his credit. He comes to Ts'e in the train of Wang Hwan, the favorite who was an offence to the philosopher, and is very sharply reproved for joining himself to such a character "for the sake of the loaves and fishes."[58] Other references to him are more favorable. Mencius declares him to be "a good man," "a real man."[59] He allows that "he is not a man of vigour," nor "a man wise in council," nor "a man of much information," but he says—"he is a man that loves what is good," and "the love of what is good is more than a sufficient qualification for the government of the kingdom;—how much more is it so for the State of Loo!"[60]

Either on his own impulse or by Yoh-ching's invitation, Mencius went himself also to Loo, hoping that the prince who had committed his government to the disciple might be willing to listen to the counsels of the master. The duke was informed of his arrival by Yoh-ching, and also of the deference which he exacted. He resolved to go and visit him and invite him to the court. The horses were put to the carriage, and the duke was ready to start, when the intervention of his favorite, a worthless creature called Tsang Ts'ang, diverted him from his good purpose. When told by the duke that he was going to visit the scholar

---

[55] Bk I. Pt II. xi.
[56] See Bk III. Pt II v. vi.
[57] Bk VI. Pt II. xiii.
[58] Bk IV. Pt I. xxv.
[59] Bk VII. Pt II. xxv.
[60] Bk VI. Pt II. xiii.

Măng, Ts'ang said, "That you demean yourself to pay the honor of the first visit to a common man, is, I apprehend, because you think that he is a man of talents and virtue. From such men the rules of ceremonial proprieties and right proceed; but on the occasion of this Măng's second mourning, his observances exceeded those of the former. Do not go to see him, my prince." The duke said, "I will not;"—and carriage and horses were ordered back to their places.

As soon as Yoh-ching had an audience of the duke, he explained the charge of impropriety which had been brought against Mencius; but the evil was done. The duke had taken his course. "I told him," said Yoh-ching, "about you, and he was coming to see you, when Tsang Ts'ang stopped him." Mencius replied to him, "A man's advancement is effected, it may be, by others, and the stopping him is, it may be, from the efforts of others. But to advance a man or to stop his advance is really beyond the power of other men; my not finding in the prince of Loo a ruler who would confide in me, and put my counsels into practice, is from Heaven. How could that scion of the Tsang family cause me not to find the ruler that would suit me?"[61]

Mencius appears to have accepted this intimation of the will of Heaven as final. He has a remarkable saying, that Heaven controls the development of a man's faculties and affections, but as there is an adaptation in his nature for these, the superior man does not say—"It is the appointment of Heaven."[62] In accordance with this principle he had striven long against the adverse circumstances which threw his hopes of influencing the rulers of his time again and again in the dust. On his first leaving Ts'e we saw how he said:—"Heaven does not yet wish that the empire should enjoy tranquility and good order." For about fifteen years, however, he persevered, if peradventure there might be a change in the Heavenly councils. Now at last he bowed in submission. The year after and he would reach his grand climacteric. We lose sight of him. He retired from courts and great officers. We can but think and conjecture of him, according to tradition, passing the last twenty years of his life amid the more congenial society of his disciples, discoursing to them, and compiling the Works which have survived as his memorial to the present day.

11. I have endeavoured in the preceding paragraphs to put together the principal incidents of Mencius' history as they may be gathered from his Writings. There is no other source of information about him, and we must regret that they tell us nothing of his domestic life and habits. In one of the stories about his mother there is an allusion to his wife, from which we may conclude that his marriage was not without its bitternesses. It is probable that the Măng Chung, mentioned in Bk II.

---

[61] Bk I. Pt II. xvi.
62 Bk III. Pt II. xiv

Pt II. ii., was his son, though this is not easily reconcilable with what we read in VI. Pt I. v., of a Măng Ke, who was, according to Chaou K'e, a brother of Măng Chung. We must believe that he loft a family, for his descendants form a large clan at the present day. He-wăn, the 56th in descent from Mencius, was, in the period Kĕa-tsing (A.D. 1522-1566), constituted a member of the Han-lin college, and of the Board in charge of the five King, which honor was to be hereditary in the family, and the holder of it to preside at the sacrifices to his ancestor.[63] China's appreciation of our philosopher could not be more strikingly shown. Honors flow back in this empire. The descendant ennobles his ancestors. But in the case of Mencius, as in that of Confucius, this order is reversed. No excellence of descendants can extend to them; and the nation acknowledges its obligations to them by nobility and distinction conferred through all generations upon their posterity.

## SECTION II. HIS INFLUENCE AND OPINIONS.

1. CONFUCIUS had hardly passed off the stage of life before his merits began to be acknowledged. The duke Gae, who had neglected his counsels when he was alive, was the first to pronounce his eulogy, and to order that public sacrifices should be offered to him. His disciples proclaimed their estimation of him as superior to all the sages whom China had ever seen. Before long this view of him took possession of the whole nation; and since the Han dynasty, he has been the man whom sovereign and people have delighted to honor.

The memory of Mencius was not so distinguished. We have seen that many centuries elapsed before his Writings were received among the classics of the empire. It was natural that under the same dynasty when this was done the man himself should be admitted to share in the sacrifices presented to Confucius.

The emperor Shin-tsung,[64] in A.D. 1083, issued a patent, constituting Mencius "duke of the State of Tsow," and ordering a temple to be built to him in the district of Tsow, at the spot where the philosopher had been interred. In the following year it was enacted that he should have a place in the temple of Confucius, next to that of Yen Yuen, the favorite disciple of the sage.

In A.D. 1330, the emperor Wăn,[65] of the Yuen dynasty, made an addition to Mencius' title, and styled him "duke of the State of Tsow, Inferior Sage." This continued till the rise of the Ming dynasty, the founder of which had his indignation excited in 1372 by one of Mencius' conversations with king Seuen. The philosopher had

---

[63] See Morrison's Dictionary, on Mencius.
[64] A.D. 1068-1085.
[65] A.D. 1330-1333.

said:—"When the ruler regards his ministers as his hands and feet, the ministers regard their ruler as their belly and heart; when he regards them as his dogs and horses, they regard him as any other man; when he regards them as the ground or as grass, they regard him as a robber and an enemy."[66] To apply such names as *robber* and *enemy* in any case to rulers seemed to the imperial reader an unpardonable outrage, and he ordered Mencius to be degraded from his place in the temples of Confucius, declaring also that if any one remonstrated on the proceeding he should be dealt with as guilty of "Contempt of Majesty."

The scholars of China have never been slow to vindicate the memory of its sages and worthies. Undeterred by the imperial threat, Ts'ëen T'ang, a president of the Board of Punishments, presented himself with a remonstrance, saying—"I will die for Mencius, and my death will be crowned with glory." The emperor was moved by his earnestness, and allowed him to go scathless. In the following year, moreover, examination and reflection produced a change of mind. He issued a second proclamation to the effect that Mencius, by exposing heretical doctrines and overthrowing perverse speakings, had set forth clearly the principles of Confucius, and ought to be restored to his place as one of his assessors.[67]

In 1530, the ninth year of the period Këa-tsing, a general revision was made of the sacrificial canon for the sage's temple, and the title of Mencius was changed into—"The philosopher Măng, Inferior Sage." So it continues to the present day. His place is the second on the west,

---

[66] Bk IV. Pt II. iii.

[67] I have taken this account from "The Sacrificial Canon of the Sage's Temples" (Vol. I. Proleg. p. 103). Dr. Morrison in his Dictionary, under the character Măng, adds that the change in the emperor's mind was produced by his reading the remarkable passage in Bk VI. Pt II. xv., about trials and hardships as the way by which Heaven prepares men for great services. He thought it was descriptive of himself, and that he could argue from it a good title to the crown;—and so he was mollified to the philosopher. It may be worth while to give here the concluding remarks in "The Paraphrase for Daily Lessons, Explaining the Meaning of the Four Books" (Vol. I. Proleg. of larger Work, p. 131), on the chapter of Mencius which was deemed by the imperial reader so objectionable:—"Mencius wished that sovereigns should treat their ministers according to propriety, and nourish them with kindness, and therefore he used these perilous words in order to alarm and rouse them. As to the other side, the part of ministers, though the sovereign regard them as his hands and feet, they ought notwithstanding to discharge most earnestly their duties of loyalty and love. Yea, though he regard them as dogs and horses, or as the ground and grass, they ought still more to perform their part in spite of all difficulties, and oblivious of their person. They may on no account make the manner in which they are regarded, whether it be of appreciation or contempt, the standard by which they regulate the measure of their grateful service. The words of Confucius, that *the ruler should behave to his ministers according to propriety, and the ministers serve their sovereign w i t h faithfulness*, contain the unchanging rule for all ages." The authors of the Daily Lessons did their work by imperial order, and evidently had the fear of the court before their eyes. Their language implies a censure of our philosopher. There will ever be a grudge against him in the minds of despots, and their creatures will be ready to depreciate him.

next to that of the philosopher Tsăng. Originally, we have seen, he followed Yen Hwuy, but Hwuy, Tsze-sze, Tsăng, and Măng were appointed the sage's four assessors, and had their relative positions fixed, in 1267.

2. The second edict in the period Hung-woo, restoring Mencius to his place in the temples of Confucius, states fairly enough the services which he is held to have rendered to his country. The philosopher's own estimate of himself has partly appeared in the sketch of his Life. He seemed to start with astonishment when his disciple Kung-sun Ch'ow was disposed to rank him as a sage;[68] but he also said on one occasion—"When sages shall rise up again, they will not change my words."[69] Evidently, he was of opinion that the mantle of Confucius had fallen upon him. A work was to be done in his generation, and he felt himself able to undertake it. After describing what had been accomplished by the great Yu, by Chow-kung, and Confucius, he adds:—"I also wish to rectify men's hearts, and to put an end to those perverse doctrines, to oppose their one-sided actions, and banish away their licentious expressions; and thus to carry on the work of the three sages."[70]

3. The place which Mencius occupies in the estimation of the literati of China may be seen by the following testimonies, selected from those appended by Choo He to the prefatory notice of his Life in the "Collected Comments."

Han Yu[71] says, "If we wish to study the doctrines of the sages, we must begin with Mencius." He also quotes the opinion of Yang Tsze-yun,[72] "Yang and Mih were stopping up the way [of truth], when Mencius refuted them, and scattered their delusions without difficulty;" and then remarks upon it:—"When Yang and Mih walked abroad, the true doctrine had nearly come to nought. Though Mencius possessed talents and virtue, even those of a sage, he did not occupy the throne. He could only speak and not act. With all his earnestness, what could he do? It is owing, however, to his words, that learners now-a-days still know to revere Confucius, to honor benevolence and righteousness, to esteem the true sovereign and despise the mere pretender. But the grand rules and laws of the sage and sage-emperors had been lost beyond the power of redemption; only one in a hundred of them was preserved. Can it be said in those circumstances that Mencius had an easy task? Yet had it not been for him, we should have been buttoning the lappets of our coats on the left side, and our discourse would have been all-confused and indistinct;—it is on this account that I have honored

---

[68] Bk II. Pt I. ii. 18, 19.
[69] Bk III. Pt II. ix. 10.
[70] *Ib.,* par. 13.
[71] See above
[72] Died A.D. 18.

Mencius, and consider his merit not inferior to that of Yu."

One asked the philosopher Ch'ing[73] whether Mencius might be pronounced to be a sage. He replied, "I do not dare to say altogether that he was a sage, but his learning had reached the extremest point." The same great scholar also said:—"The merit of Mencius in regard to the doctrine of the sages is more than can be told. Confucius only spoke of *benevolence*, but as soon as Mencius opens his mouth, we hear of *benevolence* and *righteousness*. Confucius only spoke of the *will* or *mind*, but Mencius enlarged also on *the nourishment of the passion-nature*. In these two respects his merit was great." "Mencius did great service to the world by his teaching the goodness of man's nature." "Mencius had a certain amount of the heroical spirit, and to that there always belong some jutting corners, the effect of which is very injurious. Yen Yuen, all round and complete, was different from this. He was but a hair's-breadth, removed from a sage, while Mencius must be placed in a lower rank, a great worthy, an inferior sage." Ch'ing was asked where what he called the heroical spirit of Mencius could be seen. "We have only to compare his words with those of Confucius," he said, "and we shall perceive it. It is like the comparison of ice or crystal with a precious stone. The ice is bright enough, but the precious stone, without so much brilliancy, has a softness and richness all its own."[74] (The scholar Yang Kwei-shan[75] says:—"The great object of Mencius in his writings is to rectify men's hearts, teaching them to preserve their heart and nourish their nature, and to recover their lost heart. When he discourses of benevolence, righteousness, propriety, and knowledge, he refers to the principles of these in the heart commiserating, feeling shame and dislike, affected with modesty and complaisance, approving and disapproving. When he speaks of the evils springing from perverted speakings, he says—'Growing first in the mind, they prove injurious to government.' When he shows how a prince should be served, he says—'Correct what is wrong in his mind. Once rectify the prince, and the kingdom will be settled.' With him the thousand changes and ten thousand operations of men all come from

---

[73] See Vol. I., Proleg., p. 24.

[74] This is probably the original of what appears in the "Memoires concernant les Chinois," in the notice of Mencius, vol. iii., and which Thornton (vol. ii., pp. 216, 217) has faithfully translated therefrom in the following terms:—"Confucius, through prudence or modesty; often dissimulated; he did not always say what he might have said:Măng-tsze, on the contrary, was incapable of constraining himself; he spoke what he thought, and without the least fear or reserve. He resembles ice of the purest water, through which we can see all its defects as well as its beauties: Confucius, on the other hand, is like a precious gem, which though not so pellucid as ice, has more strength and solidity." The former of these sentences is quite alien from the style of Chinese thinking and expression.

[75] One of the great scholars of the Sung dynasty, a friend of the two Ch'ing. He has a place in the temples of Confucius.

the mind or heart. If a man once rectify his heart, little else will remain for him to do. In 'The Great Learning,' the cultivation of the person, the regulation of the family, the government of the State, and the tranquillization of the empire, all have their root in the rectifying of the heart and the making the thoughts sincere. If the heart be rectified, we recognize at once the goodness of the nature. On this account, whenever Mencius came into contact with people, he testified that man's nature is good. When Ow-yang Yung-shuh[76] says, that, in the lessons of the sages, man's nature does not occupy the first place, he is wrong. There is nothing to be put before this. Yaou and Shun are the models for ten thousand ages simply because they followed their nature. And to follow our nature is just to accord with Heavenly principle. To use plans and arts, away from this, though they may be successful in great achievement, is the selfishness of human desires, and as far removed from the mode of action of the sage, as earth is from heaven." I shall close these testimonies with a sentence from Choo He himself. He says:—"Mencius, when compared with Confucius, always appears to speak in too lofty a style; but when we hear him proclaiming the goodness of man's nature, and celebrating Yaou and Shun, then we likewise perceive the solidity of his discourses."

4. The judgment concerning our philosopher contained in the above quotations will approve itself to every one who has carefully perused his Works. The long passage from Yang Kwei-shan is especially valuable, and puts the principal characteristic of Mencius' teachings in a clear light. Whether those teachings have the intrinsic value which is ascribed to them is another question. But Mencius' position with reference to "the doctrines of the sages" is correctly assigned. We are not to look for new truths in him. And this does not lead his countrymen to think less highly of him. I ventured to lay it down as one grand cause of the position and influence of Confucius, that he was simply the preserver of the monuments of antiquity, and the exemplifier and expounder of the maxims of the golden age of China. In this Mencius must share with him.

But while we are not to look to Mencius for new truths, the peculiarities of his natural character were more striking than those of his master. There was an element of "the heroical" about him. He was a dialectician, moreover. If he did not like disputing, as he protested that he did not, yet, when forced to it, he showed himself a master of the art. An. ingenuity and subtlety which we cannot but enjoy often mark his reasonings. We have more sympathy with him than with Confucius. He comes closer to us. He is not so awe-full, but he is more admirable. The

---

[76] Also one of China's greatest scholars. He has now a place in the temples of Confucius.

doctrines of the sages take a tinge from his mind in passing through it, and it is with that Mencian character about them that they are now held by the cultivated classes and by readers generally.

I will now call attention to a few passages illustrative of these remarks. Some might prefer to search them out for themselves in the body of the volume, and I am far from intending to exhaust the subject. There will be many readers, however, pleased to have the means of forming an idea of the man for themselves brought within small compass. My next object will be to review his doctrine concerning man's mental constitution and the nourishment of the passion-nature, in which he is said to have rendered special service to the cause of truth. That done, I will conclude by pointing out what I conceive to be his chief defects as a moral and political teacher. To the opinions of Yang Choo and Mih, which he took credit to himself for assailing and exposing, it will be necessary to devote another chapter.

5. It was pointed out in treating of the opinions of Confucius, that he allowed no "right divine" to a sovereign, independent of his exercising a benevolent rule. This was one of the topics, however, of which he was shy. With Mencius, on the contrary, it was a favorite theme. The degeneracy of the times and the ardour of his disposition prompted him equally to the free expression of his convictions about it.

"The people," he said, "are the most important element [in a country]; the spirits of the land and grain are the next; the ruler is the lightest. When the ruler endangers the altars of the spirits of the land and grain, he is changed, and another appointed in his place. When the sacrificial victims have been perfect, the millet in its vessels all pure, and the sacrifices offered at their proper seasons, if yet there ensue drought, or the waters overflow, the altars of the spirits of the land and grain are changed, and others appointed."[77]

"*The people are the most important element in a country, and the ruler is the lightest*;"—that is certainly a bold and ringing affirmation. Mencius was not afraid to follow it to the conclusion that the ruler who was exercising an injurious rule should be dethroned. His existence is not to be allowed to interfere with the general good. Killing in such a case is no murder. King Seuen once asked, "Was it so that T'ang banished Kěeh, and that king Woo smote Chow?" Mencius replied, "It is so in the records." The king asked, "May a minister then put his sovereign to death?" Our philosopher's reply was:—"He who outrages the benevolence proper to his nature is called a robber; he who outrages righteousness is called a ruffian. The robber and ruffian we call a mere fellow. I have heard of the cutting off of the fellow Chow, but I have

---

[77] Bk VII. Pt II. xiv.

not heard in his case of the putting a ruler to death."[78]

With regard to the ground of the relation between ruler and people, Mencius refers it very clearly to the will of God. In one place he adopts for his own purpose the language of king Woo in the Shoo-king:—"Heaven, having produced the inferior people, made for them rulers and instructors, with the purpose that they should be assisting to God, and therefore gave them distinction throughout the four quarters of the land."[79] But the question arises—How can this will of Heaven be known? Mencius has endeavoured to answer it. He says:—"Heaven gives the empire, but its appointment is not conferred with specific injunctions. Heaven does not speak. It shows its will by a, man's personal conduct and his conduct of affairs." The conclusion of the whole matter is:—"Heaven sees according as the people see; Heaven hears according as the people hear."[80]

It may not be easy to dispute these principles. I for one have no hesitation in admitting them. Their application, however, must always be attended with difficulty. Here is a sovereign who is the very reverse of a minister of God for good. He ought to be removed, but who is to remove him? Mencius teaches in one passage that the duty is to be performed by his relatives who are also ministers.

King Seuen of Ts'e asked him about the office of chief ministers. Mencius said, "Which chief ministers is your Majesty asking about?" "Are there differences among them?" inquired the king. "There are," was the reply; "there are the chief ministers who are noble and relatives of the ruler, and there are those who are of a different surname." The king said, "I beg to ask about the chief ministers who are noble and relatives of the ruler." Mencius answered, "If the ruler have great faults, they ought to remonstrate with him, and if he do not listen to them when they have done so again and again, they ought to appoint another in his place." The king on this looked moved, and changed countenance. Mencius said, "Let not your Majesty think what I say strange. You asked me, and I did not dare to reply but correctly."[81]

This plan for disposing of an unworthy sovereign has been acted on in China and in other countries. It is the best that can be adopted to secure the throne in the ruling House. But where there are no relatives that have the virtue and power to play such a part, what is to be done? Mencius has two ways of meeting this difficulty. Contrary to his general rule for the conduct of ministers who are not relatives, he allows that even they may, under certain conditions, take summary

[78] Bk I. Pt II. viii.
[79] Bk I. Pt II. iii. 7.
[80] Bk V. Pt I. v.
[81] Bk V. Pt II. ix.

measures with their sovereign.

His disciple Kung-sun Ch'ow said to him, "E Yin said, 'I cannot be near so disobedient a person,' and therewith he banished T'ae-këah to T'ung. The people were much pleased. When T'ae-këah became virtuous, he brought him back, and the people were again much pleased. When worthies are ministers, may they indeed banish their rulers in this way when they are not virtuous?" Mencius replied, "If they have the mind of E Yin, they may. If they have not that mind, it would be usurpation."[82]

His grand device, however, is what he calls "the minister of Heaven." When the sovereign has become worthless and useless, his hope is that Heaven will raise up some one for the help of the people;—some one who shall so occupy in his original subordinate position as to draw all eyes and hearts to himself.[83] Let him then raise the standard, not of rebellion but of righteousness,[84] and he cannot help attaining to the highest dignity. So it was with the great T'ang; so it was with the kings Wăn and Woo. Of the last Mencius says:—"There was one man"—*i.e.,* the tyrant Chow—"pursuing a violent and disorderly course in the land, and king Woo was ashamed of it. By one display of his anger, he gave repose to all the people."[85] He would have been glad if any one of the princes of his own time had been able to vault in a similar way to the royal throne, and he went about counseling them to the attempt. "Let your Majesty," said he to king Seuen, "in like manner, by one burst of anger, give repose to all the people of the empire." This was in fact advising to rebellion, but the philosopher would have recked little of such a charge. The House of Chow had forfeited in his view its title to the kingdom. Alas! among all the princes he had to do with, he did not find one who could be stirred to so honorable an action.

We need not wonder that Mencius, putting forth the above views so boldly and broadly, should not be a favorite with the rulers of China. His sentiments, professed by the literati, and known and read by all the people, have operated powerfully to compel the good behaviour of "the powers that be." It may be said that they encourage the aims of selfish ambition, and the lawlessness of the licentious mob. I grant it. They are lessons for the virtuous, and not for the lawless and disobedient, but the government of China would have been more of a grinding despotism, if it had not been for them.

On the readiness of the people to be governed Mencius only differs

---

[82] Bk VII. Pt I. xxxi.
[83] Bk II. Pt I. v.
[84] "Raise righteous soldiers;"—this is the profession of all rebel leaders in China.
[85] Bk I. Pt II. iii. 7.

from Confucius in the more vehement style in which he expresses his
views. He does not dwell so much on the influence of personal virtue,
and I pointed out, in the sketch of his Life, how he all but compromised
his character in his communications with king Seuen, telling him that
his love of women, of war, and of money might be so regulated as not
to interfere with his exercise of true royal government. Still he speaks
at times correctly and emphatically on this subject. He quotes
Confucius' language on the influence generally of superiors on
inferiors,—that "the relation between them is like that between the
wind and grass; the grass must bend when the wind blows upon it;"[86]
and he says himself:—"It is not enough to remonstrate with a ruler on
account of the mal-employment of ministers, nor to blame errors of
government. It is only the great man who can correct what is wrong in
the ruler's mind. Let the ruler be benevolent, and all his acts will be
benevolent. Let the ruler be righteous, and all his acts will be righteous.
Let the ruler be correct, and all his acts will be correct. Once rectify the
ruler, and the State will be firmly settled."[87]

But the misery which he saw around him, in consequence of the
prevailing anarchy and constant wars between State and State, led
Mencius to insist on the necessity of what he called "a benevolent
government." The king Sëang asked him, "Who can unite all under the
sky under one sway?" and his reply was, "He who has no pleasure in
killing men can so unite it." [88] His being so possessed with the sad
condition of his time likewise gave occasion, we may suppose, to the
utterance of another sentiment, sufficiently remarkable. "Never," said
he, "has he who would by his excellence subdue men, been able to
subdue them. Let a ruler seek by his excellence to nourish men, and he
will be able to subdue all under heaven. It is impossible that any one
should attain to the true royal sway to whom the hearts of all under
heaven are not subject."[89] The highest style of excellence will of course
have its outgoings in benevolence. Apart from that, it will be
powerless, as Mencius says. His words are akin to those of
Paul:—"Scarcely for a righteous man will one die: yet peradventure for
a good man some would even dare to die."

On the effects of a benevolent rule he says:—

"Këeh and Chow's losing the kingdom arose from their losing the
people; and to lose the people means to lose their hearts. There is a way
to get the kingdom:—get the people, and the kingdom is got. There is a
way to get the people:—get their hearts, and the people are got. There
is a way to get their hearts:—it is simply to collect for them what they

---

[86] Bk III. Pt I. ii. 4.
[87] Bk IV. Pt I. xx.
[88] Bk I. Pt I. vi.
[89] Bk IV. Pt II. xvi.

desire, and not to lay on them what they dislike.[90]The people turn to a benevolent rule as water flows downwards, and as wild beasts run to the wilds. As the otter aids the deep waters, driving the fish into them, and as the hawk aids the thickets, driving the little birds to them, so Kĕeh and Chow aided T'ang and Woo, driving the people to them. If among the present rulers throughout the kingdom there were one who loved benevolence, all the other rulers would aid him by driving the people to him. Although he wished not to exercise the royal sway, he could not avoid doing so."

Two principal elements of this benevolent rule, much insisted on by Mencius, deserve to be made prominent. They are to be found indicated in the Analects, and in the older classics also, but it was reserved for our philosopher to set them forth, sharply defined in his own style, and to show the connation between them, They are:—that the people be made well off, and that they be educated; and the former is necessary in order to the efficiency of the other.

Once, when Confucius was passing through Wei in company with Yen Yĕw, he was struck with the populousness of the State. The disciple said, "Since the people are thus numerous, what more shall be done for them?" Confucius answered, "Enrich them." "And when they have been enriched, what more shall be done for them?" The reply was—"Teach them."[91] This brief conversation contains the germs of the ideas on which Mencius delighted to dwell.

We read in one place:—

"Let it be seen to that their fields of grain and hemp are well cultivated, and make the taxes on them light:—so the people may be made rich.

"Let it be seen to that they use their resources of food seasonally, and expend them only on the prescribed ceremonies:—so they will be more than can be consumed.

"The people cannot live without water and fire; yet if you knock at a man's door in the dusk of the evening, and ask for water and fire, there is no man who will not give them, such is the great abundance of them. A sage would govern the kingdom so as cause pulse and grain to be as abundant as water and fire. When pulse and grain are as abundant as water and fire, how shall there be among the people any that are not virtuous?"[92]

---

[90] Bk IV. Pt I. ix.
[91] Con. Ana., XIII. ix.
[92] Bk VII. Pt I. xxiii.

Again he says:—

"In good years the children of the people are moat of them good, and in bad years they are most of them evil."[93]

It is in his conversations, however, with king Seuen of Ts'e and duke Wăn of T'ăng, that we find the fullest exposition of the points in hand.

"They are only men of education who, without a certain livelihood, are able to maintain a fixed heart. As to the people, if they have not a certain livelihood, it follows that they will not have a fixed heart. And if they have not a fixed heart, there is nothing which they will not do in the way of self-abandonment, of moral deflection, of depravity, and of wild license. When they have thus been involved in crime, to follow them up and punish them:—this is to entrap the people. Therefore an intelligent ruler will regulate the livelihood of the people, so as to make sure that, above, they shall have sufficient wherewith to serve their parents, and, below, sufficient wherewith to support their wives and children; that in good years they shall always be abundantly satisfied, and that in bad years they shall escape the danger of perishing. After this he may urge them, and they will proceed to what is good, for in this case the people will follow after that with readiness."[94]

It is not necessary to remark here on the measures which Mencius recommends in order to secure a certain livelihood for the people. They embrace the regulation both of agriculture and commerce.[95] And education should be directed simply to illustrate the human relations.[96] What he says on these subjects is not without shrewdness, though many of his recommendations are inappropriate to the present state of society in China itself as well as in other countries. But his principle, that good government should contemplate and will be seen in the material well-being of the people, is worthy of all honor. Whether government should interfere to secure the education of the people is questioned by not a few. The religious denomination to which I have the honor to belong has distinguished itself by opposing such a doctrine in England,—more zealously perhaps than wisely.[97] But when Mencius teaches that with the mass of men education will have little success where the life is embittered by a miserable poverty, he shows himself well acquainted

---

[93] Bk VI. Pt I vii.
[94] Bk I. Pt I. vii. 20, 21; Bk III. Pt I. iii. 3.
[95] Bk III. Pt I. iii.; Bk I. Pt II. iv; Bk II. Pt I. v.: *et al.*
[96] Bk III. Pt I. iii. 10.
[97] Its views are now, in 1874, very different.

with human nature. Educationists now seem generally to recognize it, but I think it is only within a century that it has assumed in Europe the definiteness and importance with which it appeared to Mencius here in China two thousand years ago.

We saw how Mencius, when he was residing in T'ăng, came into contact with a class of enthusiasts, who advocated a return to the primitive state of society,

"When Adam delved and Eve span."

They said that wise and able princes should cultivate the ground equally and along with their people, and eat the fruit of their labor,—that "to have granaries, arsenals, and treasuries was an oppressing of people." Mencius exposed these errors very happily, showing the necessity to society of a division of labor, and that the conduct of government should be in the hands of a lettered class.

"I suppose," he said to a follower of the strange doctrines, "that Heu Hing sows grain and eats the produce. Is it not so?" "It is so," was the answer. "I suppose that he also weaves cloth, and wears his own manufacture. Is it not so?" "No; Heu wears clothes of haircloth." "Does he wear a cap?" "He wears a cap." "What kind of cap?" "A plain cap." "Is it woven by himself?" "No; he gets it in exchange for grain." "Why does Heu not weave it himself?" "That would injure his husbandry." "Does Heu cook his food in boilers and earthen-ware pans, and does he plough with an iron share?" "Yes." "Does he make those articles himself?" "No; he gets them in exchange for grain." On these admissions Mencius proceeds:—"The getting those various articles in exchange for grain is not oppressive to the potter and the founder, and the potter and the founder in their turn, in exchanging their various articles for grain, are not oppressive to the husbandman. How should such a thing be supposed? But why does not Heu, [on his principles,] act the potter and founder, supplying himself with the articles which he uses solely from his own establishment? Why does he go confusedly dealing and exchanging with the handicraftsmen? Why does he not spare himself so much trouble?" His opponent attempted a reply:—"The business of the handicraftsman can by no means be carried on along with the business of husbandry." Mencius resumed:—"Then, is it the government of the empire which alone can be carried along with the practice of husbandry? Great men have their proper business, and little men have their proper business. Moreover, in the case of any single individual, whatever articles he can require are ready to his hand, being produced by the various handicraftsmen;—if he must first make them for his own use, this way of doing would keep all the people running about upon the roads. Hence there is the saying:—'Some men labor with their minds, and some with their strength. Those who labor with their minds govern others; those who labor with their strength are governed by others. Those who are governed by others support them; those who govern others are supported by them.' This is a principle universally recognized."[98]

Sir John Davis has observed that this is exactly Pope's line,

"And those who think still govern those who toil."[99]

Mencius goes on to illustrate it very clearly by referring to the labors of Yaou and Shun. His opponent makes a feeble attempt at the end to say a word in favor of the new doctrines he had embraced:—

"If Heu's doctrines were followed there would not be two prices in the market, nor any deceit in the kingdom. If a boy were sent to the market, no one would impose on him; linen and silk of the same length would be of the same price. So it would be with bundles of hemp and silk, being of the same weight: with the different kinds of grain, being the same in quantity; and with shoes which were the same in size." Mencius meets this with a decisive reply:—"It is the nature of things to be of unequal quality; some are twice, some five times, some ten times, some a hundred times, some a thousand times, some ten thousand times as valuable as others If you reduce them all to the same standard, that must throw the empire into confusion. If large shoes were of the same price with small shoes, who would make them? For people to follow the doctrines of Heu would be for them to lead one another on to practise deceit. How can they avail for the government of a State?"

There is only one other subject which I shall here notice, with Mencius' opinions upon it,—the position namely, which he occupied himself with reference to the princes of his time. He calls it that of "a Teacher," but that term in our language very inadequately represents it. He wished to meet with some ruler who would look to him as "guide, philosopher, and friend," regulating himself by his counsels, and thereafter committing to him the entire administration of his government. Such men, he insisted, there had been in China from the earliest ages. Shun had been such to Yaou; Yu and Kaou Yaou had been such to Shun; E Yin had been such to T'ang; T'ae-kung Wang had been such to king Wăn; Chow-kung had been such to the kings Woo and Shing; Confucius might have been such to any prince who knew his merit; Tsze-sze was such, in a degree, to the dukes Hwuy of Pe and

---

[98] Bk III. Pt iv.

[99] The Chinese, vol. ii. p. 56.

Muh of Loo.[100] The wandering scholars of his own day, who went from court to court, sometimes with good intentions and sometimes with bad, pretended to this character; but Mencius held them in abhorrence. They disgraced the character and prostituted it, and he stood forth as its vindicator and true exemplifier.

Never did Christian priest lift up his mitred front, or show his shaven crown, or wear his Geneva gown, more loftily in courts and palaces than Mencius, the Teacher, demeaned himself. We have seen what struggles sometimes arose between him and the princes who would fain have had him bend to their power and place.

"Those," said he, "who give counsel to the great should despise them, and not look at their pomp and display. Halls several fathoms high, with beams projecting several cubits:—these, if my wishes were to be realized, I would not have. Food spread before me over ten cubits square, and attendant girls to the amount of hundreds:—these, though my wishes were realized, I would not have. Pleasure and wine, and the dash of hunting, with thousands of chariots following after me:—these, though my wishes were realized, I would not have. What they esteem are what I would have nothing to do with; what I esteem are the rules of the ancients.—Why should I stand in awe of them?"[101]

Before we bring a charge of pride against Mencius on account of this language and his conduct in accordance with it, we must bear in mind that the literati in China do in reality occupy the place of priests and ministers in Christian kingdoms. Sovereign and people have to seek the law at their lips. The ground on which they stand,—"the rules of the ancients,"—affords but poor footing compared with the Word of God; still it is to them the truth, the unalterable law of life and duty, and, as the expounders of it, they have to maintain a dignity which will not compromise its claims. That "scholars are the first and head of the four classes of the people," is a maxim universally admitted. I do desiderate in Mencius any approach to humility of soul, but I would not draw my illustrations of the defect from the boldness of his speech and deportment as "a Teacher."

But in one respect I am not sure but that our philosopher failed to act worthy of the character which he thus assumed. The great men to whom he was in the habit of referring as his patterns nearly all rose from deep poverty to their subsequent eminence.

---

[100] See Bk V. Pt II. iii. vii.: *et al.*
[101] Bk VII. Pt II. xxxiv. This passage was written on the pillars of a hall in College street, East, where the gospel was first preached publicly in their own tongue to the people of Canton, in February, 1858.

"Shun rose to the Empire from among the channeled fields; Foo Yueh was called to office from the midst of his building-frames; Kaou Kih from his fish and salt."[102] "E Yin was a farmer in Sin. When T'ang sent persons with presents of silk, to entreat him to enter his service, he said, with an air of indifference and self-satisfaction, 'What can I do with those silks with which T'ang invites me? Is it not best for me to abide in the channeled fields, and there delight myself with the principles of Yaou and Shun?'"[103]

It does not appear that any of those worthies accepted favors while they were not in office, or from men whom they disapproved. With Mencius it was very different: he took largely from the princes whom he lectured and denounced. Possibly he might plead in justification the example of Confucius, but he carried the practice to a greater extent than that sage had ever done,—to an extent which staggered even his own disciples and elicited their frequent inquiries. For instance:—

P'ang Kăng asked him, saying, "Is it not an extravagant procedure to go from one prince to another and live upon them, followed by several tens of carriages, and attended by several hundred men?" Mencius replied, "If there be not a proper ground for taking it, a single bamboo-cup of rice may not be received from a man. If there be such a proper ground, then Shun's receiving the empire from Yaou is not to be considered excessive. Do you think it was excessive?" "No," said the other, "but for a scholar performing no service to receive his support notwithstanding is improper." Mencius answered, "If you do not have an intercommunication of the productions of labor, and an interchange of men's services, so that one from his overplus may supply the deficiency of another, then husbandmen will have a superfluity of grain, and women will have a superfluity of cloth. If you have such an interchange, carpenters and carriage-wrights may all get their food from you. Here now is a man who, at home, is filial, and, abroad, respectful to his elders, and who watches over the principles of the ancient kings, awaiting the rise of future learners;—and yet you will refuse to support him. How is it that you give honor to the carpenter and carriage-wright, and slight him who practices benevolence and righteousness?" P'ang Kăng said, "The aim of the carpenter and carriage-wright is by their trades to seek for a living. Is it also the aim of the superior man in his practice of principles to seek for a living?" "What have you to do," returned Mencius, "with his purpose? He is of service to you. He deserves to be supported, and should be supported. And let me ask—Do you remunerate a man's intention, or do you

---

[102] Bk VI. Pt II. xv. 1.
[103] Bk V. Pt I. vii. 2, 3.

remunerate his service?" To this Kăng replied, "I remunerate his intention." Mencius said, "There is a man here who breaks your tiles and draws unsightly figures on your walls;—his purpose may be thereby to seek for his living, but will you indeed remunerate him?" "No," said Kăng; and Mencius then concluded: "That being the case, it is not the purpose which you remunerate, but the work done."[104]

The ingenuity of Mencius in the above conversation will not be questioned. The position from which he starts in his defence, that society is based on a division of labor and an interchange of services, is sound, and he fairly hits and overthrows his disciples on the point that we remunerate a man not for his aim but for his work done. But he does not quite meet the charge against himself. This will better appear from another brief conversation with Kung-sun Ch'ow on the same subject.

"It is said, in the Book of Poetry," observed Chow,

"'He will not eat the bread of idleness.'

How is it that we see superior men eating without laboring?" Mencius replied, "When a superior man resides in a country, if the sovereign employ his counsels, he comes to tranquility, wealth, honor, and glory; if the young in it follow his instructions, they become filial, obedient to their elders, true-hearted, and faithful.—What greater example can there be than this of not eating the bread of idleness?"[105]

The argument here is based on the supposition that the superior man has free course, is appreciated by the sovereign, and venerated and obeyed by the people. But this never was the case with Mencius. Only once, the short time that he was in T'ăng, did a ruler listen favorably to his counsels. His lessons, it may be granted, were calculated to be of the greatest benefit to the communities where he was, but it is difficult to see the "work done," for which he could claim the remuneration. His reasoning might very well be applied to vindicate a government's extending its patronage to literary men, where it recognized in a general way the advantages to be derived from their pursuits. Still more does it accord with that employed in western nations where ecclesiastical establishments form one of the institutions of a country. The members belonging to them must have their maintenance, independently of the personal character of the rulers. But Mencius' position was more that of a reformer. His claims were of those of his personal merit. It seems to me that P'ang Kăng had reason to doubt the propriety of his course, and

---

[104] Bk III. Pt II. iv.
[105] Bk VII. Pt I. xxxii.

characterize it as extravagant.

Another disciple, Wan Chang, pressed him very closely with the inconsistency of his taking freely the gifts of the princes on whom he was wont to pass sentence so roundly. Mencius had insisted that, where the donor offered his gift on a ground of reason and in a manner accordant with propriety, even Confucius would have received it.

"Here now," said Chang, "is one who stops and robs people outside the city-gates. He offers his gift on a ground of reason and in a proper manner;—would it be right to receive it so acquired by robbery?" The philosopher of course said it would not, and the other pursued:—"The rulers of the present day take from their people just as a robber despoils his victim. Yet if they put a good face of propriety on their gifts, the superior man receives them. I venture to ask you to explain this." Mencius answered:—"Do you think that, if there should arise a truly royal sovereign, he would collect the rulers of the present day and put them all to death? Or would he admonish them, and then, on their not changing their ways, put them to death? Indeed to call every one who takes what does not properly belong to him a robber, is pushing a point of resemblance to the utmost, and insisting on the most refined idea of righteousness."[106]

Here again we must admire the ingenuity of Mencius; but it amuses us more than it satisfies. It was very well for him to maintain his dignity as "a Teacher," and not go to the princes when they called him, but his refusal would have had more weight, if he had kept his hands clean from all their offerings. I have said above that if less awe-full than Confucius, he is more admirable. Perhaps it would be better to say he is more brilliant. There is some truth in the saying of the scholar Ch'ing, that the one is the glass that glitters, and the other the gem that is truly valuable.

Without dwelling on other characteristics of Mencius, or culling from him other striking sayings,—of which there are many,—I proceed to exhibit and discuss his doctrine of the goodness of human nature.

6. If the remarks which I have just made on the intercourse of Mencius with the princes of his day have lowered him somewhat in the estimation of my readers, his doctrine of human nature, and the force with which he advocates it, will not fail to produce a high appreciation of him as a moralist and thinker. In concluding my exhibition of the opinions of Confucius in the former volume, I have observed that "he threw no light on any of the questions which have a worldwide interest." This Mencius did. The constitution of man's nature, and how far it supplies to him a rule of conduct and a law of duty, are inquiries

---

[106] Bk V. Pt II. iv.

than which there can hardly be any others of more importance. They were largely discussed in the Schools of Greece. A hundred vigorous and acute minds of modern Europe have occupied themselves with them. It will hardly be questioned in England that the palm for clear and just thinking on the subject belongs to Bishop Butler, but it will presently be seen that his views and those of Mencius are, as nearly as possible, identical. There is a difference of nomenclature and a combination of parts, in which the advantage is with the Christian prelate; Felicity of illustration and charm of style belong to the Chinese philosopher. The doctrine in both is the same.

The utterances of Confucius on the subject of our nature were few and brief. The most remarkable is where he says:—"Man is born for uprightness. If a man be without uprightness and yet live, his escape [from death] is the effect of mere good fortune."[107] This is in entire accordance with Mencius' view, and as he appeals to the sage in his own support,[108] though we cannot elsewhere find the words which he quotes, we may believe that Confucius would have approved of the sentiments of his follower, and frowned on those who have employed some of his sayings in confirmation of other conclusions.[109] I am satisfied in my own mind on this point. His repeated enunciation of "the golden rule," though only in a negative form, is sufficient evidence of it.

The opening sentence of "The Doctrine of the Mean,"—"What Heaven has conferred is called THE NATURE; an accordance with this nature is called THE PATH; the regulation of the path is called INSTRUCTION," finds a much better illustration from Mencius than from Tsze-sze himself. The germ of his doctrine lies in it. We saw reason to discard the notion that he was a pupil of Tsze-sze; but he was acquainted with his treatise just named, and as he has used some other parts of it, we may be surprised that in his discussions on human nature he has made no reference to the above passage.

What gave occasion to his dwelling largely on the theme was the prevalence of wild and injurious speculations about it. In nothing did the disorder of the age more appear. Kung-too, one of his disciples, once went to him and said:—

"The philosopher Kaou says:—'Man's nature is neither good nor bad.' Some say:—'Man's nature may be made to practise good, and it may be made to practise evil; and accordingly, under Wǎn and Woo, the people loved what was good, while, under Yĕw and Le, they loved what was cruel.' Others say:—'The nature of some is good, and the

[107] Ana., VI. xvii.
[108] Bk VI. Pt I. vi. 8; viii. 4.
[109] See the annotations of the editor of Yang-tsze's works in the "Complete Works of the Ten *Tsze.*"

nature of others is bad. Hence it was that under such a sovereign as Yaou there yet appeared Sěang; that with such a father as Koo-sow there yet appeared Shun; and that with Chow for their sovereign, and the son of their elder brother besides, there were found K'e, the viscount of Wei, and the prince Pe-kan.' And now you say:—'The nature is good.' Then are all those opinions wrong?"[110]

"The nature of man is good:"—this was Mencius' doctrine. By many writers it has been represented as entirely antagonistic to Christianity; and, as thus broadly and briefly enunciated, it sounds startling enough. As fully explained by himself, however, it is not so very terrible. Butler's scheme has been designated "the system of Zeno baptized into Christ."[111] That of Mencius, identifying closely with the master of the Porch, is yet more susceptible of a similar transformation.

But before endeavoring to make this statement good, it will be well to make some observations on the opinion of the philosopher Kaou. He was a contemporary of Mencius, and they came into argumentative collision. One does not see immediately the difference between his opinion, as stated by Kung-too, and the next. Might not man's nature, though neither good nor bad, be made to practise the one or the other? Kaou's view went to deny any essential distinction between good and evil,—virtue and vice. A man might be made to act in a way commonly called virtue and in a way commonly called evil,, but in the one action there was really nothing more approvable than in the other. "Life," he said, "was what was meant by nature."[112] The phenomena of benevolence and righteousness were akin to those of walking and sleeping, eating and seeing. This extravagance afforded scope for Mencius' favorite mode of argument, the *reductio ad absurdum.* He showed, on Kaou's principles, that "the nature of a dog was like the nature of an ox, and the nature of an ox like the nature of a man."

The two first conversations[113] between them are more particularly worthy of attention, because, while they are a confutation of his opponent, they indicate clearly our philosopher's own theory. Kaou compared man's nature to a willow tree, and benevolence and righteousness to the cups and bowls that might be fashioned from its wood. Mencius replied that it was not the nature of the willow to produce cups and bowls; they might be made from it indeed, by bending and cutting and otherwise injuring it; but must humanity be done such violence to in order to fashion the virtues from it? Kaou again compared the nature to water whirling round in a corner;—open a passage for it in any direction, and it will flow forth accordingly.

---

[110] Bk VI. Pt I. vi. 1-4.
[111] Wardlaw's Christian Ethics, edition of 1833, p. 119.
[112] Bk VI. Pt I. iii.
[113] Bk VI. Pt I. i. ii.

"Man's nature," said he, "is indifferent to good and evil, just as the water is indifferent to the east and west." Mencius answered him:—"Water indeed will flow indifferently to the east or west, but will it flow indifferently up or down? The tendency of man's nature to good is like the tendency of water to flow downwards. There are none but have this tendency to good, just as all water flows downwards. By striking water and causing it to leap up, you may make it go over your forehead, and, by damming and leading it, you may force it up a hill; but are such movements according to the nature of water? It is the force applied which causes them. When men are made to do what is not good, their nature is dealt with in this way."

Mencius has no stronger language than this, as indeed it would be difficult to find any stronger, to declare his belief in the goodness of human nature. To many Christian readers it proves a stumbling-block and offence. But I venture to think that this is without sufficient reason. He is speaking of our nature in its ideal, and not as it actually is,—as we may ascertain from the study of it that it ought to be, and not as it is made to become. My rendering of the sentences last quoted may be objected to, because of my introduction of the term *tendency*; but I have Mencius' express sanction for the representation I give of his meaning. (Replying to Kung-too's question, whether all the other opinions prevalent about man's nature were wrong, and his own, that it is good, correct, he said:—"From the feelings proper to it, we see that it is constituted for the practice of what is good. *This is what I mean in saying that the nature is good.* If men do what is not good, the blame cannot be imputed to their natural powers."[114] Those who find the most fault with him, will hardly question the truth of this last declaration. When a man does wrong, whose is the blame,—the sin? He might be glad to roll the guilt on his Maker, or upon his nature,—which is only an indirect charging of his Maker with it;—but it is his own burden, which he must bear himself.)

The proof by which Mencius supports his view of human nature as formed only for virtue is twofold. First, he maintains that there are in man a natural principle of benevolence, a natural principle of righteousness, a natural principle of apprehending moral truth. "These," he says, "are not infused into us from without. We are certainly possessed of them; and a different view is simply from want of reflection."[115] In further illustration of this he argued thus:—

"All men have a mind which cannot bear to see the sufferings of others. My meaning may be illustrated thus:—Even now-a-days," *i.e.*, in these degenerate times, "if men suddenly see a child about to fall

---

[114] Bk VI. Pt I. vi. 5, 6.
[115] Bk VI. Pt I. vi. 7

into a well, they will without exception experience a feeling of alarm and distress. They will feel so, not as a ground on which they may gain the favor of the child's parents, nor as a ground on which they may seek the praise of their neighbours and friends, nor from a dislike to the reputation of having been unmoved by such a thing. From this case we may see that the feeling of commiseration is essential to man, that the feeling of shame and dislike is essential to man, that the feeling of modesty and complaisance is essential to man, and that the feeling of approval and disapproval is essential to man. These feelings are the principles respectively of benevolence, righteousness, propriety, and the knowledge [of good and evil]. Men have these four principles just as they have their four limbs."[116]

Let all this be compared with the language of Butler in his three famous *Sermons upon Human Nature.* He shows in the first of these:—"First, that there is a natural principle of benevolence in man; secondly, that the several *passions* and *affections,* which are distinct both from benevolence and self-love, do in general contribute and lead us to *public* good as really as to private; and thirdly, that there is a principle of reflection in men, by which they distinguish between, approve and disapprove, their own actions."[117] Is there anything more in this than was apprehended and expressed by Mencius? Butler says in the conclusion of his first discourse that "men follow their nature to a certain degree but not entirely; their actions do not come up to the whole of what their nature leads them to; and they often violate their nature." This also Mencius declares in his own forceful manner:—"When men having these four principles, yet say of

---

[116] Bk II. Pt I. vi. 3, 4, 5, 6.

[117] I am indebted to Butler for fully understanding Mencius' fourth feeling, that of approving and disapproving, which he calls "the principle of knowledge," or wisdom. In the notes on II. Pt I. vi. 5, I have said that he gives to this term "a moral sense." It is the same with Butler's principle of reflection, by which men distinguish between, and approve or disapprove, their own actions.—I have heard gentlemen speak contemptuously of Mencius' case in point, to prove the existence of a feeling of benevolence in man. "This," they have said, "is Mencius' idea of virtue, to save a child from falling into a well. A mighty display of virtue, truly!" Such language arises from misconceiving Mencius' object in putting the case. "If there be," says Butler, "any affection in human nature, the object and end of which is the good of another, this is itself benevolence. Be it ever so short, be it in ever so low a degree, or ever so unhappily confined, it proves the assertion and points out what we were designed for, as really as though it were in a higher degree and more extensive." "It is sufficient that the seeds of it be implanted in our nature." The illustration from a child falling into a well must be pronounced a happy one. How much lower Mencius could go may be seen from his conversation with king Seuen, Bk I. Pt I. vii., whom he leads to a consciousness of his commiserating mind from the fact that he had not been able to bear the frightened appearance of a bull which was being led by to be killed, and ordered it to be spared. The kindly heart that was moved by the suffering of an animal had only to be carried out, to suffice for the love and protection of all within the four seas.

themselves that they cannot develop them, they play the thief with themselves, and he who says of his prince that he cannot develop them, plays the thief with his prince."[118] "Men differ from one another in regard to the principles of their nature;—some as much again as others, some five times as much, and some to an incalculable amount:—it is because they cannot carry out fully their natural powers."[119]

So much for the first or preliminary view of human nature insisted on by Mencius, that it contains principles which are disinterested and virtuous. But there wants something more to make good the position that virtue ought to be supreme, and that it is for it, in Second proof opposition to vice, that our nature is formed. To use some of the "licentious talk" which Butler puts into the mouth of an opponent:—"Virtue and religion require not only that we do good to others, when we are led this way, by benevolence and reflection happening to be stronger than other principles, passions, or appetites; but likewise that the *whole character* be formed upon thought and reflection; that *every* action be directed by some determinate rule, some other rule than the strength or prevalence of any principle or passion. What sign is there in our nature (for the inquiry is only about what is to be collected from thence) that this was intended by its Author? Or how does so various and fickle a temper as that of man appear adapted thereto?... As brutes have various instincts, by which they are carried on to the end the Author of their nature intended them for, is not man in the same condition, with this difference only, that to his instincts (*i.e.*, appetites and passions) is added the principle of reflection or conscience? And as brutes act agreeably to their nature in following that principle or particular instinct which for the present is strongest in them; does not man likewise act agreeably to his nature, or obey the law of his creation, by following that principle, be it passion or conscience, which for the present happens to be strongest in him?..... Let every one then quietly follow his nature; as passion, reflection, appetite, the several parts of it, happen to be the strongest; but let not the man of virtue take it upon him to blame the ambitious, the covetous, the dissolute; since these, equally with him, obey and follow their nature."[120]

To all this Butler replies by showing that the principle of reflection or conscience is "not to be considered merely as a principle in the heart, which is to have some influence as well as others, but as a faculty, in kind and in nature, supreme over all others, and which bears its own authority of being so;" that the difference between this and the other constituents of human nature is not "a difference in strength or degree,"

---

[118] Bk II. Pt I. vi. 6.

[119] Bk VI. Pt I. vi. 7.

[120] See Sermon Second.

but "a difference *in nature and in land;*" that "it was placed within to be our proper governor; to direct and regulate all under principles, passions and motives of action:—this is its right and office; thus sacred is its authority." It follows from the view of human nature thus established, that "the inward frame of man is *a system or constitution*; whose several parts are united, not by a physical principle of individuation, but by the respects they have to each other, the chief of which is the subjection which the appetites, passions, and particular affections have to the one supreme principle of reflection or conscience."[121]

Now, the *substance* of this reasoning is to be found in Mencius. Human nature—the inward frame of man—is with him *a system or constitution* as much as with Butler. He says, for instance:—

"There is no part of himself which a man does not love; and as he loves all, so he should nourish all. There is not an inch of skin which he does not love, and so there is not an inch of skin which he will not nourish. FOR EXAMINING WHETHER HIS WAY OF NOURISHING BE GOOD OR NOT, WHAT OTHER RULE IS THERE BUT THIS, THAT HE DETERMINE BY REFLECTING ON HIMSELF WHERE IT SHOULD BE APPLIED?

"Some parts of the body are noble, and some ignoble; some great and some small. The great must not be injured for the small, nor the noble for the ignoble. He who nourishes the little belonging to him is a little man, and he who nourishes the great is a great man."[122]

Again:—

"Those who follow that part of themselves which is great are great men; those who follow that part which is little are little men."[123]

The great part of ourselves is the moral elements of our constitution; the lower part is the appetites and passions that centre in self. He says finely:—

"There is a nobility of Heaven, and there is a nobility of man. Benevolence, righteousness, self-consecration, and fidelity, with unwearied joy in the goodness [of these virtues]:—these constitute the nobility of Heaven. To be a duke, a minister, or a great officer;—this constitutes the nobility of man."[124]

---

[121] See note to Sermon Third.
[122] Bk VI. Pt I. xiv.
[123] *Ib.*, ch. xv.
[124] *Ib.*, ch. xvi.

There is one passage very striking:—

"For the mouth to desire tastes, the eye colors, the ear sounds, the nose odors, and the four limbs ease and rest:—these things are natural. But there is the appointment [of Heaven] in connation with them; and the superior man does not say [in his pursuit of them], 'It is my nature.' [The exercise of] love between father and son, [the observance of] righteousness between ruler and minister, the rules of ceremony between host and guest, the [display of] knowledge in [recognizing] the able and virtuous, and [the fulfilling] the heavenly course by the sage:—these are appointed [by Heaven]. But there is [an adaptation of our] nature [for them]; and the superior man does not say, [in reference to them,] 'There is a [limiting] appointment [of Heaven].'"[125]

From these paragraphs it is quite clear that what Mencius considered as deserving properly to be called the nature of man, was not that by which he is a creature of appetites and passions, but that by which he is lifted up into the higher circle of intelligence and virtue. By the phrase, "the appointment of Heaven," most Chinese scholars understand the will of Heaven, limiting in the first case the gratification of the appetites, and in the second the exercise of the virtues. To such limitation Mencius teaches there ought to be a cheerful submission so far as the appetites are concerned, but where the virtues are in question, we are to be striving after them notwithstanding adverse and opposing circumstances. THEY ARE OUR NATURE, what we were made for, what we have to do. I will refer but to one other specimen of his teaching on this subject. "The will," he said, using that term for the higher moral nature in activity,—"the will is the leader of the passion-nature. The passion-nature pervades and animates the body. The will is first and chief, and the passion-nature is subordinate to it."[126]

My readers can now judge for themselves whether I exaggerated at all in saying that Mencius' doctrine of human nature was, as nearly as possible, identical with that of Bishop Butler. Sir James Mackintosh has said of the sermons to which I have made reference, and his other cognate discourses, that in them Butler "taught truths more capable of being exactly distinguished from the doctrines of his predecessors, more satisfactorily established by him, more comprehensively applied to particulars, more rationally connected with each other, and therefore more worthy of the name of *discovery*, than any with which we are acquainted; if we ought not, with some hesitation, to except the first

---

[125] Bk VII. Pt II. xxiv.
[126] Bk II. Pt I. ii. 9.

steps of the Grecian philosophers towards a Theory of Morals."[127] It is
to be wished that the attention of this great scholar had been called to
the writings of our philosopher. Mencius was senior to Zeno, though a
portion of their lives synchronized. Butler certainly was not indebted to
him for the views which he advocated; but it seems to me that Mencius
had left him nothing to *discover.*

But the question now arises—"Is the view of human nature
propounded by Mencius correct?" So far as yet appears, I see not how
the question can be answered otherwise than in the affirmative. Man
was formed for virtue. Be it that his conduct is very far from being
conformed to virtue, that simply fastens on him the shame of guilt.
Fallen as he may be,—fallen as I believe and know he is,—his nature
still bears its testimony, when properly interrogated, against all
unrighteousness. Man, heathen man, *a Gentile without the law, is still a
law to himself.* So the apostle Paul affirms; and to no moral teacher of
Greece or Rome can we appeal for so grand an illustration of the
averment as we find in Mencius. I would ask those whom his sayings
offend, whether it would have been better for his countrymen if he had
taught a contrary doctrine, and told them that man's nature is bad, and
that the more they obeyed all its lusts and passions, the more would
they be in accordance with it, and the more pursuing the right path?
Such a question does not need a reply. The proper use of Mencius'
principles is to reprove the Chinese—and ourselves as well—of the
thousand acts of sin of which they and we are guilty, that come within
their sweep and under their condemnation.

From the ideal of man to his actualism there is a vast descent.
Between what he ought to be and what he is, the contrast is
melancholy. "*Benevolence*" said our philosopher, "is the characteristic
of man."[128] It is "the wide house in which the world should dwell,"
while *propriety* is "the correct position in which the world should ever
be found," and *righteousness* is "the great path which men should ever
be pursuing."[129] In opposition to this, however, hatred, improprieties,
unrighteousness, are constant phenomena of human life. We find men
hateful and hating one another, quenching the light that is in them, and
walking in darkness to perform all deeds of shame. "There is none that
doeth good; no, not one." Mencius would have denied this last
sentence, claiming that the sages should be excepted from it; but he is
ready enough to admit the fact that men in general do evil and violate
the law of their nature. They sacrifice the noble portion of themselves
for the gratification of the ignoble; they follow that part which is little,
and not that which is great. He can say nothing further in explanation of

---

[127] Encyclopædia Britannica, Second Preliminary Dissertation; on Butler.
[128] Bk VII. Pt II. xvi.
[129] Bk III. Pt II. ii. 3.

the fact. He points out indeed the effect of injurious circumstances, and the power of evil example; and he has said several things on these subjects worthy of notice:—

"It is not to be wondered at that the king is not wise! Suppose the case of the most easily growing thing in the world;—if you let it have one day's genial heat, and then expose it for ten days to cold, it will not be able to grow. It is but seldom that I have an audience of the king, and when I retire, there come all those who act upon him like the cold. Though I succeed in bringing out some buds of goodness, of what avail is it?"[130] "In good years the children of the people are most of them good, while in bad years the most of them abandon themselves to evil. It is not owing to their natural powers conferred on them by Heaven that they are thus different:—the abandonment is owing to the circumstances through which they allow their minds to be ensnared and drowned in evil. There now is barley:—let it be sown and covered up; the ground being the same, and the time of sowing likewise the same, it grows rapidly up, and when the full time is come, it is all found to be ripe. Although there may be inequalities [of produce], that is owing to [the difference of] the soil as rich or poor, the unequal nourishment afforded by the rains and dews, and to the different ways in which man has performed his business."[131]

The inconsistencies in human conduct did not escape his observation. After showing that there is that in human nature which will sometimes make men part with life sooner than with righteousness, he goes on:—"And yet a man will accept of ten thousand *chung* without any consideration of propriety and righteousness. What can they add to him? When he takes them, is it not that he may obtain beautiful mansions, that he may secure the services of wives and concubines, or that the poor and needy may be helped by him?" The scalpel is used here with a bold and skilful hand. The lust of the flesh, and the lust of the eyes, and the pride of life are laid bare, nor does he stop till he has exposed the subtle workings of the delusion that the end may sanctify the means, that evil may be wrought that good may come. He pursues:—"In the former case the offered bounty was not received though it would have saved from death, and now the emolument is taken for the sake of beautiful mansions The bounty that would have preserved from death was not received, and the emolument is taken to get the services of wives and concubines. The bounty that would have saved from death was not received, and the emolument is taken that one's poor and needy acquaintance may be helped. Was it then not

---

[130] Bk VI. Pt I. ix.
[131] *Ib*. ch. vii.

possible likewise to decline this? This is a case of what is called 'Losing the proper nature of one's mind.'"[132]

To the principle implied in the concluding sentences of this quotation Mencius most pertinaciously adheres. He will not allow that original badness can be predicated of human nature from any amount of actual wickedness.

"The trees." said he, "of the Nĕw mountain were once beautiful. Being situated, however, in the suburbs of [the capital of] a large State, they were hewn down with axes and bills:—and could they retain their beauty? Still, through the growth from the vegetative life day and night, and the nourishing influence of the rain and dew, they were not without buds and sprouts springing forth;—but then came the cattle and goats, and browsed upon them. To these things is owing the bare and stript appearance [of the mountain], and when people see this they think it was never finely wooded. But is this the proper nature of the mountain? And so even of what properly belongs to man:—shall it be said that the mind [of any man] was without benevolence and righteousness? The way in which a man loses his proper goodness of mind is like the way in which those trees were denuded by axes and bills. Hewn down day after day, can the mind retain its excellence? But there is some growth of its life day and night, and in the [calm] air of the morning, just between night and day, the mind feels in a degree the desires and aversions which are proper to humanity; but the feeling is not strong, and then it is fettered and destroyed by what the man does during the day. This fettering takes place again and again; the restorative influence of the night is not sufficient to preserve [the proper goodness of the mind]; and when this proves insufficient for that purpose, the nature becomes not much different from that of the irrational animals, and when people see this, they think that it never had those powers [which I assert]. But does this condition represent the feelings proper to humanity?"[133]

Up to this point I fail to perceive anything in Mencius' view of human nature that is contrary to the teachings of our Christian Scriptures, and that may not be employed with advantage by the missionary in preaching the Gospel to the Chinese. It is far from covering what we know to be the whole duty of man, yet it is defective rather than erroneous. Deferring any consideration of this for a brief space, I now inquire whether Mencius, having an ideal of the goodness of human nature, held also that it had been and could be realized? The

---

[132] Bk VI. Pt I. xii. 7, 8.
[133] Bk VI. Pt I. ch. viii. 1, 2.

answer is that he did. The actual realization he found in the sages, and he contended that it was within the reach of every individual.

"All things which are the same in kind," he says, "are like one another;—why should we doubt in regard to man, as if he were a solitary exception to this? The sage and we are the same in kind. The feet, the mouths, the eyes of the sages were not different from those of other people, neither were their minds."[134] "Is it so," he was once asked, "that all men may be Yaous and Shuns?" and he answered, "It is," adding by way of explanation:—"To walk slowly, keeping behind his elders, is to perform the part of a younger brother, and to walk quickly and precede his elders is to violate that duty. Now, is it what a man cannot do,—to walk slowly? It is WHAT HE DOES NOT DO. The course of Yaou and Shun was simply that of filial piety and fraternal duty. Do you wear the clothes of Yaou, repeat the words of Yaou, and do the actions of Yaou;—and you will just be a Yaou."[135]

Among the sages, however, Mencius made a distinction. Yaou and Shun exceeded all the rest, unless it might be Confucius. Those three never came short of, never went beyond, the law of their nature. The ideal and the actual were in them always one and the same. The others had only attained to perfection by vigorous effort and culture. Twice at least he has told us this. "Yaou and Shun were what they were by nature; T'ang and Woo were so by returning [to natural virtue]."[136] The actual result, however, was the same, and therefore he could hold them all up as models to his countrymen of the style of man that they ought to be and might be. What the compass and square were in the hands of the workman, enabling him to form perfect circles and squares, that the sages, "perfectly exhibiting the human relations," might be to every earnest individual, enabling him to perfect himself as they were perfect.[137]

Here we feel that the doctrine of Mencius wants an element which Revelation supplies. He knows nothing of the fact that "by one man sin entered into the world, and death by sin; and so death passed" (passed on, extended, $\delta\iota\tilde{\eta}\lambda\theta\epsilon\nu$) "to all men, because all sinned." We have our ideal as well as he; but for the living reality of it we must go back to Adam, as he was made by God in His own image, after His likeness. In him the model is soon shattered, and we do not discover it again, till God's own Son appears in the world, made in the likeness of sinful flesh, yet without sin. While He died for our transgressions, He left us also an example, that we should walk in His steps; and as we do so, we

---

[134] Bk VI. Pt I. ch. vii.3.
[135] *Ib.* Pt II. ii. 1, 4, 5.
[136] Bk VII. Pt I. xxx. 1; Pt II. xxxiii. 1.
[137] Bk IV. Pt I. ii. 1.

are carried on to glory and virtue. At the same time we find a law in our members warring against the law in our minds, and bringing us into captivity to sin. However we may strive after our ideal, we do not succeed in reaching it. The more we grow in the knowledge of Christ, and see in Him the glory of humanity in its true estate, the greater do we feel our own distance to be from it, and that of ourselves we cannot attain to it. There is something wrong about us; we need help from without in order to become even what our nature, apart from Revelation, tells us we ought to be.

When Mencius therefore points us to Yaou, Shun, and Confucius, and says that they were perfect, we cannot accept his statement. Understanding that he is speaking of them only in the sphere of human relations, we must yet believe that in many things they came short. One of them, the greatest of the three in Mencius' estimation, Confucius, again and again confesses so of himself. He was seventy years old, he says, before he could follow what his heart desired without transgressing what was right.[138] It might have been possible to convince the sage that he was under a delusion in this important matter even at that advanced age; but what his language allows is sufficient to upset Mencius' appeal to him. The image of sagely perfection is broken by it. It proves to be but a brilliant and unsubstantial phantasm of our philosopher's own imagining.

When he insists again, that every individual may become what he fancies that the sages were,—*i.e.,* perfect, living in love, walking in righteousness, observant of propriety, approving whatsoever is good, and disapproving whatever is evil,—he is pushing his doctrine beyond its proper limits; he is making a use of it of which it is not capable. It supplies a law of conduct, and I have set it forth as entitled to our highest admiration for the manner in which it does so; but law only gives the knowledge of what we are required to do:—it does not give the power to do it. We have seen how when it was necessary to explain accurately his statement that the nature of man is good, Mencius defined it as meaning that "it is constituted for the practice of that which is good." Because it is so constituted, it follows that every man ought to practise what is good. But some disorganization may have happened to the nature; some sad change may have come over it. The very fact that man has, in Mencius' own words, to recover his "lost mind,"[139] shows that the object of the constitution of the nature has not been realized. Whether he can recover it or not, therefore, is a question altogether different from that of its proper design.

---

[138] Con. Ana II. iv. 6.
[139] Bk VI Pt I. xi. 4

In one place, indeed, Mencius has said that "the great man is he who does not lose his child's-heart."[140] I can only suppose that, by that expression—"the child's-heart," he intends the ideal goodness which he affirms of our nature. But to attribute that to the child as actually existing in it is absurd. It has neither done good nor evil. It possesses the capacity for either. It will by and by awake to the consciousness that it ought to follow after the one, and eschew the other; but when it does so,—I should rather say when *he* does so, for the child has now emerged from a mere creature existence, and assumed the functions of a moral being, he will find that he has already given himself to inordinate affection for the objects of sense; and in the pursuit of gratification he is reckless of what must be acknowledged to be the better and nobler part, reckless also of the interest and claims of others, and whenever thwarted glows into passion and fury. The youth is more pliant than the man in whom the dominion of self-seeking has become ingrained as a habit; but no sooner does he become a subject of law, than he is aware of the fact, that when he would do good, evil is present with him. The boy has to go in search of his "lost heart," as truly as the man of fourscore. Even in him there is an "old man, corrupt according to the deceitful lusts," which he has to put off.

Butler had an immense advantage over Mencius, arising from his knowledge of the truths of Revelation. Many, admiring his sermons, have yet expressed a measure of dissatisfaction, because he does not in them make explicit reference to the condition of man as fallen and depraved. That he fully admitted the fact we know. He says elsewhere:—"Mankind are represented in Scripture to be in a state of. ruin;" "If mankind are corrupted and depraved in their moral character, and so are unfit for that state which Christ is gone to prepare for his disciples; and if the assistance of God's Spirit be necessary to renew their nature, in the degree requisite to their being qualified for that state; all which is implied in the express, though figurative declaration, *Except a man be horn of the Spirit, he cannot see the kingdom of God*."....[141] How is it, then, that there is no mention of this in the sermons? Dissatisfaction, I have said, has been expressed on account of this silence, and it would have taken the form of more pointed utterance, and more decided condemnation, but for the awe of his great name, and the general appreciation of the service he rendered to Christianity in his work on *The Analogy of Religion to the Course of Nature*. But, in truth, dissatisfaction at all is out of place. Butler wrote his sermons as he wrote his Analogy, in consequence of the peculiar necessity of his times. More particularly against Hobbes, denying all moral sentiments and social affections, and making a regard to personal

---

[140] Bk IV. Pt II. xii.
[141] The Analogy of Religion; Part II. chap. I.

advantage the only motive of human action, it was his business to prove that man's nature is of a very different constitution, comprehending disinterested affections, and above all the supreme element of conscience, which, "had it strength as it has right, would govern the world." He proves this, and so accomplishes his work. He had merely to do with the ideal of humanity. It did not belong to him to dwell on the actual feebleness of man to perform what is good. He might have added a few paragraphs to this effect; but it was not the character of his mind to go beyond the task which he had set himself. What is of importance to be observed here is, that he does not make the application of their common principles which Mencius does. He knows of no perfect men; he does not tell his readers that they merely to set about following their nature, and, without any aid from without, they will surely and easily go on to perfection.

Mencius is not to be blamed for his ignorance of what is to us the *Doctrine of the Fall.* He had no means of becoming acquainted with it. We have to regret, however, that his study of human nature produced in him no deep *feeling* on account of men's proneness to go astray. He never betrays any consciousness of his own weakness. In this respect he is again inferior to Confucius, and far from being, as I have said of him in another aspect of his character, "more admirable" than he. In the former volume I have shown that we may sometimes recognize in what the sage says of himself the expressions of a genuine humility. He acknowledges that he comes short of what he knows he ought to be. We do not meet with this in Mencius. His merit is that of the speculative thinker. His glance is searching and his penetration deep; but there is wanting that moral sensibility which would draw us to him, in our best moments, as a man of like passions with ourselves. The absence of humility is naturally accompanied with a lack of *sympathy.* There is a hardness about his teachings. He is the professor, performing an operation in the class-room, amid a throng of pupils who are admiring his science and dexterity, and who forgets in the triumph of his skill the suffering of the patient. The transgressors of their nature are to Mencius the "tyrants of themselves," or "the self-abandoned." The utmost stretch of his commiseration is a contemptuous "Alas for them!"[142] The radical defect of the orthodox moral school of China, that there only needs a knowledge of duty to insure its performance, is in him exceedingly apparent. Confucius, Tsze-sze, and Mencius most strangely never thought of calling this principle in question. It is always as in the formula of Tsze-sze:—"Given the sincerity, and there shall be the intelligence; given the intelligence, and there shall be the sincerity."

I said above that Mencius' doctrine of human nature was defective, inasmuch as even his ideal does not cover the whole field of duty. He

---

[142] Bk IV. Pt I. x.

says very little of what we owe to God. There is no glow of natural piety in his pages. Instead of the name *God*, containing in itself a recognition of the divine personality and supremacy, we hear from him more commonly, as from Confucius, of *Heaven.* Butler has said:—"By the love of God, I would understand all those regards, all those affections of mind, which are due immediately to Him from such a creature as man, and which rest in Him as their end."[143] Of such affections Mencius knows nothing. In one place he speaks of "delighting in Heaven,"[144] but he is speaking, when he does so, of the sovereign who with a great State serves a small one, and the delight is seen in certain condescensions to the weak and unworthy. Never once, where he is treating of the nature of man, does he make mention of any exercise of the mind as due directly to God. The services of religion come in China under the principle of propriety, and are only a cold formalism; but, even here, other things come with Mencius before them. We are told:—"The richest fruit of love is this,—the service of one's parents; the richest fruit of righteousness is this,—the obeying one's elder brothers; the richest fruit of wisdom is this,—the knowing those two things, and not departing from them; the richest fruit of propriety is this,—the ordering and adorning those two things." [145] How different is this from the reiterated declaration of the Scriptures, that "the fear of the Lord is the beginning of wisdom!" The first and great commandment, "Thou shalt *love* the Lord, thy God, with all thy heart and soul and mind and strength," was never thought of, much less delivered, by any Chinese philosopher or sage. Had Mencius apprehended this, and seen how all our duties to our fellow-men are to be performed as to God, he could not have thought so highly as he did of man's powers; a suspicion might have grown up that there is a shadow on the light which he has in himself.

This absence of the recognition of man's highest obligations from Mencius' ideal of our nature is itself a striking illustration of man's estrangement from God. His talking of Heaven has combined with the similar practice of his master to prepare the way for the grosser conceptions of the modern literati, who would often seem to deny the divine personality altogether, and substitute for both God and Heaven a mere principle of order or fitness of things. It has done more: it has left the people in the mass to become an easy prey to the idolatrous

---

[143] First Sermon Upon the Love of God.

[144] Bk I. Pt II. ii. 3.

[145] Bk IV. Pt I. xxvii. My friend, the Rev. Mr Moule, of Ningpo, has supplied me with the following interesting coincidence with the sentiments of Mencius in this passage, from one of the letters of Charles Lamb to Coleridge, dated Nov. 14th, 1796:—"Oh, my friend, cultivate the filial feelings; and let no one think himself relieved from the kind charities of relationship; these shall give him peace at the last; *these are the best foundation for every species of benevolence.*"

fooleries of Buddhism. Yea, the *unreligiousness* of the teachers has helped to deprave still more the religion of the nation, such as it is, and makes its services a miserable pageant of irreverent forms.

It is time to have done with this portion of my theme. It may be thought that I have done Mencius more than justice in the first part of my remarks, and less than justice at the last; but I hope it is not so. A very important use is to be made both of what he succeeds in, and where he fails, in his discoursing upon human nature. His principles may be, and, I conceive, ought to be, turned against himself. They should be pressed to produce the conviction of sin. There is enough in them, if the conscience be but quickened by the Spirit of God, to make the haughtiest scholar cry out, "O wretched man that I am! who shall deliver me from this body of death?" Then may it be said to him with effect, "Behold the Lamb of God, who taketh away the sin of the world!" Then may Christ, as a new and true exemplar of all that man should be, be displayed, "altogether lovely," to the trembling mind! Then may a *new heart* be received from Him, that shall thrill in the acknowledgment of the claims both of men and God, and girding up the loins of the mind, address itself to walk in all His commandments and ordinances blameless! One thing should be plain. In Mencius' lessons on human duty there is no hope for his countrymen. If they serve as a schoolmaster to bring them to Christ, they will have done their part; but it is from Christ alone that the help of the Chinese can come.

7. Besides giving more explicit expression to the doctrine of the goodness of man's nature than had been done before him, Mencius has the credit also of calling attention to *the nourishment of the passion-nature.* It may be questioned whether I translate his language exactly by this phrase. What I render *the passion-nature,* Julien renders by "*vitalis spiritus.*" The philosopher says himself that it difficult to describe what he intends. Attempting such a description, he says:—"This is it:—It is exceedingly great and exceedingly strong. Being nourished by rectitude, and sustaining no injury, it fills up all between heaven and earth. This is it:—It is the mate and assistant of righteousness and reason. Without it man is in a state of starvation. It is produced by the accumulation of righteous deeds; it is not to be taken, as by surprise, by incidental acts of righteousness. If the mind does not feel complacency in the conduct, *this* is starved."[146] From such predicates we may be sure that it is not anything merely or entirely *physical* of which he is speaking. "The righteous," said Solomon, "are bold as a lion." The Hebrew saying is very much in Mencius' style. That boldness is the result of the *nourishment* for which he thought he had a peculiar aptitude. Strong in it and in a knowledge of words, a faculty of discovering the moral aberrations of others from their forms

---

[146] Bk II. Pt I. ii. 13-15.

of speech, he was able to boast of possessing "an unperturbed mind;" he could "sit in the centre" of his being, "and enjoy bright day," whatever clouds and storms gathered around him.

The nourishment, therefore, of "the passion-nature," "the vital spirit," or whatever name we choose to give to the subject, is only an effect of general good-doing. This is the practical lesson from all Mencius' high-sounding words. He has illustrated it amusingly:—

"There was a man of Sung, who was grieved that his growing corn was not longer, and pulled it up. Having done this, he returned home, looking very wearied, and said to his people, 'I am tired to-day. I have been helping the com to grow long.' His son ran to look at it, and found the com all withered. There are few in the world, who do not assist the com [of their passion-nature] to grow long. Some consider it of no benefit to them, and let it alone:—they do not weed their corn. Those who assist it to grow long, pull out their corn. What they do is not only of no benefit to the nature, but it also injures it."[147]

This portion of Mencius' teaching need not detain us. He has put a simple truth in a striking way. That is his merit. It hardly seems of sufficient importance to justify the use which has been made of it in vindicating a place for him among the sages of his country.

8. I said I should end the discussion of Mencius' opinions by pointing out what I conceive to be his chief defects as a moral and political teacher. His defects, however, in the former respect have been already not lightly touched on. So far as they were the consequence of his ignorance, without the light which Revelation sheds on the whole field of human duty, and the sanctions, which it discloses, of a future state of retribution, I do not advance any charge against his character. That he never indicates any wish to penetrate into futurity, and ascertain what comes after death; that he never indicates any consciousness of human weakness, nor moves his mind Godward, longing for more light:—these are things which exhibit strongly the contrast between the mind of the East and the West. His self-sufficiency is his great fault. To know ourselves is commonly supposed to be an important step to humility; but it is not so with him. He has spoken remarkably about the effects of calamity and difficulties. He says:—"When Heaven is about to confer a great office on a man, it first exercises his mind with suffering, and his sinews and bones with toil; it exposes his body to hunger, and subjects him to extreme poverty; it confounds his undertakings. By all these methods it stimulates his mind, hardens his nature, and supplies his incompetencies."[148] Such

---

[147] Bk II. Pt I. ii. 16.
[148] Bk VI. Pt II. xv.

have been the effects of Heaven's exercising some men with calamities; but if the issue has been a fitting for the *highest offices,* there has been a softening of the nature rather than a hardening of it. Mencius was a stranger to the humbling of the lofty looks of man, and the bowing down his haughtiness, that the Lord alone may be exalted.

His faults as a political teacher are substantially the same as those of Confucius. More than was the case with his sayings of a political character, the utterances of Mencius have reference to the condition and needs of his own age. They were for the time then being, and not for all time. He knew as little as Confucius of any other great and independent nation besides his own; and he has left one maxim which is deeply treasured by the rulers and the people of China at the present day, and feeds the supercilious idea which they are so unwilling to give up of their own superiority to foreigners. "I have heard," said he, "of men using [the doctrines of] our great land to change barbarians, but I have never yet heard of any being changed by barbarians." "I have heard of birds leaving dark valleys to remove to lofty trees, but I have not heard of their descending from lofty trees to enter into dark valleys."[149] Mongol and Tartar sway has not broken the charm of this dangerous flattery, because only in warlike energy were the Mongols and Tartars superior to the Chinese, and when they conquered the country they did homage to its sages. During the last four-and-thirty years, Christian Powers have come to ask admission into China, and to claim to be received as her equals. They do not wish to conquer her territory, though they have battered and broken her defenses. With fear and trembling their advances are contemplated. The feeling of dislike to them arises from the dread of their power, and suspicion of their faith. It is feared that they come to subdue; it is known that they come to change. The idol of Chinese superiority is about to be broken. Broken it must be ere long, and a new generation of thinkers will arise, to whom Mencius will be a study but not a guide.

## APPENDIX.

I HAVE thought it would be interesting to many readers to append here the Essays of two distinguished scholars of China on the subject of Human Nature. The one is in direct opposition to Mencius' doctrine; according to the other, his doctrine is insufficient to explain the phenomena. The author of the first, Seun K'ing, was not much posterior to Mencius. He is mentioned as in office under king Sĕang of Ts'e (B.C. 271-264), and he lived on to the times of the Ts'in dynasty. His Works which still remain form a considerable volume. The second essay is from the work of Han Yu, mentioned above, Ch. I. Sect. IV. 3.

---

[149] Bk III. Pt I iv. 12, 15.

I shall not occupy any space with criticisms on the style or sentiments of the writers. If the translation appear at times to be inelegant or obscure, the fault is perhaps as much in the original as in myself. A comprehensive and able sketch of "The Ethics of the Chinese, with special reference to the Doctrines of Human Nature and Sin," by the Rev. Griffith John, was read before the North-China Branch of the Royal Asiatic Society, in November, 1859, and has been published separately. The essays of Seun and Han are both reviewed in it.

## I. THAT THE NATURE IS EVIL.

## BY THE PHILOSOPHER SEUN.

THE NATURE of man is evil; the good which it shows is factitious. There belongs to it, even at his birth, the love of gain, and as actions are in accordance with this, contentions and robberies grow up, and self-denial and yielding to others are not to be found; there belong to it envy and dislike, and as actions are in accordance with these, violence and injuries spring up, and self-devotedness and faith are not to be found; there belong to it the desires of the ears and the eyes, leading to the love of sounds and beauty, and as the actions are in accordance with these, lewdness and disorder spring up, and righteousness and propriety, with their various orderly displays, are not to be found. It thus appears, that the following man's nature and yielding obedience to its feelings will assuredly conduct to contentions and robberies, to the violation of the duties belonging to every one's lot, and the confounding of all distinctions, till the issue will be in a state of savagism; and that there must be the influence of teachers and laws, and the guidance of propriety and righteousness, from which will spring self-denial, yielding to others, and an observance of the well-ordered regulations of conduct, till the issue will be in a state of good government.—From all this, it is plain that the nature of man is evil; the good which it shows is factitious.

To illustrate.—A crooked stick must be submitted to the pressing-frame, to soften and bend it, and then it becomes straight; a blunt knife must be submitted to the grindstone and whetstone, and then it becomes sharp; so, the nature of man, being evil, must be submitted to teachers and laws, and then it becomes correct; it must be submitted to propriety and righteousness, and then it comes under government. If men were without teachers and laws, their condition would be one of deflection and insecurity, entirely incorrect; if they were without propriety and righteousness, their condition would be one of rebellious disorder, rejecting all government. The sage kings of antiquity understanding that the nature of man was thus evil, in a state of hazardous deflection, and incorrect, rebellious and disorderly, and refusing to be governed, they set up the principles of righteousness and propriety, and framed laws and regulations to straighten and ornament the feelings of that nature and correct them, to tame and change those same feelings and guide them, so that they might all go forth in the way of moral government and in agreement with reason. Now, the man who is transformed by teachers and laws, gathers on himself the ornament of learning, and proceeds in the path of propriety and righteousness, is a superior man; and he who gives the reins to his nature and its feelings, indulges its resentments, and walks contrary to propriety and righteousness, is a mean man. Looking at the subject in this way, we see clearly that the nature of man is evil; the good which it shows is factitious.

Mencius said, "Man has only to learn, and his nature becomes good;" but I reply,—It is not so. To say so shows that he had not attained to the knowledge of man's nature, nor examined into the difference between what is natural in man and what is factitious. The natural is what the constitution spontaneously moves to:—it needs not to be learned, it needs not to be followed hard after; propriety and righteousness are what the sages have given birth to:—it is by learning that men become capable of them, it is by hard practice that they achieve them. That which is in man, not needing to be learned and striven after, is what I call natural; that in man which is attained to by learning, and achieved by hard striving, is what I call factitious. This is the distinction between those two. By the nature of man, the eyes are capable of seeing, and the ears are capable of hearing. But the power of seeing is inseparable from the eyes, and the power of hearing is inseparable from the ears;—it is plain that the faculties of seeing and hearing do not need to be learned. Mencius says, "The nature of man is good, but all lose and ruin their nature, and therefore it becomes bad;" but I say that this representation is erroneous. Man being born with his nature, when he thereafter departs from its simple constituent elements, he must lose it. From this consideration we may see clearly that man's nature is evil. What might be called the nature's being good would be if there were no departing from its simplicity to beautify it, no departing from its elementary dispositions to sharpen it. Suppose that those simple elements no more needed beautifying, and the mind's thoughts no more needed to be turned to good, than the power of vision which is inseparable from the eyes, and the power of hearing which is inseparable from the ears, need to be learned, [then we might say that the nature is good, just as] we say that the eyes see and the ears hear. It is the nature of man, when hungry, to desire to be filled; when cold, to desire to be warmed; when tired, to desire rest:—these are the feelings and nature of man. But now, a man is hungry, and in the presence of an elder he does not dare to eat before him,—he is yielding to that elder; he is tired with labor, and he does not dare to ask for rest,—he is working for some one. A son's yielding to his father and a younger brother to his elder, a son's laboring for his father and a younger brother for his elder,—these two instances of conduct are contrary to the nature and against the feelings; but they are according to the course laid down for a filial son, and the refined distinctions of propriety and righteousness. It appears that if there were an accordance with the feelings and the nature, there would be no self-denial and yielding to others. Self-denial and yielding to others are contrary to the feelings and the nature. In this way we come to see how clear it is that the nature of man is evil; the good which it shows is factitious.

An inquirer will ask, "If man's nature be evil, whence do propriety and righteousness arise?" I reply,—All propriety and righteousness are the artificial production of the sages, and are not to be considered as growing out of the nature of man. It is just as when a potter makes a vessel from the clay;—the vessel is the product of the workman's art, and is not be considered as growing out of his nature. Or it is as when another workman cuts and hews a vessel out of wood;—it is the product of his art, and is not to be considered as growing out of his nature. The sages pondered long in thought and gave themselves to practice, and so they succeeded in producing propriety and righteousness, and setting up laws and regulations. Thus it is that propriety and righteousness, laws and regulations, are the artificial product of the sages, and are not to be considered as growing properly from the nature of man.

If we speak of the fondness of the eyes for beauty, or of the mouth for [pleasant] flavors, or of the mind for gain, or of the bones and skin for the enjoyment of ease;—all these grow out of the natural feelings of man. The object is presented and the desire is felt; there needs no effort to produce it. But when the object is presented, and the affection does not move till after hard effort, I say that this effect is factitious. Those cases prove the difference between what is produced by nature and what is produced by art.

Thus the sages transformed their nature, and commenced their artificial work. Having commenced this work with their nature, they produced propriety and righteousness. When propriety and righteousness were produced, they proceeded to frame laws and regulations. It appears, therefore, that propriety and righteousness, laws and regulations, were given birth to by the sages. Wherein they agree with all other men and do not differ from them, is their nature; wherein they differ from and exceed other men, is this artificial work.

Now to love gain and desire to get;—this is the natural feeling of men. Suppose the case that there is an amount of property or money to be divided among brothers, and let this natural feeling to love gain and desire to get come into play;—why, then the brothers will be opposing, and snatching from one another. But where the changing influence of propriety and righteousness, with their refined distinctions, has taken effect, a man will give up to any other man. Thus it is that if they act in accordance with their natural feelings, brothers will quarrel together; and if they have come under the transforming influence of propriety and righteousness, men will give up to other men, to say nothing of brothers. [Again], the fact that men WISH to do what is good, is because their nature is bad. The thin wishes to be thick; the ugly wishes to be beautiful; the narrow wishes to be wide; the poor wish to be rich; the mean wish to be noble:—when anything is not possessed in one's self, he seeks for it outside himself. But the rich do not wish for wealth; the noble do not wish for position:—when anything is possessed by one's self, he does not need to go beyond himself for it. When we look at things in this way, we perceive that the fact of men's WISHING to do what is good is because their nature is evil. It is the case, indeed, that man's nature is without propriety and benevolence:—he therefore studies them with vigorous effort and seeks to have them. It is the case that by nature he does not know propriety and righteousness:—he therefore thinks and reflects and seeks to know them. Speaking of man, therefore, as he is by birth simply, he is without propriety and righteousness, without the knowledge of propriety and righteousness. Without propriety and righteousness, man must be all confusion and disorder; without the knowledge of propriety and righteousness, there must ensue all the manifestations of disorder. Man, as he is born, therefore, has in him nothing but the elements of disorder, passive and active. It is plain from this contemplation of the subject that the nature of man is evil; the good which it shows is factitious.

When Mencius says that "Man's nature is good," I affirm that it is not so. In ancient times and now throughout the empire, what is meant by good is a condition of correctness, regulation, and happy government; and what is meant by evil, is a condition of deflection, insecurity, and refusing to be under government:—in this lies the distinction between being good and being evil. And now, if man's nature be really so correct, regulated, and happily governed in itself, where would be the use for sage kings? where would be the use for propriety and righteousness? Although there were the sage kings, propriety, and righteousness, what could they add to the nature so correct, regulated, and happily ruled in itself? But it is not so; the nature of man is bad. It was on this account, that anciently the sage kings, understanding that man's nature was bad, in a state of deflection and insecurity instead of being correct, in a state of rebellious disorder instead of one of happy rule, set up therefore the majesty of princes and governors to awe it; and set forth propriety and righteousness to change it; and framed laws and statutes of correctness to rule it; and devised severe punishments to restrain it:—so that its outgoings might be under the dominion of rule, and in accordance with what is good. This is [the true account of] the governance of the sage kings, and the transforming power of propriety and righteousness. Let us suppose a state of things in which there shall be no majesty of princes and governors, no influence of propriety and righteousness, no rule of laws and statutes, no restraints of punishment:—what would be the relations of men with one another, all under heaven? The strong would be injuring the weak, and spoiling them; the many would be tyrannizing over the few, and hooting them; a universal disorder and mutual destruction would speedily ensue. When we look at the subject in this way, we see clearly that the nature of man is evil; the good which it shows is factitious.

He who would speak well of ancient times must have certain references in the present; he who would speak well of Heaven must substantiate what he says out of man. In discourse and argument it is an excellent quality when the divisions which are made can be brought together like the halves of a token. When it is so, the arguer may sit down, and discourse of his principles; and he has only to rise up, and they may be set forth and displayed and carried into action. When Mencius says that the nature of man is good, there is no bringing together in the above manner of his divisions. He sits down and talks, but there is no getting up to display and set forth his principles, and put them in operation:—is not his error very gross? To say that the nature is good does away with the sage kings, and makes an end of propriety and righteousness; to say that the nature is bad exalts the sage kings, and dignifies propriety and righteousness. As the origin of the pressing-boards is to be found in the crooked wood, and the origin of the carpenter's marking line is to be found in things' not being straight; so the rise of princes and governors, and the illustration of propriety and righteousness, are to be traced to the badness of the nature. It is clear from this view of the subject that the nature of man is bad; the good which it shows is factitious.

A straight piece of wood does not need the pressing-boards to make it straight;—it is so by its nature. A crooked piece of wood must be submitted to the pressing-boards to soften and straighten it, and then it is straight;—it is not straight by its nature. So it is that the nature of man, being evil, must be submitted to the rule of the sage kings, and to the transforming influence of propriety and righteousness, and then its outgoings are under the dominion of rule, and in accordance with what is good. This shows clearly that the nature of man is bad; the good which it shows is factitious.

An inquirer may say [again], "Propriety and righteousness, though seen in an accumulation of factitious deeds, do yet belong to the nature of man; and thus it was that the sages were able to produce them." I reply,—It is not so. A potter takes a piece of clay, and produces a dish from it; but are that dish and clay the nature of the potter? A carpenter plies his tools upon a piece of wood, and produces a vessel; but are that vessel and wood the nature of the carpenter? So it is with the sages and propriety and righteousness; they produced them, just as the potter works with the clay. It is plain that there is no reason for saying that propriety and righteousness, and the accumulation of their factitious actions, belong to the proper nature of man. Speaking of the nature of man, it is the same in all,—the same in Yaou and Shun, and in Kĕeh and in the robber Chih, the same in the superior man and in the mean man. If you say that propriety and righteousness, with the factitious actions accumulated from them, are the nature of man, on what ground do you proceed to ennoble Yaou and Yu, to ennoble [generally] the superior man? The ground on which we ennoble Yaou, Yu, and the superior man, is their ability to change the nature, and to produce factitious conduct. That factitious conduct being produced, out of it there are brought propriety and righteousness. The sages stand indeed in the same relation to propriety and righteousness, and the factitious conduct resulting from them, as the potter does to his clay:—we have a product in either case. This representation makes it clear that propriety and righteousness, with their factitious results, do not properly belong to the nature of man. [On the other hand], that which we consider mean in Kĕeh, the robber Chih, and the mean man generally, is that they follow their nature, act in accordance with its feelings, and indulge its resentments, till all its outgoings are a greed of gain, contentions, and rapine.—It is plain that the nature of man is bad; the good which it shows is factitious.

Heaven did not make favorites of Tsăng, K'ĕen, and Heaou-ke, and deal unkindly with the rest of men. How then was it that they alone were distinguished by the greatness of their filial deeds, that all which the name of filial piety implies was complete in them? The reason was that they were subject to the restraints of propriety and righteousness.

Heaven did not make favorites of the people of Ts'e and Loo, and deal unkindly with the people of Ts'in. How then was it that the latter were not equal to the former in rich manifestation of the filial piety belonging to the righteousness of the relation between father and son, and the respectful observance of the proprieties belonging to the separate functions of husband and wife? The reason was that the people of Ts'in followed the feelings of their nature, indulged its resentments, and contemned propriety and righteousness. We are not to suppose that they were different in their nature.

What is the meaning of the saying, that "Any traveler on the road may become like Yu?" I answer,—All that made Yu what he was was his practice of benevolence, righteousness, and his observance of laws and rectitude. But benevolence, righteousness, laws, and rectitude, are all capable of being known and being practiced. Moreover, any traveler on the road has the capacity of knowing these, and the ability to practise them:—it is plain that he may become like Yu. If you say that benevolence, righteousness, laws, and rectitude, are not capable of being known and practiced, then Yu himself could not have known, could not have practiced them. If you will have it that any traveler on the road is really without the capacity of knowing these things, and the ability to practise them, then, in his home, it will not be competent for him to know the righteousness that should rule between father and son, and, abroad, it will not be competent for him to know the rectitude that should rule between ruler and minister. But it is not so. There is no one who travels along the road but may know both that righteousness and that rectitude:—it is plain that the capacity to know and the ability to practise belong to every traveler on the way. Let him, therefore, with his capacity of knowing and ability to practise, take his ground on the knowableness and practicableness of benevolence and righteousness;—and it is clear that he may become like Yu. Yea, let any traveler on the way addict himself to the art of learning with all his heart and the entire bent of his will, thinking, searching, and closely examining;—let him do this day after day, through a long space of time, accumulating what is good, and he will penetrate as far as a spiritual Intelligence, he will become a ternion with Heaven and Earth. It follows that [the characters of] the sages were what any man may reach by accumulation.

It may be said:—"To be sage may thus be reached by accumulation;—why is it that all men cannot accumulate [to this extent?]" I reply,—They may do so, but they cannot be made to do so. The mean man might become a superior man, but he is not willing to be a superior man. The superior man might become a mean man, but he is not willing to be a mean man. It is not that the mean man and the superior man may not become the one the other; their not becoming the one the other is because it is a thing which may be, but cannot be made to be. Any traveler on the road may become like Yu:—the case is so; that any traveler on the road can really become like Yu:—this is not a necessary conclusion. Though any one, however, cannot really become like Yu, that is not contrary at all to the truth that he may become so. One's feet might travel all over the world, but there never was one who was really able to travel all over the world. There is nothing to prevent the mechanic, the farmer, and the merchant, from practicing each the business of the others, but there has never been a case when it has really been done. Looking at the subject in this way, we see that what may be need not really be; and although it shall not really be, that is not contrary to the truth that it might be. It thus appears that the difference is wide between what is really done or not really done, and what may be or may not be. It is plain that these two cases may not become the one the other.

Yaou asked Shun what was the character of the feelings proper to man. Shun replied, "The feelings proper to man are very unlovely; why need you ask about them? When a man has got a wife and children, his filial piety withers away; under the influence of lust and gratified desires, his good faith to his friends withers away; when he is full of dignities and emoluments, his loyalty to his ruler withers away. The natural feelings of man! The natural feelings of man! They are very unlovely. Why need you ask about them? It is only in the case of men of the highest worth that it is not so."

There is a knowledge characteristic of the sage; a knowledge characteristic of the scholar and superior man; a knowledge characteristic of the mean man; and a knowledge characteristic of the mere servant. In much speech to show his cultivation and maintain consistency, and though he may discuss for a whole day the reasons of a subject, to have a unity pervading the ten thousand changes of discourse;—this is the knowledge of the sage. To speak seldom, and in a brief and sparing manner, and to be orderly in his reasoning, as if its parts were connected with a string;—this is the knowledge of the scholar and superior man. Flattering words and disorderly conduct, with undertakings often followed by regrets;—these mark the knowledge of the mean man. Hasty, officious, smart, and swift, but without consistency; versatile, able, of extensive capabilities, but without use; decisive in discourse, rapid, exact, but the subject unimportant; regardless of right and wrong, taking no account of crooked and straight, to get the victory over others the guiding object:—this is the knowledge of the mere servant.

There is bravery of the highest order; bravery of the middle order; bravery of the lowest order. Boldly to take up his position in the place of the universally acknowledged Mean; boldly to carry into practice his views of the doctrines of the ancient kings; in a high situation, not to defer to a bad ruler, and, in a low situation, not to follow the current of a bad people; to consider that there is no poverty where there is virtue, and no wealth where virtue is not; when appreciated by the world, to desire to share in all men's joys and sorrows; when unknown by the world, to stand up grandly alone between heaven and earth, and have no fears:—this is the bravery of the highest order. To be reverently observant of propriety, and sober-minded; to attach importance to adherence to fidelity, and set little store by material wealth; to have the boldness to push forward men of worth and exalt them, to hold back undeserving men, and get them deposed;—this is the bravery of the middle order. To be devoid of self-respect and set a great value on wealth; to feel complacent in calamity, and always have plenty to say for himself; saving himself in any way without regard to right and wrong; whatever be the real state of a case, making it his object to get the victory over others:—this is the bravery of the lowest order.

The *fan-joh,* the *keu,* and the *shoo* were the best bows of antiquity; but without their regulators, they could not adjust themselves. The *tsung* of duke Hwan, the *keueh* of T'ae-kung, the *luh* of king Wăn, the *hwuh* of prince Chwang, the *kan-tsëang, moh-yay keu.-keueh,* and *p'eih-leu* of Hoh-leu:—these were the best swords of antiquity; but without the grindstone and whetstone, they would not have been sharp; without the strength of the arms that wielded them, they would not have cut anything.

The *hwa,* the *lëw,* the *le,* the *k'e,* the *sëen,* the *lei,* the *luh,* and the *urh*:—these were the best horses of antiquity; but there were still necessary for them the restraints in front of bit and bridle, the stimulants behind of cane and whip, and the management of a Tsaou-foo, and then they could accomplish a thousand *le* in one day.

So it is with man:—granted to him an excellent capacity of nature and the faculty of intellect, he must still seek for good teachers under whom to place himself, and make choice of friends with whom he may be intimate. Having got good masters and placed himself under them, what he will hear will be the doctrines of Yaou, Shun, Yu, and T'ang; having got good friends and become intimate with them, what he will see will be deeds of self-consecration, fidelity, reverence, and complaisance:—he will go on from day to day to benevolence and righteousness, without being conscious of it; a natural following of them will make him do so. On the other hand, if he live with bad men, what he will hear will be the language of deceit, calumny, imposture, and hypocrisy; what he will see will be the conduct of filthiness, insolence, lewdness, corruptness, and greed:—he will be going on from day to day to punishment and disgrace, without being conscious of it; a natural following of them will make him do so.

The Record says, "If you do not know your son, look at his friends; if you do not know your ruler, look at his confidants." All is the influence of association! All is the influence of association!

## II. AN EXAMINATION OF THE NATURE OF MAN.

### BY HAN WĂN-KUNG.

THE NATURE dates from the date of the life; THE FEELINGS date from contact with external things. There are three GRADES of the nature, and it has five CHARACTERISTICS. There are also three GRADES of the feelings, and they have seven CHARACTERISTICS. To explain myself:—The three grades of the nature are—the Superior, the Middle, and the Inferior. The superior grade is good, and good only; the middle grade is capable of being led: it may rise to the superior, or sink to the inferior; the inferior is evil, and evil only. The five characteristics of the nature are—Benevolence, Righteousness, Propriety, Sincerity, and Knowledge. In the Superior Grade, the first of these characteristics is supreme, and the other four are practiced. In the Middle Grade, the first of these characteristics is not wanting: it exists, but with a little tendency to its opposite; the other four are in an ill-assorted state. In the Inferior Grade there is the opposite of the first characteristic, and constant rebelliousness against the other four. The grade of the nature regulates the manifestation of the feelings in it. [Again]:—The three grades of the feelings are the Superior, the Middle, and the inferior; and their seven characteristics are—Joy, Anger, Sorrow, Fear, Love, Hatred, and Desire. In the Superior Grade, these seven all move, and each in its due place and degree. In the Middle Grade, some of the characteristics are in excess, and some in defect; but there is a seeking to give them their due place and degree. In the Inferior Grade, whether they are in excess or defect, there is a reckless acting according to the one in immediate predominance. The grade of the feelings regulates the influence of the nature in reference to them.

Speaking of the nature, Mencius said:—"Man's nature is g o o d ; " t h e philosopher Seun said:—"Man's nature is bad;" the philosopher Yang said:—"In the nature of man good and evil are mixed together." Now, to say that the nature, good at first, subsequently becomes bad; or that, bad at first, it subsequently becomes good; or that, mixed at first, it subsequently becomes—it may be good, it may be bad:—in each of these cases only the nature of the middle grade is dealt with, and the superior and inferior grades are neglected. Those philosophers are right about one grade, and wrong about the other two.

When Shuh-yu was born, his mother knew, as soon as she looked at him, that he would fall a victim to his love of bribes. When Yang Sze-go was born, the mother of Shuh-hëang knew, as soon as she heard him cry, that he would cause the destruction of all his kindred. When Yueh-tsëaou was born, Tsze-wăn considered it was a great calamity, knowing that through him the ghosts of the Joh-gaou family would all be famished.—With such cases before us; can it be said that the nature of man (*i.e.,* all men) is good?

When How-tseih was born, his mother had no suffering; and as soon as he began to creep, he displayed all elegance and intelligence. When king Wăn was in his mother's womb, she experienced no distress; after his birth, those who tended him had no trouble; when he began to learn, his teachers had no vexation:—with such cases before us, can it be said that the nature of man (*i.e.,* all men) is evil?

Choo was the son of Yaou, and Keun the son of Shun; Kwan and Ts'ae were sons of king Wăn. They were instructed to practise nothing but what was good, and yet they turned out villains. Shun was the son of Koo-sow, and Yu the son of K'wăn. They were instructed to practise nothing but what was bad, and yet they turned out sages.—With such cases before us, can it be said that in the nature of man (*i.e.,* all men) good and evil are blended together?

Having these things in view, I say that the three philosophers, to whom I have referred, dealt with the middle grade of the nature, and neglected the superior and the inferior; that they were right about the one grade, and wrong about the other two.

It may be asked, "Is it so, then, that the superior and inferior grades of the nature can never be changed?" I reply,—The nature of the superior grade, by application to learning, becomes more intelligent, and the nature of the inferior grade, through awe of power, comes to have few faults. The superior nature, therefore, may be taught, and the inferior nature may be restrained; but the grades have been pronounced by Confucius to be unchangeable.

It may be asked, "How is it that those who now-a-days speak about the nature do so differently from this?" I reply,—Those who now-a-days speak about the nature blend with their other views those of Laou-tsze and Buddhism; and doing so, how could they speak otherwise than differently from me?

## CHAPTER III. OF YANG CHOO AND MIH TEIH.

### SECTION I. THE OPINIONS OF YANG CHOO.

1. "THE words of Yang Choo and Mih Teih," said Mencius, "fill the empire. If you listen to people's discourses throughout it, you will find that they have adopted the views of the one or of the other. Now, Yang's principle is—'Each one for himself,' which does not acknowledge the claims of the sovereign. Mih's principle is—'To love all equally,' which does not acknowledge the peculiar affection due to a father. To acknowledge neither king nor father is to be in the state of a beast. If their principles are not stopped, and the principles of Confucius set forth, their perverse speakings will delude the people, and stop up the path of benevolence and righteousness.

"I am alarmed by these things, and address myself to the defence of the doctrines of the former sages, and to oppose Yang and Mih. I drive away their licentious expressions, so that such perverse speakers may not be able to show themselves. When sages shall rise up again, they will not change my words."[150]

His opposition to Yang and Mih was thus one of the great labors of Mencius' life, and what he deemed the success of it one of his great achievements. His countrymen generally accede to the justice of his claim; though there have not been wanting some to say—justly, as I think and will Endeavour to show in the next section—that Mih need not have incurred from him such heavy censure. For Yang no one has a

---

[150] Bk III. Pt II. ix. 9, 10.

word to say. His leading principle as stated by Mencius is certainly detestable, and so far as we can judge from the slight accounts of him that are to be gathered from other quarters, he seems to have been about "the least erected spirit," who ever professed to reason concerning the life and duties of man.

2. The generally received opinion is that Yang belonged to the period of "The Warring States," the same era of Chinese history as Mencius. He was named Choo, and styled Tsze-keu. In a note, p. 159 of my larger work, I have supposed that he was of the times of Confucius and Laou-tsze, having then before me a passage of the Taouist philosopher Chwang, in which he gives an account of an interview between Laou-tsze and Yang Choo. That interview, however, must be an invention of Chwang. The natural impression which we receive from all the references of Mencius is that Yang must have been posterior to Confucius, and that his opinions had come into vogue only in the times of our philosopher himself. This view would be placed beyond doubt if we could receive as genuine the chapter on Yang, which is contained in the writings of the philosopher Lĕeh. And so far we may accept it, as to believe that it gives the sentiments which were attributed to him in the 1st century before our era. The leading principle ascribed to him by Mencius nowhere appears in it in so many words, but the general tenor of his language is entirely in accordance with it. This will appear from the following specimens:—

"Yang Choo said, 'A hundred years are the extreme limit of longevity; and not one man in a thousand enjoys such a period of life. Suppose the case of one who does so:—infancy borne in the arms, and doting old age, will nearly occupy the half; what is forgotten in sleep, and what is lost in the waking day, will nearly occupy the half; pain and sickness, sorrow and bitterness, losses, anxieties, and fears will nearly occupy the half. There may remain ten years or so; but I reckon that not even in them will be found an hour of smiling self-abandonment, without the shadow of solicitude.—What is the life of man then to be made of? What pleasure is in it?

"'[Is it to be prized] for the pleasure of food and dress? or for the enjoyments of music and beauty? But one cannot be always satisfied with those pleasures; one cannot be always toying with beauty and listening to music. And then there are the restraints of punishments and the stimulants of rewards; the urgings and the repressings of fame and laws:—these make one strive restlessly for the vain praise of an hour, and calculate on the residuary glory after death; they keep him, as with body bent, on the watch against what his ears hear and his eyes see, and attending to the right and the wrong of his conduct and thoughts. In this way he loses the real pleasure of his years, and cannot allow himself for a moment.—In what does he differ from an individual manacled and fettered in an inner prison? The people of high antiquity knew both the shortness of life, and how suddenly and completely it might be closed by death, and therefore they obeyed the movements of their hearts, refusing not what it was natural for them to like, nor seeking to avoid any pleasure that occurred to them. They paid no heed to the incitements of fame; they enjoyed themselves according to their nature; they did not resist the common tendency of all things to self-enjoyment; they cared not to be famous after death. They managed to keep clear of punishment; as to fame and praise, being first or last, long life or short life, these things did not come into their calculations.'"

"Yang Choo said, 'Wherein people differ is the matter of life; wherein they agree is death. While they are alive, we have the distinctions of intelligence and stupidity, honorableness and meanness; when they are dead, we have so much stinking rottenness decaying away:—this is the common lot. Yet intelligence and stupidity, honorableness and meanness, are not in one's power; neither is that condition of putridity, decay, and utter disappearance. A man's life is not in his own hands, nor is his death; his intelligence is not his own, nor is his stupidity, nor his honorableness, nor his meanness. All are born and all die;—the intelligent and the stupid, the honorable and the mean. At ten years old some die; at a hundred years old some die. The virtuous and the sage die; the ruffian and the fool also die. Alive, they were Yaou and Shun; dead they were so much rotten bone. Alive they were Kĕeh and Chow; dead, they were so much rotten bone. Who could know any difference between their rotten bones? While alive, therefore, let us hasten to make the best of life; what leisure have we to be thinking of anything after death?'"

"Măng-sun Yang asked Yang-tsze, saying, 'Here is a man who sets a high value on his life, and takes loving care of his body, hoping that he will not die:—does he do right?' 'There is no such thing as not dying,' was the reply. 'But if he does so, hoping for long life, is he right?' Yang-tsze answered, 'One cannot be assured of long life. Setting value upon life will not preserve it; taking care of the body will not make it greatly better. And, in fact, why should long life be made of? There are the five feelings with their likings and dislikings,—now as in old time; there are the four limbs, now at ease, now in danger,—now as in old time; there are the various experiences of joy and sorrow,—now as in old time; there are the various changes from order to disorder, and from disorder to order,—now as in old time:—all these things I have heard of, and seen, and gone through. A hundred years of them would be more than enough, and shall I wish the pain protracted through a longer life?' Mang-sun said, 'If it be so, early death is better than long life. Let a man go to trample on the pointed steel, or throw himself into the caldron or flames, to get what he desires' Yang-tsze answered, 'No. Being once born, take your life as it comes, and endure it, and, seeking to enjoy yourself as you desire, so await the approach of death. When you are about to die, treat the thing with indifference and endure it; and seeking to accomplish your departure, so abandon yourself to annihilation. Both death and life should be treated with indifference; they should both be endured:—why trouble ones-self about earliness or lateness in connation with them?'"

"K'in-tsze asked Yang Choo, saying, 'If you could benefit the world by parting with one hair of your body, would you do it?' 'The world is not to be benefited by a hair,' replied Yang. The other urged, 'But suppose it could be, what would you do?' To this Yang gave no answer, and K'in went out, and reported what had passed to Măng-sun Yang. Măng-sun said, 'You do not understand our Master's mind:—let me explain it to you. If by enduring a slight wound in the flesh, you could get ten thousand pieces of gold, would you endure it?' 'I would' 'If by cutting off one of your limbs, you could get a kingdom, would you do it?' K'in was silent and after a little, Măng-sun Yang resumed, 'To part with a hair is a slighter matter than to receive a wound in the flesh, and that again is a slighter matter than to lose a limb:—that you can discern. But consider:—a hair may be multiplied till it become as important as the piece of flesh, and the piece of flesh may be multiplied till it becomes as important as a limb. A single hair is just one of the ten thousand portions of the body;—why should you make light of it?' K'in-tsze replied, 'I cannot answer you. If I could refer your words to Laou Tan or Kwan Yin, they would say that you were right; but if I could refer my words to the great Yu or Mih Teih, they would say that I was right.' Măng-sun Yang, on this, turned round, and entered into conversation with his disciples on another subject."

"Yang Choo said, 'The empire agrees in considering Shun, Yu, Chow-kung, and Confucius to have been the most admirable of men, and in considering Kĕeh and Chow to have been the most wicked.

"'Now, Shun had to plough the ground on the south of the Ho, and to play the potter by the Luy lake. His four limbs had not even a temporary rest; for his mouth and belly he could not find pleasant food and warm clothing. No love of his parents rested upon him; no affection of his brothers and sisters. When he was thirty years old, he had not been able to get the permission of his parents to marry. When Yaou at length resigned to him the throne, he was advanced in age; his wisdom was decayed; his son Shang-keun proved without ability; and he had finally to resign the throne to Yu. Sorrowfully came he to his death. Of all mortals never was one whose life was so worn out and empoisoned as his. K'wăn was required to reduce the deluged land to order; and when his labors were ineffectual, he was put to death on mount Yu, and Yu [his son] had to undertake the task, and serve his enemy. All his energies were spent on his labors with the land; a child was born to him, but he could not foster it; he passed his door without entering; his body became bent and withered; the skin of his hands and feet became thick and callous. When at length Shun resigned to him the throne, he lived in a low, mean house, while his sacrificial apron and cap were elegant. Sorrowfully came he to his death. Of all mortals never was one whose life was so saddened and embittered as his. On the death of king Woo [his son], king Shing was young and weak. Chow-kung had to undertake all the imperial duties. The duke of Shaou was displeased, and evil reports spread through the empire. Chow-kung had to reside three years in the east; he slew his elder brother, and banished his younger; scarcely did he escape with his life. Sorrowfully came he to his death. Of all mortals never was one whose life was so full of hazards and terrors as his. Confucius understood the ways of the ancient emperors and kings. He responded to the invitations of the princes of his time. The tree was cut down over him in Sung; the traces of his footsteps were removed in Wei; he was reduced to extremity in Shang and Chow; he was surrounded in Ch'in and Ts'ae; he had to bend to the Head of the Ke family; he was disgraced by Yang Hoo. Sorrowfully came he to his death. Of all mortals never was one whose life was so agitated and hurried as his.

"'Those four sages, during their life, had not a single day's joy. Since their death they have had a [grand] fame that will last through myriads of ages. But that fame is what no one who cares for what is real would choose. Celebrate them;—they do not know it. Reward them;—they do not know it. Their fame is no more to them than to the trunk of a tree or a clod of earth.

"'[On the other hand], Kĕeh came into the accumulated wealth of many generations; to him belonged the honor of the imperial seat; his wisdom was enough to enable him to set at defiance all below; his power was enough to shake the empire. He indulged the pleasures to which his eyes and ears prompted him; he carried out whatever it came into his thoughts to do. Brightly came he to his death. Of all mortals never was one whose life was so luxurious and dissipated as his. [Similarly], Chow came into the accumulated wealth of many generations; to him belonged the honor of the royal seat; his power enabled him to do whatever he would; his will was everywhere obeyed; he indulged his feelings in all his palaces; he gave the reins to his lusts through the long night; he never made himself bitter by the thought of propriety and righteousness. Brightly came he to his destruction. Of all mortals never was one whose life was so abandoned as his.

"'These two villains, during their life, had the joy of gratifying their desires. Since their death, they have had the [evil] fame of folly and tyranny. But the reality [of enjoyment] is what no fame can give. Reproach them;—they do not know it. Praise them;—they do not know it. Their [ill] fame is no more to them than to the trunk of a tree, or to a clod of earth.

"'To the four sages all admiration is given; yet were their lives bitter to the end, and their common lot was death. 'To the two villains all condemnation is given; yet their lives were pleasant to the last, and their common lot was likewise death.'"

3. The above passages are sufficient to show the character of Yang Choo's mind and of his teachings. It would be doing injustice to Epicurus to compare Yang with him, for though the Grecian philosopher made happiness the chief end of human pursuit, he taught also that "we cannot live pleasurably without living virtuously and justly." The Epicurean system is, indeed, unequal to the capacity, and far below the highest complacencies, of human nature; but it is widely different from the reckless contempt of all which is esteemed good and great that defiles the pages where Yang is made to tell his views.

We are sometimes reminded by him of fragmentary utterance in the Book of Ecclesiastes:—"In much wisdom is much grief; and he that increaseth knowledge increaseth sorrow." "As it happeneth to the fool, so it happeneth even to me; and why was I then more wise? Then I said in my heart, that this also is vanity. For there is no remembrance of the wise more than of the fool for ever; seeing that which now is, in the days to come shall all be forgotten. And how dieth the wise man? As the fool. Therefore I hated life; because the work that is wrought under the sun is grievous to me: for all is vanity and vexation of spirit." "There is a man whose labor is in wisdom, and in knowledge, and in equity... All his days are sorrows, and his travail grief; yea, his heart taketh not rest in the night:—this is also vanity. There is nothing better for a man than that he should eat and drink, and that he should make his soul enjoy good in his labor." "That which befalleth the sons of men befalleth beasts; even one thing befalleth them: as the one dieth, so dieth the other; yea, they have all one breath; so that a man hath no pre-eminence over a beast: for all is vanity. All go to one place; all are of the dust, and all turn to dust again... Wherefore I perceive that there is nothing better than that a man should rejoice in his own works; for that is his portion: for who shall bring him to see what shall be after him?"

But those thoughts were suggestions of evil from which the Hebrew Preacher recoiled in his own mind; and he put them on record only that he might give their antidote along with them. He vanquished them by his faith in God; and so he ends by saying, "Let us hear the conclusion of the whole matter.—Fear God, and keep His commandments: for this is the whole duty of man. For God shall bring every work into judgment with every secret thing, whether it be good, or whether it be evil." Yang Choo has no redeeming qualities. His reasonings contain no elements to counteract the poison that is in them. He never rises to the thought of God. There are, he allows, such ideas as those of propriety and righteousness, but the effect of them is merely to embitter and mar the enjoyment of life. Fame is but a phantom which only the fool will pursue. It is the same with all at death. There their being ends. After that there is but so much putridity and rottenness. With him therefore the conclusion of the whole matter is:—"Let us eat and drink; let us live in pleasure; gratify the ears and eyes; get servants and maidens, music, beauty, wine; when the day is insufficient, carry it on through the night; EACH ONE FOR HIMSELF."

Mencius might well say that if such "licentious talk" were not arrested, the path of benevolence and righteousness would be stopped up. If Yang's principles had been entertained by the nation, every bond of society would have been dissolved. All the foundations of order would have been destroyed. Vice would have become rampant, and virtue would have been named only to be scorned. There would have remained for the entire State only what Yang saw in store for the individual man—"putridity and rottenness." Doubtless it was owing to Mencius' opposition that the foul and dangerous current was stayed. He raised up against it the bulwark of human nature formed for virtue. He insisted on benevolence, righteousness, propriety, fidelity, as the noblest attributes of man's conduct. More was needed, but more he could not supply. If he had had a living faith in God, and had been in possession of His revealed will, the present state of China might have been very different. He was able to warn his countrymen of the gulf into which Yang Choo would have plunged them; but he could direct them in the way of truth and duty only imperfectly. He sent them into the dark cave of their own souls, and back to the vague lessons and imperfect examples of their sages; and China has staggered on, waxing feebler and feebler, to the present time. Her people need to be directed above themselves and beyond the present. When stars shine out to them in heaven and from eternity, the empire will perhaps renew its youth, and go forward from strength to strength.

## SECTION II. THE OPINIONS OF MIH TEIH.

1. VERY different from Yang Choo was Mih Teih. They stood at the opposite poles of human thought and sentiment; and we may wonder that Mencius should have offered the same stern opposition to the opinions of each of them. He did well to oppose the doctrine whose watch-word was—"Each one for himself;" was it right to denounce, as equally injurious, that which taught that the root of all social evils is to be traced to the want of mutual love?

It is allowed that Mih was a native and officer of the State of Sung; but the time when he lived is a matter of dispute. Sze-ma Ts'ëen says that some made him to be a contemporary of Confucius, and that others placed him later. He was certainly later than Confucius, to whom he makes many references, not always complimentary, in his writings. In one of his Treatises, moreover, mention is made of Wăn-tsze, an acknowledged disciple of Tsze-hëa, so that he must have been very

little anterior to Mencius. This is the impression also which I receive
from the references to him in our philosopher.

In Lĕw Hin's third catalogue the Mihist writers form a subdivision.
Six of them are mentioned, including Mih himself, to whom 71 *p'ëen*,
or Books, are attributed. So many were then current under his name;
but 18 of them have since been lost. He was an original thinker. He
exercised a bolder judgment on things than Confucius or any of his
followers. Antiquity was not so sacred to him, and he did not hesitate to
condemn the literati—the orthodox—for several of their doctrines and
practices.

Two of his peculiar views are adverted to by Mencius, and
vehemently condemned. The one is about the regulation of funerals,
where Mih contended that a spare simplicity should be the rule.[151] On
that I need not dwell. The other is the doctrine of "Universal Love."[152]
A lengthy exposition of this remains in the Writings which go by Mih's
name, though it is not from his own pen, but that of a disciple. Such as
it is, with all its repetitions, I give a translation of it. My readers will be
able, after perusing it, to go on with me to consider the treatment which
the doctrine received at the hands of Mencius.

## UNIVERSAL LOVE. PART I.

It is the business of the sages to effect the good government of the
empire. They must know, therefore, whence disorder and confusion
arise, for without this knowledge their object cannot be effected. We
may compare them to a physician who undertakes to cure a man's
disease:—he must ascertain whence the disease has arisen, and then he
can assail it with effect, while, without such knowledge, his endeavours
will be in vain. Why should we except the case of those who have to
regulate disorder from this rule? They must know whence it has arisen,
and then they can regulate it.

It is the business of the sages to effect the good government of all
under heaven. They must examine therefore into the cause of disorder;
and when they do so, they will find that it arises from the want of
mutual love. When a minister and a son are not filial to their sovereign
and their father, this is what is called disorder. A son loves himself, and
does not love his father;—he therefore wrongs his father and
advantages himself: a younger brother loves himself, and does not love
his elder brother;—he therefore wrongs his elder brother, and
advantages himself: a minister loves himself, and does not love his

---

[151] Bk III. Pt I. v.

[152] In the phrase for this the former character represents *a hand grasping two stalks
of grain*, so the phrase denotes, "a love that grasps or unites many in its embrace." I do
not know how to render it better than by "universal love." Mencius and the literati
generally find the idea of equality in it also, and it is with them—"To love all equally."

sovereign:—he therefore wrongs his sovereign, and advantages himself:—all these are cases of what is called disorder. Though it be the father who is not kind to his son, or the elder brother who is not kind to his younger brother; or the sovereign who is not gracious to his minister:—the case comes equally under the general name of disorder. The father loves himself, and does not love his son;—he therefore wrongs his son, and advantages himself: the elder brother loves himself, and does not love his younger brother;—he therefore wrongs his younger brother, and advantages himself: the sovereign loves himself, and does not love his minister;—he therefore wrongs his minister, and advantages himself. How do these things come to pass? They all arise from the want of mutual love. Take the case of any thief or robber:—it is just the same with it. The thief loves his own house, and does not love his neighbor's house;—he therefore steals from his neighbor's house to advantage his own: the robber loves his own person, and does not love his neighbor;—he therefore does violence to his neighbor to advantage himself. How is this? It all arises from the want of mutual love. Come to the case of great officers throwing each other's families into confusion, and of princes attacking one another's States:—it is just the same with them. The great officer loves his own family, and does not love his neighbor's;—he therefore throws his neighbor's family into disorder to advantage his own: the prince loves his own State, and does not love his neighbor's;—he therefore attacks his neighbor's State to advantage his own. All disorder in the empire has the same explanation. When we examine into the cause of it, it is found to be the want of mutual love.

Suppose that universal mutual love prevailed throughout the kingdom;—if men loved others as they love themselves, disliking to exhibit what was unfilial......[150] And moreover would there be those who were unkind? Looking on their sons, younger brothers, and ministers as themselves, and disliking to exhibit what was unkind.... the want of filial duty would disappear. And would there be thieves and robbers? When every man regarded his neighbor's house as his own, who would be found to steal? When every one regarded his neighbor's person as his own, who would be found to rob? Thieves and robbers would disappear. And would there be great officers throwing one another's families into confusion, and princes attacking one another's States? When officers regarded the families of others as their own, what one would make confusion? When princes regarded other States as their own, what one would begin an attack? Great officers throwing one another's families into confusion, and princes attacking one another's States, .would disappear.

If, indeed, universal mutual love prevailed throughout the

---

[150] There are evidently some omissions and confusion here in the Chinese text.

kingdom; one State not attacking another, and one family not throwing another into confusion; thieves and robbers nowhere existing;—rulers and ministers, fathers and sons, all being filial and kind:—in such a condition the kingdom would be well governed. On this account, how may sages, whose business it is to effect the good government of the kingdom, do other than prohibit hatred and advise to love? On this account it is affirmed that universal mutual love throughout the kingdom will lead to its happy order, and that mutual hatred leads to confusion. This was what our master, the philosopher Mih, meant, when he said, "We must not but advise to the love of others."

## UNIVERSAL LOVE. PART II.

OUR Master, the philosopher Mih, said, "That which benevolent men consider to be incumbent on them as their business, is to stimulate and promote all that will be advantageous to the kingdom, and to take away all that is injurious to it. This is what they consider to be their business."

And what are the things advantageous to the kingdom, and the things injurious to it? Our Master said, "The mutual attacks of State on State; the mutual usurpations of family on family; the mutual robberies of man on man; the want of kindness on the part of the sovereign and of loyalty on the part of the minister; the want of tenderness and filial duty between father and son:—these, and such as these, are the things injurious to the empire."

And from what do we find, on examination, that these injurious things are produced? Is it not from the want of mutual love?

Our Master said, "Yes, they are produced by the want of mutual love. Here is a prince who only knows to love his own State, and does not love his neighbor's;—he therefore does not shrink from raising all the power of his State to attack his neighbor. Here is the chief of a family who only knows to love it, and does not love his neighbor's;—he therefore does not shrink from raising all his powers to seize on that other family. Here is a man who only knows to love his own person, and does not love his neighbor's;—he therefore does not shrink from using all his strength to rob his neighbor. Thus it happens that the princes, not loving one another, have their battle-fields; and the chiefs of families, not loving one another, have their mutual usurpations; and men, not loving one another, have their mutual robberies; and sovereigns and ministers, not loving one another, become unkind and disloyal; and fathers and sons, not loving one another, lose their affection and filial duty; and brothers, not loving one another, contract irreconcilable enmities. Yea, men in general not loving one another, the strong make prey of the weak; the rich do despite to the poor; the noble are insolent to the mean; and the deceitful impose upon the stupid. All the miseries, usurpations, enmities, and hatreds in the world, when traced to their origin, will be found to arise from the want of mutual love. On this account, the benevolent condemn it."

They may condemn it; but how shall they change it?

Our Master said, "They may change it by universal mutual love, and by the interchange of mutual benefits."

How will this law of universal mutual love and the interchange of mutual benefits accomplish this?

Our Master said, "[It would lead] to the regarding another kingdom as one's own; another family as one's own; another person as one's own. That being the case, the princes, loving one another, would have no battle-fields; the chiefs of families, loving one another, would attempt no usurpations; men, loving one another, would commit no robberies; rulers and ministers, loving one another, would be gracious and loyal; fathers and sons, loving one another, would be kind and filial; brothers, loving one another, would be harmonious and easily reconciled. Yea, men in general loving one another, the strong would not make prey of the weak; the many would not plunder the few; the rich would not insult the poor; the noble would not be insolent to the mean; and the deceitful would not impose upon the simple. The way in which all the miseries, usurpations, enmities, and hatreds in the world may be made not to arise, is universal mutual love. On this account, the benevolent value and praise it."

Yes; but the scholars of the empire and superior men say, "True; if there were this universal love, it would be good. It is, however, the most difficult thing in the world."

Our Master said, "This is because the scholars and superior men simply do not understand the advantageousness [of the law], and to conduct their reasonings upon that. Take the case of assaulting a city, or of a battle-field, or of the sacrificing one's life for the sake of fame;—this is felt by the people everywhere to be a difficult thing. Yet, if the sovereign be pleased with it, both officers and people are able to do it:—how much more might they attain to universal mutual love, and the interchange of mutual benefits, which is different from this! When a man loves others, they respond to and love him; when a man benefits others, they respond to and benefit him; when a man injures others, they respond to and injure him: when a man hates others, they respond to and hate him:—what difficulty is there in the matter? It is only that rulers will not carry on the government on this principle, and so officers do not carry it out in their practice.

"Formerly, the duke Wăn of Tsin liked his officers to be badly dressed, and, therefore, they all wore rams' furs, a leathern swordbelt, and a cap of bleached cotton. Thus attired, they went in to the prince's levee, and came out and walked through the court. Why did they do

this? The sovereign liked it, and therefore the ministers did it. The duke
Ling of Ts'oo liked his officers to have small waists, and, therefore,
they all limited themselves to a single meal. They held in their breath in
putting on their belts, and had to help themselves up by means of the
wall. In the course of a year, they looked black, and as if they would
die of starvation. Why did they do this? The sovereign liked it, and,
therefore, the ministers were able to do it. Kow-tsëen, the king of Yueh,
liked his ministers to be brave, and taught them to be accustomed to be
so. At a general assembly of them, he set on fire the ship where they
were, and to try them, said, "All the precious things of Yueh are here."
He then with his own hands beat a drum, and urged them on. When
they heard the drum thundering, they rushed confusedly about, and
trampled in the fire, till more than a hundred of them perished, when he
struck the gong, and called them back.

"Now, little food, bad clothes, and the sacrifice of life for the sake
of fame,—these are what it is difficult for people to approve of. Yet,
when the sovereign was pleased with it, they were all able [in those
cases] to bring themselves to them. How much more could they attain
to universal mutual love, and the .interchange of mutual benefits, which
is different from such things! When a man loves others, they respond to
and love him; when a man benefits others, they respond to and benefit
him; when a man hates others, they respond to and hate him; when a
man injures others, they respond to and injure him. It is only that rulers
will not carry on their government on this principle, and so, officers do
not carry it out in their practice."

Yes; but now the officers and superior men say, "Granted; the
universal practice of mutual love would be good; but it is an
impracticable thing. It is like taking up the T'ae mountain, and leaping
with it over the Ho or the Tse."

Our Master said, "That is not the proper comparison for it. To take
up the T'ae mountain, and leap with it over the Ho or the Tse, may be
called an exercise of most extraordinary strength; it is, in fact, what no
one, from antiquity to the present time, has ever been able to do. But
how widely different from this is the practice of universal mutual love,
and the interchange of mutual benefits!

"Anciently, the sage kings practiced this. How do we know that
they did so? When Yu reduced the empire to order:—in the west he
made the western Ho and the Joo-tow, to carry off the waters of K'eu-
sun-wang; in the north, he made the Fang-yuen, the Koo, How-che-te,
and the Tow of Foo-t'o; setting up also the Te-ch'oo, and chiseling out
the Lung-mun, to benefit Yen, Tae, Hoo, Mih, and the people of the
western Ho; in the east, he drained the waters to Luh-fang and the
marsh of Măng-choo, reducing them to nine channels, to limit the
waters of the eastern country, and benefit the people of K'e-chow; and
in the south, he made the Kёang, the Han, the Hwae, the Joo, the course

of the eastern current, and the five lakes, to benefit King, Ts'oo, and Yueh, the people of the wild south. These were the doings of Yu; and I am now for practicing the [same] universal [mutual love].

"When king Wăn brought the western country to good order, his light spread, like the sun or the moon, over its four quarters. He did not permit great States to insult small ones; he did not permit the multitude to oppress the fatherless and the widow; he did not permit violence and power to take from the husbandmen their millet pannicled millet, dogs, and swine. Heaven, as if constrained, visited king Wăn with blessing. The old and childless were enabled to complete their years; the solitary and brother-less could yet mingle among the living; the young and parentless found those on whom they could depend, and grew up. These were the doings of king Wăn; and I am now for practicing the same universal [mutual love].

"King Woo tunneled through the T'ae mountain. The Record says, 'There is a way through the mountain, made by me, the descendant of the kings of Chow:—I have accomplished this great work. I have got my virtuous men, and rise up full of reverence for Shang, Hĕa, and the tribes of the south, the east, and the north. Though he has his multitudes of relatives, they are not equal to my virtuous men. If guilt attach to the people anywhere throughout the empire, it is to be required of me, the One man.' This describes the doings of king Woo, and I am now for practicing the [same] universal mutual love.

"If, now, the rulers of the kingdom truly and sincerely wish all in it to be rich, and dislike any being poor; if they desire its good government, and dislike disorder; they ought to practise universal mutual love, and the interchange of mutual benefits. This was the law of the sage kings; it is the way to effect the good government of the kingdom; it may not but be striven after."

## UNIVERSAL LOVE. PART III.

OUR Master, the philosopher Mih, said, "The business of benevolent men requires that they should strive to stimulate and promote what is advantageous to the empire, and to take away what is injurious to it."

Speaking, now, of the present time, what are to be accounted the most injurious things to the empire? They are such as the attacking of small States by great ones; the inroads on small families of great ones; the plunder of the weak by the strong; the oppression of the few by the many; the scheming of the crafty against the simple; the insolence of the noble to the mean. To the same class belong the ungraciousness of rulers, and the disloyalty of ministers; the unkindness of fathers, and the want of filial duty on the part of sons. Yea, there is to be added to these the conduct of the mean men, who employ their edged weapons and poisoned stuff, water and fire, to rob and injure one another.

Pushing on the inquiry now, let us ask whence all these injurious things arise. Is it from loving others and advantaging others? It must be answered "No;" and it must likewise be said, "They arise clearly from hating others and doing violence to others." [If it be further asked] whether those who hate and do violence to others hold the principle of loving all, or that of making distinctions, it must be replied, "They make distinctions." So then, it is this principle of making distinctions between man and man, which gives rise to all that is most injurious in the empire. On this account we conclude that that principle is wrong.

Our Master said, "He who condemns others must have whereby to change them." To condemn men, and have no means of changing them, is like saving them from fire by plunging them in water. A man's language in such a case must be improper. On this account our Master said, "There is the principle of loving all, to change that which makes distinctions." If, now, we ask, "And how is it that universal love can change [the consequences of] that other principle which makes distinctions?" the answer is, "If princes were as much for the States of others as for their own, what one among them would raise the forces of his State to attack that of another?—he is for that other as much as for himself. If they were for the capitals of others as much as for their own, what one would raise the forces of his capital to attack that of another?—he is for that as much as for his own. If chiefs regarded the families of others as their own, what one would lead the power of his family to throw that of another into confusion?—he is for that other as much as for himself. If, now, States did not attack, nor holders of capitals smite, one another, and if families were guilty of no mutual aggressions, would this be injurious to the empire, or its benefit?" It must be replied, "This would be advantageous to the empire." Pushing on the inquiry, now, let us ask whence all these benefits arise. Is it from hating others and doing violence to others? It must be answered, "No;" and it must likewise be said, "They arise clearly from loving others and doing good to others." [If it be further asked] whether those who love others and do good to others hold the principle of making distinctions between man and man, or that of loving all, it must be replied, "They love all." So then it is this principle of universal mutual love which really gives rise to all that is most beneficial to the empire. On this account we conclude that that principle is right.

Our Master said, a little ago, "The business of benevolent men requires that they should strive to stimulate and promote what is advantageous to the kingdom, and to take away what is injurious to it." We have now traced the subject up, and found that it is the principle of universal love which produces all that is most beneficial to the kingdom, and the principle of making distinctions which produces all that is injurious to it. On this account what our Master said—"The principle of making distinctions between man and man is wrong, and the principle of universal love is right," turns out to be correct as the sides of a square.

If, now, we just desire to promote the benefit of the kingdom, and select for that purpose the principle of universal love, then the acute ears and piercing eyes of people will hear and see for one another; and the strong limbs of people will move and be ruled for one another; and men of principle will instruct one another. It will come about that the old, who have neither wife nor children, will get supporters who will enable them to complete their years; and the young and weak, who have no parents, will yet find helpers that shall bring them up. On the contrary, if this principle of universal love is held not to be correct, what benefits will arise from such a view? What can be the reason that the scholars of the empire, whenever they hear of this principle of universal love, go on to condemn it? Plain as the case is, their words in condemnation of this principle do not stop;—they say, "It may be good, but how can it be carried into practice?"

Our Master said, "Supposing that it could not be practiced, it seems hard to go on likewise to condemn it. But how can it be good, and yet incapable of being put into practice?"

Let us bring forward two instances to test the matter.—Let any one suppose the case of two individuals, the one of whom shall hold the principle of making distinctions, and the other shall hold the principle of universal love. The former of these will say, "How can I be for the person of my friend as much as for my own person? how can I be for the parents of my friend as much as for my own parents?" Reasoning in this way, he may see his friend hungry, but he will not feed him; cold, but he will not clothe him; sick, but he will not nurse him; dead, but he will not bury him. Such will be the language of the individual holding the principle of distinction, and such will be his conduct. The language of the other, holding the principle of universality, will be different, and also his conduct. He will say, "I have heard that he who wishes to play a lofty part among men, will be for the person of his friend as much as for his own person, and for the parents of his friend as much as for his own parents. It is only thus that he can attain his distinction? Reasoning in this way, when he sees his friend hungry, he will feed him; cold, he will clothe him; sick, he will nurse him; dead, he will bury him. Such will be the language of him who holds the principle of universal love, and such will be his conduct.

The words of the one of these individuals are a condemnation of those of the other, and their conduct is directly contrary. Suppose now that their words are perfectly sincere, and that their conduct will be carried out,—that their words and actions will correspond like the parts of a token, every word being carried into effect; and let us proceed to put the following questions on the case:—Here is a plain in the open country, and an officer, with coat of mail, gorget, and helmet, is about to take part in a battle to be fought in it, where the issue, whether for life or death, cannot be fore-known; or here is an officer about to be despatched on a distant commission from Pa to Yueh, or from Ts'e to King, where the issue of the journey, going and coming, is quite uncertain:—on either of these suppositions, to whom will the officer entrust the charge of his house, the support of his parents, and the care of his Wife and children?—to one who holds the principle of universal love? or to one who holds that which makes distinctions? I apprehend there is no one under heaven, man or woman, however stupid, though he may condemn the principle of universal love, but would at such a time make one who holds it the subject of his trust. This is in words to condemn the principle, and when there is occasion to choose between it and the opposite, to approve it;—words and conduct are here in contradiction. I do not know how it is, that, throughout the empire, scholars condemn the principle of universal love, whenever they hear it.

Plain as the case is, their words in condemnation of it do not cease, but they say, "This principle may suffice perhaps to guide in the choice of an officer, but it will not guide in the choice of a sovereign."

Let us test this by taking two illustrations:—Let any one suppose the case of two sovereigns, the one of whom shall hold the principle of mutual love, and the other shall hold the principle which makes distinctions. In this case, the latter of them will say, "How can I be as much for the persons of all my people as for ray own? This is much opposed to human feelings. The life of man upon the earth is but a very brief space; it may be compared to the rapid movement of a team of horses whirling past any particular spot." Reasoning in this way, he may see his people hungry, but he will not feed them; cold, but he will not clothe them; sick, but he will not nurse them; dead, but he will not bury them. Such will be the language of the sovereign who holds the principle of distinctions, and such will be his conduct. Different will be the language and conduct of the other who holds the principle of universal love. He will say, "I have heard that he who would show himself a [virtuous and] intelligent sovereign, ought to make his people the first consideration, and think of himself only after them." Reasoning in this way, when he sees any of the people hungry, he will feed them; cold, he will clothe them; sick, he will nurse them; dead, he will bury them. Such will be the language of the sovereign who holds the principle of universal love, and such his conduct. If we compare the two sovereigns, the words of the one are condemnatory of those of the other, and their actions are opposite. Let us suppose that their words are equally sincere, and that their actions will be made good,—that their words and actions will correspond like the parts of a token, every word being carried into effect; and let us proceed to put the following questions on the case:—Here is a year when a pestilence walks abroad among the people; many of them suffer from cold and famine; multitudes die in the ditches and water-channels. If at such a time they might make an election between the two sovereigns whom we have supposed, which would they prefer? I apprehend there is no one under heaven, however stupid, though he may condemn the principle of universal love, but would at such a time prefer to be under the sovereign who holds it. This is in words to condemn the principle, and, when there is occasion to choose between it and the opposite, to approve it;—words and conduct are here in contradiction. I do not know how it is that throughout the empire scholars condemn the principle of universal love, whenever they hear it.

Plain as the case is, their words in condemnation of it do not cease; but they say, "This universal [mutual love] is benevolent and righteous. That we grant, but how can it be practiced? The impracticability of it is like that of taking up the T'ae mountain, and leaping with it over the Kĕang or the Ho. We do, indeed, desire this universal love, but it is an impracticable thing!"

Our Master said, "To take up the T'ae mountain, and leap with it over the Kĕang or the Ho, is a thing which never has been done, from the highest antiquity to the present time, since men were; but the exercise of mutual love and the interchange of mutual benefits,—this was practiced by the ancient sages and six kings."

How do you know that the ancient sages and the six kings practiced this?

Our Master said, "I was not of the same age and time with them, so that I could myself have heard their voices, or seen their faces; but I know what I say from what they have transmitted to posterity, written on bamboo or cloth, cut in metal or stone, engraven on their vessels."

It is said in "The Great Declaration,"—"King Wăn was like the sun or like the moon; suddenly did his brightness shine through the four quarters of the western region."

According to these Words, king Wăn exercised the principle of universal love on a vast scale. He is compared to the sun or moon which shines on all, without partial favor to any spot under the heavens;—such was the universal love of king Wăn. What our Master insisted on was thus exemplified in him.

Again, not only does "The Great Declaration" speak thus;—we find the same thing in "The Declaration of Yu." Yu said, "Ye multitudes, listen all to my words. It is not only I who dare to say a word in favor of war;—against this stupid prince of Mĕaou we must execute the punishment appointed by Heaven. I am therefore leading your hosts, and go before you all to punish the prince of Mĕaou."

Thus Yu punished the prince of Mĕaou, not to increase his own riches and nobility, nor to obtain happiness and emolument, nor to gratify his ears and eyes;—he did it, seeking to promote what was advantageous to the empire, and to take away what was injurious to it. It appears from this that Yu held the principle of universal love. What our Master insisted on may be found in him.

And not only may Yu thus be appealed to;—we have "The words of T'ang" to the same effect. T'ang said, "I, the child Le, presume to use a dark-colored victim, and announce to Thee, O supreme Heavenly Sovereign.—Now there is a great drought, and it is right I should be held responsible for it. I do not know but that I have offended against the Powers above and below. But the good I dare not keep in obscurity, and the sinner I dare not pardon. The examination of this is with Thy mind, O God. If the people throughout the empire commit offences, it is to be required of me. If I commit offences, it does not concern the people." From these words we perceive that T'ang, possessing the dignity of supreme king, and the wealth of the kingdom, yet did not shrink from offering himself as a sacrifice which might be acceptable to God and [other] spiritual Beings. It appears from this that T'ang held the principle of universal love. What our Master insisted on was exemplified in T'ang.

And not only may We appeal in this way to the "Declarations," "Charges," and "The Words of T'ang,"—we find the same thing in "The Poems of Chow." One of those poems says,

> "Wide and long is the Royal way,
>      It is straight as an arrow,
> Without deflection, without injustice.
>      It is smooth as a whetstone.
> The Royal way is plain and level,
>      The officers tread it;
> Without injustice, without deflection.
>      The lower people see it."

Is not this speaking of the [Royal] way in accordance with our style? Anciently, Wăn and Woo, acting with exact justice and impartiality, rewarded the worthy and punished the oppressive, allowing no favoritism to influence them towards their own relatives. It appears from this that Wăn and Woo held the principle of universal love. What our Master insisted on was exemplified in them.—How is it that the scholars of the empire condemn this universal love, whenever they hear of it? Plain as the case is, the words of those who condemn the principle of universal love do not cease. They say, "It is not advantageous to the entire devotion to parents which is required;—it is injurious to filial piety." Our Master said, "Let us bring this objection to the test:—A filial son, having [the happiness of] his parents at heart, considers how it is to be secured. Now, does he, so considering, wish men to love and benefit his parents? or does he wish them to hate and injure his parents?" On this view of the question, it must be evident that he wishes men to love and benefit his parents. And what must he himself first do in order to gain this object? If I first address myself to love and benefit men's parents, will they for that return love and benefit to my parents? or if I first address myself to hate men's parents, will they for that return love and benefit to my parents? It is clear that I must first address myself to love and benefit men's parents, and they will return to me love and benefit to my parents. The conclusion is that a filial son has no alternative.—He must address himself in the first place to love and do good to the parents of others. If it be supposed that this is an accidental course, to be followed on emergency by a filial son, and not sufficient to be regarded as a general rule, let us bring it to the test of what we find in the Books of the ancient kings. It is said in the Ta Ya,

> "Every word find its answer;
>     He threw me a peach;
> Every action its recompense.
>     I returned him a plum."

These words show that he who loves others will be loved, and that he who hates others will be hated. How is it that the scholars of the empire condemn this principle of universal love, when they hear it?

Is it that they deem it so difficult as to be impracticable? But there have been more difficult things, which yet have been done. [For instance], king Ling of King was fond of small waists. In his time, the officers of King restricted themselves to a handful of rice, till they required a stick to raise themselves, and in walking had to hold themselves up by the wall. Now, it is a difficult thing to restrict one's-self in food, but they were able to do it, because it would please king Ling.—It needs not more than a generation to change the manners of the people, such is their desire to move after the pattern of their superiors.

[Again], Kow-tsëen the king of Yueh, was fond of bravery. He spent three years in training his officers to be brave; and then, not knowing fully whether they were so, he set fire to the ship where they were, and urged them forward by a drum into the flames. They advanced, one rank over the bodies of another, till an immense number perished in the water or the flames; and it was not till he ceased to beat the drum, that they retired. Those officers of Yueh might be pronounced to be full of reverence. To sacrifice one's life in the flames is a difficult thing, but they were able to do it, because it would please their king.—It needs not more than a generation to change the manners of the people, such is their desire to move after the pattern of their superiors. [Once more], duke Wăn of Tsin was fond of garments of coarse flax. In his time, the officers of Tsin wore wide clothes of that fabric, with rams' furs, leathern swordbelts, and coarse canvas sandals. Thus attired, they went in to the duke's levee, and went out and walked through the court. It is a difficult thing to wear such clothes, but they were able to do it, because it would please duke Wăn.—It needs but a generation to change the manners of the people, such is their desire to move after the pattern of their superiors.

Now, little food, a burning ship, and coarse clothes,—these are among the most difficult things to endure; but because the ruler would be pleased with the enduring them, they were able [in those cases] to do it. It needs no more than a generation to change the manners of the people. Why? Because such is their desire to move after the pattern of their superiors. And now, as to universal mutual love, it is an advantageous thing and easily practiced,—beyond all calculation. The only reason why it is not practiced is, in my opinion, because superiors do not take pleasure in it. If superiors were to take pleasure in it, stimulating men to it by rewards and praise, and awing them from opposition to it by punishments and fines, they would, in my opinion, move to it,—the practice of universal mutual love, and the interchange of mutual benefits,—as fire rises upwards, and as water flows downwards:—nothing would be able to check them. This universal love was the way of the sage kings; it is the principle to secure peace for kings, dukes, and great men; it is the means to secure plenty of food and clothes for the myriads of the people. The best course for the superior man is to well understand the principle of universal love, and exert himself to practise it. It requires the ruler to be gracious, and the minister to be loyal; the father to be kind, and the son to be filial; the elder brother to be friendly, and the younger to bo obedient. Therefore the superior man, with whom the chief desire is to see gracious rulers and loyal ministers; kind fathers and filial sons; friendly elder brothers and obedient younger ones, ought to insist on the indispensableness of the practice of universal love. It was the way of the sage kings; it would be the most advantageous thing for the myriads of the people.

2. Notwithstanding the mutilations and corruptions in the text of the preceding Essay, its general scope is clearly discernible, and we obtain from it a sufficient account of Mih's doctrine on the subject of "Universal Love." We have now to consider the opposition offered to this doctrine by Mencius. He was not the first, however, to be startled and offended by it. The Essay shows that it was resented as an outrage on the system of orthodox belief during all the lifetime of Mih and his immediate disciples. Men of learning did not cease to be clamorous against it. From the allusions made by Mencius to its prevalence in his days, it would appear that it had overcome much of the hostility which it at first encountered. He stepped forward to do battle with it; and

though he had no new arguments to ply, such was the effect of his onset, that "Universal Love" has ever since been considered, save by some eccentric thinkers, as belonging to the Limbo of Chinese Vanity, among other things "abortive, monstrous, or unkindly mixed."

We may approach the question conveniently by observing that Mih's attempts to defend his principle were in several points far from the best that could be made. His references to the examples of Yu, T'ang, and the kings Wăn and Woo, are of this nature. Those worthies well performed the work of their generation. They punished the oppressor, and delivered the oppressed. Earnest sentiments of justice and benevolence animated their breasts and directed their course. But they never laid down the doctrine of "Universal Love," as the rule for themselves or others.

When he insists, again, that the people might easily be brought to appreciate and practise his doctrine, if their rulers would only set them the example, he shows the same overweening idea of the influence of superiors, and the same ignorance of human nature, which I have had occasion to point out in both Confucius and Mencius. His references to duke Wăn of Tsin, king Ling of Ts'oo, and Kow-tsëen of Yueh, and his argument from what they are said to have effected, only move us to smile. And when he teaches that men are to be *awed* to love one another *"by punishments and fines,"* we feel that he is not understanding fully what he says nor whereof he affirms.

Still, he has broadly and distinctly laid it down, that if men would only universally love one another, the evils which disturb and embitter human society would disappear. I do not say that he has taught the *duty* of universal love. His argument is conducted on the ground of *expediency*. Whether he had in his own mind a truer, nobler foundation for his principle, does not immediately appear. Be that as it may, his doctrine was that men were to be exhorted to love one another,—to love one another as themselves. According to him, "princes should be as much for the States of others as for their own. One prince should be for every other as for himself." So it ought to be also with the heads of clans, with ministers, with parents, and with men generally.

Here it was that Mencius joined issue with him. He affirmed that "to love all equally did not acknowledge the peculiar affection due to a parent." It is to be observed that Mih himself nowhere says that his principle was that of loving all EQUALLY. His disciples drew this conclusion from it. In the third Book of Mencius' Works, we find one of them, E Che, contending that the expression in the Shoo-king, about the ancient kings acting towards the people "as if they were watching over an infant," sounded to him as if love were to be *without difference of degree*, the manifestation of it simply commencing with our parents. To this Mencius replied conclusively by asking, "Does E really think that a man's affection for the child of his brother is merely like his affection for the child of his neighbor?" With still more force might he have asked, "Is a man's affection for his father merely like his affection for the father of his neighbor?" Such a question, and the necessary reply to it, are implied in his condemnation of Mih's system, as being "without father," that is, denying the peculiar affection due to a father. If Mih had really maintained that a man's father was to be no more to him than the father of any other body, or if his system had necessitated such a consequence, Mencius would only have done his duty to his country in denouncing him, and exposing the fallacy of his reasonings. As the case is, he would have done better if he had shown that no such conclusion necessarily flows from the doctrine of Universal Love, or its preceptive form that we are to love our neighbor as ourselves.

Of course it belonged to Mih himself to defend his views from the imputation. But what he has said on the point is not satisfactory. In reply to the charge that his principle was injurious to filial piety, he endeavoured to show, that, by acting on it, a man would best secure the happiness of his parents:—as he addressed himself in the first place to love, and do good to, the parents of others, they would recompense to him the love of, and good-doing to, his parents. It might be so, or it might not. The reply exhibits strikingly in what manner Mih was conducted to the inculcation of "universal love," and that really it had in his mind no deeper basis than its expediency. This is his weak point; and if Mencius, whose view of the constitution of human nature, and the obligation of the virtues, apart from all consideration of consequences, was more comprehensive and correct than that of Mih, had founded his opposition on this ground, we could in a measure have sympathized with him. But while Mih appeared to lose sight of the other sentiments of the human mind too much, in his exclusive contemplation of the power of love, he did not doubt but his principle would make sons more filial, and ministers more devoted, and subjects more loyal. The passage which I have just referred to, moreover, does not contain the admission that the love was to be *without any difference of degree*. The fact is, that he hardly seems to have realized the objection with which Mencius afterwards pressed the advocacy of his principle by his followers. If he did do so, he blinked the difficulty, not seeing his way to give a full and precise reply to it.

This seems to be the exact state of the case between the two philosophers.—Mih stumbled on a truth, which, based on a right foundation, is one of the noblest that can animate the human breast, and affords the surest remedy for the ills of society. There is that in it, however, which is startling, and liable to misrepresentation and abuse. Mencius saw the difficulty attaching to it, and unable to sympathize with the generosity of it, set himself to meet it with a most vehement opposition. Nothing, certainly, could be more absurd than his classing Yang Choo and Mih Teih together, as equally the enemies of benevolence and righteousness. When he tries to ridicule Mih, and talks contemptuously about him, how, if he could have benefited the kingdom, by toiling till he had rubbed off every hair of his body, he would have done it,—this only raises up a barrier between himself and us. It reminds us of the *hardness* of nature which I have elsewhere charged against him.

3. Confucius, I think, might have dealt more fairly and generously with Mih. In writing of him, I called attention to his repeated enunciation of "the golden rule" in a negative form,—"What you do not wish done to yourself, do not do to others."[151] In one place, indeed, he rises for a moment to the full apprehension of it, and recognizes the duty of taking the initiative,—of behaving to others in the first instance as he would that they should behave to him.[152] Now, what is this but the practical exercise of the principle of universal love? "All things whatsoever ye would that men should do to you, do ye even so to them:"—this is simply the manifestation of the requirement, "Thou shalt love thy neighbor as thyself." Confucius might have conceded, therefore, to Mih, that the rule of conduct which he laid down was the very best that could be propounded. If he had gone on to remove it from the basis of expediency, and place it on a better foundation, he would have done the greatest service to his countrymen, and entitled himself to a place among the sages of the world.

On this matter I am happy to find myself in agreement with the "prince of literature," Han Yu. "Our literati," says he, "find fault with Mih because of what he has said on 'The Estimation to be attached to Concord,'[153] on 'Universal Love' on 'The Estimation to be given to Men of Worth,' on 'The Acknowledging of Spiritual Beings,'[154] and on

---

[151] Vol. I., Proleg., p. 111.

[152] See Proleg. on the Doctrine of the Mean, p. 48.

[153] This is the title of one of Mih's Essays,—forming the third Book of his Works. Generalizing after his fashion, he traces all evils up to a want of concord, or agreement of opinion; and goes on to assert that the sovereign must be recognized as the "Infallible Head," to lay down the rule of truth and right, saying, "What the sovereign approves, all must approve; what the sovereign condemns, all must condemn." It is an unguarded utterance; and taken absolutely, apart from its connection, may be represented very much to Mih's disadvantage. See "Supplemental Observations on the Four Books," on Mencius, Book I. art. lix. The coincidence between this saying and the language of Hobbes is remarkable,—"Quod legislator præceperit, id pro bono, quod vetuerit, id pro malo habendum esse." (*De Cive*, cap. xii. 1.)

[154] This is found in the 8th Book of Mih. The first and second parts of the essay, however, are unfortunately lost. In the third he tells several queer ghost stories, and adduces other proofs, to show the real existence of spiritual Beings, and that they take account of men's actions to reward or to punish them. He found another panacea for the ills of the kingdom in this truth. His doctrine here, however, is held to be inconsistent with Confucius' reply to Fan Ch'e, Ana. VI. xx., that wisdom consists in respecting spiritual Beings, but at the same time keeping aloof from them. As between Confucius and Mih, on this point we would agree rather with the latter. He holds an important truth, mingled with superstition; the sage is sceptical.

'Confucius' being in awe of great men, and, when he resided in any State, not blaming its great officers.'[155] But when the Ch'un Ts'ĕw finds fault with assuming ministers, is not this attaching a similar value to concord? When Confucius speaks of 'overflowing in love to all, and cultivating the friendship of the good,' and of how 'the extensive conferring of benefits constitutes a sage,' does he not teach universal love? When he advises 'the esteem of the worthy;' when he arranged his disciples into 'the four classes,' so stimulating and commending them; when he says that 'the superior man dislikes the thought of his name not being mentioned after death:'—does not this show the estimation he gave to men of worth? When 'he sacrificed as if the spiritual Beings were present' and condemned 'those who sacrificed as if they were not really sacrificing,' when he said, 'When I sacrifice, I shall receive blessing:'—was not this acknowledging spiritual Beings? The literati and Mih equally approve of Yaou and Shun, and equally condemn Kĕeh and Chow; they equally teach the cultivation of the person, and the rectifying of the heart, reaching on to the good government of the kingdom, with all its States and families:—why should they be so hostile to each other? In my opinion, the discussions which we hear are the work of their followers, vaunting on each side the sayings of their Teacher; there is no such contrariety between the real doctrines of the two Teachers. Confucius would have used Mih; and Mih would have used Confucius. If they would not have used each other, they could not have been K'ung and Mih."

4. It seems proper, in closing this discussion of Mih's views, to notice the manner in which the subject of "universal love" appears in Christianity. Its whole law is comprehended in the one word—Love; but how wide is the scope of the term compared with all which it ever entered into the mind of Chinese sage or philosopher to conceive!

It is most authoritative where the teachers of China are altogether silent, and commands:—"Thou shalt love the Lord, thy God, with all thy heart, and with all thy soul, and with all thy strength, and with all thy mind." For the Divine Being Christianity thus demands from all men supreme love;—the love of all that is majestic, awing the soul; the love of all that is beautiful, wooing the heart; the love of all that is good, possessing and mastering the entire nature. Such a love, existing, would necessitate obedience to every law, natural or revealed. Christianity, however, goes on to specify the duties which every man owes, as the complement of love to God, to his fellow-men:—"Owe no man anything, but to love one another, for he that loveth another hath fulfilled the law. For this—'Thou shalt not commit adultery,' 'Thou shalt not kill,' 'Thou shalt not steal,' 'Thou shalt not bear false witness,' 'Thou shalt not covet;' and if there be any other

---

[155] Han avoids saying anything on this point.

commandment:—the whole is briefly comprehended in this saying, 'Thou shalt love thy neighbor as thyself.'" This commandment is "like to" the other, only differing from it in not requiring the *supreme* love which is due to God alone. The rule which it prescribes,—such love to others as we feel for ourselves,—is much more definitely and intelligibly expressed than anything we find in Mih, and is not liable to the cavils with which his doctrine was assailed. Such a love to men, existing, would necessitate the performance of every relative and social duty; we could not help doing to others as we would that they should do to us.

Mih's universal love was to find its scope and consummation in the good government of China. He had not the idea of man as man, any more than Confucius or Mencius. How can that idea be fully realized, indeed, where there is not the right knowledge of one living and true God, the creator and common parent of all? The love which Christianity inculcates is a law of humanity; paramount to all selfish, personal feelings; paramount to all relative, local, national attachments; paramount to all distinctions of race or of religion. Apprehended in the spirit of Christ, it will go forth even to the love of enemies; it will energize in a determination to be always increasing the sum of others' happiness, limited only by the means of doing so.

But I stop. These prolegomena are the place for disquisition; but I deemed it right to say thus much here of that true, universal love, which at once gives glory to God and effects peace on earth.

*The Works of Mencius.*

## BOOK I. KING HWUY OF LËANG.[156] PART I.

CHAPTER I.[157] 1. MENCIUS [went to] see king Hwuy of Lëang.[158] 2. The king said, "Venerable Sir, since you have not counted it far to come here, a distance of a thousand *le*, may I presume that you are likewise provided with [counsels] to profit my kingdom?"[159]

---

[156] The *title of the Work* in Chinese is simply Măng-tsze, or "The Philosopher Măng;" thus simply bearing the name, or surname rather, of him whose conversations and opinions it relates, and which, it is said, were compiled in their present form by himself. He is always called Măng-tsze, or Mencius, throughout the work, and not "the Master," which epithet is confined to Confucius. See on the Analects, I. i. See also the sketch of Mencius' life in the Prolegomena.

The *title of this Book* in Chinese is—"King Hwuy of Lëang; in chapters and sentences. Parts I. and II." Like the Books of the Confucian Analects, those of this work are headed by two or three words at or near the commencement of them. Each Book is divided into two parts. This arrangement was made by Chaou K'e, who has been spoken of in the Prolegomena, and to him are due also the divisions into chapters, and sentences or paragraphs containing, it may be, many sentences.

[157] CH. I. BENEVOLENCE AND RIGHTEOUSNESS MENCIUS' ONLY TOPICS WITH THE PRINCES OF HIS TIME; AND THE ONLY PRINCIPLES WHICH CAN MAKE A COUNTRY PROSPEROUS.

[158] *Par.* 1. "King Hwuy of Lëang."—In the time of Confucius, Tsin was one of the great States, perhaps the greatest State, of the kingdom,—but the power of it was usurped by six great families or clans. By B.C. 452, three of these were absorbed by the other three, the clans, namely, of Wei, Chaou, and Han, which continued to encroach on the small remaining authority of their princes, till at last they divided the whole territory among themselves. King Wei-lëeh, in B.C. 402, granted to the chief of each family the title of Marquis. Wei, called also, from the name of its capital, Lëang, occupied what had been the south-eastern part of Tsin, Han and Chaou lying to the west and north-west of it. The Lëang, where Mencius visited king Hwuy, is said to have been in the present district of Ts'ëang-foo, department K'ae-fung. Hwuy—"of soft disposition and kind to the people"—was the posthumous or sacrificial epithet of the king, whose name was Yung. He had usurped the title of king, as the princes of many other States did about the same time, before Mencius visited him, which it is said was in the 35th year of his government, B.C. 335. The philosopher, it is supposed, visited him on invitation.

[159] *Par.* 2. Mencius, we have seen, was a native of Tsow in Loo, the name of which still remains in the Tsow district of the department Yen-chow, in Shantung. The king in complimentary style calls the distance from Tsow to Lëang a thousand *le*, though in reality it was not half so much. The "venerable Sir," with which he salutes the philosopher, should also be taken as complimentary, and we cannot draw any inference from it as to the age of Mencius at this time. The "likewise" has led to much speculation to bring out its meaning. Some think that the king is referring to the many scholars of that age, who made it their business to wander from State to State to counsel the princes, so that his meaning was:—"You *also*, like other scholars," &c. Then when Mencius in reply uses the same term, they think that he is referring to the ancient sages as his models:—"I *also*, like them," &c. This is too farfetched. I suppose that the king's "likewise" follows the clause "You have come a thousand *le*," and means, "That is one favour, but you probably have others to confer also." Then Mencius' "likewise" refers to the king's, and = "You say I likewise have counsels to profit you. What I likewise have is benevolence," &c.

3. Mencius replied, "Why must your Majesty use that word 'profit'? What I am likewise provided with are [counsels to] benevolence and righteousness; and these are my only topics.[160]

4. "If your Majesty say, 'What is to be done to profit , my kingdom?' the great officers will say, 'What is to be done to profit our families?, and the [inferior] officers and the common people will say, 'What is to be done to profit our persons?' Superiors and inferiors will try to take the profit the one from the other, and the kingdom will be endangered. In the kingdom of ten thousand chariots, the murderer of his ruler will be [the chief of] a family of a thousand chariots. In the State of a thousand chariots, the murderer of his ruler will be [the chief of] a family of a hundred chariots. To have a thousand in ten thousand, and a hundred in a thousand, cannot be regarded as not a large allowance; but if righteousness be put last and profit first, they will not be satisfied without snatching all.[161]

5. "There never was a man trained to benevolence who neglected his parents. There never was a man trained to righteousness who made his ruler an after-consideration.[162]

6. "Let your Majesty likewise make benevolence and righteousness your only themes;—why must you speak of profit?"

II.[163] 1. When Mencius [another day] was seeing king Hwuy of Lëang, the king [went and] stood [with him] by a pond, and, looking round on the wild geese and deer, large and small, said, "Do wise and good [princes] also take pleasure in these things?"

2. Mencius replied, "Being wise and good, they then have pleasure in these things. If they are not wise and good, though they have these things, they do not find pleasure.[164]

3. "It is said in the Book of Poetry:—

---

[160] *Par.* 3. Benevolence is defined by Choo He as "the virtue of the mind, the principle of love," and righteousness as "the regulation of the mind, the fitness of things." Mencius had in mind the benevolent government of which he speaks at length in many places. See especially the 7th chapter of this Part.

[161] *Par.* 4. By "the kingdom of ten thousand chariots" is meant the royal domain, which, according to the theory of the kingdom, could send into the field 10,000 chariots; and by "the chief of a family of a thousand chariots," one of the king's principal ministers, whose territory, which was in the royal domain, was supposed to be able to send forth a thousand chariots. "A State of a thousand chariots" was one of the largest of the feudal States, and "the chief of a family of a hundred chariots" was one of its principal ministers, the head of a powerful clan.

[162] *Par.* 5. In the "likewise" here Mencius turns the tables on the king. Let him follow the example of the philosopher, confident in the truth of the positions which he had stated.

[163] CH. II. RULERS MUST SHARE THEIR PLEASURES WITH THE PEOPLE. THEY CAN ONLY BE HAPPY WHEN THEY RULE OVER HAPPY SUBJECTS.

[164] *Parr.* 1, 2. *Par.* 1 must be supplemented as I have done. Mencius would go to the court; and then the king would go with him, or have left orders for him to be brought to the park. Observe the "also" in the king's question, and the "then" in Mencius' reply.

'When he planned the commencement of the Marvelous
    tower,
He planned it, and defined it,
And the people in crowds undertook the work,
And in no time completed it.
When he planned the commencement, [he said], "Be not in a
    hurry;"
But the people came as if they were his children.
The king was in the Marvelous park,
Where the does were lying down,—
The does so sleek and fat;
With the white birds glistening.
The king was by the Marvelous pond;—
How full was it of fishes leaping about!'

King Wăn used the strength of the people to make his tower and pond,
and the people rejoiced [to do the work], calling the tower 'the
Marvelous tower' and the pond 'the Marvelous pond,' and being glad
that he had his deer, his fishes, and turtles. The ancients caused their
people to have pleasure as well as themselves, and therefore they could
enjoy it.[165]

4. "In the Declaration of T'ang it is said, 'O sun, when wilt thou
expire? We will die together with thee.' The people wished [for Kĕeh's
death, though] they should die with him. Although he had his tower, his
pond, birds and animals, how could he have pleasure alone?"[166]

III.[167] 1. King Hwuy of Lĕang said, "Small as my virtue is, in [the
government of] my kingdom, I do indeed exert my mind to the utmost.
If the year be bad inside the Ho, I remove [as many of] the people [as] I
can to the east of it, and convey grain to the country inside. If the year
be bad on the east of the river, I act on the same plan. On examining the
governmental methods of the neighbouring kingdoms, I do not find
there is any [ruler] who exerts his mind as I do. And yet the people of
the neighbouring kings do not decrease, nor do my people
increase;—how is this?"[168]

---

[165] *Par.* 3. Here is an instance of a wise and good prince happy with his happy
subjects in his park and tower and pond. See the Book of Poetry, III. i. VIII. The last
sentence shows what we are to understand by a prince's sharing his pleasure with his
subjects.

[166] *Par.* 4. Here is an instance of an oppressive prince, and of his discontented
subjects. They were weary of their lives, and would die with him, rather than live on as
they were; how could he be happy in such circumstances? See the Shoo, IV. i. 3.

[167] CH. III. HALF MEASURES ARE OF LITTLE USE. IF A PRINCE CARRY OUT
FAITUFULLY THE GREAT PRINCIPLES OF ROYAL GOVERNMENT, THE PEOPLE WILL MAKE
HIM KING.

[168] *Par.* 1. A prince was wont to speak of himself as "the small or deficient man,"

2. Mencius replied, "Your Majesty loves war; allow me to take an illustration from war. [The soldiers move forward at] the sound of the drum; and when the edges of their weapons have been crossed, [on one side] they throw away their buff-coats, trail their weapons behind them, and run. Some run a hundred paces and then stop; some run fifty paces and stop. What would you think if these, because [they had run but] fifty paces, should laugh at [those who ran] a hundred paces?" The king said, "They cannot do so. They only did not run a hundred paces; but they also ran." [Mencius] said, "Since your Majesty knows this, you have no ground to expect that your people will become more numerous than those of the neighbouring kingdoms.

3. "If the seasons of husbandry be not interfered with, the grain will be more than can be eaten. If close nets are not allowed to enter the pools and ponds, the fish and turtles will be more than can be consumed. If the axes and bills enter the hill-forests [only] at the proper times, the wood will be more than can be used. When the grain and fish and turtles are more than can be eaten, and there is more wood than can be used, this enables the people to nourish their living and do all offices for their dead, without any feeling against any. [But] this condition, in which [the people] nourish their living, and do all offices to their dead without having any feeling against any, is the first step in the Royal way.[169]

4. "Let mulberry-trees be planted about the homesteads with their five acres, and persons of fifty years will be able to wear silk. In keeping fowls, pigs, dogs, and swine, let not their times of breeding be neglected, and persons of seventy years will be able to eat flesh. Let there not be taken away the time that is proper for the cultivation of the field-allotment of a hundred acres, and the family of several mouths will not suffer from hunger. Let careful attention be paid to the teaching in the various schools, with repeated inculcation of the filial and fraternal duties, and gray-haired men will not be seen upon the roads, carrying burdens on their backs or on their heads. It has never been that [the ruler of a State] where these results were seen, persons of seventy wearing silk and eating flesh, and the black-haired people suffering

---

and so king Hwuy calls himself here. I have translated it by "small as my virtue is, I;" but hereafter I will generally translate the phrase simply by I. "Inside the Ho" and "East of the Ho" were the names of two tracts in Wei. The former remains in the district of Ho-nuy (meaning inside the Ho), in the department of Hwae-k'ing, Ho-nan. The latter, according to the geographers, should be found in the present Hëae Chow, Shan-se; but this seems too far away from the other.

[169] *Par.* 3 contains the first principles of Royal government, in contrast with the king's expedients as detailed by him in par. 1. The seasons of husbandry were spring, summer, and autumn. The government should undertake no military expeditions or public works in them. Close nets would take the small fish, whereas these, if left untouched, would grow and increase. Generally the time to take firewood from the forests was when the growth for the year was over; but there were many regulations on this point.

neither from hunger nor cold, did not attain to the Royal dignity.[170]

5. "Your dogs and swine eat the food of men, and you do not know to store up [of the abundance]. There are people dying from famine on the roads, and you do not know to issue [your stores for their relief]. When men die, you say, 'It is not owing to me; it is owing to the year.' In what does this differ from stabbing a man and killing him, and then saying, 'It was not I; it was the weapon'? Let your Majesty cease to lay the blame on the year, and instantly the people, all under the sky, will come to you."[171]

IV.[172] 1. King Hwuy of Lĕang said, "I wish quietly to receive your instructions."

2. Mencius replied, "Is there any difference between killing a man with a stick and with a sword?" "There is no difference," was the answer.[173]

3. [Mencius continued,] "Is there any difference between doing it with a sword and with governmental measures?" "There is not," was the answer [again].

4. [Mencius then] said, "In [your] stalls there are fat beasts; in [your] stables there are fat horses. [But] your people have the look of hunger, and in the fields there are those who have died of famine. This is leading on beasts to devour men.[174]

---

[170] *Par.* 4 continues the description of the measures of Royal government to secure plenty for the people. What I translate by "acre" was anciently a space of 100 paces square,—very large paces apparently, of six cubits each, but the cubit was not so long as it is now. The land was marked off in squares of 900 acres, of which we shall read more at length by and by, the middle square containing what was called "the public field," belonging to the government. The other eight squares were allotted to eight families, each one having 100 acres, which it cultivated for itself, and all uniting in the cultivation of the central or government square. But from this 20 acres were cut off, and assigned in portions of 2½ acres to the farmers, to build their huts on, and cultivate vegetables, &c. The same amount of 2½ acres was assigned to each family in their villages, where they lived in winter when their labors were not required in the fields. Thus each family had five acres where they might build their dwellings and field-huts, and cultivate their kitchen-vegetables; and on this space also they reared their mulberry-trees round their houses and huts. In this way the large portion of the ground was left for grain produce, while they could nourish enow of silk-worms to produce the silk which they required for the use of those who were 50 years of age and over. The saying that persons of 70 years might eat flesh means that they might always have it at their meals, and in no stinted supply. On the schools, see III. Pt I. iii. 10. Education thus completes Mencius' theory of Royal government, the elements in which were, provision for the maintenance of all, the comfort of the aged, and a moral education and training for the young.

[171] *Par.* 5. Application to king Hwuy of the above principles. The two first sentences refer to the bad years of his opening remarks. If he took proper advantage of the good years, he would not be obliged to resort to such extreme expedients in bad ones.

[172] CH. IV. A CONTINUATION OF THE FORMER CHAPTER, AND FURTHER EXPOSURE OF THE CHARACTER OF KING HWUY'S GOVERNMENT.

[173] *Par.* 2. The "stick" may be a staff or a club, and "the sword" any sharp-edged weapon.

[174] *Par.* 4. The first sentence is literally—"The stalls have fat flesh," and by stalls we are to understand the house or houses where cattle were fed for the king's table. "The

5. 'Beasts devour one another, and men hate them [for doing so]. When he who is [called] the parent of the people conducts his government so as to be chargeable with leading on beasts to devour men, where is that parental relation to the people?

6. "Chung-ne said, 'Was he not without posterity who first made wooden images [to bury with the dead]?' [So he said,] because that man made the semblances of men and used them [for that purpose];—what shall be thought of him who causes his people to die of hunger?"[175]

V.[176] 1. King Hwuy of Lëang said, "There was not in the kingdom a stronger State than Ts'in, as you, venerable Sir, know. But since it descended to me, on the east we were defeated by Ts'e, and then my eldest son perished; on the west we lost seven hundred *le* of territory to Ts'in; and on the south we have sustained disgrace at the hands of Ts'oo. I have brought shame on my departed predecessors, and wish on their account to wipe it away once for all. What course is to be pursued to accomplish this?"[177]

2. Mencius replied, "With a territory [only] a hundred *le* square it has been possible to obtain the Royal dignity.[178]

3. "If your Majesty will [indeed] dispense a benevolent government to the people, being sparing in the use of punishments and fines, and making the taxes and levies of produce light, [so causing that] the fields shall be ploughed deep, and the weeding well attended to, and that the able-bodied, during their days of leisure, shall cultivate their filial piety, fraternal duty, faithfulness, and truth, serving thereby,

---

fields" are literally—"the wilds;" meaning here the open country, away from the capital, and generally away from cities and towns. The "leading on beasts to devour men" is merely a forcible way of describing the king's measures, careful for the good condition of his cattle and horses, and so negligent of the well-being of his people.

[175] *Par.* 6. In high antiquity, it is said, bundles of straw were formed to represent men imperfectly, and then buried with the dead, as attendants upon them. After the rise of the Chow dynasty, wooden figures, with springs in them by which they could move, were used for those bundles; and this, as Confucius thought, led to the practice of burying living persons with the dead, and he branded the inventor of the images as in the text. Mencius thought his words suited his purpose, and used them accordingly. We know that the practice of burying living persons with the dead existed in China in the time of Confucius, and has been practiced even in the present dynasty; and the true explanation of it is very different from that suggested by the sage's words. Chung-ne;—see the Life of Confucius in Volume I.

[176] CH. V. HOW A RULER MIGHT BEST MAKE HIMSELF STRONG, AND REGARD WITH INDIFFERENCE ANY EFFORTS OF HIS ENEMIES TO ATTACK OR INJURE HIM.

[177] *Par.* 1. In the note on par. 1, ch. i. I have spoken of the breaking up of the old State of Tsin into the three States of Wei or Lëang, Chaou, and Han. They were often called "the three Tsin;" and here king Hwuy appears to call Wei alone by the name of Tsin. Ts'e was the most powerful State, at this time styled kingdom, lying north and east from Wei; Ts'in was on the west of it; and Ts'oo on the south.

[178] *Par.* 2. The case which Mencius, probably, had in view here was that of king Wăn, the founder of the Chow dynasty.

at home, their fathers and elder brothers, and, abroad, their elders and superiors; you will then have a people who can be employed with sticks which they have prepared to oppose the strong buff-coats and sharp weapons of [the troops of] Ts'in and Ts'oo.[179]

4. "[The rulers of] those [States] rob their people of their time, so that they cannot plough and weed their fields in order to support their parents. Parents suffer from cold and hunger; elder and younger brothers, wives and children, are separated and scattered abroad.

5. "Those [rulers] drive their people into pitfalls or into the water; and your Majesty will go to punish them. In such a case, who will oppose your Majesty?

6. "In accordance with this is the saying,—'The benevolent has no enemy!' I beg your Majesty not to doubt [what I said]."[180]

VI.[181] 1. Mencius had an interview with king Sëang of Lëang.[182]

2. When he came out, he said to some persons, "When I looked at him from a distance, he did not appear like a ruler; when I drew near to him, I saw nothing venerable about him. Abruptly he asked me, 'How can the kingdom, all under the sky, be settled?'

2. "I replied, 'It will be settled by being united under one [sway].'

3. "'Who can so unite it?, [he asked].

4. "I replied, 'He who has no pleasure in killing men can so unite it.'

5. "'Who can give it to him?' [he asked].[183]

6. "I replied, 'All under heaven will give it to him. Does your Majesty know the way of the growing grain? During the seventh and eighth months, when drought prevails, the plants become dry. Then the clouds collect densely in the heavens, and send down torrents of rain, so that the grain erects itself as if by a shoot. When it does so, who can

---

[179] *Par.* 3. Here among the elements of a benevolent government, there appear a gentle rule and light taxation. These being exercised, the people would feel free to give their strength to agriculture, and have leisure to attend to their social and moral duties, and would moreover be ruled by a most powerful gratitude to their ruler. Mencius' doctrine of the goodness of human nature, though it is not expressed, underlies all this.

[180] *Par.* 6. The remarkable saying about "the benevolent" has a special reference to a benevolent ruler such as Mencius had sketched; but I have preferred to retain it in the translation without any limitation. The concluding remark was designed to caution the king against regarding the philosopher's remarks as merely transcendental.

[181] CH. VI. DISAPPOINTMENT OF MENCIUS WITH KING SËANG OF WEI. BY WHAT RULER THE WHOLE KINGDOM MIGHT BE UNITED UNDER ONE SWAY.

[182] *Par.* 1. Sëang was the son of king Hwuy. The first year of his reign is commonly assigned to B.C. 317; but this cannot be regarded as certain. Sëang's name was Hih. As a posthumous epithet, Sëang has various meanings:—"Land-enlarger and Virtuous;" "Successful in arms;" "Successful in the conduct of affairs." The interview here recorded seems to have taken place immediately after Hih's accession, and Mencius, it is said, was so disappointed by it that he soon after left the country.

[183] *Par.* 5. "Who can give it to him?" is by the Chinese critics understood as = "Who can go to him?" I prefer my own meaning, which accords equally well with the scope of the chapter, and is supported by the usage of the original term in V. i. V.

keep it back? Now among those who are shepherds of men throughout the kingdom, there is not one who does not find pleasure in killing men. If there were one who did not find pleasure in killing men, all the people under the sky would be looking towards him with outstretched necks. Such being indeed the case, the people would go to him as water flows downwards with a rush, which no one can repress."

VII.[184] 1. King Seuen of Ts'e asked, saying, "May I be informed by you of the transactions of Hwan of Ts'e and Wăn of Tsin?"[185]

2. Mencius replied, "There were none of the disciples of Chung-ne who spoke about the affairs of Hwan and Wăn, and therefore they have not been transmitted to [these] after-ages; your servant has not heard of them. If you will have me speak, let it be about [the principles of attaining to] the Royal sway."[186]

3. [The king] said, "Of what kind must his virtue be who can [attain to] the Royal sway?" [Mencius] said, "If he loves and protects the people, it is impossible to prevent him from attaining it."[187]

4. [The king] said, "Is such an one as poor I competent to love and protect the people?" "Yes," was the reply. "From what do you know that I am competent to that?" "I have heard," said [Mencius], "from Hoo Heih the following incident:—'The king' said he, 'was sitting aloft in the hall, when some people appeared leading a bull past below it. The king saw it, and asked where the bull was going, and being answered that they were going to consecrate a bell with its blood, he said, "Let it go, I cannot bear its frightened appearance as if it were an

---

[184] CH. VII. LOVING AND PROTECTING THE PEOPLE IS THE GRAND CHARACTERISTIC OF ROYAL GOVERNMENT; AND THE SURE PATH TO THE ROYAL DIGNITY. HOW THIS PRINCIPLE WOULD BE MANIFESTED.

This long and interesting chapter has been arranged in five parts. In the first part, parr. 1-5, Mencius unfolds the principle of Royal government, and tells the king of Ts'e that he possessed it. In the second, parr. 6-8, he leads the king on to understand his own mind, and how he might exercise the Royal government. In the third, parr. 9-12, he unfolds how the king might and ought to carry out the kindly heart which was natural to him. In the fourth, parr. 13-18, he shows the absurdity of the king's expecting to gain his end by the course he was pursuing, and how rapid would be the response to an opposite one. In the last part he shows the government that loves and protects the people in full development, and crowned with Royal sway.

[185] *Par.* 1. Seuen was the second of the Tĕen family who ruled in Ts'e with the title of king. The date of his accession is not fully ascertained, but it is generally placed in B.C. 332. His name was P'eih-kĕang. The epithet Seuen means—"A skilful questioner and universally informed," or "Sage, good, and universally informed." Hwan of Ts'e and Wăn of Tsin were the greatest of the five presiding princes, who played so conspicuous a part in the Ch'un Ts'ĕw period, which Confucius has chronicled. From king Seuen's question, it would appear that he wished to distinguish himself as Hwan had done.

[186] *Par.* 2. Mencius, no doubt, could have discoursed sufficiently about the affairs of Hwan and Wăn, but he did not wish to do so, and therefore gave this evasive reply. To have a real king was the necessity of his time; but there was more of loyalty in the idea of a presiding prince than in the counsels which our philosopher gave.

[187] *Par.* 3. "To love and protect the people" lay at the foundation of the "benevolent government" of which Mencius always spoke.

innocent person going to the place of death." They asked in reply whether, if they did so, they should omit the consecration of the bell; but [the king] said, "How can that be omitted? Change it for a sheep."' I do not know whether this incident occurred."[188]

5. "It did," said [the king], and [Mencius] replied, "The heart seen in this is sufficient to carry you to the Royal sway. The people all supposed that your Majesty grudged [the animal], but your servant knows surely that it was your Majesty's not being able to bear [the sight of the creature's distress which made you do as you did]."[189]

6. The king said, "You are right; and yet there really was [an appearance of] what the people imagined. [But] though Ts'e be narrow and small, how should I grudge a bull? Indeed it was because I could not bear its frightened appearance, as if it were an innocent person going to the place of death, that therefore I changed it for a sheep."

7. Mencius said, "Let not your Majesty deem it strange that the people should think you grudged the animal. When you changed a large one for a small, how should they know [the true reason]? If you felt pained by its [being led] without any guilt to the place of death, what was there to choose between a bull and a sheep?" The king laughed and said, "What really was my mind in the matter? I did not grudge the value of the bull, and yet I changed it for a sheep! There was reason in the people's saying that I grudged [the creature]."[190]

8. [Mencius] said, "There is no harm [in their saying so]. It was an artifice of benevolence. You saw the bull, and had not seen the sheep. So is the superior man affected towards animals, that, having seen them alive, he cannot bear to see them die, and, having heard their [dying] cries, he cannot bear to eat their flesh. On this account he keeps away from his stalls and kitchen."

9. The king was pleased and said, "The Ode says,

'What other men have in their minds,
I can measure by reflection.'

---

[188] *Par.* 4. Hoo Heih must have been an officer of the court of Ts'e. The hall here mentioned was probably that where the king was giving audience to his ministers. In the court below the hall, the parties would appear leading the bull past. When a bell was cast they killed an animal, and with its blood smeared over the crevices. But the act was a religious one, and a consecration of the bell for religious or other important use. Almost all things connected with their worship were among the ancient Chinese purified with blood,—their temples and the vessels used in them.

[189] *Par.* 5. Mencius would thus bring home to the king the conviction that benevolence was natural to him. He often reasons on the constitution of human nature as he does here. He pursues the subject in the parr. of the second part of the chapter.

[190] *Par.* 7. The king here is nonplussed, and hardly knows what was his own mind in the matter; but in par. 8 Mencius relieves him from his perplexity.

This might be spoken of you, my Master. I indeed did the thing, but when I turned my thoughts inward and sought for it, I could not discover my own mind. When you, Master, spoke those words, the movements of compassion began to work in my mind. [But] how is it that this heart has in it what is equal to the attainment of the Royal sway?"[191]

10. [Mencius] said, "Suppose a man were to make this statement to your Majesty, 'My strength is sufficient to lift three thousand catties, but it is not sufficient to lift one feather; my eyesight is sharp enough to examine the point of an autumn hair, but I do not see a wagon-load of faggots,' would your Majesty allow what he said?" "No," was the [king's] remark, [and Mencius proceeded], "Now here is kindness sufficient to reach to animals, and yet no benefits are extended from it to the people;—how is this? is an exception to be made here? The truth is, the feather's not being lifted is because the strength was not used; the wagon-load of firewood's not being seen is because the eyesight was not used; and the people's not being loved and protected is because the kindness is not used. Therefore your Majesty's not attaining to the Royal sway is because you do not do it, and not because you are not able to do it."[192]

11. [The king] asked, "How may the difference between him who does not do [a thing] and him who is not able to do it be graphically set forth?" [Mencius] replied, "In such a thing as taking the T'ae mountain under your arm, and leaping with it over the North sea, if you say to people, 'I am not able to do it,' that is a real case of not being able. In such a matter as breaking off a branch from a tree at the order of a superior, if you say to people, 'I am not able to do it,' it is not a case of not being able to do it. And so your Majesty's not attaining to the Royal sway is not such a case as that of taking the T'ae mountain under your arm and leaping over the North sea with it; but it is a case like that of breaking off a branch from a tree.

12. "Treat with the reverence due to age the elders in your own family, so that those in the families of others shall be similarly treated; treat with the kindness due to youth the young in your own family, so that those in the families of others shall be similarly treated:—do this and the kingdom may be made to go round in your palm. It is said in the Book of Poetry,

---

[191] *Par.* 9. See the She. II. v. Ode IV. 4.

[192] *Parr.* 10, 11, contain the famous distinction of physical and moral ability; and I like Mencius' way of putting it. The case of a thing that might easily be done, and yet is not done, is very differently understood. I have followed Choo He in taking the terms in what is their natural meaning,—"breaking off the branch of a tree." Ch'aou Ke understood them as meaning "the rubbing or manipulating the elbow or any other joint of the arm;"—a service which was often required from servants by their masters. Maou K'e-ling and others cry out against Choo's interpretation, showing there-by, it seems to me, only their own want of the critical faculty.

'His example acted on his wife,
Extended to his brethren,
And was felt by all the clans and States;'

telling us how [King Wăn] simply took this [kindly] heart, and exercised it towards those parties. Therefore the carrying out the [feeling of] kindness [by a ruler] will suffice for the love and protection of all within the four seas; and if he do not carry it out, he will not be able to protect his wife and children. The way in which the ancients came greatly to surpass other men was no other than this, that they carried out well what they did, so as to affect others. Now your kindness is sufficient to reach to animals, and yet no benefits are extended from it to the people. How is this? Is an exception to be made here?[193]

13. "By weighing we know what things are light, and what heavy. By measuring we know what things are long, and what short. All things are so dealt with, and the mind requires specially to be so. I beg your Majesty to measure it.

14. "Your Majesty collects your equipments of war, endangers your soldiers and officers, and excites the resentment of the various princes:—do these things cause you pleasure in your mind?"[194]

15. The king said, "No. How should I derive pleasure from these things? My object in them is to seek for what I greatly desire."

16. [Mencius] said, "May I hear from you what it is that your Majesty greatly desires?" The king laughed, and did not speak. [Mencius] resumed, "[Are you led to desire it], because you have not enough of rich and sweet [food] for your mouth? or because you have not enough of light and warm [clothing] for your Body? or because you have not enow of beautifully colored objects to satisfy your eyes? or because there are not voices and sounds enow to fill your ears? or because you have not enow of attendants and favorites to stand before you and receive your orders? Your Majesty's various officers are sufficient to supply you with all these things. How can your Majesty have such a desire on account of them?" "No," said the king, "my desire is not on account of them." [Mencius] observed, "Then, what your Majesty greatly desires can be known. You desire to enlarge your territories, to have Ts'in and Ts'oo coming to your court, to rule the Middle States, and to attract to you the barbarous tribes that surround

---

[193] *Par.* 12. Compare with the opening sentence what is said in "The Great Learning," Comm., Chapters ix, and x. The Ode quoted is the She, III. 1. VI.

[194] In *Parr.* 14-18, Mencius measures or weighs the king's mind for him, and shows the object he is bent on, with the absurdity of seeking for it by the course which he pursued, and also how rapid would be the response to a different course. All the people in the kingdom, high and low, would wish to be his subjects.

them. But to do what you do in order to seek for what you desire is like climbing a tree to seek for fish."

17. "Is it so bad as that?" said [the king]. "I apprehend it is worse," was the reply. "If you climb a tree to seek for fish, although you do not get the fish, you have no subsequent calamity. But if you do what you do in order to seek for what you desire, doing it even with all your heart, you will assuredly afterwards meet with calamities." The king said, "May I hear [what they will be]?" [Mencius] replied, "If the people of Tsow were lighting with the people of Ts'oo, which of them does your Majesty think would conquer?" "The people of Ts'oo would conquer," was the answer, and [Mencius] pursued, "So then, a small State cannot contend with a great, few cannot contend with many, nor can the weak contend with the strong. The territory within the seas would embrace nine divisions, each of a thousand *le* square. All Ts'e together is one of them. If with one part you try to subdue the other eight, what is the difference between that and Tsow's contending with Ts'oo? [With the desire which you have], you must turn back to the proper course [for its attainment].

18. "Now if your Majesty will institute a government whose action shall all be benevolent, this will cause all the officers in the kingdom to wish to stand in your Majesty's court, the farmers all to wish to plough in your Majesty's fields, the merchants, both travelling and stationary, all to wish to store their goods in your Majesty's market-places, travelers and visitors all to wish to travel on your Majesty's roads, and all under heaven who feel aggrieved by their rulers to wish to come and complain to your Majesty. When they are so bent, who will be able to keep them back?"

19. The king said, "I am stupid, and cannot advance to this. [But] I wish you, my Master, to assist my intentions. Teach me clearly, and although I am deficient in intelligence and vigour, I should like to try at least [to institute such a government]."

20. [Mencius] replied, "They are only men of education, who, without a certain livelihood, are able to maintain a fixed heart. As to the people, if they have not a certain livelihood, they will be found not to have a fixed heart. And if they have not a fixed heart, there is nothing which they will not do in the way of self-abandonment, of moral deflection, of depravity, and of wild license. When they have thus been involved in crime, to follow them up and punish them, is to entrap the people. How can such a thing as entrapping the people be done under the rule of a benevolent man?[195]

21. "Therefore an intelligent ruler will regulate the livelihood of

---

[195] *Par.* 20, brings in the subjects of "a fixed heart," or a mind always firm to do what is good, and of "a certain livelihood," or a sure provision of the necessaries of life, and of the necessity of the latter to the former. We shall meet with these topics in Mencius again and again.

the people, so as to make sure that, above, they shall have sufficient wherewith to serve their parents, and, below, sufficient wherewith to support their wives and children; that in good years they shall always be abundantly satisfied, and that in bad years they shall not be in danger of perishing. After this he may urge them, and they will proceed to what is good, for in this case the people will follow after that with readiness.

22. "But now, the livelihood of the people is so regulated, that, above, they have not sufficient wherewith to serve their parents, and, below, they have not sufficient where-with to support their wives and children; [even] in good years their lives are always embittered, and in bad years they are in danger of perishing. In such circumstances their only object is to escape from death, and they are afraid they will not succeed in doing so;—what leisure have they to cultivate propriety and righteousness?

23. "If your Majesty wishes to carry out [a benevolent government], why not turn back to what is the essential step [to its attainment]?[196]

24. "Let mulberry-trees be planted about the homesteads with their five acres, and persons of fifty years will be able to wear silk. In keeping fowls, pigs, dogs, and swine, let not their times of breeding be neglected, and persons of seventy years will be able to eat flesh. Let there not be taken away the time that is proper for the cultivation of the field-allotment of a hundred acres, and the family of eight mouths will not suffer from hunger. Let careful attention be paid to the teaching in the various schools, with repeated inculcation of the filial and fraternal duties, and gray-haired men will not be seen upon the roads, carrying burdens on their backs or on their heads. It has never been that [the ruler of a State] where these results were seen, the old wearing silk and eating .flesh, and the black-haired people suffering neither from hunger nor cold, did not attain to the Royal dignity."[197]

---

[196] *Par.* 23. "The essential step to a benevolent government" is the sure provision of the necessaries of life, and the elements of moral instruction.

[197] *Par.* 24, Compare par. 4 of ch. iii. The two are nearly identical.

## BOOK I. KING HWUY OF LËANG. PART II.

CHAPTER I.[198] 1. CHWANG PAOU, [having gone to] see Mencius, said to him, "I had an audience of the king. His Majesty told me about his loving music, and I was not prepared with anything to reply to him. What do you pronounce concerning [that] love of music?" Mencius said, "If the king's love of music were very great, the kingdom of Ts'e would be near to [being well governed]."[199]

2. Another day, Mencius had an audience of the king, and said, "Your Majesty, [I have heard,] told the officer Chwang about your love of music;—was it so?" The king changed color, and said, "I am unable to love the music of the ancient kings; I only love the music that suits the manners of the [present] age."[200]

3. [Mencius] said, "If your Majesty's love of music were very great, Ts'e, I apprehend, would be near to [being well governed]. The music of the present day is just like the music of antiquity [for effecting that]."

4. [The king] said, "May I hear [the proof of what you say]?" "Which is the more pleasant," was the reply,—"to enjoy music by yourself alone, or to enjoy it along with others?'" "To enjoy it along with others," said [the king]. "And which is the more pleasant," pursued [Mencius],—"to enjoy music along with a few, or to enjoy it along with many?" "To enjoy it along with many," replied [the king].

5. [Mencius went on], "Will you allow your servant to speak to your Majesty about music?

6. "Your Majesty is having music here.—The people hear the sound of your bells and drums, and the notes of your reeds and flutes, and they all, with aching heads, knit their brows, and say to-one another, 'That's how our king loves music! But why does he reduce us to this extremity [of distress]? Fathers and sons do not see one another; elder brothers and younger brothers, wives and children, are separated

---

[198] CH. I. HOW THE LOVE OF MUSIC MAY BE MADE SUBSERVIENT TO GOOD GOVERNMENT, AND WHEN SHARED WITH THE PEOPLE LEAD ON TO THE ROYAL SWAY. The chapter is a good specimen of Mencius' manner. The moral of it is the same as that of chapter ii. Part I. Mencius slips cleverly from the point in hand to introduce his own notions, and tries to win king Seuen over to benevolent government by his vice itself. It is on this account that Chinese thinkers say that Mencius was wanting in the consistency of a moral teacher, and refuse to rank him with Confucius.

[199] *Par.* 1. The king here was, it is understood, king Seuen of last chapter. Chwang Paou must have been a minister or officer about his court. He was evidently on good terms with Mencius, but his name does not occur in the list of his disciples. The king must have been notorious for his love of music, and Mencius' remark that, if his love for it were very great, Ts'e would be in a happy state, only commends itself when we find what the philosopher included in his idea of greatly loving music.

[200] *Par.* 2. The king changed color, being conscious of the charges to which he was open in connection with his love of music.

and scattered abroad.' Again, your Majesty is hunting here. The people hear the noise of your carriages and horses, and see the beauty of your plumes and pennons, and they all, with aching heads, knit their brows, and say to one another, 'That's how our king loves hunting! But why does he reduce us to this extremity of distress? Fathers and sons do not see one another; elder brothers and younger brothers, wives and children, are separated and scattered abroad.' This is from no other cause, but that you do not give the people to have pleasure as well as yourself.

7. "Your Majesty is having music here.—The people hear the sound of your bells and drums, and the notes of your reeds and flutes, and they all, delighted and with joyful looks, say to one another, 'That sounds as if our king were free from all sickness! What fine music he is able to have!' Again, your Majesty is hunting here.—The people hear the noise of your carriages and horses, and see the beauty of your plumes and pennons, and they all, delighted and with joyful looks, say to one another, 'That looks as if our king were free from all sickness! How he is able to hunt!' This is from no other reason but that you cause the people to have pleasure as well as yourself.

8. "If your Majesty now will make pleasure a thing common to the people and yourself, the Royal sway awaits you."[201]

II.[202] 1. King Seuen of Ts'e asked, "Was it so that the park of king Wăn contained seventy square *le*?" Mencius replied, "It is so in the Records."[203]

2. "Was it so large as that?" said [the king]. "The people," said [Mencius], "still considered it small." "My park," responded [the king], "contains [only] forty square *le*, and the people still consider it large. How is this?" "The park of king Wăn,"—said [Mencius], "contained seventy square *le*, but the grass-cutters and fuel-gatherers [had the privilege of] resorting to it, and so also had the catchers of pheasants and hares. He shared it with the people, and was it not with reason that they looked on it as small?

3. "When I first arrived at your frontiers, I enquired about the great prohibitory regulations before I would venture to enter [the country];

---

[201] *Par.* 8. This and other similar passages, it is argued, are to be understood with reference to the great distress of the times, which made Mencius express himself as he did. There was, no doubt, a great difference between the music of antiquity, and that in which king Seuen delighted; but if Seuen and other princes could only be led on to make the comfort and happiness of the people their principal object, everything that was wrong would rectify itself.

[202] CH. II. THAT A RULER MUST NOT INDULGE HIS LOVE FOR PARKS AND HUNTING TO THE DISCOMFORT OF THE PEOPLE. The moral of this chapter is the same as that of the preceding,—that a ruler must share his pleasures with the people, or see it that they have pleasures of a similar kind.

[203] *Par.* 1. This is understood to have been the park of king Wăn after two-thirds of the States of the kingdom had given in their adhesion to him.

and I heard that inside the border-gates there was a park of forty square *le*, and that he who killed a deer in it, whether large or small, was held guilty of the same crime as if he had killed a man. In this way those forty square *le* are a pit-fall in the middle of the kingdom. Is it not with reason that the people look upon [your park] as large?"[204]

III.[205] 1. King Seuen of Ts'e asked, saying, "Is there any way [to regulate one's maintenance] of intercourse with neighbouring States?" Mencius replied, "There is. But it requires a benevolent [ruler] to be able with a great State to serve a small;—as, for instance, T'ang served Koh, and king Wăn served the hordes of the Keun. And it requires a wise [ruler] to be able with a small State to serve a great,—as, for instance, king T'ae served the Heun-yuh, and Kow-tsëen served Woo.[206]

2. "He who with a great [State] serves a small is one who delights in Heaven; and he who with a small [State] serves a great is one who fears Heaven. He who delights in Heaven will affect with his love and protection all under the sky; and he who fears Heaven will so affect his own State.[207]

3. "It is said in the Book of Poetry,[208]

'I revere the majesty of Heaven,
And thus preserve its [favor].'"

4. The king said, "A great saying! [But] I have an infirmity,—I love valour."[209]

---

[204] *Par.* 3. Mencius seems to distinguish here between what I have called "the frontiers" of Ts'e, and the *kaou*, or the country at the distance of a hundred *le* from the capital. Both at the frontiers and at the point where the *kaou* commenced, there were, I believe, barrier gates through which travelers had to pass. He seems to say that the park was inside the circle of the *kaou*. These forest laws of Ts'e were hardly worse than those enacted by the first Norman sovereigns of England, when whoever killed a deer, a boar, or even a hare, was punished with the loss of his eyes, and with death if the statute was repeatedly violated.

[205] CH. III. HOW INTERCOURSE WITH NEIGHBOURING STATES MAY BE MAINTAINED, AND THE LOVE OF VALOUR MADE SUBSERVIENT TO THE GOOD OF THE PEOPLE AND THE GLORY OF THE PRINCE.

[206] *Par.* 1. "A benevolent ruler" here is one who is very slow to shed blood, and will bear and forbear much before he will adopt violent measures of war to endanger the lives of his people. On the case of T'ang and Koh, see III. ii. V; on that of Wăn and the hordes of the Keun we have not much information;—see the She, III. i. III. 8, and VII. 2. On king T'ae and the Heun-yuh, see ch. xv. below; for Kow-tsëen and Woo, see Tso's Chuen, after XII. i. 2, *et al* and the "History of the various States," Bk lxxx.

[207] *Par.* 2. Choo He says on the word "Heaven" here, "Heaven is just principle, *i.e.,* the reason of things, and nothing more." The instance is a good one of the way in which he and others try to expunge the idea of a governing power and a personal God from their classics. Heaven is here evidently the loving and directing Power of the universe, or the will of that Power as indicated in the course of its Providence.

[208] *Par.* 3. See the She, IV. i. [i.] VII.

[209] *Par.* 4. From this par. Mencius deals with Seuen's love of valour just as in ch. i.

5. [Mencius] replied, "I beg your Majesty not to love small valour. If a man brandishes his sword, looks fierce, and says, 'How dare he withstand me? , this is the valour of a common man, and can only be used against one individual. I beg your Majesty to change it into great valour.

6. "It is said in the Book of Poetry,

> 'The king rose majestic in his wrath.
> He marshaled his troops,
> To stop the march to Keu;
> To consolidate the prosperity of Chow;
> To meet the expectations of all under heaven.'

This was the valour of king Wăn. King Wăn, by one burst of his anger, gave repose to all the people under heaven.[210]

7. "It is said in the Book of History, 'Heaven, having produced the inferior people, made for them rulers, and made for them instructors, with the purpose that they should be aiding to God, and gave them distinction through-out the four quarters [of the land]. Whoever are offenders, and whoever are innocent, here am I [to deal with them]. How dare any under heaven give indulgence to their refractory wills? , One man was pursuing a violent and disorderly course in the kingdom, and king Woo was ashamed of it. This was the valour of king Woo, and he also, by one burst of his anger, gave repose to all the people under heaven.[211]

8. "Let now your Majesty, in one burst of anger, give repose to all the people under heaven. The people are only afraid that your Majesty does not love valour."

IV.[212] 1. King Seuen of Ts'e [went to] see Mencius in the Snow palace, and said to him, "Do men of talents and virtue likewise find pleasure in [such a place as] this?" Mencius replied, "They do. And if people [generally] do not get [similar pleasure], they condemn their superiors.[213]

---

he deals with his love of music.

[210] *Par.* 6. See the She, III. i. VII. 5. Mencius gives the third line differently from the common reading in the She.

[211] *Par.* 7. See the Shoo, V. i. Pt I. 7, but the quotation here is still more different from the classical text. The sentiment that rulers and instructors are intended to be aiding to God is the same as that of Paul, in Romans, xiii. 1-4, that "the powers ordained of God are the ministers of God."

[212] CH. IV. A RULER'S PROSPERITY DEPENDS ON HIS EXERCISING A RESTRAINT ON HIS OWN LOVE OF PLEASURE, AND SYMPATHIZING WITH HIS PEOPLE IN THEIR JOYS AND SORROWS;—ILLUSTRATED BY THE EXAMPLE OF DUKE KING OF TS'E.

[213] *Par.* 1. The Snow palace was a pleasure palace of the princes of Ts'e, and is said to have been in the present district of Lin-tsze, department Ts'ing-chow. Most of the critics say that the king had lodged Mencius there and went to see him in it; and this is the most natural inference from the language. The king's question was in the same words

2. "For them, when they do not get that, to condemn their superiors is wrong; but when the superiors of the people do not make [such] pleasure a thing common to the people and themselves, they also do wrong.

3. "When [a ruler] rejoices in the joy of his people, they also rejoice in his joy; when he sorrows for the sorrow of his people, they also sorrow for his sorrow. When his joy extends to all under heaven, and his sorrow does the same, it never was that in such a case [the ruler] did not attain to the Royal sway.

4. "Formerly, duke King of Ts'e asked the minister Gan, saying, 'I wish to make a tour to Chuen-foo and Chaou-woo, and then to bend my way southward, along the shore, till I come to Lang-yay. What shall I do specially, that my tour may be fit to be compared with those made by the former kings?'[214]

5. "The minister Gan replied, 'An excellent inquiry! When the son of Heaven visited the feudal princes, it was called "a tour of inspection;" that is, he surveyed the States under their care. When the princes attended at his court, it was called "a report of office;" that is, they reported [their administration of] their offices. [Thus] neither of those proceedings was without its proper object. [And moreover], in the spring they examined the plowing, and supplied any deficiency [of seed]; in the autumn they examined the reaping, and assisted where there was any deficiency [of yield]. There is the saying of the Hëa dynasty,

> "If our king go not from home,
> Whence to us will comfort come?
> If our king make not his round,
> Whence to us will help be found?"

That excursion and that round were a pattern for the princes.[215]

---

as that of king Hwuy of Lëang in ch. ii. of Part I.; but there it had to be understood of rulers, while here its application is to Mencius himself, and there is in it an undertone of self-congratulation by the king on his handsome treatment of the philosopher. Mencius, however, starts off from it in his usual way to introduce his great theme of benevolent government, and benevolent feeling towards the people in the prince's heart; and this is developed in parr. 2 and 3.

[214] *Par*. 4. On duke King of Ts'e and his minister Gan, see the Ana XII. xi.; V. xvi.; *et al*. King was marquis of Ts'e for 58 years, from B.C. 546 to 489. Mencius here presents his character in a more favorable light than Confucius does. Chuen-foo and Chaou-woo were two hills which must have been in the north-east of Ts'e, and looking on the waters now called the Gulf of Pih-chih-le. Lang-yay was the name both of a hill and an adjacent city, in the present district of Choo-shing, department Ts'ing-chow. The duke was bent evidently on pleasure, and his last words were simply intended to gloss that over.

[215] *Par*. 5. On the royal tours of inspection see the Shoo, II. i. 8, 9. Under the Chow dynasty the kings were understood to make such tours once in 12 years, and the feudal princes had to present themselves in their court once in six years. The spring and autumn

6. "'Now the state of things is different. A host marches [in attendance on the ruler], and the provisions are consumed. The hungry are deprived of their food, and there is no rest for those who are called to toil. Maledictions are uttered by one to another with eyes askance, and the people proceed to the commission of wickedness. The [Royal] orders are violated and the people are oppressed; the supplies of food and drink flow away like water. The [rulers] yield themselves to the current; or they urge their way against it; they are wild; they are lost:—[these things proceed] to the grief of the [smaller] princes.[216]

7. "'Descending along with the current, and forgetting to return,' is what I call yielding to it. 'Going against it, and forgetting to return,' is what I called urging their way against it. 'Pursuing the chase without satiety' is what I call being wild. 'Delighting in spirits without satiety' is what I call being lost.

8. "'The former kings had no pleasures to which they gave themselves as on the flowing stream, no doings which might be so characterized as wild and lost.

9. "'It is for you, my ruler, to take your course'[217]

10. "Duke King was pleased. He issued a grand proclamation through the State, and went out [himself] and occupied a shed in the suburbs. From that time he began to open [his granaries] for the relief of the wants [of the people], and, calling the grand music master, said to him, 'Make for me music to suit a prince and his minister well pleased with each other' It was then that the Che Shaou and Kĕ'oh Shaou was made, in the poetry to which it was said,

'What fault is it one's ruler to restrain?'

He who restrains his ruler loves him."[218]

---

movements were common to the king in his domain, and to the feudal princes in their States; but they are mentioned here, as appears from the conclusion of the paragraph, with special reference to the king.

[216] *Par.* 6. What is here called "a host" was a body of 2,500 men, by which the ruler of a State was accompanied when he went abroad; but the term is often used generally of a body of followers or an army. It is the picture of a wretched State which appears in this and the next paragraph. The "smaller princes" in the end of this paragraph denote the lords of the small, "attached" principalities in the larger States, and perhaps also the governors of the cities, on whom requisitions would be made to supply the wants of the ruler and his followers.

[217] *Par.* 9 means that his minister would have duke King choose between the ways of the ancient kings and those of the princes of his time. Other meanings have been assigned to it, but incorrectly.

[218] *Par.* 10. I believe the proper rendering of "issued a grand proclamation" would be "proclaimed a grand fast;" but I have not ventured to give the original words a meaning which none of the critics have adopted;—though it is quite allowable. The duke's own occupancy of the shed was the way he took to "afflict his soul." *Shaou* was the name given to a piece of music said to be transmitted from the ancient Shun, and is used here to signify that made to celebrate the good understanding between King and his minister. It appears to have consisted of two parts, one beginning with the note *che,* and

V.[219] 1. King Seuen of Ts'e asked saying, "People all tell me to pull down the Brilliant hall and remove it;—shall I pull it down, or stop [the movement for that object]?"[220]

2. Mencius replied, "The Brilliant hall is the hall appropriate to the kings. If your Majesty wishes to practise Royal government, do not pull it down."[221]

3. The king said, "May I hear from you what Royal government is?" "Formerly," was the reply, "king Wăn's government of K'e was the following:—From the husband-man [there was required the produce of] one ninth [of the land]; the descendants of officers were salaried; at the passes and in the markets, [strangers] were inspected, but goods were not taxed; there were no prohibitions respecting the ponds and weirs; the wives and children of criminals were not involved in their guilt. There were the old and wifeless, or widowers, the old and husbandless, or widows; the old and childless, or solitaries; and the young and fatherless, or orphans:—these four classes are the most destitute under heaven, and have none to whom they can tell [their wants], and king Wăn, in the institution of his government with its benevolent action, made them the first objects of his regard. It is said in the Book of Poetry,[222]

---

the other with the note *kĕoh*. I do not know enough of music myself to explain these.

[219] CH. V. ON THE PURPOSE TO PULL DOWN THE BRILLIANT HALL IN TS'E. CERTAIN PRINCIPLES OF ROYAL GOVERNMENT; AND THAT NEITHER GREED OF SUBSTANCE NOR LOVE OF BEAUTY NEED INTERFERE WITH THE PRACTICE OF IT. There can be no doubt that in this chapter Mencius suggests, if he does not directly incite to, rebellion. It is a graver charge against him that, after his usual fashion, he here overlooks the selfish vices of the rulers of his day, and thinks that, while still practicing them, they could be transformed into true kings.

[220] *Par.* 1. The "Brilliant hall" was a name given to the principal apartment of the palaces where the kings in their tours of inspection, spoken of in the last chapter, received the feudal princes of the different quarters of the kingdom. See the Le Ke, XIV. The one in the text was near the foot of mount T'ae, and had originally been within the limits of the State of Loo. Now the territory where it was belonged to Ts'e, and as the Royal tours of inspection had fallen into disuse, it was proposed to king Seuen to remove the Brilliant hall.

[221] *Par.* 2. Here certainly Mencius suggests to king Seuen the idea of his superseding the kings of Chow.

[222] *Par.* 3. K'e was a double-peaked hill, giving its name to the adjacent country which formed the old State of Chow, after the removal of the tribe, under T'an-foo afterwards styled king T'ae, from its older seat in Pin. The mountain gives its name to the present district of K'e-shan, department Fung-ts'eang, in the south-west of Shen-se. It was in K'e that king Wăn succeeded to his father, and laid the foundations of the Royal sway, to which his son Woo attained. On the 1st point of Wăn's government of K'e see under Pt II. iii. 4. According to the 2nd, descendants of meritorious officers, if men of ability, received office, and even, if they were not so, they had pensions in acknowledgment of the services of their fathers. The ponds and weirs were free to the people, with the restriction as to the size of their nets referred to in Pt I. iii. 3. It is not said what measures were adopted by king Wăn for the relief of the four destitute classes who are mentioned. They must have been mainly provisions for their maintenance.

The concluding lines are from the She, II. iv. VIII. 13.

'The rich may get through,
But alas for the helpless and solitary!'"

4. The king said, "Excellent words!" [Mencius] said, "Since your
Majesty deems them excellent, why do you not put them into practice?"
"I have an infirmity," said the king; "I am fond of substance."
"Formerly," replied [Mencius], "duke Lĕw was fond of substance. It is
said in the Book of Poetry,

'He stored up [the produce] in the fields and in barns;
He tied up dried meat and grain
In bottomless bags and sacks;
That he might hold [his people] together, and glorify [his
    tribe].
Then with bows and arrows all ready,
With shields and spears, and axes, large and small,
He commenced his march.'

In this way those who remained in their old seat had their stores in the
fields and in barns, and those who marched had their bags of grain. It
was not till after this that he commenced his march. If your Majesty is
fond of substance, let the people have the opportunity to gratify the
same feeling, and what difficulty will there be in your attaining to the
Royal sway?"[223]

5. The king said, "I have an infirmity; I am fond of beauty." The
reply was, "Formerly king T'ae was fond of beauty, and loved his wife.
It is said in the Book of Poetry,

'The ancient duke T'an-foo
Came in the morning, galloping his horses,
Along the banks of (he western rivers,
To the foot of Mount K'e;
And there he and the lady Kĕang
Came, and together looked out for a site on which to settle.'

At that time, in the seclusion of the house, there were no dissatisfied
women, and, abroad, there were no unmarried men. If your Majesty is
fond of beauty, let the people be able to gratify the same feeling, and
what difficulty will there be in your attaining to the Royal sway?"[224]

---

[223] *Par.* 4. See the She, III. ii. VI. i.
[224] *Par.* 5. See the She, III. i. III. 2. We may admire the ingenuity of Mencius in the
illustrations in these two paragraphs; but they would have little power with a sensual,
self-indulgent man like king Seuen.

VI.[225] 1. Mencius said to king Seuen of Ts'e, "[Suppose that] one
of your Majesty's servants were to entrust his wife and children to the
care of his friend, while he went [himself] into Ts'oo to travel, and that,
on his return, [he should find] that [the friend] had caused his wife and
children to suffer from cold and hunger,—how ought he to deal with
him?" The king said, "He should cast him off."

2. [Mencius] proceeded, "[Suppose that] the chief criminal judge
could not regulate the officers of justice under him, how should he be
dealt with?" The king said, "He should be dismissed."[226]

3. [Mencius again] said, "When within the four borders [of your
kingdom] there is not good government, what is to be done?" The king
looked to the right and left, and spoke of other matters.

VII.[227] 1. Mencius, having [gone to] see king Seuen of Ts'e, said to
him, "When men speak of 'an ancient kingdom,' it is not meant thereby
that. it has lofty trees in it, but that it has ministers [sprung from
families that have been noted in it] for generations. Your Majesty has
no ministers with whom you are personally intimate. Those whom you
advanced yesterday are gone to-day, and you do not know it."[228]

2. The king said, "How shall I know that they have no ability, and
avoid employing them at all?"

3. The reply was, "A ruler advances to office [new] men of talents
and virtue [only] as a matter of necessity. As he thereby causes the low
to overstep the honorable and strangers to overstep his relatives, ought
he to do so but with caution?[229]

4. "When all those about you say [of a man], 'He is a man of
.talents and virtue,' do not immediately [believe them]. When your
great officers all say, 'He is a man of talents and virtue,' do not
immediately [believe them]. When your people all say, 'He is a man of
talents and virtue,' then examine into his character; and, when you find
that he is such indeed, then afterwards employ him. When all those
about you say, 'He will not do,' do not listen to them. When your great
officers all say, 'He will not do' do not listen to them. When your
people all say, 'He will not do' then examine into his character; and

[225] CH. VI. BRINGING HOME HIS BAD GOVERNMENT TO THE KING OF TS'E. This is
a good specimen of the bold manner in which Mencius was not afraid to tell the truth to
the kings and princes of his time.

[226] *Par.* 2. For the office of "chief criminal judge" see under the Analects, XVIII. ii.

[227] CH. VII. WHAT IS MEANT BY AN ANCIENT KINGDOM; AND THE CAUTION TO BE
EXERCISED BY A RULER IN RAISING MEN TO OFFICE. HIS GREAT CARE MUST BE TO
HAVE THE SYMPATHY AND APPROVAL OF THE PEOPLE.

[228] *Par.* 1. If the king had no intimate ministers, men who had his familiar
confidence and affection, he could not have men of old families in his service.

[229] *Par.* 3. The "low" are new men who had not previously been in office.
"Strangers" means literally "distant in relationship." It appears from the Ch'un Ts'ëw and
Tso Chuen that the ministers in the different feudal States were nearly all of families
which were offshoots from the ruling Houses.

when you find that .he will not do, then afterwards send him away.

5. "When those about you all say [of a man], 'He deserves death' do not listen to them. When your great officers all say, 'He deserves death,' do not listen to them. When your people all say, 'He deserves death' then examine into his case; and when you find that he deserves death, then afterwards put him to death. In accordance with this we have the saying, 'The people put him to death'

6. "Act in this way and you will be the parent of the people."[230]

VIII.[231] 1. King Seuen of Ts'e asked, saying, "Was it so that T'ang banished Këeh, and king Woo smote Chow?" Mencius replied, "It is so in the Records."[232]

2. [The king] said, "May a subject put his ruler to death?"

3. The reply was, "He who outrages benevolence is called a ruffian; he who outrages righteousness is called a villain. The ruffian and villain we call a mere fellow. I have heard of the cutting off of the fellow Chow; I have not heard of the putting a ruler to death [in his case]."[233]

IX.[234] 1. Mencius, [having gone to] see king Seuen of Ts'e, said, "If you are going to build a large mansion, you will surely cause the Master of the workmen to look out for large trees; and when he has found them, your Majesty will be glad, thinking they will be fit for the object. Should the workmen hew them so as to make them too small, then you will be angry, thinking that they will not answer for the purpose. Now a man spends his youth in learning [the principles of right government], and, when grown up to vigour, he wishes to put them in practice:—if your Majesty say to him, 'For the present put aside what you have learned, and follow me,' what shall we say?

2. "Here now you have a gem in the stone. Although it be worth 240,000 [taels], you will surely employ your chief lapidary to cut and

---

[230] *Par.* 6. See the Great Learning, Commentary, x. 3.

[231] CH. VIII. KILLING A SOVEREIGN IS NOT NECESSARILY REBELLION NOR MURDER. We have here one of Mencius' boldest utterances.

[232] *Par.* 1. T'ang was the founder of the dynasty of Shang, and Këeh was the last of the sovereigns of Hëa, a tyrant, whom T'ang defeated and banished to Nan-ts'aou, where he died. Chow was the last of the sovereigns of Shang, also a tyrant who burned himself to death, after his defeat by king Woo in the wild of Muh.

[233] *Par.* 3. In calling Chow "a mere fellow" Mencius probably borrowed from king Woo, who in the Shoo, V. i Part iii. 4, calls Chow, while still alive, "this solitary fellow Show."

[234] CH. IX. THE ABSURDITY OF A RULER'S NOT ACTING ACCORDING TO THE COUNSEL OF THE MEN OF TALENTS AND VIRTUE WHOM HE CALLS TO AID IN HIS GOVERNMENT, BUT REQUIRING THEM TO FOLLOW HIS OWN WAYS. In one point the illustrations of Mencius here fail. A prince is not supposed to understand either house-building or gem-cutting;—he must delegate these to other men who do. But government he ought to understand, and he may not delegate the responsibility of it to any scholars or officers. No doubt, however, there was that about king Seuen's procedures which made our philosopher's lesson to him quite appropriate.

polish it. But when you come to the government of your kingdom, you say, 'For the present put aside what you have learned and follow me;—how is it that you herein act differently from your calling in the lapidary to cut and polish the gem?"

X.[235] 1. The people of Ts'e attacked Yen, and conquered it.[236]

2. King Seuen asked, saying, "Some tell me not to take possession of it, and some tell me to take possession of it. For a kingdom of ten thousand chariots to attack another of the same strength, and to complete, the conquest of it in fifty days, is an achievement beyond [mere] human strength. If I do not take it, calamities from Heaven will surely come upon me:—what do you say to my taking possession of it?"[237]

3. Mencius replied, "If the people of Yen will be pleased with your taking possession of it, do so.—Among the ancients there was [one] who acted in this way, namely king Woo. If the people of Yen will not be pleased with your taking possession of it, do not. Among the ancients there was one who acted in this way, namely king Wăn.[238]

4. "When with [the strength of] your kingdom of ten thousand chariots you attacked another of the same strength, and they met your Majesty's army with baskets of rice and vessels of congee, was there any other reason for this but that they [hoped to] escape out of fire and water? If [you make] the water more deep and the fire more fierce, they will just in like manner make another revolution."[239]

XI.[240] 1. The people of Ts'e having attacked Yen and taken possession of it; the [other] princes proposed to take measures to deliver Yen. King Seuen said, "As the princes are many of them

---

[235] CH. X. THE DISPOSAL OF KINGDOMS RESTS WITH THE MINDS OF THE PEOPLE. NO CONQUEST AND SUBSEQUENT ANNEXATION CAN BE VINDICATED AS ACCORDING TO THE WILL OF HEAVEN, UNLESS THE PEOPLE OF THE CONQUERED KINGDOM ARE CONTENT AND SATISFIED.

[236] *Par.* 1. Yen lay north-west from Ts'e, forming part of the present province of Chih-le. Its princes had in former times been marquises or earls, but in the age of Mencius they, like those of many other States, had assumed the title of king. At the time to which this chapter refers, though the question of the chronology is much disputed, its king, a poor weakling, had resigned the throne to his chief minister, and great confusion ensued, so that the people welcomed the appearance of the troops of Ts'e and made no resistance to them.

[237] *Par.* 2. King Seuen by calling both Ts'e and Yen "States of 10,000 chariots" plainly intimates that their rulers had taken the royal title, and wished to establish their sway over all the land.

[238] *Par.* 3. The common saying is that "King Wăn had possession of two of the three parts of the kingdom." But he did not think that the people were prepared for the extinction of the dynasty of Shang or Yin, and left the completion of the fortunes of his house to his son Woo.

[239] *Par.* 4. Mencius disabuses the king, and gives a natural explanation of the success he had met with.

[240] CH. XI. AMBITION AND GREED ONLY RAISE ENEMIES AND BRING DISASTERS. SAFETY AND PROSPERITY LIE IN BENEVOLENT GOVERNMENT. King Seuen, it appears, was unwilling to give up his appropriation of Yen, on which, however, Mencius insists.

consulting to attack me, how shall I prepare myself for them?" Mencius replied, "I have heard of one who with seventy *le* gave law to the whole kingdom, but I have not heard of [a ruler] who with a thousand *le* was afraid of others.[241]

2. "The Book of History says, 'When T'ang began his work of punishment, he commenced with Koh. All under heaven had confidence in him. When the work went on in the east, the wild tribes of the west murmured. When it went on in the south, those of the north murmured. They said, "Why does he make us the last?" The looking of the people for him was like the looking in a time of great drought for clouds and rainbows. The frequenters of the markets stopped not; the husbandmen made no change [in their operations]. While he took off their rulers, he consoled the people. [His progress] was like the falling of seasonable rain, and the people were delighted.' It is said [again] in the Book of History, 'We have waited for our prince [long]; the prince's coming is our reviving.'[242]

3. "Now [the ruler of] Yen was tyrannizing over his people, and your Majesty went and punished him. The people supposed that you were going to deliver them out of the water and the fire, and with baskets of rice and vessels of congee they met your Majesty's host. But you have slain their fathers and elder brothers, and put their sons and younger brothers in chains; yon have pulled down the ancestral temple [of the rulers], and are carrying away its precious vessels:—how can such a course be admitted? [The other States of] the kingdom were afraid of the strength of Ts'e before; and now when with a doubled territory you do not exercise a benevolent government, this puts the arms of the kingdom in motion [against you].

4. "If your Majesty will make haste to issue an order, restoring [your captives] old and young, and stopping [the removal of] the precious vessels; [and if then] you will consult with the people of Yen, appoint [for them] a [new] ruler, and afterwards withdraw from the country:—in this way you may still be able to stop [the threatened attack]."

XII.[243] 1. There had been a skirmish between [some troops of] Tsow and Loo, [in reference to which,] duke Mih asked, saying, "Of my officers there were killed thirty-three men and none of the people would die in their defence. If I would put them to death, it is impossible

---

[241] *Par.* 1. When T'ang commenced his operations against Kĕeh of Shang, he was the occupant of a small principality, being part of the present department of Kwei-tih, Ho-nan.

[242] *Par.* 2. See the Shoo, IV. ii. 6. But the Book of the Shoo, which gave a full account of Tang's dealings with the chief of Koh, has been lost. See the Preface to the Shoo, Par. 10.

[243] CH. XII. THE AFFECTIONS OF THE PEOPLE CAN ONLY BE SECURED BY BENEVOLENT GOVERNMENT; AS THEY ARE DEALT WITH BY THEIR RULERS, SO WILL THEY DEAL BY THEM. ILLUSTRATED BY A CASE IN THE STATE OF TSOW.

to deal so with so many; if I do not put them to death, then there is [the crime unpunished of] their looking on with evil eyes at the death of their officers, and not saving them:—how is the exigency of the case to be met?"[244]

2. Mencius replied, "In calamitous years and years of famine, the old and weak of your people who have been found lying in ditches and water-channels, and the able-bodied who have been scattered about to the four quarters, have amounted to thousands. All the while, your granaries, O prince, have been stored with rice and other grain, and your treasuries and arsenals have been full, and not one of your officers has told you [of the distress];—so negligent have the superiors [in your State] been, and cruel to their inferiors. The philosopher Tsăng said, 'Beware, beware. What proceeds from you will return to you.' Now at last the people have had an opportunity to return [their conduct]; do not you, O prince, blame them.[245]

3. "If you will practise a benevolent government, then the people will love all above them, and will die for their officers."

XIII.[246] 1. Duke Wăn of T'ăng asked, saying, "T'ăng is a small State, and lies between Ts'e and Ts'oo. Shall I serve Ts'e? or shall I serve Ts'oo?"[247]

2. Mencius replied, "This is a matter in which I cannot counsel you. If you will have me speak, there is but one thing [I can suggest]. Dig [deep] your moats; build [strong] your walls; then guard them along with the people; be prepared to die [in their defence], and [have] the people [so that] they will not leave you:—this is a course which may be put in practice."[248]

---

[244] *Par.* 1. Tsow was the principality of which Mencius was a native:—see in the Prolegomena, at the beginning of his Life. Its power was much inferior to that of Loo, and therefore the engagement between their troops is not called a "battle," but merely "a skirmish," or "a noisy brush." Its ruler's precise rank at this time I have not been able to ascertain. He is called here by his honorary or sacrificial epithet of "duke Muh," Muh in such application meaning, "Dispenser of virtue and maintainer of righteousness, outwardly showing inward feeling."

[245] *Par.* 2. "Calamitous years" are years of pestilence, inundations, fires, &c. The "ditches and water-channels" were numerous, being much used in connection with the system of agriculture. The former are characterized as "long and small," the latter as "deep and large." "The philosopher Tsăng" we became familiar with in the Analects as one of the principal disciples of. Confucius.

[246] CH. XIII. IT IS BETTER FOR A PRINCE, EVEN THOUGH HIS STATE BE SMALL, TO RELY ON HIMSELF THAN TO DEPEND ON, OR TRY TO PROPITIATE, GREATER POWERS.

[247] *Par.* 1. T'ăng was a small State, whose lords were Kes, marquises, in early times, but now only viscounts,—in the present district of T'ăng, department Yen-chow. North of it was the kingdom of Ts'e, and, in the time of Mencius, Ts'oo had so far extended its power northwards as to threaten it from the south. Wăn is the posthumous epithet of the viscount of this time, meaning "Loyally truthful and courteous."

[248] *Par.* 2. Mencius could have given counsel on the questions proposed by the prince, but he thought he could give him better advice. He says that the course he suggested might be put in practice, not that it would be successful.

XIV.[249] 1. Duke Wăn of T'ăng asked, saying, "The people of Ts'e are going to fortify Sěeh, and [the movement] occasions me great alarm; what is the proper course for me to take in the case?"[250]

2. Mencius replied, "Formerly, when king T'ae dwelt in Pin, the Teih were [continually] making incursions upon it. He [therefore] left it, and went to the foot of Mount K'e, and there took up his residence. He did not take that situation as having selected it;—it was a matter of necessity.[251]

3. "If you do good, among your descendants in future generations there shall be one who will attain to the Royal sway. The superior man lays the foundation of the inheritance, and hands down the beginning [which he has made], doing what can be continued [by his successors]. As to the accomplishment of the great result, that is with Heaven. What is that [Ts'e] to you, O prince? you have simply to make yourself strong to do good."[252]

XV.[253] 1. Duke Wăn of T'ăng asked, saying, "T'ăng is a small State. I do my utmost to serve the great kingdoms [on either side of it], but I cannot escape [suffering from them]. What is the proper course for me to pursue in the case?" Mencius replied, "Formerly, when king T'ae dwelt in Pin, the Teih were continually making incursions upon it. He served them with skins and silks, and still he suffered from them. He served them with dogs and horses, and still he suffered from them. He served them with pearls and pieces of jade, and still he suffered from them. On this he assembled his old men, and announced to them, saying, 'What the Teih want is my territory. I have heard this,—that the superior man does not injure his people for that which he nourishes them with. My children, why should you be troubled about having no ruler. I will leave this' [Accordingly] he left Pin, crossed over Mount Lĕang, [built] a town at the foot of Mount K'e, and dwelt there. The people of Pin said, 'He is a benevolent man;—we must not lose him.' Those who followed him [looked] like crowds going to market.[254]

---

[249] CH. XIV. A PRINCE, THREATENED BY A POWERFUL NEIGHBOUR, WILL FIND HIS BEST DEFENCE AND CONSOLATION IN DOING WHAT IS GOOD AND RIGHT. Mencius was at his wit's end, I suppose, to give duke Wăn an answer. It was all very well to tell him to do good, but the promise of a royal descendant would hardly afford him much comfort.

[250] *Par.* 1. Sěeh was a small principality, adjoining T'ăng, and like it referred to the same present district in department Yen-chow. It had long been incorporated with Ts'e, which now proposed to fortify its principal town, as a basis of operations, probably, against T'ăng.

[251] *Par.* 2. See par. 2 of next chapter on king T'ae's removal from Pin to K'e.

[252] *Par.* 3. In his first sentence here, Mencius, no doubt, was thinking, and would have duke Wăn think, of the kings Wăn and Woo, the descendants of king T'ae.

[253] CH. XV. TWO HONOURABLE COURSES OPEN TO A PRINCE THREATENED BY ENEMIES WHOM HE CANNOT RESIST,—REMOVAL OR ABDICATION, AND DEATH IN A GALLANT DEFENCE.

[254] *Par.* 2. Some of the particulars which Mencius gives here of king T'ae's dealings with the Teih are also found in Fuh-săng's Introduction to the Shoo. They were no doubt

4. "On the other hand [a prince] may say, '[The country] has been held [by my ancestors] for generations, and is not what I can undertake to dispose of in my person. I will go to the death for it, and will not leave it.'

5. "I beg you, O prince, to make your election between these two courses."

XVI.[255] 1. Duke P'ing of Loo was about to go out [one day], when his favorite Tsang Ts'ang begged [to ask] him, saying, "On other days, when your lordship has gone out, you have given instructions to the officers as to where you were going. But now the horses have been put to your carriage, and the officers do not yet know where you are going. I venture to request your orders." The duke said, "I am going to see the philosopher Măng." "What!" said the other. "That you demean yourself, O prince, by what you are doing, to pay the first visit to a common man, is, I apprehend, because you think that he is a man of talents and virtue. [Our rules of] propriety and righteousness must have come from such men; but on the occasion of this Măng's second mourning, his observances exceeded those of the former. Do not go to see him, O prince." The duke said, "I will not."[256]

2. The officer Yoh-ching entered [the court], and had an audience. "Prince," said he, "why have you not gone to see Măng K'o?" "One told me," was the reply, "that on the occasion of Mr. Mang's second mourning, his observances exceeded those of the former, and therefore I did not go to see him." [Yoh-ching] said, "How is this? By what your lordship calls 'exceeding,' you mean, I suppose, that on the former occasion he used the ceremonies appropriate to an inferior officer, and on the latter those appropriate to a great officer; that he first used three tripods, and afterwards five." "No," said the duke, "I refer to the greater

---

from traditional accounts still floating among the people towards the end of the Chow dynasty.

[255] CH. XVI. DISAPPOINTMENT OF MENCIUS' PROSPECTS OF USEFULNESS IN LOO, AND HIS REMARKS UPON IT. A MAN'S WAY IN LIFE IS ORDERED BY HEAVEN; THE INSTRUMENTALITY OF OTHER MEN IN FORWARDING OR OBSTRUCTING HIS OBJECTS IS ONLY SUBORDINATE. Mencius' presence in Loo at this time is referred to B.C. 309, and he is supposed to have hence-forth given up the idea of doing anything for his age by his labors with its kings and princes. His prospects of doing anything with duke P'ing could not have been great, for Loo had for a considerable time lost its independence, and the descendants of the duke of Chow were suffered to drag out an unhonored existence only by the contemptuous forbearance of Ts'oo.

[256] *Par.* 1. Yoh-ching, mentioned in par. 2, was a disciple of Mencius, with whom we shall meet again. He had found employment at the court of P'ing, and had spoken to him of his master, so that now the duke was about to proceed in his carriage to invite Mencius to his court, as his counselor and guide. Wishing to do him honour, he would in the first place visit him at his lodging. His favorite Tsang Ts'ang knew all this, and took measures accordingly to prevent the meeting of the duke and the philosopher. The first occasion of Mencius' mourning was, it is said, on the death of his father. But according to the received accounts Mencius' father died when he was only three years old. We must suppose that the favorite invented the account that he gave.

excellence of the coffin, the shell, the grave-clothes, and the shroud."
[Yoh-ching] replied, "That cannot be called 'exceeding.' That was the
difference between being poor and being rich."[257]

3. [After this] the officer Yoh-ching [went to] see Mencius, and
said, "I told the ruler about you, and he was consequently coming to see
you, when his favorite Tsang Ts'ang stopped him, and he did not carry
his purpose into effect." [Mencius] said, "A man's advance is effected,
it may be, by others, and the stopping him is, it may be, from the efforts
of others. But to advance a man or to stop his advance is [really]
beyond the power of other men. My not finding [the right prince] in the
marquis of Loo, is from Heaven. How could that scion of the Tsang
family cause me not to find [the ruler that would suit me]?"

## BOOK II. KUNG-SUN CH'OW.[258] PART I.

CHAPTER I.[259] 1. KUNG-SUN CH'OW said, "Master, if you were to
obtain the ordering of the government in Ts'e, could you promise
yourself the accomplishment of such successful results as were realized
by Kwan Chung and the minister Gan?"[260]

2. Mencius said, "You, Sir, are indeed a [true] man of Ts'e. You
know about Kwan Chung and the minister Gan, and nothing more.

3. "One asked Tsăng Se, saying, 'To which, my [good] Sir, do you
give the superiority,—to yourself or to Tsze-loo?' Tsang Se looked
uneasy, and said, 'He was an object of veneration to my grandfather.'
'Then,' pursued the man, 'do you give the superiority to yourself, or to
Kwan Chung?' Tsăng Se flushed with anger, was displeased, and said,
'How do you compare me to Kwan Chung? Considering how entirely
he possessed [the confidence of] his ruler, how long he had the
direction of the government of the State, and how low [after all] was

---

[257] *Par.* 2. The tripods here mentioned contained the offerings of meat used in the
funeral, sacrificial rites. The king used nine, a feudal prince seven, a great officer five,
and a scholar or inferior officer three. To each tripod belonged its appropriate kind of
flesh.

[258] TITLE OF THIS BOOK. The name of Kung-sun Ch'ow, one of Mencius' disciples,
heading the first chapter, the Book is named from him accordingly.

[259] CH. I. WHILE MENCIUS WISHED TO SEE A TRUE ROYAL GOVERNMENT, AND
COULD EASILY HAVE REALIZED IT HAD HE BEEN IN OFFICE, SO THAT THE KING OF TS'E
WOULD SOON HAVE BECOME SOVEREIGN OF THE WHOLE KINGDOM FROM THE PECULIAR
CIRCUMSTANCES OF THE TIME, HE WOULD NOT HAVE HAD RECOURSE TO ANY WAYS
INCONSISTENT WITH ITS IDEA.

[260] *Par.* 1. It appears from par. 2 that Kung-sun Ch'ow was a native of Ts'e. He
must have been a cadet of the old ducal family. The sons of the feudal princes were styled
Kung-tsze, and their sons again Kung-sun, "ducal grandsons." Those two characters
might become the surname of their descendants, who mingled with the undistinguished
masses of the people. Kwan Chung,—see on Ana. III. xxii.; *et al.* He was the chief
minister of duke Hwan, the famous leader of all the feudal princes. The minister
Gan,—see on Ana. V. xvi.; *et al.* He was mentioned above in Book I. ii. IV.

what he accomplished, how is it that you compare me to him?'[261]

4. "Thus," added Mencius, "Tsăng Se would not play Kwan Chung, and is it what you desire for me, that I should do so?"

5. [Kung-sun Ch'ow] said, "Kwan Chung raised his ruler to be the leader of all the other princes, and the minister Gran made his ruler illustrious; and do you still think that it would not be enough for you to do what they did?"

6. "To raise [the ruler of] Ts'e to the .Royal dignity would [simply] be like turning round the hand," was the reply.[262]

7. "So!" returned the other. "The perplexity of your disciple is hereby very much increased! And there was king Wăn, with all the virtue which belonged to him, and who did not die till he had reached a hundred years; yet his influence had not penetrated to all under heaven. It required king Woo and the duke of Chow to continue his course, before that influence greatly prevailed. And now you say that the Royal dignity may be so easily obtained:—is king Wăn then not worthy to be imitated?"[263]

8. [Mencius] said, "How can king Wăn be matched? From T'ang to Woo-ting there had arisen six or seven worthy and sage sovereigns; all under heaven had been long attached to Yin. The length of time made a change difficult, and Woo-ting gave audience to all the princes and possessed the whole kingdom, as if it had been a thing which he turned round in his palm. [Then] Chow was removed from Woo-ting by no great interval of time. There were still remaining some of the ancient families, and of the old manners, of the influence which had emanated [from the earlier sovereigns], and of their good government. Moreover, there were the viscount of Wei and his second son, his Royal Highness Pe-kan, the viscount of Ke, and Kaou Kih, all men of ability and virtue, who gave their joint assistance to Chow [in his government]. In consequence of these things it took him a long time to lose the kingdom. There was not a foot of ground which he did not possess; there was not one of all the people who was not his subject. So it was on his side, while king Wăn made his beginning from a territory of [only] a hundred square *le,* and therefore it was difficult for him

---

[261] *Par.* 3. Tsăng Se was, according to some, the son, according to others, the grandson of Tsăng Sin, one of Confucius' most famous disciples. With Sin and with Tsze-loo the readers of the Analects must be familiar.

[262] *Par.* 6. Here Mencius states his thesis, according to his fashion, in the broadest and most unlimited manner;—giving him the opportunity to explain and vindicate it as he does below.

[263] *Par.* 7. King Wăn died at the age of 97;—Ch'ow uses the round number 100. According to the representations of Chinese writers two-thirds of the kingdom then acknowledged his supremacy. His son king Woo continued his work, and overthrew the dynasty of Shang, while another son, the duke of Chow, regulated the constitution and all the ceremonies of the new dynasty; and then the principles of Wăn received their full development.

[immediately to attain to the Royal dignity].[264]

9. "The people of Ts'e have the saying, 'A man may have wisdom and discernment, but that is not like embracing the favorable opportunity; a man may have [good] hoes, but that is not like waiting for the [favorable] seasons.' The present time is one in which [the Royal dignity] may be easily attained.[265]

10. "In the flourishing periods of the sovereigns of Hĕa, of Yin, and of Chow, the [Royal] territory did not exceed a thousand *le* and Ts'e embraces as much. Cocks crow and dogs bark to one another all the way to its four borders, so that Ts'e also possesses the [requisite number of] people. No change is needed for the enlargement of its territory, nor for the collecting of a population. If [its ruler] will put in practice a benevolent government, no power can prevent his attaining to the Royal sway.

11. "Moreover, never was there a time farther removed than this from the appearance of a true king; never was there a time when the sufferings of the people from oppressive government were more intense than this. The hungry are easily supplied with food, and the thirsty with drink.

12. "Confucius said, 'The flowing progress of virtue is more rapid than the transmission of orders by stages and couriers.'

13. "At the present time, in a country of ten thousand chariots, let a benevolent government be exercised, and the people will be delighted with it, as if they were relieved from hanging by the heels. With half the merit of the ancients, double their achievement is sure to be realized. It is only at this time that such could be the case."

II.[266] 1. Kung-sun Ch'ow asked [Mencius], saying, "Master, if you

---

[264] *Par.* 8. From T'ang to Woo-ting there were altogether 18 sovereigns, or, according to the Bamboo Annals, 20, exclusive of themselves; and from Woo-ting to Chow there were seven. In the former period T'ae-kĕah, T'ae-mow, Ts'oo-yih, and Pwan-kăng are specified as "worthy and sage," in addition to T'ang and Woo-ting. From Woo-ting to Chow there elapsed about a century and a quarter. The viscount of Wei was an elder brother of Chow, and many say by the same mother, but she was not queen, but only a member of the harem, when he was born. Some critics will have it that the next faithful adherent of Chow who is mentioned was the viscount's brother and not his son. The viscount of Ke was a king's son as well as Pe-kan. They were both, probably, uncles of Chow. Kaou Kih did not belong to the royal House of Shang, but was a faithful adherent of it.

[265] *Par.* 9. Ability and instruments are good; but there must also be the favorable opportunity.

[266] CH. II. THAT MENCIUS HAD ATTAINED TO AN UNPERTURBED MIND; THAT THE MEANS BY WHICH HE HAD DONE SO WAS HIS KNOWLEDGE OF WORDS, AND THE NOURISHMENT OF HIS PASSION-NATURE; AND THAT CONFUCIUS WAS THE GREAT OBJECT OF HIS IMITATION, FOR THERE NEVER HAD BEEN ANOTHER MAN WHO COULD BE REGARDED AS HIS EQUAL. The chapter is divided into four parts; the first, parr. 1-8, showing generally that there are various ways to attain an unperturbed mind; the second, parr. 9, 10, exposing the error of the way taken by the philosopher Kaou; the third, parr. 11-17, unfolding Mencius' own way; and the fourth, parr. 18-28, showing that Mencius

were to be appointed a high noble and prime minister of Ts'e, so as to carry your principles into practice, though you should thereupon [raise the ruler to] be head of all the other princes or [even] to be king, it would not be to be wondered at; but in such a position would your mind be perturbed or not?" Mencius replied, "No. At forty I attained to an unperturbed mind."[267]

2. [Chow] said, "Then, Master, you are far beyond Măng Pun." "[The mere attainment of] that," said [Mencius], "is not difficult. The scholar Kaou attained to an unperturbed mind at an earlier period of life than I did."[268]

3. "Is there any [proper] way to an unperturbed mind?" asked [Chow]; and the reply was, "Yes.

4. "Pih-kung Yĕw had this way of nourishing his valour:—His flesh did not shrink [from a wound], and his eyes did not turn aside [from any thrusts at them]. He considered that to submit to have a hair pulled out by any one was as great [a disgrace] as to be beaten in the market-place, and that what he would not receive from [a common man in his] loose garments of hair-cloth, neither should he receive from the ruler of ten thousand chariots. He viewed stabbing the ruler of ten thousand chariots just as stabbing a fellow in cloth of hair. He feared not any of the princes. A bad word addressed to him he always

---

followed Confucius, and praising that sage as the first of mortals. It is in a great measure owing to what Mencius says in this chapter about the nourishment of the passion-nature that a place has been accorded to him among the sages of China, or in immediate proximity to them. His views are substantially these:—Man's nature is composite. He possesses moral and intellectual powers (comprehended under the terms "heart" and "mind," interchanged with "will"), and active powers (summed up under the term *k'e*, and embracing the emotions, desires, and appetites). The moral and intellectual powers should be supreme and govern, but there is a close connection between them and the others which give effect to them. The active powers should not be stunted, for then the whole character will be feeble. But on the other hand they must not be allowed to take the lead. They must get their tone from the mind, and the way to develop them in all their completeness is to do good. Let them be vigorous, and the mind clear and pure, and we shall have the man whom nothing external to himself can perturb,—Horace's *justum et tenacem propositi virum*. In brief, if we take the *sanum corpus* of the Roman adage as not expressing merely the physical body, but the whole physical and emotional nature, what Mencius exhibits here may be said to be *"mens sana in corpore sano."*

The attentive reader will find the above thoughts dispersed through this chapter, and be able to separate them from the irrelevant matter—that especially relating to Confucius—with which they are set forth.

[267] *Par.* 1. The questioner here is the same who discourses with our philosopher in the preceding chapter;—see there on par. 1. The one chapter may indeed be considered as the sequel of the other. The disciple allows that the master could achieve what he had asserted, and asks whether the being placed in a position to do so would disturb his mind.

It was a maxim with the ancient Chinese that a man was in his greatest vigour at 40, and able to encounter all the difficulties of official service; see the Le Ke, I. Pt I. i. 27. Compare Confucius' account of himself in Ana. II. iv.

[268] *Par.* 2. Măng Pun was a celebrated bravo, probably of Ts'e, of whom various feats of strength and daring are recorded. The scholar Kaou is probably the same who gives name to the sixth Book of Mencius, which see.

returned.[269]

5. "The valour which Măng She-shay nourished spoke on this wise:—'I look upon conquering and not conquering in the same way. To measure the enemy and then advance; to calculate the chances of victory and then engage:—this is to stand in awe of the opposing force. How can I make certain of conquering? I can only rise superior to all fear.'[270]

6. "Măng She-shay resembled the philosopher Tsăng, and Pih-kung Yĕw resembled Tsze-hĕa. I do not know to the valour of which the superiority should be ascribed; but Măng She-shay attended to what was of the greater importance.[271]

7. "Formerly, the philosopher Tsăng said to Tsze-seang, 'Do you love valour? I heard an account of great valour from the Master, [who said that it speaks thus]:—"If on self-examination I find that I am not upright, shall I not be afraid of [a common man in his] loose garments of hair-cloth; if on self-examination I find that I am upright, I will go forward against thousands and tens of thousands."'[272]

8. "What Măng She-shay maintained, however, was his physical energy merely, and was not equal to what the philosopher Tsăng maintained, which was [indeed] of the greater importance."[273]

9. [Ch'ow] said, "May I venture to ask [the difference between] your unperturbed mind, Master, and that of the scholar Kaou?" [Mencius] answered, "Kaou says, 'What you do not find in words, do not seek for in your mind; what you do not find in your mind, do not seek for by passion-effort.' [This last]—not to seek by passion-effort

---

[269] *Par.* 4. Pih-kung Yĕw belonged, probably, to the State of Wei, and was a cadet of one of the principal clans in it, sprung from the ruling House. There was, however, a clan also in Ts'e with the surname of Pih-kung. Yĕw evidently was a bold and reckless fellow.

[270] *Par.* 5. Of Măng She-shay we know nothing but what we are told here. He was evidently a bold and fearless man.

[271] *Par.* 6. Pih-kung Yĕw thought of others, and was determined to conquer, if he could; Măng She-shay thought only of himself, and allowed no fear to enter his mind. It is on this account that Mencius gives Măng the preference. The basis of the reference to the two disciples of Confucius was the commonly received idea of their several characters. Tsăng (see on Ana. I. iv.) was reflective, and dealt with himself; Tsze-hĕa was learned and ambitious, and would not be inferior to others.

[272] *Par.* 7. Tsze-sĕăng was a disciple of Tsăng. The sentiment of Confucius is the same as that of Solomon, with a characteristic difference of expression:—"The wicked flee when no man pursueth; but the righteous are bold as a lion."

[273] *Par* 8. Here we first meet with the character *k'e* so important in this chapter. Originally it was the same in form as another meaning "cloudy vapor." With the addition of the character for "rice," or that for "fire," it should indicate "steam of rice," or "steam" generally. The sense in which Mencius uses it is indicated in the translation and in the preliminary note. That sense springs from its being used as correlate to *sin*, "the mind," taken in connection with the idea of "energy" inherent in it from its composition. Thus it signifies the lower but active portion of man's constitution; and in this paragraph, that lower part in its lowest sense,—animal vigour or courage.

for what you do not find in your mind—may be conceded; but not to seek in your mind for what you do not find in words ought not to be conceded. For the will is the leader of the passion-nature; and the passion-nature pervades and animates the body. The will is [first and] chief, and the passion-nature is subordinate to it. Therefore [I] say, Maintain firm the will, and do no violence to the passion-nature.[274]

10. [Ch'ow observed], "Since you say that the will is chief and the passion-nature subordinate to it, how do you also say, Maintain firm the will, and do no violence to the passion-nature?" The reply was, "When the will is exclusively active, then it moves the passion-nature; and when the passion-nature is exclusively active, it moves the will. For instance now, the case of a man falling or running is an exertion of his passion-nature, and yet it moves his mind."[275]

11. "I venture to ask" [said Ch'ow again], "wherein you, Master, have the superiority" [Mencius] said, "I understand words. I am skilful in nourishing my vast, flowing, passion-nature."[276]

12. [Ch'ow pursued,] "I venture to ask what you mean by your vast, flowing, passion-nature." The reply was, "It is difficult to describe it.

13. "This is the passion-nature:—It is exceedingly great, and exceedingly strong. Being nourished by rectitude and sustaining no injury, it fills up all between heaven and earth.

14. "This is the passion-nature:—It is the mate and assistant of righteousness and reason. Without this [man's nature] is in a state of starvation.

15. "It is produced by the accumulation of righteous deeds, and cannot be attained by incidental acts of righteousness. If the mind do not feel complacency in the conduct, [the nature becomes] starved.

---

[274] *Par.* 9. Kaou's principle seems to have been this,—indifference to everything external and entire passivity of mind. Modern writers are fond of saying that in his words are to be found the essence of Buddhism, and that his aim was to obtain a sort of Buddhistic *nirvana*; and perhaps this helps us to a glimpse at his meaning, which is far from being evident. Mencius' concession of the second of his instructions is not to be understood as an approval of it, but simply that he did not consider it so objectionable as the other; and he goes on to show wherein he considered it to be defective.

[275] *Par.* 10. Ch'ow did not understand what his master had said about the relation between the mind and the passion-nature: and as the latter was subordinate, he would have had it disregarded altogether. Hence his question; but Mencius shows that the passion-nature is really a part of our constitution, acts upon the mind, and is acted on by it, and ought not to be disregarded.

[276] *Parr.* 11-16. There is much vain babbling in the Chinese commentators about "the vast, flowing, passion-nature," to show how the *k'e* of heaven and earth is the *k'e* also of man. Mencius, it seems to me, has before his mind the idea of a perfect man, complete in all the parts of his constitution; and it is this which gives its elevation to his language. There is much that is good and important in what he says. A *course* of righteous action, where the character is at all heroic, as that of Mencius was, produces a wonderful boldness and vigour of character. While a bad conscience makes men cowards, a good conscience operates as effectually in the contrary direction.

Hence it is that I say that Kaou has never understood righteousness, because he makes it something external.

16. "There must be the [constant] practice [of righteousness], but without the object [of thereby nourishing the passion-nature]. Let not the mind forget [its work], but let there be no assisting the growth. Let us not be like the man of Sung. There was a man at Sung who was grieved that his growing corn was not longer, and so he pulled it up. He then returned home, looking very stupid, and said to his people, 'I am very tired to-day; I have been helping the corn to grow long.' His son ran to look at it, and found the corn all withered. There are few people in the world who [do not deal with their passion-nature as if they] were thus assisting their corn to grow long. Some indeed consider it of no benefit to them, and neglect it;—they do not weed their corn. They who assist it to grow long pull out their corn. [What they do is] not only of no benefit [to the nature], but it also injures it."

17. [Kung-sun Ch'ow further asked,] "What do you mean by saying that you understand words?" [Mencius] replied, "When speeches are one-sided, I know how [the mind of the speaker] is clouded over; when they are extravagant, I know wherein [the mind] is snared; when they are all-depraved, I know how [the mind] has departed [from principle]; when they are evasive, I know how [the mind] is at its [wit's] end. [These evils], growing in the mind, injure the [principles of the] government, and, displayed in the government, are hurtful to the conduct of affairs. When a sage shall again arise, he will certainly agree with [these] my words."[277]

18. On this Ch'ow observed, "Tsae Wo and Tsze-kung were clever in making speeches; Jen Něw, the disciple Min, and Yen Yuen, while their words were good, were distinguished for their virtuous conduct. Confucius united both the qualities, [but still he] said, 'In the matter of speeches I am not competent.'—Then, Master, have you attained to be a sage?"[278]

19. [Mencius] replied, "Oh! what words are these? Formerly Tsze-

---

[277] *Par.* 17. With regard to the first ground of Mencius' superiority over Kaou,—his "knowledge of words," as he is briefer than on the other, so, to my mind, he is less satisfactory. Perhaps he meant to say that, however great the dignity to which he might be raised, his knowledge of words and ability to refer incorrect and injurious speeches to the mental defects from which they sprang would keep him from being deluded, and preserve his mind unperturbed. One of the scholars, Ch'ing, uses this illustration:—"Mencius, with his knowledge of words was like a man seated in a hall, who can distinguish all the movements of the people below it, which he could not do if it were necessary for him to descend and mingle with the crowd."

The concluding remark gives rise to the rest of the chapter, it seeming to Ch'ow that Mencius placed himself by it on the platform of sages.

[278] *Par.* 18. Compare Ana. XI ii. 2, to the enumeration in which of the excellencies of several of Confucius disciples there seems to be here a reference. But the point of Ch'ow's question lies in the remark of the sage about himself, found nowhere else, and obscure enough. He thinks that Mencius is taking more upon himself than Confucius did.

kung asked Confucius, saying, 'Master, are you a sage?' and was answered, 'To be a sage is what I cannot [claim]; but I learn without satiety, and teach without being tired.' Tsze-kung rejoined, 'You learn without satiety;—that shows your wisdom. You teach without being tired;—that shows your benevolence. Benevolent and wise:—Master, you are a sage.' Now, since Confucius would not accept the position of a sage, what words were those [you spake about me]?"[279]

20. [Ch'ow said], "Formerly, it seems to me, I have heard that Tsze-hĕa, Tsze-yĕw, and Tsze-chang had each one member of a sage, and that Jen Nĕw, the disciple Min, and Yen Yuen had all the members, but in small proportions. I venture to ask with which of these you are pleased to rank yourself."

21. [Mencius] replied, "Let us drop [speaking about] these if you please."

22. [Ch'ow then] asked, "What do you say of Pih-e and E Yin?" "Their ways," said [Mencius], "were different [from mine]. Not to serve a prince nor employ a people whom he did not approve; in a time of good government to take office, and in a time of disorder to retire;—this was [the way of] Pih-e. [To say], 'Whom may I not serve as my ruler? Whom may I not employ as my people?' In a time of good government to take office, and in a time of disorder to do the same:—this was [the way of] E Yin. When it was proper to go into office, then to go into office, and when it was proper to keep aloof from office, then to keep aloof; when it was proper to continue in it long, then to do so, and when it was proper to withdraw from it quickly, then so to withdraw:—that was [the way of] Confucius. These were all sages of antiquity, and I have not attained to do what they did; but what I wish to do is to learn to be like Confucius."[280]

23. [Ch'ow] said, "Comparing Pih-e and E Yin with Confucius, are they to be placed in the same rank with him?" The reply was, "No. Since there were living men until now, there never was [another] Confucius."

24. "Then," said [Ch'ow], "did they have any points of agreement [with him]?" "Yes," said [Mencius]; "if they had been rulers over a hundred *le* of territory, they would all of them have brought all the

---

[279] *Parr.* 19-21. Mencius disclaims being regarded as a sage; but does he indicate that he thought himself superior to all the disciples of Confucius mentioned by Ch'ow,—even to Yen Yuen? Hardly so much as that; but that he would not be content with them as his model.

[280] *Parr.* 22-24. Pih-e,—see on Ana. V. xxii. E Yin,—see my note on the title of Book IV. Part IV. of the Shoo. Mencius discourses fully on both these ancient worthies in V. ii. I., *et al.* The different ways of them and of Confucius have been thus expressed:—"The principle of Pih-e was to keep himself pure; that of E Yin, to take office; and that of Confucius, to do what the time required." But while thus differing, they would equally keep aloof from whatever was unrighteous, however they might be tempted.

feudal princes to attend at their court, and would have possessed all under the sky. And none of them, to obtain that, would have committed one act of unrighteousness, or put to death one innocent person. In these points they agreed with him."

25. [Ch'ow] said, "I venture to ask wherein he differed from them." [Mencius] replied, "Tsae Wo, Tsze-kung, and Yew Joh had wisdom sufficient to know the sage. [Even if we rank them] low, they would not have demeaned themselves to flatter their favorite.[281]

26. "Tsae Wo said, 'According to my view of the Master, he is far superior to Yaou and Shun'

27. "Tsze-kung said, 'By viewing the ceremonial ordinances [of a ruler] we know [the character of] his government; and by hearing his music we know [that of] his virtue. Along the distance of a hundred ages, I can arrange, [according to their merits], the line of their kings, so that not one can escape me; and from the birth of mankind downwards there has not been [another like our] Master.'

28. "Yew Joh said, 'Is it only among men that it is so? There is the *k'e-lin* among quadrupeds, the phoenix among birds, the T'ae mountain among ant-hills, the Ho and the sea among rain-pools. [Though different in degree], they are the same in kind. And so the sages among mankind are the same in kind. But they stand out from their fellows, and rise up above the crowd; and from the birth of mankind till now there never has been one so complete as Confucius.'"

III.[282] 1. Mencius said, "He who, using force, makes a pretence to benevolence becomes the leader of the princes, and he must be possessed of a large State. He who, using virtue, practices benevolence becomes the king, and he need not wait till he has a large State. T'ang did it with [only] seventy *le*, and king Wan with [only] a hundred *le*.[283]

2. "When one by force subdues men they do not submit to him in

<hr/>

[281] *Par.* 25. Yĕw Joh,—see on Ana. I. ii. With parr. 26-28 compare the eulogium of Confucius in the Doctrine of the Mean, chh. xxx.-xxxii., and also Ana. XIX. chh. xxiii.-xxv. It is in vain the western reader tries to quicken himself to any corresponding appreciation of the sage. We look for the being whom his disciples describe as vainly as we do for the fabulous *k'e-lin* and phoenix, to which they compare him. The *k'e* is properly the male, and the *lin* the female of the animal referred to,—a monster with a deer's body, an ox's tail, and a horse's feet, &c., which appears to greet the birth of a sage, or the reign of a sage sovereign. So in *fung-hwang*, which I have rendered *phoenix*, the names of the male and female are put together to denote one individual of either sex. In the words "rise up above the crowd," the image is that of stalks of grass or grain, shooting high above the level of the waving field.

[282] CH. III. THE DIFFERENCE BETWEEN A LEADER OF THE PRINCES AND A TRUE SOVEREIGN ARISES FROM SUBMISSION CONSTRAINRD BY FORCE AND THAT ACCORDED TO VIRTUE AND BENEVOLENCE.

[283] *Par.* 1. T'ang was the founder of the Shang dynasty, as king Wăn was of that of Chow. The size of their States is that of their hereditary possessions; though we know that those of the House of Chow had increased very largely before the final struggle between it and that of Shang, conducted by king Woo, the son of Wăn.

heart, but because their strength is not adequate [to resist]. When one subdues men by virtue, in their hearts' core they are pleased, and sincerely submit, as was the case with the seventy disciples in their submission to Confucius. What is said in the Book of Poetry,

> 'From the west to the east,
> From the south to the north,
> There was not a thought but did him homage,'

is an illustration of this."[284]

IV.[285] 1. Mencius said, "Benevolence brings glory, and the opposite of it brings disgrace. For [the rulers of] the present day to hate disgrace, and yet live complacently doing what is not benevolent, is like hating moisture and yet living in a low situation.[286]

2. "If [a ruler] hates disgrace, his best course is to esteem virtue and honor [virtuous] scholars, giving the worthiest of them places [of dignity] and the able offices [of trust]. When throughout the State there is leisure and rest [from external troubles], taking advantage of such a season, let him clearly digest the measures of his government with their penal sanctions, and even great States will stand in awe of him.[287]

3. "It is said in the Book of Poetry,

> 'Before the sky was dark with rain,
> I gathered the roots of the mulberry tree,
> And bound round and round my window and door.
> Now, ye people below,
> Dare any of you despise my house?'

"Confucius said, 'Did not he who made this ode understand the way [of governing]?' Who will dare to insult him who is able rightly to govern his State?[288]

---

[284] *Par.* 2. "The seventy disciples" is a round number. See on the disciples of Confucius in the Prolegomena to vol. i. of my larger Work. The ode from which the quotation is made is the last of the first Book of the third Part of the She, celebrating the kings Wăn and Woo. The lines quoted refer specially to Woo. Tsow Haou, a statesman and scholar of the 11th century, says on this chapter:—"He who subdues men by force has the intention of subduing them, and they dare not but submit. He who subdues them by virtue has no intention to subdue them, and they cannot but submit. From antiquity downwards there have been many dissertations on the leader of the princes and the true sovereign, but none so deep, incisive, and perspicuous as this chapter."

[285] CH. IV. THE INCONSISTENCY OF A RULER'S SEEKING TO BE GREAT AND GLORIOUS BY ANY OTHER COURSE BUT THAT OF BENEVOLENCE. CALAMITY AND HAPPINESS ARE MEN'S OWN SEEKING.

[286] *Par.* 1. "Glory" here is not only the glory of reputation, but specially that of success and high position.

[287] *Par.* 2. Compare with this the 20th chapter of the "Doctrine of the Mean."

[288] *Par.* 3. See the She, Pt I. xv. Ode II., where the duke of Chow personating a

4. "[But] now [the rulers] take advantage of the time when throughout their States there is leisure and rest [from external troubles] to abandon themselves to pleasure and indolent indifference,—thus seeking calamities for themselves.[289]

5. "Calamity and happiness are in all cases men's own seeking.

6. "This is illustrated by what is said in the Book of Poetry,

'Always strive to accord with the will [of heaven],
So shall you be seeking for much happiness;'

and by the passage of the T'ae-keah, 'Calamities sent by Heaven may be avoided, but when we bring on the calamities ourselves, it is not possible to live.'"

V.[290] 1. Mencius said, "If [a ruler] give honor to men of talents and virtue and employ the able, so that offices shall all be filled by individuals of the highest distinction, then all the scholars of the kingdom will be pleased, and wish to stand in his court.[291]

2. "If in the market-places he levy a ground-rent on the shops but do not tax the goods, or enforce the [proper] regulations without levying a ground-rent, then all traders of the kingdom will be pleased, and wish to store their goods in his market-places.[292]

---

small bird addressing an owl, vindicates the vigour of his measures in suppressing rebellion. Mencius adduces the stanza, with the moral of it as expounded by Confucius, to show how a ruler should strengthen himself by vigorous and precautionary measures.

[289] *Parr.* 4-6. Par. 4 shows how the rulers of his time took no such measures, but pursued a thoughtless, reckless course of an opposite tendency. For the poetry quoted in par. 6, see the She, III. i. Ode I.; and for the passage from the T'ae-kĕah, see the Shoo, IV. v., Pt ii. 3.

[290] CH. V. FIVE POINTS OF TRUE ROYAL GOVERNMENT, THE PRACTICE OF WHICH WOULD HAVE CARRIED ANY OF THE PRINCES OF MENCIUS' TIME TO THE THRONE OF THE WHOLE KINGDOM ON THE TIDE OF UNIVERSAL POPULARITY.

[291] *Par.* 1. Compare the first part of par. 2 in the previous chapter. The point described here would have brought all the scholars, or the official class, of the different States to the court of the ruler who practiced it.

[292] *Par.* 2 describes the second point which would have attracted all the traders and men of business from the four quarters. According to Choo He, the capitals and large cities in those ancient times were laid out after the fashion of the division of the land in portions of nine equal squares as in the figure ⊞, where the central square contained the fields of the State. The central square in the cities contained the palace and buildings connected with it; that in front of it, the ancestral and other temples, the government treasuries, arsenals, &c.; that behind it was the market-place, or place of business; and the three squares on each side were occupied by the dwellings of the people. He adds that when traders became too many, a ground-rent was levied on their stances or shops; and that when they were few, it was remitted, and only a surveillance of the markets was exercised by the proper officers. That surveillance consisted in the inspection of weights and measures, regulation of prices, &c. This view seems to give us a satisfactory meaning for this paragraph. Chaou K'e understands the second clause in it of the tithe of the produce of the ground; but it is foreign to the object of Mencius to introduce that subject in speaking of the traders in the market-place.

3. "If at the frontier-gates there be an inspection of the persons, but no charges levied, then all the travelers of the kingdom will be pleased, and wish to be found on his roads.[293]

4. "If the husbandmen be required to give their material aid [in cultivating the public field], and no levies be made [of the produce of their own], then all the farmers in the kingdom will be pleased, and wish to plough in his fields.[294]

5. "If from the [occupiers of the] people's dwellings he do not exact the cloth required from the individual [idler] or the quota for residences, then all the people in the kingdom will be pleased, and wish to be his people.[295]

6. "If [a ruler] can truly practise these five things, then the people of neighbouring States will look up to him as a parent. From the first birth of mankind until now never has any one led children to attack their parents, and succeeded in his enterprise. Such [a ruler] will not have an enemy under the sky, and he who has no enemy under the sky is the minister of Heaven. Never has there been such a case where [the ruler] did not attain to the royal dignity."[296]

VI.[297] 1. Mencius said, "All men have a mind which cannot bear

---

[293] *Par.* 3. See I. Pt i. VII. 18; Pt ii. V. 3. The "travelers," I suppose, would mostly consist of men moving' from State to State in the prosecution of business.

[294] *Par.* 4. The levying of a tax, an additional tithe, on the produce of the fields which by the theory of the division of the land were the private possession of the husbandmen, commenced in Loo in the 16th year of duke Seuen:—see in the Ch'un Ts'ĕw and the Tso Chuen, on VII. xvi. 8. Other States, no doubt, had adopted the practice of Loo in the matter.

[295] *Par.* 5. It is difficult to determine the meaning of this paragraph. Anciently a fine had been levied on the idlers who neglected to plant mulberry-trees and hemp about the ground assigned to them for their huts and dwellings besides the fields which were devoted to the cultivation of grain;—being at first so much cloth, and subsequently the equivalent of that in money. Then some ground-rent was levied perhaps from all the husband-men for the ground so assigned for their dwellings. These two taxes appear in Mencius' time to have been levied from all occupying the three side-spaces of the cities to which I have referred in par. 2; and it is this exaction which Mencius here condemns.—Many of the residents in those spaces would be the mechanics of the States; and thus the five points recommended in this chapter would secure the good-will of the four classes into which the population was anciently divided:—scholars or the official class, husband-men, mechanics, and traders.

[296] *Par.* 6. "The minister of Heaven" appears again in Pt ii. VIII. 2. On this designation one commentator observes: "An officer is one commissioned by his ruler; the officer of Heaven is he who is commissioned by Heaven. He who bears his ruler's commission can punish men and put them to death;—he may deal so with all criminals. He who bears the commission of Heaven can execute judgment on men and smite them;—he can deal so even with all who are oppressing and misgoverning their States."

[297] CH. VI. THAT THE PRINCIPLES OF BENEVOLENCE, RIGHTEOUSNESS, PROPRIETY, AND KNOWLEDGE BELONG TO MAN AS NATURALLY AS HIS FOUR LIMBS, AND MAY AS EASILY BE EXERCISED. This chapter is important in its connection with the doctrine of Mencius respecting the goodness of human nature; but while the assertions of it are universally true, they are to be understood as introduced here with special reference to the oppressive ways and government of the princes of his time.

[to see the sufferings of] others.[298]

2. "The ancient kings had this commiserating mind, and they had likewise, as a matter of course, a commiserating government. When with a commiserating mind there was practiced a commiserating government, to bring all under heaven to order was [as easy] as to make [a small thing] go round in the palm.

3. "The ground on which I say that all men have a mind which cannot bear [to see the suffering of] others is this:—Even now-a-days, when men suddenly see a child about to fall into a well, they will all experience a feeling of alarm and distress. They will feel so not that they may thereon gain the favor of the child's parents; nor that they may seek the praise of their neighbours and friends; nor from a dislike to the reputation of [being unmoved by] such a thing.[299]

4. "Looking at the matter from this case, [we may see that] to be without this feeling of distress is not human, and that it is not human to be without the feeling of shame and dislike, or to be without the feeling of modesty and complaisance, or to be without the feeling of approving and disapproving.[300]

5. "That feeling of distress is the principle of benevolence; the feeling of shame and dislike is the principle of righteousness; the feeling of modesty and complaisance is the principle of propriety; and the feeling of approving and disapproving is the principle of knowledge.

6. "Men have these four principles just as they have their four limbs. When men, having these four principles, yet say of themselves that they cannot [manifest them], they play the thief with themselves; and he who says of his ruler that he cannot [manifest them], plays the thief with his ruler.[301]

---

[298] *Par.* 1. Compare parr. 4, 5, 6 in I. Pt i. VII. Chaou K'e and many others understand the language about "the mind that cannot bear other men," as if it meant "the mind that cannot bear [to injure] others." But it is not so much—cannot bear to inflict suffering, as—cannot bear to see suffering. Those paragraphs make this plain, as well as the illustration which immediately follows here in par. 3.

[299] *Par.* 3. The object here is to prove that the feeling of commiseration is instinctive, and does not spring up from any considerations of interest or advantage to be got by it.

[300] *Parr.* 4, 5. In par. 4 we have Mencius' account of the moral constitution of human nature. "The feeling of distress, of shame," &c., is in the original "the mind that feels distress, shame," &c. The mind is one, but all these feelings are natural to it, and make it what it is. "Principle" in par. 5, is the right translation of the original term, meaning "the beginning," as the end of a clue, &c. The feeling of distress is in itself benevolent, and from the primary feeling all benevolent feelings and actions may be developed. "Knowledge" is the only term with which I am not satisfied. Would "wisdom" be a better word, with the meaning it has in such passages of the Bible as "The fear of the Lord is the beginning of wisdom?"

[301] *Parr.* 6, 7. "To play the thief with one's self, or with one's ruler," is to injure and rob one's self or one's ruler, taking away from him that which properly belongs to him. In par. 7 Mencius must begin the application of his principles with an "if." His analysis of

7. "Since we all have the four principles in ourselves, let us know to give them all their development and completion, and the issue will be like that of a fire which has begun to burn, or of a spring which has begun to find vent. Let them have their full development, and they will suffice to love and protect all [within] the four seas; let them be denied that development, and they will not suffice for a man to serve his parents with."

VII.[302] 1. Mencius said, "Is the arrow-maker [naturally] more wanting in benevolence than the maker of mail? [And yet], the arrow-maker's only fear is lest [his arrows] should not wound men, and the fear of the maker of mail is lest men should be wounded. So it is as between the priest and the coffin-maker. [The choice of] a profession therefore is a thing in which it is very necessary to be careful.[303]

2. "Confucius said, 'The excellence of a neighborhood consists in its virtuous manners. If a man, in selecting a residence, do not fix on one where such prevail, how can he be wise?' Now benevolence belongs to the most honorable nobility of Heaven, and is the quiet home where man should dwell. Since no one can hinder us from being so, if we are not benevolent, this shows our want of wisdom.[304]

3. "He who is [thus] neither benevolent nor wise will be without propriety and righteousness, and must be the servant of [other] men. To be the servant of men and yet ashamed of such servitude is like a bow-maker's being ashamed to make bows, or an arrow-maker's being ashamed to make arrows.[305]

4. "If [a man] be ashamed of being in such a case, his best course is to practise benevolence.

5. "He who [would be] benevolent is like the archer. The archer adjusts himself, and then shoots. If he shoot and do not hit, he does not murmur against those who surpass himself:—he simply turns round, and seeks the [cause of failure] in himself."[306]

---

human nature is admirable, but something is the matter with it of which he is not aware.

[302] CH. VII. THE PRINCIPLE OF BENEVOLENCE SHOULD DOMINATE IN ALL THE PROFESSIONS OF LIFE,—IN THE BUSINESS OF GOVERNMENT AND IN THE ARTS OF LOWER WALKS. THE BENEVOLENT RULER WILL NEVER BE A SERVANT OF OTHERS, AND HE WHO IS SO HAS ONLY HIMSELF TO BLAME. The argument of Mencius in this chapter is more loosely put forth than in his general practice, and it is more difficult to set it forth concisely.

[303] *Par.* 1. The term which I have translated "priest" here occurs in the Analects, XIII. xxii., where it is translated by "wizard." See the passage. As opposed to a "coffin-maker," who makes provision for the death of men, It indicates one by whose prayers and other methods it is sought to procure life and prosperity for men.

[304] *Par.* 2. See Ana. IV. i.

[305] *Par.* 3. The first clause here flows from the previous par., and the next seems to show what will be the consequence of being devoid of benevolence and wisdom; and the whole will result in servitude to others. That result is natural, and he who grieves under it has only himself to blame.

[306] *Par.* 5. Compare Ana. III. vii. and xvi.

VIII.[307] 1. Mencius said, "When any one told Tsze-loo that he had a fault, he was glad.[308]

2. "When Yu heard good words, he bowed [to the speaker].[309]

3. "The great Shun had a [still] greater [quality]:—he regarded goodness as the common property of himself and others, giving up his own way to follow others, and delighting to copy [the example of] others,—in order to practise what was good.[310]

4. "From the time that he ploughed and sowed, exercised the potter's art and was a fisherman, to that when he was emperor, he was always learning from others.[311]

5. "To take example from others to practise what is good is to help men in the same practice. Therefore there is no attribute of the superior man greater than his helping men to practise what is good."

IX.[312] 1. Mencius said, "Pih-e would not serve a ruler whom he did not approve, nor be friendly with any one whom he did not esteem. He would not stand in the court of a bad man, nor speak with a bad man. To stand in a bad man's court, or to speak with a bad man, would have been in his estimation the same as to stand with his court robes and court cap amid mire and charcoal. Pursuing our examination of his dislike to what was evil, [we find] that he thought it necessary, if he were standing with a villager whose cap was not rightly adjusted, to leave him with a high air as if he were going to be defiled. Hence it was, that, though some of the princes made application to him with very proper messages, he would not accept [their invitations]. That refusal to accept [their invitations] was because he counted it inconsistent with his purity to go to them.[313]

2. "Hwuy of Lĕw-hĕa was not ashamed [to serve] an impure ruler, nor did he think it low to be in a small office. When called to employment, he did not keep his talents and virtue concealed, but made it a point to carry out his principles. When neglected and left out of

---

[307] CH. VIII. HOW SAGES AND WORTHIES DELIGHTED IN WHAT WAS GOOD. TO HELP OTHERS TO PRACTISE GOODNESS IS A GREAT INSTANCE OF VIRTUE.

[308] *Par.* 1. Tsze-loo's ardor in pursuing his self-improvement appears in Ana. V. xiii., and other places; but the particular point mentioned here is not mentioned anywhere else.

[309] *Par,* 2. See the Shoo, II. iii. 1.

[310] *Par.* 3. Shun's distinction was that he did not think of himself as Tsze loo did, nor of others as Yu did, but only of what was good, and was unconsciously carried to it wherever he saw it.

[311] *Par.* 4. It is related of Shun that in his early days he ploughed at the foot of the Leih mountain, did potter's work on the banks of the Ho, fished in the Luy lake, made various implements on the Show mountain, and often resided at Foo-hĕa. There will be occasion to consider where these places were in connection with some of Mencius' future references to him. On his elevation to be emperor see the first Book of the Shoo.

[312] CH. IX. PICTURES OF PIH-E AND HWUY OF LEW-HEA; AND MENCIUS' JUDGMENT CONCERNING THEM.

[313] *Par.* 1. Pih-e,—see on ch. ii. 22.

office, he did not murmur; and when straitened by poverty, he did not grieve. Accordingly, he would say, 'You are you, and I am I. Although you stand by my side with bare arms and breast, how can you defile me?' In this way, self-possessed, he associated with men indifferently, and did not feel that he lost himself. If pressed to remain in office, he would remain. He would remain in office when so pressed, because he did not feel that his purity required him to go away."[314]

3. Mencius said, "Pih-e was narrow-minded, and Hwuy of Lĕw-hĕa was wanting in self-respect. The superior man will not follow either narrow-mindedness or the want of self-respect."[315]

## BOOK II. KUNG-SUN CH'OW. PART II.

CHAPTER I.[316] 1. MENCIUS said, "Opportunities of time [vouchsafed by] Heaven are not equal to advantages of situation [afforded by] the earth, and advantages of situation [afforded by] the earth are not equal to the strength [arising from the] accord of men.[317]

2. "[There is a city], with an inner wall of three *le* in circumference and an outer wall of seven. [The enemy] surround and attack it, but are not able to take it. Now, to surround and attack it, there must have been vouchsafed to them by Heaven the opportunity of time, and in such case their not taking it is because opportunities of time [vouchsafed by] Heaven are not equal to advantages of situation [afforded by] the earth.[318]

3. "[There is a city] whose walls are as high and moats as deep as could be desired, and where the arms and mail [of its defenders] are distinguished for their sharpness and strength, and the [stores of] rice and grain are abundant; yet it has to be given up and. abandoned. This

---

[314] *Par.* 2. Hwuy of Lĕw-hĕa,—see on Ana. XV. xiii.; XVIII. ii.; viii.

[315] *Par.* 3. By "the superior man," Mencius, perhaps, tacitly refers to himself as having taken Confucius for his model. One commentator says on this paragraph;—"Elsewhere Mencius advises men to imitate E and Hwuy, but he is there speaking to the weak; when here he advises not to follow them, he is speaking for those who wish to do the right thing at the right time."

[316] CH. I. NO ADVANTAGES WHICH A RULER CAN OBTAIN FOR THE PURPOSE OF DEFENCE, OR TO EXALT HIM OVER OTHERS, ARE EQUAL TO HIS POSSESSING THE HEARTS OF MEN. Because of this chapter Mencius has got a place in China among the writers on the art of war, which surely he would not have wished to claim for himself, his design being to supersede the recourse to arms altogether.

[317] *Par.* 1. Chinese commentators have much to say about ascertaining the "time of Heaven" by divination and astrology; but all this is to be set aside as foreign to the mind of Mencius in the text, though many examples of the resort to those arts can be adduced from ancient records. "The accord of men" is the loyal union of the people with their ruler.

[318] *Par.* 2. The city here supposed, with its double circle of fortification, is a small one, the better to illustrate the superiority of advantage of situation, just as that in the next par. is a large one, to bring out the still greater superiority of the union of men. A city of the dimensions specified here was the capital of a baronial State.

is because advantages of situation [afforded by] the earth are not equal to the [strength arising from the] accord of men.

4. "In accordance with these principles it is said, 'A people is bounded in not by the limits of dykes and borders; a State is secured not by the strengths of mountains and streams; the kingdom is overawed not by the sharpness of arras [and strength] of mail.' He who finds the proper course has many to assist him, and he who loses it has few. When this—the being assisted by few—reaches the extreme point, [a ruler's] own relatives and connections revolt from him. When the being assisted by many reaches its extreme point, all under heaven become obedient [to the ruler].[319]

5. "When one to whom all under heaven are prepared to become obedient attacks one from whom his own relatives and connections are ready to revolt, [what must the result be?] Therefore the true ruler will [prefer] not [to] fight, but if he do fight, he is sure to overcome."

II.[320] 1. As Mencius was about to go to court to the king, the king sent a person to him with this message:—"I was wishing to come and see you. But I have got a cold, and may not expose myself to the wind. In the morning I will hold my court. I do not know whether you will give me the opportunity of seeing you?" [Mencius] replied, "Unfortunately I am unwell, and not able to go to court."[321]

2. Next day he went out to pay a visit of condolence to the Tung-kwoh family, when Kung-sun Ch'ow said to him, "Yesterday you declined [going to the court] on the ground of being unwell, and to-day you are paying a visit of condolence:—may not this be regarded as improper?" "Yesterday" said [Mencius], "I was unwell; to-day I am better:—why should I not pay this visit?"[322]

---

[319] *Par.* 4. "The proper course" intended is that style of government on the principles of benevolence and righteousness which is sure to unite the hearts of the people to their ruler. "Relatives" are relatives by blood; "connections," merely relatives by affinity.

[320] CH. II. HOW MENCIUS CONSIDERED THAT IT WAS SLIGHTING HIM FOR THE KING OF TS'E TO CALL HIM BY MESSENGERS TO GO TO COURT TO SEE HIM; AND THE SHIFTS HE WAS PUT TO TO GET THIS UNDERSTOOD. It must be understood that Mencius was in Ts'e simply as an honored guest, in his capacity of teacher or philosopher, and had not accepted any official position with the salary attached to it. It was for him to pay his respects at court, if he wished to do so; but if the king wished to show him respect and to ask his counsel, it was for him to go to him, and beg his instructions.

[321] *Par.* 1. The morning, as soon as it was light, was the regular time for the king and feudal princes to give audience to their ministers and officers, and arrange about the administration of affairs; and this is also the modern practice in China. The king's saying that he had a cold was merely a pretence;—he wanted to get Mencius to come to him. Mencius' saying that he was unwell was equally a pretence. Compare Confucius' conduct in Ana. XVII. xx.

[322] *Par.* 2. Tung-kwoh was a clan name in Ts'e, taking its rise from the quarter where the founder of it had lived. Some member of the family had died, and Mencius now went to it to pay a visit of condolence, that the king might hear of his doing so, and understand the lesson he had meant to give him the day before by saying that he was

3. [In the mean time] the king sent a messenger to inquire about his illness, and a physician [also] came [from the court]. Măng Chung replied to them, "Yesterday, when the king's order came, he was feeling a little unwell, and could not go to the court. Today he was a little better and hastened to go to court. I do not know whether he can have reached it [by this time] or not." [Having said this,] he sent several men to intercept [Mencius] on the way, and say to him that he begged him, before he returned, to be sure and go to the court.[323]

4. [On this, Mencius] felt himself compelled to go to King Ch'ow's, and there stop the night. The officer King said to him, "In the family there is [the relation of] father and son; beyond it there is [that of] ruler and minister. These are the greatest relations among men. Between father and son the ruling principle is kindness; between ruler and minister the ruling principle is respect. I have seen the respect of the king to you, Sir, but I have not seen in what way you show respect to him." The reply was, "Oh! what words are these? Among the people of Ts'e there is no one who speaks to the king about benevolence and righteousness. Is it because they think that benevolence and righteousness are not admirable? No; but in their hearts they say, 'This man is not fit to be spoken with about benevolence and righteousness.' Thus they manifest a disrespect than which there can be none greater. I do not dare to set forth before the king any but the ways of Yaou and Shun. There is therefore no man of Ts'e who respects the king so much as I do."[324]

5. King-tsze said, "Not so; that was not what I meant. In the Book of Rites it is said, 'When a father calls, the son must go to him without a moment's hesitation; when the prince's order calls, the carriage must not be waited for.' You were certainly going to court, but when you heard the king's message, you did not carry the purpose out. This does seem as if your conduct were not in accordance with that rule of propriety."[325]

---

unwell. The disciple did not understand the reason of his proceeding, and our philosopher, we think, had better have told it to him plainly than go on to further prevarication.

[323] *Par.* 3. Măng Chung must have been a near relative of Mencius:—some say that he was a son; others, a nephew. "He was a little unwell" is in Chinese "he had anxiety about gathering firewood." To do this was the business of the children of the common people, from which sickness alone could give them a dispensation. Used of Mencius it was an expression of humility. Neither did Măng Chung understand the conduct of his father or uncle; and having committed himself to a falsehood about it, he took the step which is related to get Mencius to go to court to make his own words good.

[324] *Par.* 4. Mencius was resolved that the king should know the reason of his not going to court; and as the words of Măng Chung interfered with his first plan for that purpose, he now went to another officer of Ts'e whose acquaintance he enjoyed, and talked the matter over with him fully, that through him the whole thing might reach the king's ears.

[325] *Par.* 5. The passages quoted by the officer King from the Book of Rites (I. Pt I.

6. [Mencius] answered him, "How can you give that meaning to my conduct? The philosopher Tsăng said, 'The wealth of Tsin and Ts'oo cannot be equaled. Their [rulers] have their wealth, and I have my benevolence. They have their rank; and I have my righteousness. Wherein should I be dissatisfied [as inferior to them]? Now were these sentiments not right? Seeing that the philosopher Tsăng gave expression to them, there is in them, I apprehend, a [real] principle. Under heaven there are three things universally acknowledged to be honorable:—rank; years; and virtue. In courts, rank holds the first place of the three; in villages, years; and for helping one's generation and presiding over the people, virtue. How can the possession of only one of them be presumed on to despise one who possesses the other two?

7. "Therefore, a prince who is to accomplish great deeds will certainly have ministers whom he does not call to go to him. When he wishes to consult with them, he goes to them. [The ruler] who does not honor the virtuous and delight in their ways of doing to this extent is not worth having to do with.

8. "Accordingly, so did T'ang behave to E Yin:—he learned of him, and then employed him as his minister, and so without difficulty he became king. And so did duke Hwan behave to Kwan Chung:—he learned of him, and then employed him as his minister, and so without difficulty he became leader of the princes.[326]

9. "Now throughout the kingdom [the territories of] the princes are of equal extent and in their achievements they are on a level. Not one of them is able to exceed the others. This is from no other reason but that they love to make ministers of those whom they teach, and do not love to make ministers of those by whom they might be taught.[327]

10. "So did T'ang behave to E Yin, and duke Hwan to Kwan Chung, that they would not venture to call them [to them]. If even Kwan Chung could not be called to him [by his ruler], how much less may he be called who would not play the part of Kwan Chung!"[328]

III.[329] 1. Ch'in Tsin asked [Mencius], saying, "Formerly, when you

---

iii. 14; XIII. iii. 2) were not fully applicable to Mencius, who did not consider himself a minister of Ts'e. He was there as an honored visitor, and would only take office if he saw reason to believe that the king would follow his counsels.

[326] *Par.* 8. We are told that it was only after T'ang had five times solicited the presence of E Yin by special messengers that that worthy was induced to go to him. See the confidence reposed by duke Hwan in Kwan Chung in Pt I. i. 3. Kwan was taken to Ts'e originally as a prisoner to be put to death, but the duke, knowing his ability and worth, had determined to make him his chief minister, and therefore, having first caused him to be relieved of his fetters, he drove himself out of his capital and met him with all distinction, listening to a long discourse from him on government.

[327] *Par.* 9. All things were ready for one prince to exceed all the others, and to be made king; but no one would follow the counsels of Mencius which would have resulted in such an issue.

[328] *Par.* 10. Compare Pt I. i. 4.

[329] CH. III. BY WHAT PRINCIPLES MENCIUS WAS GUIDED IN RECEIVING OR

were in Ts'e, the king sent you a present of 2,000 taels of fine silver, and you refused to accept it. When you were in Sung, 1,400 taels were sent to you, which you accepted; and when you were in Sëeh, 1,000 taels were sent, which you [likewise] accepted. If your declining the gift in the first case was right, your accepting it in the latter cases was wrong. If your accepting it in the latter cases was right, your declining it in the first case was wrong. You must accept, Master, one of these alternatives."[330]

2. Mencius said, "I did right in all the cases.

3. "When I was in Sung, I was about to take a long journey. Travellers must be .provided with what is necessary for their expenses. The [prince's] message was—'A present against travelling expenses.' Why should I not have received it?[331]

4. "When I was in Sëeh, I was apprehensive for my safety, and wished to take measures for my protection. The message [with the gift] was—'I have heard that you are apprehensive for your safety, and therefore I send you this to help you in procuring weapons.' Why should I not have received it?

5. "But as to the case in Ts'e, I had then no occasion for money. To send a man a gift, when he has no occasion for it, is to bribe him. How can one claim to be a superior man, and allow himself to be taken with a bribe?"

IV.[332] 1. Mencius, having gone to P'ing-luh, said to the governor of it, "If [one of] your spearmen should lose his place in the ranks three times in one day, would you, Sir, put him to death or not?" "I would not wait till he had done so three times," was the reply.[333]

---

DECLINING THE GIFTS TENDERED TO HIM BY THE PRINCES. The practice of receiving gifts from the princes whom he condemned was one of the weak points in Mencius' life, and his disciples were evidently stumbled by it. He had always something to say, however, in reply to their doubts and questions;—ingenious, if not altogether satisfactory.

[330] *Par.* 1. Ch'in Tsin was one of Mencius' disciples, but this is all that is known of him. Nor can we tell to what period of our philosopher's life this conversation should be referred. Fine silver, is, literally, "double metal;" *i.e.*, silver (not gold) worth twice as much as that in ordinary circulation. Sung was the dukedom over which the representatives of the kings of the Shang dynasty ruled, having as its capital Shang-këw, which name remains in the district so called of the department Kwei-tih in Ho-nan. Sëeh,—see on I. Pt II. xiv. 1. I suppose that though Sëeh in Mencius' time belonged to Ts'e the descendants of its former princes were permitted to administer it, and that it was one of them who sent to him the present here mentioned.

[331] *Parr.* 3-5. These contain the explanation which Mencius gives of his conduct. He took gifts when he had occasion for them;—it would have been better if he had not taken them at all.

[332] CH. IV. HOW MENCIUS BROUGHT CONVICTION OF THEIR FAULTS TO AN OFFICER OF TS'E AND TO THE KING. This brief chapter is a good instance of Mencius' manner, and of the ingenuity which he displayed in bringing his counsels before those whom he wished most to influence.

[333] *Par.* 1. P'ing-luh was a city—one of those called *capitals*, as having in them an ancestral temple of the princes of the State—in the south of Ts'e, somewhere, probably,

2. [Mencius] continued, "Well then, you, Sir, have lost your place in the ranks many times. In calamitous years and years of famine, the old and feeble of your people who have been found lying in ditches and water-channels, and the able-bodied who have been scattered about to the four quarters, have amounted to thousands." "This is not a case in which I, Keu-sin, can take it upon me to act."[334]

3. "Here," said [Mencius], "is a man who receives charge of the sheep and cattle of another, and undertakes to feed them for him;—of course he must seek for pasture-ground and grass for them. If, after seeking for these, he cannot find them, will he return his charge to the owner? or will he stand [by] and see them die?" "Herein," said [the governor], "I am guilty."[335]

4. Another day Mencius had an audience of the king, and said to him, "Of the governors of your Majesty's cities I am acquainted with five; but the only one who knows his fault is K'ung Keu-sin." He then related to the king the conversation which he had had [with that officer], and the king said, "In this matter I am the guilty one."

V.[336] 1. Mencius said to Ch'e Wa, "There seemed to be reason in your declining [the governorship] of Ling-k'ew, and requesting to be appointed chief criminal judge, because the [latter office] would afford you the opportunity of speaking your mind. But now several months have elapsed; and have you found nothing about which you might speak?"[337]

2. [On this] Ch'e Wa remonstrated [on some matter] with the king; and, his counsel not being taken, he resigned his office, and went away.[338]

---

in the present department of Yen-chow. Its governor or commandant, presiding also over the country around it, was K'ung Keu-sin.

[334] *Par.* 2. The governor's saying that the case which Mencius described was not one in which he could act meant that the measures to provide for it, such as opening the public granaries, could only emanate from the king.

[335] *Par.* 3. Mencius wished the governor to understand that he ought not in such circumstances to retain his office.

[336] CH. V. THE FREEDOM WHICH MENCIUS CLAIMED FOR HIMSELF IN RETAINING HIS POSITION IN TS'E, NOTWITHSTANDING OBJECTIONABLE MEASURES OF THE KING, WAS BECAUSE HE WAS UNSALARIED.

[337] *Par.* 1. Of Ch'e Wa we only know what is related here. Ling-k'ew was a city in the borders of Ts'e, remote from the court. Ch'e Wa had been governor of it, but got himself appointed chief criminal judge, wishing to be near the king, with whom this office would give him the opportunity to remonstrate on measures of which he did not approve. Perhaps he found it easier to resolve to discharge that disagreeable duty, than to carry the resolution into practice.

[338] *Parr.* 2-4. Ch'e Wa, stimulated by Mencius, did remonstrate and then felt it necessary to retire from office. We cannot wonder at the remarks of the people on Mencius' conduct.

Kung-too was one of his disciples with whom we shall meet again. Mencius thought highly of him, but this is nearly all we know about him. He appears to have been descended from a prince of Ts'oo, who held the city of Too; and hence the surname.

3. The people of Ts'e said, "In the course which he marked out for Ch'e Wa he did well; but as to the course which he pursues for himself, we do not know."

4. His disciple Kung Too told him these remarks.

5. [Mencius] said, "I have heard that when he, who is in charge of an office, is prevented from performing its duties, he should take his departure, and that he on whom is the responsibility of giving his opinions, when his words are disregarded, should do the same. [But] I am in charge of no office, and on me is no responsibility to speak out my views;—may not I act freely and without restraint either in going forward or in retiring?"

VI.[339] 1. Mencius, occupying the position of a high dignitary in Ts'e, went from it on a mission of condolence to T'ăng, and the king sent Wang Hwan, governor of Kah, [with him] as assistant-commissioner. Wang Hwan, morning and evening, waited upon him, but, during all the way to T'ăng and back to Ts'e, [Mencius] never spoke to him about the affairs of the mission.[340]

2. Kung-sun Ch'ow said [to Mencius], "The position of a high dignitary of Ts'e is not a small one, and the way from Ts'e to T'ăng is not short;—how was it that during all the way from Ts'e to T'ăng and back, you never spoke [to Hwan] about the affairs of the mission?" "There were the proper parties to attend to them; why should I speak [to him about them]?"[341]

VII.[342] 1. Mencius [went] from Ts'e to bury [his mother] in Loo. When he returned to Ts'e, he stopped at Ying, and Ch'ung Yu begged [to put a question to] him, saying, "Formerly, in ignorance of my incompetency, you employed me to superintend the business of making the coffin. As [you were then pressed by] the urgency [of the business], I did not venture to put any question to you; but now I wish to take the liberty to submit the matter. The wood, it appeared to me, was too good."[343]

---

[339] CH. VI MENCIUS' BEHAVIOUR TOWARDS AN UNWORTHY ASSOCIATE.

[340] *Par.* 1. Mencius' situation as a "noble" or "high dignitary" of Ts'e appears to have been honorary only, without emolument, and the king employed him on this occasion to give weight by his character to the mission. But he associated with him Wang Hwan, an unworthy favorite. I think Mencius had better have declined the mission, and escaped from the association altogether, than behave as he did.

[341] *Par.* 2. Chaou K'e understands the first part of Mencius' reply to Ch'ow as relating to Wang Hwan, and = "The fellow attended to them—managed them—himself;" but the interpretation followed in the version is more natural, and in harmony with the ordinary usage of the terms.

[342] CH. VII. THAT ONE OUGHT TO DO HIS UTMOST IN THE BURIAL OF HIS PARENTS;—ILLUSTRATED BY THE STYLE IN WHICH MENCIUS BURIED HIS MOTHER. Compare I. Pt II. xvi.

[343] *Par.* 1. The tradition is that Mencius had had his mother with him in Ts'e, and that on her death he carried the coffin to the family sepulchre in Tsow, which now was part of Loo. How long he remained in Loo is uncertain; perhaps the whole three years

2. [Mencius] replied, "Anciently, there was no rule for [the thickness of] either the inner or the outer coffin. In middle antiquity, the inner coffin was made seven inches thick, and the outer the same. This was done by all from the son of Heaven down to the common people, and not simply for the beauty of the appearance, but because they thus satisfied [the natural feelings of] the human heart.[344]

3. "If prevented [by statutory regulations] from making their coffins thus, men cannot have the feeling of pleasure; and if they have not the money [to make them thus], they cannot have that feeling. When they were not prevented, and had the money, the ancients all used this style;—why should I alone not do so?

4. "And moreover, is this alone no satisfaction to a man's heart—to prevent the earth from getting near to the bodies of his dead?

5. "I have heard that the superior man will not for all the world be niggardly to his parents."

VIII.[345] 1. Shin T'ung, on his private authority, asked [Mencius], saying, "May Yen be attacked?" Mencius said, "It may. Tsze-k'wae had no right to give Yen to another man; and Tsze-che had no right to receive Yen from Tsze-k'wae. [Suppose] there were an officer here, with whom you, Sir, were pleased, and that, without announcing the matter to the king, you were privately to give to him your salary and rank, and [suppose that] this officer, also without the king's orders, were privately to receive them from you;—would [such a transaction] be allowable? And where is the difference between [the case of Yen and] this?"[346]

---

proper to the mourning for a parent. Ying was a city in the south of Ts'e, and it is also disputed whether his stopping at it was for a night merely, or for a longer period. Ch'ung Yu was one of Mencius' disciples, and it has been deemed strange, if the philosopher completed the period of mourning in Loo, that Yu should have submitted his doubts to him after the lapse of so long a time. But it has been replied that this only illustrates how fond Mencius' disciples were of applying to him for a solution of their doubts; and the instance of Ch'in Tsin in chapter iii. is another case in point of the length of time they would keep things in mind. The different speculations on the points thus indicated are endless.

[344] *Par.* 2. "Middle antiquity" commences with the Chow dynasty, and Mencius has reference especially to the statutes settled by the duke of Chow for the regulation of funeral and other rites; though what he says about the equal thickness of the inner and outer coffins does not agree with what we find in the Le Ke, XXII. ii. 31. It must be borne in mind also that seven inches of the Chow dynasty were only equal to rather more than four inches of the present day.

[345] CH. VIII. EVEN DESERVED PUNISHMENT OUGHT NOT TO BE INFLICTED BY ANY BUT THE PROPER AUTHORITY. AN OFFENDING STATE CAN ONLY BE ATTACKED BY THE MINISTER OF HEAVEN;—ILLUSTRATED FROM THE CASE OF TS'E AND YEN. See on Book 1. Pt II. x. and xi. This chapter should come in perhaps, in point of time, before ch. x. there. Tsze-k'wae was the name of the weak king of Yen who had resigned his portion to his favorite minister Tsze-che.

[346] *Par.* 1. Shin T'ung must have been a minister of Ts'e; and though he consulted Mencius, as is here related, about attacking Yen, on his own private impulse, he must have informed the king and others of the answer of the philosopher which was supposed

2. The people of Ts'e attacked Yen, and some one asked [Mencius] saying, "Is it true that you advised Ts'e to attack Yen?" He replied, "No. Shin T'ung asked me whether Yen might be attacked, and I replied that it might, on which they proceeded to attack it. If he had asked me who might attack it, I would have answered him that the minister of Heaven might do so. Suppose the case of a murderer, and that one asked me, 'May this man be put to death?' I would answer him, 'He may.' If he [further] asked me, 'Who may put him to death?' I would answer him, 'The chief criminal judge.' But now with [one] Yea to attack [another] Yen:—how should I have advised this?"[347]

IX.[348] 1. The people of Yen having rebelled, the king said, "I am very much ashamed [when I think] of Mencius"[349]

2. Ch'in Kĕa said [to him], "Let not your Majesty be troubled. Whether does your Majesty consider yourself or the duke of Chow the more benevolent and wise?" The king replied, "Oh! what words are these?" [Ch'in Kĕa] rejoined, "The duke of Chow employed Kwan-shuh to over-see [the heir of] Yin, but Kwan-shuh rebelled with [the people of] Yin. If, knowing [that this would happen], he yet employed him, he was not benevolent. If he employed him without knowing it, he was not wise. The duke of Chow was [thus] not perfectly benevolent and wise, and how much less can your Majesty be expected to be so! I beg to [go and] see Mencius, and relieve [your Majesty] of that [feeling]."[350]

3. [Accordingly] he saw Mencius, and asked him, saying, "What kind of man was the duke of Chow?" "An ancient sage," was the reply. "Is it true," pursued [the other], "that he employed Kwan-shuh to oversee [the heir of] Yin, and that Kwan-shuh rebelled with [the people of] Yin?" "It is," said [Mencius]. [Ch'in Kĕa] asked, "Did the duke of Chow know that he would rebel, and [thereupon] employ him?" "He

---

to justify the movement of Ts'e against the neighboring State.

[347] *Par.* 2. Compare what Mencius did really say to the king of Ts'e on the subject of his appropriating the vanquished Yen in I. Pt II. x. and xi.

[348] CH. IX. How MENCIUS EXPOSED THE ATTEMPT TO ARGUE IN EXCUSE OF ERRORS AND MISCONDUCT:—REFERRING ALSO TO THE CASE OF TS'E AND YEN. This chapter should come in after ch. xi. of I. Pt. II.

[349] *Par.* 1. The king was naturally ashamed of himself for having misinterpreted what Mencius had said to Shin T'ung, and neglected the advice which he had given to himself.

[350] *Par.* 2. Ch'in Kĕa was, like Shin T'ung, an officer of Ts'e. The case of the duke of Chow to which Kĕa referred was this:—On king Woo's extinction of the dynasty of Shang, having spared the life of the son of the last sovereign, he farther conferred on him the small State of Yin from which the dynasty had taken one of its names, but placed him under the surveillance of two of his own brothers, Sĕen and Too, one of them older and the other younger than another brother, Tan the duke of Chow, by whose advice, we must understand, the step was taken. Sĕen has come down to us with the title of Kwan-shuh, Kwan being the name of the principality which he had received for himself. After Woo's death, Sĕen and Too joined the heir of Yin in rebelling against the new dynasty, when the duke of Chow took action against them, put the former to death and banished the other.

did not know it," was the reply. "Then though a sage, he still fell into error." "The duke of Chow," said [Mencius], "was the younger brother, and Kwan-shuh the elder. Was not the error of the duke of Chow reasonable?[351]

4. "Moreover, when the superior men of old had errors, they reformed them; but when the superior men of the present day have errors, they persist in them. The errors of the superior men of old were like the eclipses of the sun and moon. All the people witness them; and when they have resumed their usual appearance, all the people look up to them [with their former admiration]. But do superior men of the present day merely persist [in their errors]?—they go on to make excuses for them as well."[352]

X.[353] 1. Mencius gave up his office [in Ts'e], and [was preparing to] return [to his native State].[354]

2. The king went to see him, and said, "Formerly I wished to see you, but found no opportunity to do so. When I got that opportunity, and stood by you in the same court, I was exceedingly glad. [But] now again you are abandoning me and returning home;—I do not know if here-after I may have another opportunity of seeing you." "I do not venture to make any request," was the reply, "but indeed it is what I desire."[355]

3. Another day, the king said to the officer She, "I wish to give Mencius a house in the centre of the kingdom, and to support his disciples with [an allowance of] 10,000 *chung*, so that all the great officers and people may have [such an example] to reverence and imitate. Had you not better tell him this for me?"[356]

---

[351] *Par.* 3. What Mencius means in the conclusion of this paragraph is, that brother ought not to be suspicious of brother, and that it is better, between brothers, to be deceived than to impute evil.

[352] *Par.* 4. In the phrase—"the superior men of the present day," "the superior men" has to be taken vaguely, and merely means—those who wish to be regarded as superior men.

[353] CH X. MENCIUS, IN LEAVING A STATE OR REMAINING IN IT, WAS NOT INFLUENCED BY PECUNIARY CONSIDERATIONS, BUT BY THE OPPORTUNITY DENIED OR ACCORDED TO HIM OF CARRYING HIS LESSONS INTO PRACTICE:—ILLUSTRATED BY THE CIRCUMSTANCES ATTENDING HIS LEAVING TS'E.

[354] *Par.* 1. Mencius had given the king of Ts'e a long trial, and it was clear that nothing really great was to be accomplished with him. He therefore resigned his honorary office, and prepared to withdraw from the State or kingdom. I think I have given the true meaning of the paragraph. Chaou K'e indeed makes the "returning" to be only to Mencius' own house in the capital of Ts'e; but according to that view, the "I do not venture to make any request," in the next par. = "I do not venture to ask you to come again in person to see me;" which is surely flat and absurd.

[355] *Par.* 2. Mencius sees that the king, with all his complimentary expressions, is really bidding him adieu, and answers accordingly, in as complimentary a way, intimating his purpose to be gone.

[356] *Par.* 3. The king after all does not like the idea of Mencius' going away, and thinks of this plan to retain him, which was in reality what Mencius calls in ch. iii. trying

4. The officer She conveyed this message by means of the disciple Ch'in, who reported his words to Mencius.[357]

5. Mencius said, "Yes; but how should the officer She know that the thing may not be? Supposing that I wanted to be rich, having declined 100,000 *chung*, would my accepting 10,000 be the conduct of one desiring riches?[358]

6. "Ke-sun said, 'A strange man was Tsze-shuh E! Suppose that he himself was a high minister, if [his prince would] no longer employ him, he had to retire; but he would again [try to] get one of his younger relatives to be high minister. Who indeed is there of men that does not wish to be rich and noble, but he only, among the rich and noble, sought to monopolize the conspicuous mound.'[359]

7. "In old time the market-dealers exchanged the articles which they had for others which they had not, and simply had certain officers to keep them in order. There was a mean fellow, who made it a point to look out for a conspicuous mound, and get up upon it. Thence he looked right and left to catch in his net the whole gain of the market. People all thought his conduct mean, and therefore they proceeded to lay a tax upon his wares. The taxing of traders took its rise from this mean fellow."[360]

XI.[361] 1. Mencius, having left [the capital of] T'se, was passing the night in Chow.[362]

---

to take him with a bribe. She was an officer at the court of Ts'e.

The *chung* was the name of a large measure of grain, equal to 64 *tow* or pecks, amounting to about seven hundred-weight. "The centre of the kingdom" is to be understood of the capital, as in the She, III. ii. IX.

[357] *Par.* 4. "The disciple Ch'in" here is the Ch'in Tsin of ch. iii.

[358] *Par.* 5. Mencius does not care to state plainly here his real reason for going,—that he was not permitted to see his principles carried into practice; and therefore contents himself with repelling the idea that he was accessible to pecuniary considerations. 100,000 *chung* was the regular allowance for a high minister, which Mencius had declined to receive.

[359] *Par.* 6. Ke-sun was the clan name of the greatest of the families of Loo, but which of the Heads of that clan was here intended we do not know. Tsze-shuh was also a clan name in Loo, but of E, the member of it who is mentioned, we know nothing beyond what is here told. Mencius quotes the remarks of Ke-sun about Tsze-shuh E, to show that they would be applicable to himself, if he were to take the course suggested to him from the king of Ts'e. Chaou K'e makes out Ke-sun and Tsze-shuh to have been disciples of Mencius, and according to his view we should have to translate, "Ke-sun said, 'How strange [is this course]!'" Tsze-shuh [also] doubted [about it]. "Suppose," [they thought,] "he himself is no longer employed as a high minister, let him go away, but let him get his disciples into the situation," &c. But all this is plainly inadmissible.

[360] *Par.* 7. Mencius here explains the expression in the end of Ke-sun's speech about "monopolizing the conspicuous mound,"—explains it in a way to show still more pointedly his sense of the proposal of the king of Ts'e.

[361] CH. XI. HOW MENCIUS REPELLED A MAN, WHO, OFFICIOUSLY AND ON HIS OWN IMPULSE, WISHED TO DETAIN HIM IN TS'E.

[362] *Par.* 1. Chow was a city on the south-western border of Ts'e, at which Mencius had arrived in his progress to Loo. He had conducted his departure leisurely, hoping that

2. A person who wished for the king to detain him [came and] sat down [to speak with him]. [Mencius] gave him no answer, but leant upon his stool and slept.[363]

3. The stranger was displeased, and said, "I have fasted for two days before I would venture to speak with you, and [now], Master, you sleep and do not listen to me. Allow me to request that I may not again presume to see you." [Mencius] said, "Sit down, and I will explain the matter clearly to you. Formerly, if duke Muh of Loo had not had persons [continually] by the side of Tsze-sze, he could not have kept Tsze-sze [in his State]; and if Sëeh Lëw and Shin Ts'ëang had not had persons by the side of duke Muh, they would not have been able to feel at rest [in remaining in Loo].[364]

4. "You, Sir, are concerned and plan about an old man like me, but I have not been treated as Tsze-sze was. Is it you, Sir, who cut me? Or is it I who cut you?"[365]

XII.[366] 1. Mencius having left Ts'e, Yin Sze spake about him to others, saying, "If he did not know that the king could not be made a T'ang or a Woo, that showed his want of intelligence. If he knew that he could not be made such, and yet came [to Ts'e] notwithstanding, that he was seeking for favors. He came a thousand *le* to wait upon the king. Because he did not find in him the ruler he wished, he took his leave. Three nights he stayed, and then passed from Chow;—how dilatory and lingering [was his departure]! I am dissatisfied on account of this."[367] [368]

---

the king would recall him ere he had left the State, and pledge himself to follow his counsels.

[363] *Par.* 2. Who the person that thus intruded himself into Mencius' company was we do not know. All that is meant by "for the king" is that he knew that it would please the king if he could induce Mencius to remain. "Leant upon his stool;"—the stool was small, and could be carried in the hand. Parties leant forward, or back, on it, as they sat upon the mat, which was spread for them on the floor.

[364] *Par.* 3. "I fasted for two days" is literally "I fasted and passed the night;" that is, "I fasted over the night," = "I have fasted two days." Tsze-sze was the well-known grandson of Confucius. Shin Ts'ëang was the son of Tsze-chang, one of Confucius' disciples. Sëeh Lew was also a native of Loo. and belonged to the Confucian school. Tsze-sze required great respect to be shown to him, and he had an attendant appointed by duke Muh always in waiting on him, to assure him of the respect with which he was cherished. The two others had not such attendants, but they knew that there were always officers by the duke's side to admonish him not to forget them.

[365] *Par.* 4. The stranger's thinking that he could retain Mencius, without any such demonstrations from the king, show how little store he set by the philosopher,—was really cutting him.

[366] CH. XII. HOW MENCIUS EXPLAINED HIS SEEMING TO LINGER IN TS'E AFTER HE HAD RESIGNED HIS OFFICE AND QUITTED THE COURT.

[367] *Par.* 1. Nothing more can be said of Yin Sze than that he was a man, a scholar, of Ts'e. What he chiefly charged against Mencius was the lingering nature of his departure.

[368] *Par.* 2. The disciple Kaou appears again in VII. Pt II. xxi., from which it would appear that there was something not satisfactory about him.

3. The disciple Kaou informed [Mencius] of these remarks.[369]

4. [Mencius] said, "How should Yin Sze know me? When I came a thousand *le* to see the king, it was what I desired to do. When I went away, not finding in him the ruler that I wished, was that what I desired to do? I felt myself constrained to do it.

5. "When I stayed three nights before I passed from Chow, in my own mind I still considered my departure speedy. I was hoping that the king might change. If the king had changed, he would certainly have recalled me.

6. "When I passed from Chow, and the king had not sent after me, then, and only then, was my mind resolutely bent on returning [to Tsow]. But notwithstanding that, was I giving the king up? He is after all one who may be made to do what is good. If the king .were to use me, would it be for the happiness of the people of Ts'e only? It would be for the happiness of all under heaven. Would the king but change! I am daily hoping for this.

7. "Am I like one of your little-minded people? They will remonstrate with their ruler, and when their remonstrance is not accepted, they get angry, and with their passion displayed in their countenance, they take their leave, and travel with all their strength for a whole day before they will stop for the night."[370]

8. When Yin Sze heard this [explanation], he said, "I am indeed a small man."

XIII.[371] 1. When Mencius left Ts'e, Ch'ung Yu questioned him on the way, saying, "Master, you look like one who carries an air of dissatisfaction in his countenance. [But] formerly I heard you say that the superior man does not murmur against Heaven, nor cherish a grudge against men."[372]

2. [Mencius] said, "That was one time, and this is another.

3. "It is a rule that a true sovereign should arise in the course of five hundred years, and that during that time there should be men illustrious in their generation.[373]

---

[369] *Par.* 3. Mencius was constrained to leave Ts'e by the conviction forced at last upon him that he would not get the king to carry his counsels into practice.

[370] *Par.* 7. Compare with this paragraph Confucius' defense of Kwan Chung in Ana. XIV. xviii.

[371] CH. XIII. MENCIUS' GRIEF AT NOT FINDING THE OPPORTUNITY TO ACCOMPLISH FOR THE KINGDOM THE GOOD WHICH HE WAS CONSCIOUS HE HAD IN HIM THE POWER TO DO.

[372] *Par.* 1. Ch'ung Yu has appeared before in ch. vii. We find the saying which he here attributes to his master used by Confucius of himself in Ana. XIV. xxxvii. 2.

[373] *Par.* 3. "Five hundred years;"—this is speaking in round and loose numbers, even if we judge of the sentiment from the history of China prior to Mencius. "During that time" would seem to mean that, in addition to the true king, all along the centuries there would be men of distinguished ability and virtue; but Mencius is generally understood as referring to the men who should arise at the same time with the true sovereign, and assist him by their counsels.

4. "From the commencement of the Chow dynasty till now, more than seven hundred years have elapsed. Judging numerically, the date is passed. Considering the matter from the [character of the present] time, we might expect [a true king to arise].[374]

5. "But Heaven does not yet wish that tranquility and good order should prevail all under the sky. If it wished this, who is there besides me to bring it about? How should I be otherwise than dissatisfied?"[375]

XIV.[376] 1. When Mencius left Ts'e, he dwelt in Hĕw. [There] Kung-sun Ch'ow asked him, "Was it the way of the ancients to hold office without receiving salary?"[377]

2. [Mencius] said, "No. When I first saw the king in Ts'ung, it was my intention, on retiring from the interview, to go away. Because I did not wish to change this intention, I would not receive [any salary].[378]

3. "Immediately after, orders were issued for [the collection of] troops, when it would have been improper for me to beg [permission to leave]. [But] to remain long in Ts'e was not my purpose."[379]

---

[374] *Par.* 4. Nearly 800 years must have elapsed from the rise of the Chow dynasty, when Mencius thus spoke. He seems for the time to have been oblivious of Confucius; but he was merely a sage, and had not the power to carry out his principles on a grand scale. What had been wanting in his time, and was wanting still, was a true king.

[375] *Par.* 5. It cannot be said that Mencius had not a sufficiently high opinion of himself. Compare with this paragraph the sentiments of Confucius in Ana. IX. v.

[376] CH. XIV. THE REASON OF MENCIUS' HOLDING MERELY AN HONORARY OFFICE IN TS'E, WITHOUT RECEIVING SALARY, WAS BECAUSE FROM THE FIRST HE HAD LITTLE CONFIDENCE IN THE KING, AND WISHED TO BE FREE IN HIS MOVEMENTS.

[377] *Par.* 1. Hĕw was in the present district of T'ăng, in the department of Yen-chow. Kung-sun Ch'ow's inquiry, as appears from the style in the Chinese of Mencius' reply, was simply for information.

[378] *Par.* 2. Ts'ung was the name of a city in Ts'e, the situation of which cannot now be more exactly determined. There Mencius first met with king Seuen, and received an unfavorable impression of him.

[379] *Par.* 3. Perhaps "the collection of troops" was connected with Tse's relations with Yen. See the conversation of king Seuen with Mencius in I. Pt II. xi.; at such a time Mencius could not well ask leave to quit the State. Another interpretation of the phrase has been proposed, making it refer to the proposal to retain him in Ts'e, which is mentioned in ch. x.; but this is quite unreasonable.

## BOOK III. T'ÄNO WÄN KUNG.[380] PART I.

CHAPTER I.[381] 1. WHEN duke Wăn of T'ang was heir-son, being on a journey to Ts'oo he passed by [the capital of] Sung, and had an interview with Mencius.[382]

2. Mencius discoursed to him how the nature of man is good, and, in speaking, made laudatory appeal to Yaou and Shun.[383]

3. When the heir-son was returning from Ts'oo, he again saw Mencius, when the latter said to him, "Prince, do you doubt my words? The path is one, and only one.[384]

4. "Ch'ing Kan said to duke King of Ts'e, 'They were men, [and] I am a man;—why should I stand in awe of them?' (Yen Yuen said, 'What kind of man was Shun? What kind of man am I? He who exerts himself will also become such as he was.' Kung-ming E said, 'King Wăn is my teacher and model;—how should the duke of Chow deceive me [by these words]?'[385]

5. "Now T'ăng, taking its length with its breadth, will amount to

---

[380] The TITLE OF THE BOOK is taken from duke Wăn of T'ăng, who is prominent in the first three chapters of it Wăn of course is the honorary or sacrificial title which he received after his death. We have already met with him in confidential intercourse with Mencius, in chapters xiii. to xv. of Book I. Part II., the date of which must be subsequent to that of the chapters in this Book. Chaou K'e compares the title of this Book with that of the 15th Book of the Analects.

[381] CH. I. THAT ALL MEN BY DEVELOPING THEIR NATURAL GOODNESS MAY BECOME EQUAL TO THE ANCIENT SAGES. ADDRESSED BY MENCIUS TO THE HEIR-SON OF T'ĂNG.

[382] *Par.* 1. "Heir-son," and "eldest son" were applied indifferently to the eldest sons, or the declared successors, of the kings and feudal princes during the Chow dynasty. Since the Han dynasty, "heir-son" has been discontinued as a denomination of the eldest son of the emperor, the crown prince. Mencius at this time was in the State of Sung, and some have tried to fix the date of the chapter to B.C. 317. Ts'oo had so far extended its territories to the north, that it was there conterminous with T'ăng; but as the prince would be going to its capital it would not take him much out of his way to go through Sung. Possibly that route was the most convenient for him to take, though the language of the text would seem to be intended to give us the idea that he took it in order that he might see Mencius.

[383] *Par.* 2. For the full exposition of Mencius' doctrine of the goodness of human nature, see Book VI.

[384] *Par.* 3. We must suppose that Mencius had been told that the prince doubted the correctness of what he had said at their former interview; or it may be, the remark here preserved occurred in the course of a conversation, of the previous part of which we have no record. "The way is one and only one" probably means the way of human duty, the course to which Mencius felt that he ought to call all who wished to learn of him.

[385] *Par.* 4. Mencius here fortifies himself with the opinions of other worthies. Of Ch'ing Kan we know nothing but what we read here. Whom he intended by "they" we cannot well say. Yen Yuen was the favorite disciple of Confucius. Kung-ming E was a great officer of Loo, a disciple, first, of Tsze-chang, and afterwards of Tsăng-tsze. The remark about king Win's being his model and teacher would seem to have been made by the duke of Chow.

about fifty square le. [Though small,] it may still be made a good kingdom. It is said in the Book of History, 'If medicine do not distress the patient, it will not cure his sickness.'"[386]

II.[387] 1. When duke Ting of T'ăng died, the heir-son said to Jen Yĕw, "Formerly, Mencius spoke with me in Sung, and I have never forgotten his words. Now, alas! this great affair [of the death of my father] has happened, and I wish to send you, Sir, to ask Mencius, and then to proceed to the services [connected with it]."[388]

2. Jen Yĕw [accordingly] proceeded to Tsow, and consulted Mencius. Mencius said, "Is not this good? The mourning rites for parents are what men feel constrained to do their utmost in. The philosopher Tsăng said, 'When parents are alive, they should be served according to [the rules of] propriety; when dead, they should be buried, and they should be sacrificed to, according to the same:—this may be called filial piety.' I have not learned [for myself] the ceremonies to be observed by the feudal princes, but nevertheless I have heard these points:—Three years' mourning, with the wearing the garment of coarse cloth with its lower edge even, and the eating of thin congee, have been equally prescribed by the three dynasties, and are binding on all, from the son of Heaven to the common people."[389]

3. Jen Yĕw reported the execution of his commission, and [the prince] determined that the three years' mourning should be observed. His uncles and elder cousins, and the body of the officers, did not wish it, and said, "The former rulers of Loo, the State which we honor, have, none of them, observed this mourning, nor have any of our own former rulers observed it. For you to change their practice is improper; and moreover, the History says, 'In mourning and sacrifice ancestors are to be followed,' meaning that we have received those things from a

---

[386] *Par.* 5. "A good kingdom" is such an one as is described in ch. iii. For the quotation from the Book of History, see the Shoo, IV. viii. Pt I. 8. Mencius would seem to say that his lesson was all the more likely to be beneficial, because it had perplexed and disturbed the prince.

[387] CH. II. HOW MENCIUS ADVISED THE PRINCE OF T'ĂNG TO CONDUCT THE MOURNING FOR HIS FATHER WITH EVERY DEMONSTRATION OF GRIEF.

[388] *Par.* 1. Duke Ting was the father of duke Wăn, the heir-son of last chapter. Ting was his honorary epithet Jen Yĕw had been the prince's tutor.

[389] *Par.* 2. On children's feeling constrained to do their utmost in the mourning rites for their parents,—see Ana. XIX. xvii.

The remarks here attributed to Tsăng-tsze were at first addressed by Confucius to another disciple. Tsăng may have appropriated them, so that they came to be regarded as his own; or Mencius here makes a slip of memory. I suppose that Mencius means to say that he could not speak of the mourning rites of the princes from personal observation; but he could speak of the observances which were common to prince and peasant. "The three years' mourning,"—see Ana. XVII. xxi. "The garment of coarse cloth with the lower edge even" was that appropriate to the mourning for a mother, and less intense than that used in mourning for a father, when the lower edge was all frayed, as if chopped with a hatchet. It would appear, however, that either of the phrases might be used to denote mourning of the deepest kind;—see Ana. IX. ix.

[proper] source."[390]

4. [The prince again] said to Jen Yĕw, "Hitherto I have not given myself to the pursuit of learning, but have found my pleasure in driving my horses and in sword-exercise. Now my uncles and elder cousins and the body of officers are not satisfied with me. I am afraid I may not be able to carry out [this] great business; do you, Sir, [again go and] ask Mencius for me." Jen Yĕw went again to Tsow, and consulted Mencius, who said, "Yes, but this is not a matter in which he has to look to any one but himself. Confucius said, 'When a ruler died, his successor entrusted the administration to the prime minister. He sipped the congee, and his face looked very dark. He went to the [proper] place, and wept. Of all the officers and inferior employees there was not one who did not dare not to be sad, when [the prince thus] set them the example. What the superior loves, his inferiors will be found to love still more. The relation between superiors and inferiors is like that between, the wind and the grass. The grass must bend when the wind blows upon it.' The [whole thing] depends on the heir-son."[391]

5. Jen Yĕw returned with this answer to his commission, and the prince said, "Yes; it does indeed depend on me." For five months he dwelt in the shed, and did nonissue an order or a caution. The body of officers and his relatives [said], "He may be pronounced acquainted [with all the ceremonies] When the time of interment arrived, they came from all quarters to see it, with the deep dejection of his countenance, and the mournfulness of his wailing and weeping. Those who [had come from other States to] condole with him were greatly pleased.[392]

---

[390] *Par.* 3. The lords of T'ăng were descended from Shuh-sĕw, one of the sons of king Wăn, but by an inferior wife, while the duke of Chow, the ancestor of Loo, was in the true royal line; and hence all the other States ruled by descendants of king Wăn were supposed to look up to Loo. But we are not to suppose that the early princes of Loo and of T'ăng had not observed the mourning for three years. The remonstrants were wrong in attributing to them the neglect of later rulers. What "History" or "Record" they refer to we cannot tell. The last clause of the paragraph is not by any means clear. Chaou K'e mentions a view of it, which I have felt strongly inclined to adopt:—"[The prince] said, 'I have received my view from a [proper] source.'"

[391] *Par.* 4. In the quotations from Confucius, Mencius has blended different places in the Analects together, or enlarged them to suit his own purpose;—see Ana. XIV. xliii.; XII. xix.

[392] *Par.* 5. "The shed" was built of boards and straw, outside the centre door of the palace, against the surrounding wall, and this the mourning prince tenanted till the interment,—see the Le Ke, XXII. ii. 16. Choo He, at the close of his notes on this chapter, introduces the following remarks from the commentator Lin Che-k'e:—"In the time of Mencius, although the rites to the dead had fallen into neglect, yet the three years' mourning, with the sorrowing heart and afflictive grief, being the expression of what really belongs to man's mind, had not quite perished. Only, sunk in the slough of manners becoming more and more corrupt, men were losing all their moral nature without being conscious of it. When duke Wăn saw Mencius, and heard him speak of the goodness of man's nature, and of Yaou and Shun, that was the occasion of moving and

III.[393] 1. Duke Wăn of T'ăng asked [Mencius] about [the proper way of] governing a State.[394]

2. Mencius said, "The business of the people must not be remissly attended to. It is said in the Book of Poetry,[395]

'In the daytime collect the grass,
And at night twist it into ropes.
Then get up quickly on our roofs:—
We shall have to recommence our sowing.'

3. "The way of the people is this:—Those who have a certain livelihood have a fixed heart, and those who have not a certain livelihood have not a fixed heart. If they have not .a fixed heart, there is nothing which they will not do in the way of self-abandonment, of moral deflection, of depravity, and of wild license. When they have thus been involved in crime, to follow them up and punish them is to entrap the people. How can such a thing as entrapping the people be done under the rule of a benevolent man?[396]

4. "Therefore a ruler endowed with talents and virtue will be gravely complaisant and economical, showing a respectful politeness to his ministers, and taking from the people only according to definite

---

bringing forth his better heart; and, on this occasion of the death of his father, he felt sincerely all the stirrings of sorrow and grief. Then, moreover, when his older relatives and his officers wished not to act as he desired, he turned inwards to reprove himself, and lamented his former conduct which made him not be believed in his present course, not presuming to blame his officers and relatives:—although we must concede an extraordinary natural excellence and ability to him, yet his energy in learning must not be impeached. Finally, when we consider with what decision he acted at last, and how all, near aid far, who saw and heard him, were delighted to acknowledge and admire his conduct, we have an instance of how, when that which belongs to all men's minds is in the first place exhibited by one, others are brought, without any previous purpose, to the pleased acknowledgment and approval of it:—is not this a proof that it is indeed true that [the nature of man] is good?"

[393] CH. III. MENCIUS' LESSONS TO DUKE WĂN OF T'ĂNG FOR THE GOVERNMENT OF HIS STATE. AGRICULTURE AND EDUCATION ARE THE CHIEF POINTS TO BE ATTENDED TO. THE FORMER INDEED IS FUNDAMENTAL TO PROSPERITY, AND A STATE PROSPEROUS BY ITS AGRICULTURE IS THE PROPER FIELD FOR THE APPLIANCES OF EDUCATION.

[394] *Par.* 1. We must suppose that the three years of mourning have passed, and that the heir-son has fully taken his position as marquis of T'ăng, one of his first measures having been to get Mencius to come into his State.

[395] *Par.* 2. By "the business of the people" we must understand agriculture. The promotion this required the attention of the government before all other things. That promotion would involve the establishment of the agricultural system of the State or the best principles.

For the lines of poetry, see the She, I. xv. I. 7. They are not much to the point; but the whole ode to which they belong is understood as showing how attention to agriculture was the chief thing required in the kings of Chow.

[396] *Par.* 3. See I. Pt I. vii. 20. This paragraph shows how essential it was there should be a sure provision for the support of the people, and that therefore their business should not be remissly attended to.

regulations.[397]

5. "Yang Hoo said, 'He who seeks to be rich will not be benevolent; .and he who seeks to be benevolent will not be rich.'[398]

6. "[Under] the sovereigns of Hëa, [each farmer received] fifty acres, and contributed [a certain tax]. [Under] those of Yin, [each farmer received] seventy acres, and [eight families] helped [to cultivate the public acres]. Under those of Chow, [each farmer received] a hundred acres, and [the produce] was allotted in shares. In reality what was paid in all these was a tithe. The share system means division; the aid system means mutual dependence.[399]

7. "Lung-tsze said, 'For regulating the land there is no better system than that of mutual aid, and none worse than that of contributing a certain tax. According to the tax system it was fixed by taking the average of several years. In good years, when the grain lies about in abundance, much might be taken without its being felt to be oppressive, and the actual exaction is small. In bad years, when [the produce] is not sufficient to [repay] the manuring of the fields, this system still requires the taking of the full amount. When he who should be the parent of the people causes the people to wear looks of distress, and, after the whole year's toil, yet not to be able to nourish their parents, and moreover to set about borrowing to increase [their means of paying the tax]; till their old people and children are found lying in the ditches and water-channels:—where [in such a case] is his parental relation to the people?'[400]

---

[397] *Par.* 4 interjects two attributes of the good ruler, which are necessary to his carrying out the government which Mencius had at heart.

[398] *Par.* 5. This Yang Hoo is the Yang Ho of the Analects, XVII. i. A worthless man, he made the observation given with a bad object; but there was a truth in it, and Mencius adduces it for a good purpose.

[399] *Par.* 6. By the Hëa statutes, every (husbandman—head of a family—received 50 acres, and paid the produce of live of them, or one-tenth of the whole, to the government. This was called kung or tribute. Under the Shang dynasty, 630 acres were divided into nine portions of 70 acres each, the central portion belonging to the government, and being cultivated by the united labors of the holders of the other portions. Under the Chow dynasty, in the portions of the State distant from the capital eight husbandmen received each a hundred acres, and the same space in the centre was cultivated by them all together for the government. Yet they all united also in the cultivation of the other portions, and each one family received an equal share of the produce, the whole being divided into eight portions. Deducting twenty acres from the government portion which was given to the farmers for building huts on, &c., there remained eighty acres, or ten acres for the cultivation of each of the eight families; that is, in the country parts of the States of Chow the amount of the produce paid to the government was one-tenth. In the more central parts, however, the system of the Hëa dynasty was in force. According to the above accounts, the contribution under the Shang dynasty amounted to one-ninth, but there was, no doubt, some assignment of a portion of the public fields to the cultivators, which reduced it to one-tenth.

[400] *Par.* 7. Nothing certain is known of the Lung who is here introduced, but he was "an ancient worthy." He gives us an important point of information about the way in which the amount of contribution according to the Hëa system was determined, and

8. "As to the system of hereditary salaries, that is already observed in T'ăng.[401]

9. "It is said in the Book of Poetry,

'May it rain first on our public fields.
And then come to our private!'

It is only in the system of mutual aid, that there are the public fields, and from this passage we perceive that even in the Chow dynasty this system has been recognized.[402]

10. "Establish *ts'eang, seu, hëoh,* and *hëaou,*—[all these educational institutions]—for the instruction [of the people]. The name *ts'ëang* indicates nourishing; *hëaou* indicates teaching; and seu indicates archery. By the Hëa dynasty the name *hëaou* was used; by the Yin dynasty that of seu; and by the Chow dynasty that of *ts'ëang.* As to the *hëoh,* they belonged equally to the three dynasties, [and by that name]. The object of them all is to illustrate the [duties of the] human relations. When these are [thus] illustrated by superiors, mutual affection will prevail among the smaller people below.[403]

11. "Should a [true] king arise, he will certainly come and take an example [from you], and thus you will be the teacher of the [true] king.[404]

12. "It is said in the Book of Poetry,

'Although Chow was an old State,
The [favoring] appointment lighted on it recently.'

That is said with reference to king Wăn. Do you practise those things with vigour, and you will also give a new history to your State."

13. [The duke afterwards] sent Peih Chen to ask about the nine-squares system of dividing the land. Mencius said to him, "Since your ruler, wishing to put in practice a benevolent government, has made

---

shows how objectionable the whole system was.

[401] *Par.* 8. See on I. Pt II. v. 3.

[402] *Par.* 9. See the She, II. vi. VIII. 3. The quotation is intended to show that the system of cultivation according to the system of mutual aid, which Mencius recommended, though it was fallen in his time into disuse, had at one time obtained under the Chow dynasty.

[403] *Par.* 10. The pith of Mencius' advice here is that education should be provided for all, and that it might be provided with advantage, when measures had been taken for the support of all by husbandry. Ah to the names and characters of the different institutions which he mentions, the discussions are endless. When he speaks of the human relations being illustrated by superiors, it is foreign to the object of the paragraph to suppose that he means the illustration of them in their personal conduct;—he means, I think, the inculcation of them by the institution of those educational establishments.

[404] *Parr.* 11, 12 show what duke Wăn would be sure to accomplish by following the advice which he had received. See the She, III. i. I. 1.

choice of you, and put you into this employment, you must use all your efforts. Benevolent government must commence with the definition of the boundaries. If the boundaries be not defined correctly, the division of the land into squares will not be equal, and the produce [available for] salaries will not be evenly distributed. On this account, oppressive rulers and impure ministers are sure to neglect the defining of the boundaries. When the boundaries have been defined correctly, the division of the fields and the regulation of the salaries may be determined [by you] sitting [at your ease].[405]

14. "Although the territory of T'ăng be narrow and small there must be in it, I apprehend, men of a superior grade, and there must be in it country-men. If there were not men of a superior grade, there would be none to rule the country-men; if there were not country-men, there would be none to support the men of superior grade.[406]

15. "I would ask you, in the [purely] country districts, to observe the nine-squares division, having one square cultivated on the system of mutual aid; and in the central parts of the State, to levy a tenth, to be paid by the cultivators themselves.[407]

16. "From the highest officers downwards, each one must have [his] holy field, consisting of fifty acres.[408]

17. "Let the supernumerary males have [their] twenty-five acres.[409]

18. "On occasions of death, or of removing from one dwelling to another, there will be no quitting the district. In the fields of a district,

---

[405] *Par.* 13. Peih Chen must have been the minister employed by duke Wăn to organize the agricultural system of the State according to the views of Mencius. He is here sent to the philosopher to get more particular instructions for his guidance. On the nine-squares system of dividing the land, see the note on II. i. V. 2. By defining the boundaries must be meant, I think, the boundaries of each space of nine squares, and not, as Chaou K'e supposes, the boundaries of the State. How the unequal division of the fields would affect the salaries of officers we have not sufficient information on the subject to enable us to speak exactly. But it is difficult to conceive of the division of the fields of a State on this plan, especially when it had become pretty thickly peopled. The natural irregularities of the surface would be one great obstacle. and we find, below, "the holy field," and other assignments, which must continually have been requiring new arrangements of the boundaries.

[406] *Par.* 14. "Men of a superior grade" are men in office, who did not have to earn their bread by the sweat of their brow. All other classes may be supposed to be comprehended under the denomination of country-men.

[407] *Par.* 15. See the note on par. 6.

[408] *Par.* 16. These 50 acres were in addition to the hereditary salary alluded to in par. 8. I call them "the holy field," because Chaou K'e and Choo He explain the term by which they are called by "pure," and the produce was intended to supply the means of sacrifice. Other explanations of the term have been proposed.

[409] *Par.* 17. A family was supposed to consist of the grandfather and grandmother, the husband, wife, and children, the husband being the grandparents' eldest son. The extra fields were for other sons of the grandparents, and were given to them when they reached the age of sixteen. When they married and became the heads of families themselves, they received the regular allotment of a family. In the mean time they were called "supernumerary males." Other explanations of this phrase have been proposed.

those who belong to the same nine-squares render all friendly offices to one another in their going out and coming in, aid one another in keeping watch and ward, and sustain one another in sickness. Thus the people will be led to live in affection and harmony.[410]

19. "A square le covers nine squares of land, which nine squares contain nine hundred acres. The central square contains the public fields; and eight families, each having its own hundred acres, cultivate them together. And it is not till the public work is finished that they presume to attend to their private fields. [This is] the way by which the country-men are distinguished [from those of a superior grade].[411]

20. "These are the great outlines [of the system]. Happily to modify and adapt them depends on your ruler and you."

IV.[412] 1. There came from Ts'oo to T'ăng one Heu Hing, who gave out that he acted according to the words of Shin-nung. Coming right to his gate, he addressed duke Wăn, saying, "A man of a distant region, I have heard that you, O ruler, are practicing a benevolent government, and I wish to receive a site for a house, and to become one of your people." Duke Wăn gave him a dwelling-place. His disciples, amounting to several tens, all wore clothes of hair-cloth, and made sandals of hemp and wove mats for a living.[413]

---

[410] *Par.* 18 sets forth various social and moral advantages flowing from the nine-squares division of the land.

[411] *Par.* 19. Under the Chow dynasty, 100 *poo*, or paces, made the length or Bide of a mow, or acre; but the exact length of the pace is not exactly determined. Some will have it that the 50 acres of Hĕa, the 70 of Shang, and the 100 of Chow were actually of the same dimensions.

[412] CH. IV. MENCIUS' REFUTATION OF THE DOCTRINE THAT THE RULER OUGHT TO LABOUR AT HUSBANDRY WITH HIS OWN HANDS. HE SHOWS THE NECESSITY OF A DIVISION OF LABOUR, AND OF A LETTERED CLASS CONDUCTING GOVERNMENT. The first three paragraphs, it is said, relate how Heu Hing, the heresiarch, and Ch'in Sĕang, his follower, sought to undermine the arrangements advised by Mencius for the division of the land. The next eight paragraphs expose the fundamental error of Heu Hing that the ruler must labor at the toils of husbandry equally with the people. From the 12th paragraph to the 16th, Sĕang is rebuked for forsaking his master, and taking up with the heresy of Heu Hing. In the last two paragraphs Mencius proceeds, from the evasive replies of Sĕang, to give the *coup de grace* to the new pernicious teachings.

[413] *Par.* 1. All that we know of Heu Hing is from this chapter. He was a native of Ts'oo, and had evidently got in his seething brain the idea of a new moral world where there would be no longer the marked distinctions of ranks in which society had arranged itself. Shin-nung, "Wonderful husbandman," is the designation of the second of the five famous emperors of Chinese prehistoric times. He is also called *Yen-te*, "the Blazing emperor." He is placed between Fuh-he, and Hwang-te, though separated from the latter by the intervention of seven reigns, making with his own over 500 years. If any faith could be placed in this chronology, it would place him B.C. 3272. In the appendix to the Yih King he is celebrated as the Father of husbandry. Other traditions make him the Father of medicine also. Those who, like Heu Hing, in the time of Mencius, gave out that they were his followers, had no record of his words or, principles, but merely used his name to recommend their own wild notions. "The benevolent government" was the division of the laud on the principles described in last chapter. According to par. 4, the "hair-cloth" seems to have been quite an inartificial affair. The sandals, which I have said

2. Ch'in Sëang, a disciple of Ch'in Lëang, with his younger brother Sin, with their plough-handles and shares on their backs, came [at the same time] from Sung to T'ăng, saying, "We have heard that you, O ruler, are putting into practice the government of the [ancient] sages, [showing that] you are likewise a sage: we wish to be the subjects of a sage."[414]

3. When Ch'in Seang saw Heu Hing, he was very much pleased with him, and, abandoning all which he had learned, he set about learning from him. Having an interview with Mencius, he repeated to him the words of Heu Hing to this effect:—"The ruler of T'ăng is indeed a worthy prince, but nevertheless he has not yet heard the [real] ways [of antiquity], Wise and able rulers should cultivate the ground equally and along with their people, and eat [the fruit of their own labor]. They should prepare their morning and evening meals [themselves], and [at the same time] carry on the business of government. But now [the ruler of] T'ăng has his granaries, treasuries, and arsenals, which is a distressing of the people to support himself;—how can he be deemed a [real] ruler of talents and virtue?"[415]

4. Mencius said, "Mr. Heu, I suppose, sows grain and eats [the produce]." "Yes," was the reply. "I suppose he [also] weaves cloth, and wears his own manufacture." "No, he wears clothes of hair-cloth." "Does he wear a cap?" "He wears a cap." "What kind of cap?" "A plain cap." "Is it woven by himself?" "No; he gets it in exchange for grain." "Why does he not weave it himself?" "That would be injurious to his husbandry." "Does he cook his food with boilers and earthenware pans, and plough with an iron share?" "Yes." "Does he make them himself?" "No; he gets them in exchange for grain."[416]

5. [Mencius then said], "The getting such articles in exchange for grain is not oppressive to the potter and founder; and are the potter and founder oppressive to the husbandman, when they give him their various articles in exchange for grain? Moreover, why does Heu not act the potter and founder, and supply himself with the articles which he uses solely from his own establishment? Why does he go confusedly

---

Hing's followers "made," appear to have been manufactured by beating and tying the materials together, and not by any process of weaving. It has been supposed that their manufacture of sandals and mats was only a temporary employment, till lands should be assigned them.

[414] *Par.* 2. Ch'in Lëang appears in par. 12 to have been a native of Ts'oo, but to have come to the northern States, and distinguished himself as a scholar. We know nothing more of him, nor do we know anything of Ch'in Sëang and his brother Sin but what we are told in this chapter. The "share," the invention of which is ascribed to Shin-nung, was of wood;—in Mencius time, as appears in par. 4, it was made of iron.

[415] *Par.* 3. The object of Heu Hing, in the remarks given here, would be to invalidate Mencius' doctrine, put forth especially in par. 14 of last chapter, that there must be the ruler and the ruled, and that the former must be supported by the latter.

[416] *Parr.* 4, 5. Mencius skillfully leads Sëang on here to an admission which is fatal to the doctrine of his new master, that every man ought to do everything for himself.

dealing and exchanging with the handicraftsmen? Why is he so indifferent to the trouble that he takes?" [Ch'in Sëang replied], "The business of the handicraftsmen can by no means be carried on along with that of husbandry."

6. [Mencius resumed], "Then is it the government of all under heaven which alone can be carried on along with the business of husbandry? Great men have their proper business, and little men have theirs. Moreover, in the case of any single individual, [whatever articles he can require are] ready to his hand, being produced by the various handicraftsmen:—if he must first make them himself for his own use, this would keep all under heaven running about on the roads. Hence there is the saying, 'Some labor with their minds, and some labor with their strength. Those who labor with their minds govern others, and those who labor with their strength are governed by others. Those who are governed by others support them, and those who govern others are supported by them/ This is a thing of right universally recognized.[417]

7. "In the time of Yaou, when the world had not yet been perfectly reduced to order, the vast waters, flowing out of their channels, made a universal inundation. Vegetation was luxuriant, and birds and beasts swarmed. The five kinds of grain could not be grown, and the birds and beasts pressed upon men. The paths marked by the feet of beasts and prints of birds crossed one another throughout the Middle States. To Yaou especially this caused anxious sorrow. He called Shun to office, and measures to regulate the disorder were set forth. Shun committed to Yih the direction of the fire to be employed, and he set fire to, and consumed, [the forests and vegetation on] the mountains and [in] the marshes, so that the birds and beasts fled away and hid themselves. Yu separated the nine [streams of the] Ho, cleared the courses of the Tse and the T'ah, and led them to the sea. He opened a vent for the Joo and the Han, removed the obstructions in the channels of the Hwae and the Sze, and led them to the Këang. When this was done, it became possible for [the people of] the Middle States to [cultivate the ground, and] get food [for themselves]. During that time, Yu was eight years away from his house, thrice passing by his door without entering it. Although he had wished to cultivate the ground, could he have done it?[418]

---

[417] *Par.* 6. Mencius reiterates here his doctrine, which indeed had been proved by the admissions of Ch'in Sëang, that there are two classes, the ruling and the ruled, the former supported by the latter.

[418] *Par.* 7. seems to carry our thoughts back to a time antecedent even to Yaou. We have presented to us the world—all "under heaven"—in a wild, confused, chaotic state, the attempts to bring which into order had not been attended with any great success, and which was waiting for the labours of Yu, whom Yaou brought into the field. Mencius did not go, 1.or ought we to go, beyond Yaou for the founding of the Chinese empire. Then in par. 8 we have How-tseih doing over again the work of Shin-nung, and teaching men husbandry.

8. "How-tseih taught the people to sow and reap, cultivating the five kinds of grain; and when these were brought to maturity, the people all enjoyed a comfortable subsistence. [But] to men there belongs the way [in which they should go]; and if they are well fed, warmly clad, and comfortably lodged, without being taught [at the same time], they become almost like the beasts. This also was a subject of anxious solicitude to the sage [Shun]; and he appointed Sëeh to be minister of Instruction, and to teach the relations of humanity!—how, between father and son, there should be affection; between ruler and subject, righteousness; between husband and wife, attention to their separate functions; between old and young, a proper distinction; and between friends, fidelity. Fang-heun said, 'Encourage them; lead them on; rectify them; straighten them; help them; give them wings; causing them to become masters of their own [nature] for themselves.' When the sages were exercising their solicitude for the people in this way, had they leisure to cultivate the ground?[419]

9. "What Yaou felt as peculiarly giving him anxiety was the not getting Shun; and what Shun felt as peculiarly giving him anxiety was the not getting Yu and Kaou Yaou. But he whose anxiety is about his

---

In regard to the calamity spoken of in this paragraph, it is to be observed that it is not presented to us as a deluge or sudden accumulation of water, but as arising from the natural river-channels being all choked up, and disordered. For the labours of Shun, Yih, and Yu, see the Shoo, Parts II and III. By the "Middle States" is to be understood the portion of the country which wa3 first occupied by the Chinese settlers. The "nine streams" all belonged to the Ho or Yellow river, and by them Yu led off a large portion of the inundating waters. The Këang is what we now call the Yang-tsze. Choo He observes that of the rivers mentioned as being led into the Keang only the Han flows into that stream, while the Hwae receives the Joo and the Sze, and makes a direct course to the sea. He supposes that there is some error in the text.

[419] *Par.* 8. How-tseih, which is now received as a kind of proper name, was properly the official designation of K'e, Shun's minister of Agriculture. Sëeh was the name of Shun's minister of Instruction. For these two men and their works, see the Shoo, Part. II. The "five kinds of grain" are paddy, millet, sacrificial millet, wheat, and pulse; but each of these terms must be taken as comprehending several varieties under it. "To men there belongs the way [in which they should go]" carries our thoughts to the duties of the five relations of society, which are immediately specified. In my larger volume I have translated the clause by "Men possess a moral nature," but in the note have suggested whether the original characters may not be translated as the clause at the commencement of ch. iii. 2,—"The way of men is this." Dr Plath, in his work which I have referred to in the Preface, insists that this is the only correct meaning, and says that I have made a mistake in rendering by—"Men possess a moral nature." That rendering, however, or the more literal one which I have now given, is the only one which has the sanction of Chinese critics and commentators. The other which I suggested, and which Dr Plath vaunts as entirely his, has never occurred to any one of them; and a deeper study of the text has satisfied me that it is inadmissible. This cannot be shown, however, without appealing to the Chinese characters, and the Chinese structure of the whole paragraph. Fang-heun appears in the very first paragraph of the Shoo as the name of the emperor Yaou. The address here given, however, is not found in the Shoo, and it was Shun who appointed Sëeh and gave to him his instructions. Perhaps it was addressed to Shun himself;—only on this supposition can I account for its introduction here.

hundred acres' not being properly cultivated is a [mere] husbandman.[420]

10. "The imparting by a man to others of his wealth is called 'a kindness' The teaching others what is good is called 'an exercise of fidelity' The finding a man who shall benefit all under heaven is called 'benevolence' Hence to give the kingdom to another man would be easy; to find a man who shall benefit it is difficult.[421]

11. "Confucius said, 'Great was Yaou as a ruler! Only Heaven is great, and only Yaou corresponded to it. How vast [was his virtue]! The people could find no name for it. Princely indeed was Shun! How majestic was he, possessing all under heaven, and yet seeming as if it were nothing to him!' In their governing all under heaven, had Yaou and Shun no subjects with which they occupied their minds? But they did not occupy them with their own cultivation of the ground.[422]

12. "I have heard of men using [the ways of our] great land to change barbarians, but I have not yet heard of any being changed by barbarians.; Ch'in Lĕang was a native of Ts'oo. Pleased with the doctrines of the dukes of Chow and Chung-ne, he came north to the Middle States and learned them. Among the learners of the northern regions, there were perhaps none who excelled him;—he was what you call a scholar of high and distinguished qualities. You and your younger brother followed him for several tens of years, but on his death you forthwith turned the back on him.[423]

13. "Formerly, when Confucius died, after three years had elapsed the disciples put their baggage in order, intending to return to their homes. Having entered to take leave of Tsze-kung, they looked towards one another and wailed, till they all lost their voices. After this they returned to their homes, but Tsze-kung built another house for himself on the altar-ground, where he lived alone for [other] three years, after which he returned home. Subsequently, Tsze-hĕa, Tsze-chang, and Tsze-yĕw, thinking that Yĕw Joh resembled the sage, wished to pay to him the same observances which they had paid to Confucius, and [tried to] force Tsăng-tsze [to join with them]. He said, [however], 'The thing must not be done. What has been washed in the waters of the Keang and Han, and bleached in the autumn sun:—how glistening it is! Nothing can be added to it.'[424]

---

[420] *Par.* 9. is an illustration of what is said in par. 6, that "great men have their proper business, and little men theirs."

[421] *Par.* 10. Compare Ana. VI. xxviii.

[422] *Par.* 11. See Ana. VIII. xviii. and xix., which two chapters Mencius blends together, with the omission of some parts and alterations of others.

[423] *Par.* 12. Observe how here Ts'oo is excluded from the Middle States, the China proper of the time of Mencius.

[424] *Par.* 13. On the death of Confucius, his disciples generally remained by his grave for three years, mourning for him as for a father, but without wearing the mourning dress. During ail that time Tsze-kung acted as master of the ceremonies, and when the others left, he continued by the grave for another period of three years nominally, but in reality

14. "Now here is this shrike-tongued barbarian of the south, whose doctrines are not those of the ancient kings. You turn your back on your [former] master, and learn of him;—different you are indeed from Tsăng-tsze.

15. "I have heard of [birds] leaving the dark valleys, and removing to lofty trees, but I have not heard of their descending from lofty trees, and entering the dark valleys.[425]

16. "In the Praise-odes of Loo it is said,

'He smote the tribes of the west and the north;
He punished King and Shoo.'

Thus the duke of Chow then smote those [tribes], and you are become a disciple of [one of] them;—the change which you have made is indeed not good."[426]

17. [Ch'in Sëang said], "If Heu's doctrines were followed, there would not be two prices in the market, nor any deceit in the State. Though a lad of five cubits were sent to the market, nobody would impose on him. Linens and silks of the same length would be of the same price. So would it be with [bundles of] hemp and silk, being of the same weight; with the different kinds of grain, being the same in quantity; and with shoes which were of the same size."[427]

18. [Mencius] replied, "It is in the nature of things to be of unequal quality. Some are twice, some five times, some ten times, some a hundred times, some a thousand times, some ten thousand times as valuable as others. If you reduce them all to the same standard, that would throw all under heaven into confusion. If large shoes and small shoes were of the same price, would people make them? If people were to follow the doctrines of Heu, they would [only] lead on one another to practise deceit;—how can they avail for the government of a State?"

V.[428]  1. The Mihist E Che sought, through Seu Peih, to see

---

of two years and three months. On Yĕw Joh's resemblance to Confucius, see the Le Ke, II. i. III. 4.

[425] *Par.* 15. See the She, II. i. Ode V. 1.

[426] *Par.* 16. See the She, IV. ii. Ode IV. 5. The lines contain an auspice of what the poet hoped would be accomplished by duke He of Loo; but Mencius seems to apply them to the achievements of his ancestor, the duke of Chow.

[427] *Parr.* 17, 18. I suppose that Ch'in Sëang made this final attempt to defend the doctrines which he had adopted without well knowing what to say. It is difficult to imagine the wildest dreamer really holding that the question of quality was not to enter at all into the price of things.

"A boy of five cubits" would be a boy of about ten years old, who might easily be imposed upon. See on Ana. VIII. vi.

[428] CH. V. HOW MENCIUS CONVINCED A MIHIST OF HIS ERROR THAT ALL MEN WERE TO BE LOVED EQUALLY, WITHOUT DIFFERENCE OF DEGREE, BY SETTING FORTH THE FEELING OUT OF WHICH GREW THE RITES OF BURIAL, ESPECIALLY IN THE CASE OF ONE'S PARENTS.

Mencius. Mencius said, "I indeed wished to see him; but at present I am still unwell. When I am better, I will myself go and see him; he need not come [to me]."[429]

2. Next day, [E Che] again sought to see Mencius, who said, "Yes, to-day I can see him. But if I do not correct [his errors], the [true] principles will not clearly appear; let me first correct him. I have heard that Mr. E is a Mihist. Now Mih thinks that in the regulation of the rites of mourning a spare simplicity should be the rule. E thinks [with Mih's doctrines] to change [the customs of] all under heaven; but how does he [himself] regard them as if they were wrong, and not honor them? Thus when E buried his parents in a sumptuous manner, he was doing them service in a way which [his doctrines] discountenanced."[430]

3. The disciple Seu informed Mr. E of these remarks. E said, "[Even according to] the principles of the learned, the ancients, [though sages, dealt with the people] as if they were loving and cherishing their children. What does this expression mean? To me it sounds that we are to love all without difference of degree, the manifestation of it [simply] beginning with our parents;" Seu reported this reply to Mencius, who said, "Does Mr. E really think that a man's affection for the child of his elder brother is [merely] like his affection for the child of his neighbor? What is to be taken hold of in that [expression] is simply this:—[that the peopled offences are no more than] the guiltlessness of an infant, which, crawling, is about to fall into a well. Moreover, Heaven gives birth to creatures in such a way that they have [only] one root, while Mr. E makes them to have two roots;—this is the cause [of his error].[431]

---

[429] *Par.* 1. Of Mih and his doctrines I have spoken in the Prolegomena. Mencius thought it was one of the principal missions of his life to expose and beat back his principles.

Of E Che we have no information beyond what we learn from this chapter. From the Tso Chuen we know that there were families of the surname E both in Ts'e and Choo.

Seu Peih was a disciple of Mencius, with whom E Che seems to have had some acquaintance. Our philosopher, probably, was well enough, but feigned sickness that he might test, by interposing delay, the sincerity of the Mihist's wish to see him. The same purpose was also served by his saying that he would go to see E Che, when lie was better. He did not, indeed, mean to do so; but having been told that he would do it, E Che, if he had not been in earnest, might have given up his desire to have an interview.

[430] *Par.* 2. E Che showed his sincerity in again seeking so soon after to have an interview with Mencius. Mencius knew that in one point his practice disagreed with the principles of Mih which he professed to follow, and resolved from that point to commence his communications with him. According to Chwang-tsze, Mih all his life-time did not Bing, nor did he permit mourning for the dead. He would have no outer coffin, and the inner one which he allowed was to be only three inches in thickness.

[431] *Par.* 3. Up to this time Mencius had not seen E Che, nor does it appear that he subsequently did so. The intercourse between them was conducted by Seu Peih. E Che does not try to vindicate his sumptuous interment of his parents, but proceeds to state and argue for the notable dogma of his master, that all men are to be loved equally. In support of this he refers to an expression in the Shoo, V. ix. 9, where the prince of K'ang is exhorted to deal with the people as he would do in protecting his own infant children. Mencius shows that that expression is merely metaphorical, and meant that the people

4. "Indeed, in the most ancient times there were some who did not inter their parents, but [simply] took their dead bodies up and threw them into a ditch. Afterwards, when passing by them, [they saw] foxes and wild-cats devouring them, and flies and gnats gnawing at them. The perspiration started out upon their foreheads, and they looked away, because they could not bear the sight. It was not because of [what] other people [might say] that this perspiration flowed. The emotions of their hearts affected their faces and eyes, and so they went home, and returned with baskets and spades, and covered the [bodies]. If this covering them was indeed right, then filial sons and virtuous men must be guided by a certain principle in the burial of their parents."[432]

5. Seu informed Mr. E of what Mencius had said. Mr. E seemed lost in thought, and after a little said, "He has instructed me."[433]

## BOOK III. T'ĂNO WĂN KUNG. PART II.

CHAPTER I.[434] 1. CH'IN TAE said [to Mencius], "In not [going to] see any of the princes, you seem to me to be standing out on a small point. If now you were once to wait upon them, the result might be so great that you would make one of them king, or, if smaller, you might yet make one of them leader of the [other] princes. And moreover, the History says, 'By bending only to the extent of one cubit, you make eight cubits straight.' It appears to me like a thing which might be done."[435]

---

were to be dealt with with a very kindly consideration of their weakness and liability to err. Nature itself, he says, teaches us to regard with peculiar feelings our parents and all related to us by blood. If we were to regard them and all others not related to us in the same way, that would be to make us sprung from two roots,—to be connected equally with our parents and with other men.

[432] *Par.* 4. Mencius tries to confirm his position by showing the origin of burial rites in the most ancient times, that is, before the sages had delivered their rules on the subject. Even then the natural feelings of men made them bury their parents, and where some neglected to do so, remorse speedily supervened. What affection thus prompted in the first place was prompted similarly in its more sumptuous exhibition in the progress of civilization. If any interment were called for by nature, a handsome one must have our approbation.

[433] *Par.* 5. E Che was satisfied of the truth of what Mencius had said, and probably ceased to be a Mihist.

[434] CH. I. HOW MENCIUS DEFENDED THE DIGNITY OF RESERVE, BY WHICH HE REGULATED HIS INTERCOURSE WITH THE PRINCES OF HIS TIME. To understand this chapter, it must be borne in mind that there were many wandering scholars in the days of Mencius,—men who went from court to court, recommending themselves to the various princes, and trying to influence the course of events by their counsels. They would stoop for place and employment. Not so with our philosopher. He required that there should be shown to himself a portion of the respect which was due to the principles of which he was the expounder. Compare chapter vii.

[435] *Par.* 1. Ch'in Tae was one of Mencius' disciples; and this is all that we know of him. "The thing that might be done" was Mencius' going to wait upon the princes,—taking the initiative in seeking employment from them.

2. Mencius said, "Formerly, duke King of Ts'e, [once] when he was hunting, called the forester to him by a flag. [The forester] would not come, and [the duke] was going to kill him. [With reference to this incident], Confucius said, 'The resolute officer does not forget [that his end may be] in a ditch or stream; the brave officer does not forget that he may lose his head.' What was it [in the forester] that Confucius thus approved? He approved his not going [to the duke], when summoned by an article that was not appropriate to him. If one go [to see the princes] without waiting to be called, what can be thought of him?[436]

3. "Moreover, [that sentence,] 'By bending to the extent of one cubit you make eight cubits straight,' is spoken with reference to the gain [that may be got]. If gain be the rule, then we may seek it, I suppose, by bending to the extent of eight cubits to make one cubit straight.[437]

4. "Formerly, the minister Chaou Këen made Wăng Lëang act as charioteer to his favorite He, and in the course of a whole day they did not get a single bird. The favorite He reported this result, saying, 'He is the poorest charioteer in the world.' Some one informed Wang Lëang of this, who said, 'I beg to try again,' By dint of pressing, he got this accorded to him, and in one morning they got ten birds. The favorite He [again] reported the result, saying, 'He is the best charioteer in the world.' The minister Këen said, 'I will make him be the driver of your carriage;' but when he informed Wang Lëang of this, he refused, saying, 'I [drove] for him, strictly observing the rules for driving, and in the whole day he did not get one bird. I [drove] for him so as deceitfully to intercept [the birds], and in one morning he got ten. The Book of Poetry says,

"No error in driving was committed,
And the arrows went forth like downright blows."

---

[436] *Par.* 2. The forester was an officer as old as the time of Shun, who in the Shoo, II. i. 22., appoints Yih, saying that "he could rightly superintend the birds and beasts of the fields and trees on his hills and in his forests." In the Official Book of Chow, XVII. vi., we have an account of the office and its duties. In those days the various officers had their several tokens, which the prince's or king's messenger bore when he was sent to summon any one of them. The forester's token was a fur cap, and the one in the text could not answer to a summons with a flag. We find the incident mentioned by Mencius given in the Tso Chuen under the 20th year of duke Ch'aou;—but with variations:—"In the 12th month, the marquis of Ts'e was hunting in P'ei, and summoned the forester to him with a bow. The forester did not come forward, and the marquis caused him to be seized, when he explained his conduct, saying, 'At the huntings of our former rulers, a flag was used to call a great officer, a bow to call an inferior one, and a fur cap to call a forester. Not seeing the fur cap, I did not venture to come forward.' On this he was let go. Confucius said, 'To keep the rule [of answering a prince's summons] is not so good as to keep [the special rule for one's] office. Superior men will hold this man right.'"

[437] *Par.* 3. This is the decisive paragraph in the conversation.

I am not accustomed to drive for a mean man. I beg to decline the office.'[438]

5. "[Thus this] charioteer even was ashamed to bend improperly to the will of [such] an archer. Though by bending to it they would have caught birds and animals enow to form a hill, he would not do it. If I were to bend my principles and follow those [princes], of what course would my conduct be? Moreover you are wrong. Never has a man who has bent himself been able to make others straight."

II.[439] 1. King Ch'un said [to Mencius], "Are not Kung-sun Yen and Chang E really great men? Let them once be angry, and all the princes are afraid; let them live quietly, and the flames of trouble are extinguished throughout the kingdom."[440]

2. Mencius said, "How can they be regarded as great men? Have you not read the Ritual [usages];—'At the capping of a young man, his father admonishes him. At the marrying away of a daughter, her mother admonishes her, accompanying her to the door, and cautioning her in these words, "You are going to your home. You must be respectful; you must be cautious. Do not disobey your husband."' [Thus,] to look upon compliance as their correct course is the rule for concubines and wives.[441]

3. "To dwell in the wide house of the world; to stand in the correct position of the world; and to walk in the great path of the world; when he obtains his desire [for office], to practise his principles for the good of the people; and when that desire is disappointed, to practise them alone; to be above the power of riches and honors to make dissipated, of poverty and mean condition to make swerve [from principle], and of power and force to make bend:—these characteristics constitute the

---

[438] *Par.* 4. Këen was the honorary or sacrificial epithet of Chaou Yang, the chief minister of Tsin, in the time of Confucius. He is constantly appearing in the Tso Chuen after the 24th year of duke Ch'aou; and Wang Lëang was his charioteer, who appears in the Tso Chuen and the narratives of the States also as Yëw Lëang, Yëw Woo-seuh, Yëw Woo-ching. I have not met with any further reference to Chaou Yang's favorite He. The ode in the Book of Poetry from which the quotation is made is II. iii. V.

[439] CH. II. MENCIUS' CONCEPTION OF THE GREAT MAN.

[440] *Par.* 1. King Ch'un was a contemporary of Mencius, who occupied himself with the intrigues of the time, designed to unite the other States in opposition to Ts'in or to induce them to submit to it. He was an admirer of Kung-sun Yen and Chang E, two principal leaders in those intrigues, and whose influence was very great on the fortunes of the time. They were both of them natives of Wei, but were generally opposed to each other in their schemes. Yen was a grandson of one of the rulers of Wei, and hence his surname of Kung-sun. He is often mentioned by the designation of Se-nëw;—see the "Historical Records," Book C. Chang E was perhaps the abler man of the two.

[441] *Par.* 2. The Ritual usages, to which Mencius here refers, is the collection known by the name of E Le. Our philosopher throws various passages together, and, according to his wont, is not careful to quote correctly. Obedience was the rule for women, and especially so for concubines or secondary wives. Mencius introduces them to show his contempt for Yen and E, who, with all their bluster, only pandered to the passions of the princes.

great man."[442]

III.[443] 1. Chow Sĕaou asked [Mencius], saying, "Did superior men of old time take office?" Mencius said, "They did." The Record says, "When Confucius was three months without [being employed by] some ruler, he looked disappointed and unhappy. When he passed over the boundary [of a State], he was sure to carry with him his proper gift of introduction." Kung-ming E said, "Among the ancients, when [an officer] was three months without [being employed by] some ruler, he was condoled with."[444]

2. [Sĕaou said,] "Did not this condoling, on being three months unemployed by a ruler, show a too great urgency?"

3. "The loss of his place," was the reply, "is to an officer like the loss of his State to a prince. It is said in the Book of Rites, 'The prince ploughs [himself], and is afterwards assisted [by others], in order to supply the millet-vessels [for sacrifice]. His wife keeps silk-worms and unwinds their cocoons, to make the robes [used in sacrificing]. If the victims be not perfect, the millet in the vessels not pure, and the robes not complete, he does not presume to sacrifice. And the scholar, who, [out of office], has no [holy] field, also does not sacrifice. The victims for slaughter, the vessels, and the robes, not being all complete, he does not presume to sacrifice, and then he does not presume to feel at ease and happy.' Is there not in all this sufficient ground for condolence?"[445]

---

[442] *Par.* 3. "The wide house of the world" *is benevolence or love,* the chief and home of all the virtues; "the correct seat" *is propriety;* and "the great path" *is righteousness.*

[443] CH. III. OFFICE IS TO BE EAGERLY DESIRED; AND YET IT SHOULD NOT BE SOUGHT BY ANY BUT ITS PROPER PATH. It will be seen that the questioner of Mencius in this chapter wished to condemn him for the dignity of reserve which he maintained in his intercourse with the princes, and which is the subject of the 1st chapter of this Part. Mencius does not evade any of his questions, and defends himself very ingeniously.

[444] *Par.* 1. Chow Sĕaou was one of the wandering scholars of Mencius' time. In the "Plans of the Warring States," under the division of Wei, of which he was a native, he appears as an opponent of Kung-sun Yen of last chapter. The "Record," from which Mencius quotes about Confucius, whatever it was, is now lost. Every person waiting on another—a superior—was supposed to pave his way by some introductory gift; and each official rank had its proper article to be used for that purpose by all belonging to it;—see the Le Ke, I. ii. III. 18. Confucius carried his gift with him, that he might not lose any opportunity of being in office again. Kung-ming E,—see on Part I. i.

[445] *Par.* 3. In his quotations here from the Le Ke, Mencius combines and adapts to his purpose different passages, with more than his usual freedom. Choo He, to illustrate the text, gives his own summary of the same passages thus:—"It is said in the Book of Bites that the feudal princes had their special field of a hundred acres, in which, wearing their crown, with its blue flaps turned up, they held the plough to commence the plowing, which was afterwards completed with the help of the common people. The produce of this field was reaped and stored in the ducal granary, to supply the vessels of millet in the ancestral temple. They also cause the noble women of their harem to attend to the silkworms in the silkworm house attached to the State mulberry trees, and to bring the cocoons to them. These were then presented to their wives, who received them in their sacrificial head-dress and robe, soaked them, and thrice drew out a thread. The cocoons

4. [Sëaou again asked], "What was the meaning of [Confucius']
always carrying his proper gift of introduction with him, when he
passed over the boundary [of a State]?"

5. "An officer's being in office," was the reply, "is like the
plowing of a husbandman. Does a husbandman part with his plough
because he goes from one State to another?"

6. [Sëaou] pursued, "The kingdom of Tsin is one, as well as others,
of official employments, but I have not heard of any being thus earnest
about being in office in it. If there should be this urgency about being in
office, why does a superior man make any difficulty about taking it?"
[Mencius] replied, "When a son is born, what is desired for him is that
he may have a wife; and when a daughter is born, what is desired for
her is that she may have a husband. This is the feeling of the parents,
and is possessed by all men. [If the young people], without waiting for
the orders of the parents and the arrangements of the go-betweens, shall
bore holes to steal a sight of each other, or get over the wall to be with
each other, then their parents and all other people will despise them.
The ancients did indeed always desire to be in office, but they also
hated being so by any but the proper way. To go [to see the princes] by
any but the proper way is of a class with [young people's] boring
holes."[446]

IV.[447] 1. P'ăng Kăng asked [Mencius], saying, "Is it not an
extravagant procedure to go from one prince to another and live upon
them, followed by several tens of carriages and attended by several
hundred men?" Mencius replied, "If there be not a proper ground [for
taking it], a single bamboo-cup of rice should not be received from a
man; if there be such a ground for it, Shun's receiving from Yaou all
under heaven is not to be considered excessive? Do you think it was
excessive?"[448]

2. [Kăng] said, "No. [But] for a scholar performing no service to

---

were then distributed among the ladies of the three palaces to prepare the threads for the
ornaments of the robes to be worn in sacrificing to the former kings and dukes."

The officer's field is the "holy" field of Pt i. III. 16. The argument is that it was not
the loss of office which was a proper subject for grief and condolence, but the
consequences of it in not being able, especially, to continue the proper sacrifices;—as
here set forth.

[446] *Par.* 6. By the "superior man" and his making a difficulty in taking office, Sëaou
evidently intended Mencius himself, who, however, does not take any notice of the
insinuation. The method of contracting marriages here referred to by Mencius still exists,
and seems to have been the rule of the Chinese race from time immemorial.

[447] CH. IV. THE LABOURER IS WORTHY OF HIS HIRE: AND THERE IS NO LABORER
SO WORTHY AS THE SCHOLAR WHO INSTRUCTS MEN IN THE PRINCIPLES, AND GUIDES
MEN IN THE PRACTICE, OF VIRTUE.

[448] *Par.* 1. P'ăng Kăng was a disciple of Mencius. Whether his own mind was really
perplexed as to the character of his master's way of life, or he simply wished to stir, him
up to visit the princes and go into office, we cannot tell.

receive his support notwithstanding is improper."[449]

3. [Mencius] answered, "If you do not have an intercommunication of the productions of labor and an inter-change of [men's] services, so that [one from his] overplus may supply the deficiency of another, then husbandmen will have a superfluity of grain, and women a superfluity of cloth. If you have such an interchange, then cabinet-makers, builders, wheel-wrights, and carriage-builders may all get their food from you. Here is a man, who, at home, is filial, and, abroad, respectful to his elders; and who watches over the principles of the ancient kings to be ready for [the use of] future learners:—and yet he will not be able to get his support from you. How is it that you give honor to the cabinet-makers, and the others I have mentioned, and slight him who practices benevolence and righteousness."

4. [P'ăng Kăng] said, "The aim of the cabinet-maker, and others of his class, is [by their trades] to seek for a living;—is it also the aim of the superior man, in his practice of the principles [you mention], to seek for a living?" "What have you to do with his aim?" was the reply. "He renders services to you. He deserves to be supported, and you support him. And [let me ask],—do you remunerate a man for his intention? or do you remunerate him for his service?" [To this Kang] replied, "I remunerate him for his intention."

5. [Mencius] said, "There is a man here who breaks your tiles, and draws [unsightly] ornaments on your walls, his purpose being thereby to seek for his living; but will you indeed remunerate him?" "No," was the reply; and [Mencius then] concluded, "Then, it is not for his purpose that you remunerate a man, but for the work done."

V.[450] 1. Wan Chang said [to Mencius], "Sung is a small State; but [its ruler] is now setting about to practise the [true] royal government, and Ts'e and Ts'oo hate and attack him;—what is to be done in the case?"[451]

---

[449] *Parr.* 2-5. We cannot but admire the ingenuity which Mencius displays here in the turn which he gives to the conversation. and he is right in saying that it is not the purpose which we remunerate, but the work which is done for us. Yet his argument, as a defense of himself and his own practice, fails to carry conviction to the mind. Men in general will give honour to him who holds the principles of benevolence and righteousness, inculcating them, moreover, and exemplifying them; but it does not follow that they are bound to support him, nor can he accept their support without some loss of character.

[450] CH. V. THE PRINCE WHO WILL SET HIMSELF TO PRACTICE A BENEVOLENT GOVERNMENT ON THE PRINCIPLES OF THE ANCIENT KINGS HAS NONE TO FEAR:—WITH REFERENCE TO THE CASK OF A DUKE OF SUNG WHO CLAIMED THE TITLE OF KING.

[451] *Par.* 1. Wan Chang was a disciple of Mencius, the fifth Book of whose Works is named from him. The ruler of Sung to whom reference is made was Yen, who raised himself by violence to the dukedom in B.C. 328, and in .317 assumed the title of king, when he gained some successes over the States of Ts'e on the north, of Ts'oo on the south, and of Wei on the west. He probably gave out at first that he meant to imitate the ancient kings in his government, but he was very far from doing so. In the Historical

2. Mencius said, "When T'ang dwelt in Poh, he adjoined to [the State of] Koh, the earl of which was living in a dissolute state, and neglecting [his proper] sacrifices. T'ang sent messengers to ask why he did not sacrifice, and when he said that he had no means of supplying the [necessary] victims, T'ang caused sheep and oxen to be sent to him. The earl, however, ate them, and still continued not to sacrifice. T'ang again sent messengers to ask him the same question as before, and when he said that he had no means of supplying the vessels of millet, T'ang sent the people of Poh to go and till the ground for him, while the old and feeble carried their food to them. The earl led his people to intercept those who were thus charged with spirits, cooked lice, millet and paddy, and took their stores from them, killing those who refused to give them up. There was a boy with millet and flesh for the laborers, who was thus killed and robbed. What is said in the Book of History, 'The earl of Koh behaved as an enemy to the provision-carriers,' has reference to this.[452]

3. "Because of his murder of this boy, [T'ang] proceeded to punish him. All within the four seas said, 'It is not because he desires the riches of the kingdom, but to avenge the common men and women.'[453]

4. "When T'ang began his work of executing justice, he commenced with Koh; and though he punished eleven [States], he had not an enemy under heaven. When he pursued his work in the east, the rude tribes in the west murmured. So did those in the north, when he pursued it in the south. Their cry was, 'Why does he make us last?' The people's longing for him was like their longing for rain in a time of great drought. The frequenters of the markets stopped not; those engaged in weeding made no change [in their operations]. While he punished their rulers, he consoled the people. [His progress was] like the falling of opportune rain, and the people were delighted. It is said in the Book of History, 'We have waited for our prince. When our prince comes, we shall escape the misery [under which we suffer].'[454]

---

Records, Book XXXVIII., he appears as a worthless and oppressive ruler, and his ambition, which led him into collision with the great States mentioned above, precipitated the extinction of the dukedom of Sung, which took place in B.C. 285. Wan Chang gives a too favorable account of him to our philosopher, who, however, was not deceived by it.

[452] *Par.* 2. Compare I. ii. III. 1, and XI. 2. Poh, the capital of T'ang's principality (though there were three places of the same name), is referred to a place in the present district of Shang-k'ëw, in the department of Kwei-tih, Ho-nan; and the capital of the earldom of Koh was in the district of Ning-ling in the same department, so that Mencius might say well enough that Poh adjoined to Koh, and T'ang might render to the earl of Koh the services which are mentioned. The passage of the Shoo referred to at the end is from IV. ii. 6.

[453] *Par.* 3. "To avenge the common men and women" is spoken generally, but the words have a special application to the father and mother of the murdered boy.

[454] *Par.* 4. Compare I. ii. XI. 2; and for the quotations from the Shoo, see IV. ii. 6, and v. Pt II. 5. The eleven punitive expeditions of T'ang cannot all be made out. In the Shoo and the She we find only six. By a peculiar construction of the text here, Ch'aou

5. "There being some who would not become the subjects [of Chow, king Woo] proceeded to punish them on the east. He gave tranquility to [their people, both] men and women, who [welcomed him] with baskets full of their dark and yellow silks, [saying,] 'From henceforth [we shall serve] our king of Chow, and be made happy by him.' So they gave in their adherence as subjects to the great State of Chow. The men of station [of Shang] took baskets full of dark and yellow silks, to meet the men of station [of Chow], and the lower classes of the one met those of the other with bamboo-cups of cooked rice and vessels of congee. [Woo] saved the people from the midst of fire and water, seizing only their oppressors, [and destroying them].[455]

6. "It is said in 'The Great Declaration:'—'My military prowess is displayed, and I enter his territories, and will seize the oppressor. My execution and punishment of him shall be displayed, more glorious than the work of T'ang.'[456]

7. "[Sung] is not practicing royal government, as you say among other things about it. If it were practicing royal government, all within the four seas would be lifting up their heads, and looking for [its king], wishing to have him for their ruler. Great as Ts'e and Ts'oo are, what would there be to fear from them?"[457]

VI.[458] 1. Mencius said to Tae Puh-shing, "Do you indeed, Sir, wish your king to be virtuous? Well, I will plainly tell you [how he may be made so]. Suppose that there is here a great officer of Ts'oo, who wishes his son to learn the speech of Ts'e, will he employ a man of Ts'e as his tutor, or a man of Ts'oo?" "He will employ a man of Ts'oo to teach him," was the reply, and [Mencius] went on, "If [but] one man of Ts'e be teaching him, and there be a multitude of men of Ts'oo shouting out about him, although [his father] beat him every day, wishing him to learn the speech of Ts'e, it will be impossible for him to do so. [But] in the same way, if he were to be taken and placed for several years in the Chwang [street], or the Yoh [quarter], although [his father] should beat him every day, wishing him to speak the language of Ts'oo, it would be impossible for him to do so.[459]

---

K'e makes them to have been 22; others have put them down at as many as 27.

[455] *Par.* 5. The first half of this paragraph is substantially a quotation from the Shoo, V. iii. 7; but that Book of the Shoo is supposed to be imperfect, and to require considerable emendation.

[456] *Par.* 6. See the Shoo, V. i. Pt II. 6.

[457] *Par.* 7. Here is the conclusion of the matter. The king of Sung, having taken the sword in a different spirit from T'ang and Woo, would perish by the sword.

[458] CH. VI. THE ALL-POWERFUL INFLUENCE OF EXAMPLE AND ASSOCIATION. THE IMPORTANCE OF HAVING VIRTUOUS MEN ABOUT A RULER'S PERSON. This chapter may be considered as connected with the preceding.

[459] *Par.* 1. Tae Puh-shing was a minister, probably the chief minister, of Sung, a descendant from one of its dukes, who had received the posthumous epithet of Tae, which had been adopted as their clan-name by a branch of his posterity. Chwang and Yoh were two well-known quarters in the capital of Ts'e. They are both mentioned in the Tso

2. "You say that Sëeh Keu-chow is a scholar of virtue, and you have got him placed in attendance on the king. If all that are in attendance on the king, old and young, high and low, were Sëeh Keu-chows, whom would the king have to do evil with? [But] if those that are in attendance on the king, old and young, high and low, are all not Sëeh Keu-chows, whom will the king have to do good with? What can one Sëeh Keu-chow do alone for the king of Sung?"[460]

VII.[461] 1. Kung-sun Ch'ow asked [Mencius], saying, "What is the point of righteousness in your not going to see the princes?" Mencius said, "Anciently, if one had not been a minister [in the State], he did not go to see [the ruler].[462]

2. "Twan Kan-muh leaped over a wall to avoid [the prince]; Sëeh Lew shut the door and would not admit him. These two, however, [carried their scrupulosity] to excess. When a prince is urgent, it is not improper to see him.[463]

3. "Yang Ho wished to get Confucius to go to see him, but disliked [that he should be charged himself with] any want of propriety. [As it was the rule, therefore, that] when a great officer sends a gift to a scholar, if the latter be not at home to receive it, he must go and make his acknowledgments at the gate of the other, Yang Ho watched when Confucius was out and sent him a steamed pig. Confucius, in his turn, watched when Ho was out, and went to pay his acknowledgments to him. At that time Yang Ho had taken the initiative;—how could [Confucius] avoid going to see him?[464]

4. "The philosopher Tsăng said, 'Those who shrug up their shoulders and laugh in a flattering way toil harder than the summer

---

Chuen under par. 6 of the 28th year of duke Sëang. Some will have it that Chwang was the name of a street merely, and Yoh of a neighborhood.

[460] *Par.* 2. Sëeh Keu-chow was also a minister of Sung, recommended as tutor or adviser to the king by Tae Puh-shing. He was a man of virtue and acquirements,—a descendant of the lords of Sëeh, which principality dates at least from the time of Yu.

[461] CH. VII. MENCIUS DEFENDS HIS NOT GOING TO SEE THE PRINCES BY THE EXAMPLE AND MAXIMS OF THE ANCIENTS. Akin to the first and other chapters of this Book.

[462] *Par.* 1. In Ana. XIV. xxii. we have an example of how Confucius, not then actually in office, but having been so, went to see the marquis of Loo. He had a good reason, however, for doing so, independently of his having been in office. Mencius is never altogether satisfactory in vindicating his own conduct in the matters affecting his intercourse with the princes, which staggered the faith of his followers.

[463] *Par.* 2. Twan Kan-muh, or Twan-kan Muh (the surname and name are not clearly ascertained), was a native of Tsin, and a disciple of Tsze-Hëa. The prince whom he avoided in the way which Mencius refers to was Sze, the first marquis of Wei, known as duke Wăn, who died in B.C. 386. He never drove past Twan's door, it is said, without bowing forward to the front bar of his carriage in token of respect; but Twan stood out upon his purity, and would not go to see him.

Sëeh Lew has been mentioned in II. ii. XI. 3.

[464] *Par.* 3. See Ana. XVII. i. In the incident which is here related few will see anything more or higher than the ingenuity of Confucius in getting out of a difficulty.

[laborer in the] fields.' Tsze-loo said, 'There are those who will talk with people with whom they have no agreement. If you look at their countenances, they are full of blushes, and are not such as I [care to] know.' By looking at the matter in the light of these remarks, [the spirit] which the superior man nourishes may be known."[465]

VIII.[466] 1. "Tae Ying-che said [to Mencius], "I am not able at present and immediately to do with a tithe [only], and abolish [at the same time] the duties charged at the passes and in the markets. With your leave I will lighten all [the present extraordinary exactions] until next year, and then make an end of them. What do you think of such a course?"[467]

2. Mencius said, "Here is a man who every day appropriates the fowls of his neighbours that stray to his premises. Some one says to him, 'Such is not the way of a good man,' and he replies, 'With your leave I will diminish my appropriations, and will take only one fowl a month, until next year, when I will make an end of the practice altogether.'

3. "If you know that the thing is unrighteous, then put an end to it with all dispatch;—why wait till next year?"

IX.[468] 1. The disciple Kung-too said [to Mencius], "Master, people beyond [our school] all say that you are fond of disputing. I venture to ask why you are so." Mencius replied, "How should I be fond of disputing? But I am compelled to do it.[469]

2. "A long period has elapsed since this world [of men] received its being, and there have been [along its history] now a period of good order, and now a period of confusion.[470]

---

[465] *Par.* 4. We must understand Tsze-loo as speaking of those men who gave their counsels freely to princes and men of influence of whom they disapproved.

[466] CH. VIII. WHAT IS WRONG SHOULD BE PUT AN END TO AT ONCE, WITHOUT RESERVE, AND WITHOUT DELAY.

[467] *Par.* 1. Tae Ying-che was a minister of Sung;—supposed by some to have been the same with the Tae Puh-shing of chapter vi. I think it likely they were the same. We must suppose that Mencius had been talking with him on the points indicated in his remarks, and insisting on them as necessary to the benevolent government, which, it was pretended, was being instituted in Sung. See 1. ii. V. 3; II. i. V. 3; and III. i. III.

[468] CH. IX. MENCIUS DEFENDS HIMSELF AGAINST THE CHARGE OF BEING FOND OF DISPUTING. WHAT LED TO HIS APPEARING TO BE SO WAS THE NECESSITY OF THE TIME. Compare II. i. II. It would appear from that chapter and this that our philosopher believed that the mantle of Confucius had fallen upon him, and that he was in the position of a sage on whom it devolved to live and labor for the world.

[469] *Par.* 1. Kung-too,—see II. ii. V. 4. There was some truth, no doubt, in the common opinion about Mencius reported to him by Kung-too.

[470] *Parr.* 2, 3. Commentators are unanimous in understanding Mencius to be speaking here not of the material world, but of the first appearance of men; and it is remarkable that in his review of the history of mankind, he does not go beyond the time of Yaou, and that at its commencement he places a period of disorder. Compare Pt i. IV. 7. The "nests" were huts on high-raised platforms. In the Le Ke, IX. i. 8, it is said that these were the summer habitations of the earliest men, who made caves for themselves in

3. "In the time of Yaou, the waters, flowing out of their channels, inundated all through the States, snakes and dragons occupied the country, and the people had no place where they could settle themselves. In the low grounds they made [as it were] nests for themselves, and in the high grounds they made caves. It is said in the Book of History, 'The vast waters filled me with dread.' What are called 'the vast waters' were those of the [above] great inundation.

4. "[Shun] employed Yu to reduce the waters to order. He dug open the ground [which impeded their flow], and led them to the sea. He drove away the snakes and dragons, and forced them into the grassy marshes. [On this] the waters pursued their course in their channels,—[the waters of] the Këang, the Hwae, the Ho, and the Han. The [natural] difficulties and obstructions being thus removed, and the birds and beasts which had injured the people having disappeared, men found the plains [available for them], and occupied them.[471]

5. "After the death of Yaou and Shun, the principles of [those] sages fell into decay. Oppressive rulers arose one after another, who pulled down the houses [of the people] to make ponds and lakes, so that the people could nowhere rest in quiet, and threw fields out of cultivation to form gardens and parks, so that the people could not get clothes and food. [Afterwards], corrupt speakings and oppressive deeds also became rife; gardens and parks, ponds and lakes, thickets and marshes were numerous; and birds and beasts made their appearance. By the time of Chow, all under heaven was again in a state of great confusion.[472]

6. "The duke of Chow assisted king Woo, and destroyed Chow. He attacked Yen, and in three years put its ruler to death. He drove Fei-lëen to a corner by the sea, and slew him. The States which he extinguished amounted to fifty. He drove far away the tigers, leopards, rhinoceroses, and elephants. All under heaven were greatly pleased. It is said in the Book of History, 'How great and splendid were the plans of king Wăn! How greatly were they carried out by the energy of king Woo. They are for the help and guidance of us their descendants,—all in principle correct, and deficient in nothing.'[473]

---

the winter, and lived in them. For the words of the Shoo, see that work, II iii. 14.

[471] *Par.* 4. "The waters pursued their course in their channels;"—or, it may be, "the waters pursued their course through the country," that is, no more overflowed it.

[472] *Par.* 5. The dynasties of Hëa and Shang have their history summed up here in very small compass. Yu and T'ang, and various worthy, if not sage, sovereigns are passed over without ceremony. Does not the account thus given imply that down to the rise of the Chow dynasty the country was very thinly peopled?

[473] *Par.* 6. Yen was a State in the present district of K'ëuh-fow, department Yen-chow, Shan-tung. From the specification of it here, it must have been of considerable note and influence. Fei-lëen was a favorite minister of Chow, who abetted him in his enormities. It would be vain to try to enumerate the "fifty States," which the duke of Chow is said to have extinguished. "The tigers," &c., spoken of here, are said to have

7. "[Again] the world fell into decay, and principles faded away. Perverse speakings and oppressive deeds again became rife. There were instances of ministers who murdered their rulers, and of sons who murdered their fathers.[474]

8. "Confucius was afraid and made the Ch'un Ts'ëw. What the Ch'un Ts'ëw contains are matters proper to the son of Heaven. On this account Confucius said, 'It is the Ch'un Ts'ëw which will make men know me, and it is the Ch'un Ts'ëw which will make men condemn me.'

9. "[Once more] sage kings do not arise, and the princes of the States give the reins to their lusts. Unemployed scholars indulge in unreasonable discussions. The words of Yang Choo and Mih Teih fill the kingdom. [If you listen to] people's discourses throughout it, [you will find that] if they are not the adherents of Yang, they are those of Mih. Yang's principle is—'Each one for himself;' which leaves no [place for duty to] the ruler. Mih's principle is—'To love all equally;' which leaves no place for [the peculiar affection due to] a father. But to acknowledge neither ruler nor father is to be in the state of a beast. Kung-ming E said, 'In their stalls there are fat beasts, and in their stables there are fat horses, but their people have the look of hunger, and in the fields there are those who have died of famine. This is leading on beasts to devour men.' If the principles of Yang and Mih are not stopped, and the principles of Confucius are not set forth, then those perverse speakings will delude the people, and stop up [the path of] benevolence and righteousness. When benevolence and righteousness are stopped up, beasts will be led on to devour men, and men will devour one another.[475]

10. "I am alarmed by these things, and address myself to the defence of the principles of the former sages. I oppose Yang and Mih, and drive away their licentious expressions, so that such perverse speakers may not be able to show themselves. When [their errors] spring up in men's minds, they are hurtful to the conduct of affairs.

---

been those kept by the tyrant Chow, and those infesting the country, as in earlier times. The text of Mencius, however, produces a different impression on my mind. He would have us think of much of the country as being, even in the time of the duke of Chow, still over-run by wild animals. See the Shoo, V. xxv. 6.

[474] *Parr.* 7, 8. What Mencius says hereabout the "Spring and Autumn" is very perplexing, and the reader will find the passages discussed at length in the first chapter of my Prolegomena to Vol. V. of my larger work. It is difficult to believe that our philosopher can be speaking of the "Spring and Autumn" which we now have; and yet the evidence seems complete that the present classic of that name is what came from the *stylus* of the sage.

[475] *Par.* 9. From Confucius to Mencius was but a short time compared with that which intervened between Confucius and the duke of Chow, and that again between the duke of Chow and Yaou and Shun. The process of decay was going on with unexampled rapidity. Of Yang Choo, as well as of Mih Teih, and of the principles of them both, I have spoken in the Prolegomena. See the words here attributed to Kung-ming E in I. i. IV. 4.

When they are thus seen in their affairs, they are hurtful to their government. When a sage shall again arise, he will certainly not change [these] ray words.[476]

11. "Formerly, Yu repressed the vast waters [of the inundation], and all under the sky was reduced to order. The duke of Chow's achievements extended to the wild tribes of the east and north, and he drove away all ferocious animals, so that the people enjoyed repose. Confucius completed the Spring and Autumn, and rebellious ministers and villainous sons were struck with terror.[477]

12. "It is said in the Book of Poetry,

'He smote the tribes of the west and the north;
He punished King and Shoo;
And no one dared to resist us.'

These father-deniers and king-deniers would have been smitten by the duke of Chow.[478]

13. "I also wish to rectify men's hearts, and to put an end to [those] perverse speakings, to oppose their one-sided actions, and banish away their licentious expressions;—and thus carry on the [work of the] three sages. Do I do so because I am fond of disputing? I am constrained to do it.[479]

14. "Whoever can by argument oppose Yang and Mih is a disciple of the sages."[480]

X.[481] 1. K'wang Chang said [to Mencius], "Is not Mr. Ch'in Chung a man of true self-denying purity? He was living in Woo-ling, and for three days was without food, till he could neither hear nor see. Over a well there grew a plum tree, a fruit of which had been, more than half of it, eaten by worms. He crawled to it, and tried to eat [some of this fruit], when, after swallowing three mouthfuls, he recovered his sight and hearing."[482]

---

[476] *Par.* 10. Compare II. i. II. 17.

[477] *Par.* 11. The way in which the duke of Chow's driving away "all ferocious animals" is here mentioned seems inconsistent with the view of the expression of which I have spoken under par. 6.

[478] *Par.* 12. See on Pt i. IV. 16.

[479] *Par.* 13. Compare II. i. II. 17.

[480] *Par.* 14. Mencius seems here to call on all disciples of Confucius to cooperate with him in upholding the doctrines of the sage, and yet the sentence was perhaps intended to take away from the forcible assertion to which he had given utterance, and by which he claimed for himself a place in the line of sages.

[481] CH. X. THE MAN WHO WILL AVOID ALL ASSOCIATION WITH, AND OBLIGATION TO, THOSE OF WHOM HE DOES NOT APPROVE MUST NEEDS GO OUT OF THE WORLD.—ILLUSTRATED BY THE CASE OF CH'IN CHUNG OF TS'E.

[482] *Par.* 1. K'wang Chang and Ch'in Chung (called also Ch'in Tsze-chung) were both natives of Ts'e. The former was high in the confidence and employment of the kings Wei and Seuen, and did good service to the State on more than one occasion;—see on IV.

2. Mencius replied, "Among the scholars of Ts'e I must regard Chung as the thumb [among the fingers]. But still, how can he be regarded as having that self-denying purity? To carry out the principles which he holds, one must become an earth-worm, for so only can it be done.[483]

3. "Now an earth-worm eats the dry mould above, and drinks the yellow spring below. Was the house in which Mr. Chung lives built by a Pih-e? or was it built by a robber like Chih? Was the grain which he eats planted by a Pih-e? or was it planted by a robber like Chih? These are things which cannot be known."[484]

4. "But," said [Chang], "what does that matter? He himself weaves sandals of hemp, and his wife twists hempen threads, which they exchange [for other things]."[485]

5. [Mencius] rejoined, "Mr. Chung belongs to an ancient and noble family of Ts'e. His elder brother Tae received from Kah a revenue of 10,000 *chung*, but he considered his brother's emolument to be unrighteous, and would not dwell in the place. Avoiding his brother, and leaving his mother, he went and dwelt in Woo-ling. One day afterwards, he returned [to their house], when it happened that some one sent his brother a present of a live goose. He, knitting his brows, said, 'What are you going to use that cackling thing for?' By-and-by, his mother killed the goose, and gave him some of it to eat. [Just then] his brother came into the house and said, 'It's the flesh of that cackling thing,' on which he went out, and vomited it.

6. "Thus what his mother gave him he would not eat, but what his

---

ii. xxx. The latter, as we learn from this chapter, belonged to an old and noble family of the State. His principles appear to have been those of Heu Hing, mentioned in Pt i. IV., or even more severe. We may compare him with the recluses of Confucius' time. Woo-ling was a poor, wild place, where Chung and his wife, likeminded with himself, lived in retirement. It was somewhere in the present department of Tse-nan. Chaou K'e thinks that it is said the plum was half-eaten, to show how Mr. Chung had really all but lost his eye-sight.

[483] *Par.* 2. Mencius' idea is that Ch'in Chung's principles were altogether impracticable.

[484] *Par.* 3. Pih-e,—see II i. II. 22, *et al.* Chih was a famous robber chief of Confucius' time, a younger brother of Hwuy of Lĕw-hea, celebrated by Mencius in II. i. IX. 2, *et al.* There was, however, it is said, in high antiquity in the time of Hwang-te, a noted robber so called, whose name was given to Hwuy's brother because of the similarity of their course. "The robber Chih" had come to be used like a proper name.—As Chung withdrew from human society lest he should be defiled by it, Mencius shows that unless he were a worm, he could not be independent of other men. Even the house he lived in, and the grain he ate, might be the result of the labor of a villain like Chih, or of a worthy like Pih-e, for anything he could tell.

[485] *Parr.* 4, 5. K'wang Chang says that the lodging and food of Mr. Ch'in were innocently and righteously come by; and it was not necessary to push one's inquiries further back. Mencius does not reply to him directly, but throws ridicule on the self-denying recluse by the ridiculous story which he tells; and concludes by reiterating what he had affirmed as to the impracticability of the man and of his principles.

wife gives him he eats. He will not dwell in his brother's house, but he dwells in Woo-ling. How can he in such circumstances complete the style of life which he professes? With such principles as Mr. Chung holds, [a man must be] an earth-worm, and then he can carry them out."

## BOOK IV. LE LOW. PART I.

CHAPTER I.[486] 1. MENCIUS said, "The power of vision of Le Low, and the skill of hand of Kung-shoo, without the compass and square, could not form squares and circles. The acute ear of the [music]-master Kwang, without the pitch-tubes, could not determine correctly the five notes. The principles of Yaou and Shun, without a benevolent government, could not secure the tranquil order of the kingdom.

With this Book commences what is commonly called the second or lower Part of the Works of Mencius; but that division is not recognized in the critical editions. It is called Le Low from its commencing with those two characters, and contains twenty-eight chapters which are most of them shorter than those of the preceding Books.[487]

2. "There are now [princes] who have benevolent hearts and a reputation for benevolence, while yet the people do not receive any benefits from them, nor will they leave any example to future ages;—all because they do not put into practice the ways of the ancient kings.[488]

---

[486] CH. I. THERE IS AN ART OF GOVERNMENT, AS WELL AS A WISH TO GOVERN WELL, TO BE LEARNED FROM THE EXAMPLE AND PRINCIPLES OF THE ANCIENT KINGS, AND WHICH MUST BE STUDIED AND PRACTISED BY RULERS AND THEIR MINISTERS.

[487] *Par.* 1. Le Low, called also Le Choo, carries us back to the highest Chinese antiquity. He was, it is said, of the time of Hwang-te, and so acute of vision that at the distance of a hundred paces he would see the point of the smallest hair. Kung-shoo, named Pan, was a celebrated mechanist of Loo, contemporary with Confucius, if, as some think, he was a son of duke Ch'aou. He is fabled to have made birds of bamboo which could continue flying for three days, and other marvelous contrivances. He is now the tutelary spirit of carpenters, under the name of Loo Pan or Pan of Loo; but many critics contend that the Kung-shoo of Mencius and Loo Pan ought not to be identified. See the Le Ke, II. ii. II. 21. Kwang, styled Tsze-yay, was a famous music-master of Tsin, a little before the time of Confucius. There is an interesting conversation between him and the marquis of Tsin in the Tso Chuen, under the 14th year of duke Sëang. The pitch-tubes, here called "six," by synecdoche for "twelve," were invented in the earliest times, to determine by their various lengths the notes of the musical scale, and for other purposes. See some account of them under par. 8 in the Shoo, II. i. "The five notes" are the five full notes of the octave, omitting the semitones. The word "principles" in the phrase, "the principles of Yaou and Shun," must be taken vaguely, and as meaning simply the wish to govern rightly, subsequently embodied in "benevolent government," such as Mencius delighted to dwell on in many chapters of the previous Books. The use of "principles," however, in this vague and uncertain way, introduces au inconsistency and ambiguity into the chapter. Mencius exhorts to follow the *ways* or "principles" of the ancient kings, and yet they are here said to be insufficient for good government.

[488] *Par.* 2. One of the early commentators of the Sung dynasty refers to king Seuen

3. "Hence we have the saying, 'Goodness alone is not sufficient for the exercise of government; laws alone cannot carry themselves into practice.'[489]

4. "It is said in the Book of Poetry,

'Erring in nothing, forgetful of nothing,
Observing and following the old statutes.'

Never has any one fallen into error who followed the laws of the ancient kings.[490]

5. "When the sages had used all the power of their eyes, they called in to their aid the compass, the square, the level, and the line; and the ability to make things square, round, level, and straight was inexhaustible. When they had used all the power of their ears, they called in the aid of the pitch-tubes; and the ability to determine correctly the five notes was inexhaustible. When they had used all the thoughts of their hearts, they called in to their aid a government that could not bear [to witness the suffering of] men; and their benevolence overspread all under heaven.[491]

6. "Hence we have the saying, 'To raise a thing high we must begin from [the top of] a mound or a hill; to dig to a [great] depth, we must commence in [the low ground of] a stream or a marsh.' Can he be pronounced wise who, in the exercise of government, does not start from the ways of the ancient kings.[492]

7. "Therefore only the benevolent ought to be in high stations. When a man destitute of benevolence is in a high station, he thereby disseminates his wickedness among the multitudes [below him].[493]

8. "When the ruler has not principles by which he examines [his administration], and his ministers have no laws by which they keep themselves [in the discharge of their duties], then in the court obedience is not paid to principle, and in the office obedience is not paid to rule. Superiors violate [the laws of] righteousness, and inferiors

---

of Ts'e of I. i. VII. *et al.*, as an instance of the rulers who have a benevolent heart, and to the first emperor of the Lĕang dynasty, (A.D. 502-549), whose Buddhistic scrupulosity about taking life made him have a reputation for benevolence. Yet the heart of the one and the reputation of the other proved of little benefit to their people.

[489] *Par.* 3. "Goodness alone" is the benevolent heart without the method. "Laws alone" is the benevolent government without the heart.

[490] *Par.* 4. See the She, III. ii. V. 2.

[491] *Par.* 5. According to the views of Chinese writers, the *lever* was the first of the mechanical powers which was invented. "The lever revolving produced the *circle*. The circle produced the *square*. The square produced the *line*; and the line produced the *level*." On government as "not bearing to witness the sufferings of men," see II. i. VI.

[492] *Par.* 6. The saying is found in the Le Ke, X. ii. 10.

[493] *Par.* 7. The "therefore" expresses a consequence from what has been said in all the previous paragraphs. "High stations" should perhaps be "the highest station." The ruler is indicated.

violate the penal laws. It is only by a fortunate chance that a State in such a case is preserved.[494]

9. "Therefore it is said, 'It is not the interior and exterior walls being incomplete, nor the supply of weapons offensive and defensive not being large, which constitutes the calamity of a State. It is not the non-extension of the cultivable area, nor the non-accumulation of stores and wealth, which is injurious to a State.' When superiors do not observe the rules of propriety, and inferiors do not learn [anything better], then seditious people spring up, and [that State] will perish in no time.

10. "It is said in the Book of Poetry,[495]

'Heaven is now producing such movements;—
Do not be so indifferent'

11. "'Indifferent,' that is, careless and dilatory.

12. "And so may [those officers] be deemed who serve their ruler without righteousness, who take office and retire from office without regard to propriety, and in their words disown the ways of the ancient kings.

13. "Therefore it is said, 'To urge one's ruler to difficult achievements should be called showing respect for him; to set before him what is good and repress his perversities should be called showing reverence for him. [He who does not do these things, but says to himself], 'My ruler is incompetent to this,' should be said to play the thief with him."[496]

II.[497] 1. Mencius said, "The compass and square produce perfect circles and squares. By the sages the human relations are perfectly exhibited.[498]

2. "He who, as a ruler, would perfectly discharge the duties of a ruler, and he who, as a minister, would perfectly discharge the duties of a minister, have only to imitate,—the one Yaou, and the other Shun. He who does not serve his ruler as Shun served Yaou does not reverence his ruler, and he who does not rule the people as Yaou ruled them

---

[494] *Par.* 8 is an illustration of the concluding clause of par. 7, showing how wickedness flows downwards, with its consequences.

[495] *Par.* 10. See the She, III. ii. X. 2.—From this paragraph Mencius has the ministers of a ruler in view. They have their duties to perform, in order that the benevolent government may be realized.

[496] *Par.* 13. Compare II. ii. II. 4.

[497] CH. II. A CONTINUATION OF LAST CHAPTER.—THAT YAOU AND SHUN WERE PERFECT MODELS FOR RULERS AND MINISTERS; AND THE CONSEQUENCES OF NOT IMITATING THEM.

[498] *Par.* 1. The "human relations" are the five specified in III. i. IV. 8. "The sages," according to this par., were not only models for rulers and ministers, but showed human nature in all its relations according to its ideal.

injures his people.[499]

3. "Confucius said, 'There are but two courses, that of benevolence and its opposite.'[500]

4. "[A ruler] who carries the oppression of his people to the highest pitch will himself be slain, and his State will perish. If one stop short of the highest pitch, his life will be in danger, and his State will be weakened. He will be styled 'The Dark' or 'The Cruel;' and though he may have filial sons and affectionate grandsons, they will not be able in a hundred generations to change [the designation].[501]

5. "This is what is intended in the words of the Book of Poetry,[502]

> 'The beacon of Yin is not far distant;—
> It is in the age of the [last] sovereign of Hëa.'"

III.[503] 1. Mencius said, "It was by benevolence that the three dynasties gained the kingdom, and, by not being benevolent that they lost it.[504]

2. "It is in the same way that the decaying and flourishing, the preservation and perishing, of States are determined.

3. "If the son of Heaven be not benevolent, he cannot preserve [all within] the four seas [from passing from him]. If a feudal prince be not benevolent, he cannot preserve his altars. If a noble or great officer be not benevolent, ho cannot preserve his ancestral temple. If a scholar or common man be not benevolent, he cannot preserve his four limbs.[505]

4. "Now they hate death and ruin, and yet delight in not being benevolent;—this is like hating to be drunk, and yet being strong [to

---

[499] *Par.* 2. We have no particular account of how Shun discharged his duties as a minister, nor of how Yaou discharged his as a ruler. All our information about them is comprised in a short space at the beginning of the Shoo. We must believe that Shun was all that a minister could be, and Yaou all that a ruler could be.

[500] *Par.* 3. This is a saying of Confucius for the preservation of which we are indebted to Mencius. By the course of benevolence is intended the imitation of Yaou and Shun; by its opposite the neglect of them as models.

[501] *Par.* 4. By rulers who carry oppression to the highest pitch Mencius intends Këeh and Chow, the last sovereigns of the Hëa and Yin dynasties; by "The Dark" and "The Cruel," he intends the twelfth and tenth kings of the Chow dynasty, who received those posthumous, but indelible, designations.

[502] *Par.* 5. See the She, III. iii. I. 6.

[503] CH. III. THE IMPORTANCE TO ALL, BUT ESPECIALLY TO RULERS, OF EXERCISING BENEVOLENCE.

[504] *Par.* 1. "The three dynasties" are of course those of Hëa, Shang or Yin, and Chow. It is a bold utterance, seeing that the dynasty of Chow was still existing in the time of Mencius; but he regarded it as old and ready to vanish away.

[505] *Par.* 3. "The four seas" is here equivalent to "all beneath the sky," which means the empire or kingdom of China. See on the Shoo, II. i. 13. "The altars" are in the Chinese text specifically those to the spirits of the land and the grain. The phrase is here equivalent to "his State."

drink] spirits."[506]

IV.[507] 1. Mencius said, "If a man love others, and no [responsive] affection is shown to him, let him turn inwards and examine his own benevolence; if he [is trying to] rule others, and his government is unsuccessful, let him turn inwards and examine his own wisdom. If he treats others politely and they do not return his politeness, let him turn inwards and examine his own [feeling of] respect.

2. "If we do not by what we do realize [what we desire], we should turn inwards, and examine ourselves in every point. When a man is himself correct, all under heaven will turn to him [with recognition and submission].

3. "It is said in the Book of Poetry,

'Always strive to accord with the will [of Heaven];
So shall you be seeking for much happiness.'"

V.[508] 1. Mencius said, "People have this common saying,—'The kingdom, the State, the clan.' The root of the kingdom is in the State; the root of the State is in the clan; the root of the clan is in the person.

VI.[509] Mencius said, "The administration of government is not

---

[506] *Par.* 4 has for its subject the princes of Mencius' time.

[507] CH. IV. WITH WHAT MEASURE A MAN METES IT WILL BE MEASURED TO HIM AGAIN; AND CONSEQUENTLY BEFORE A MAN DEALS WITH OTHERS, EXPECTING THEM TO BE AFFECTED BY HIM, HE SHOULD FIRST DEAL WITH HIMSELF. The sentiment is expressed quite generally, but a particular reference is to be understood to the princes of the time. The lines quoted are from the She, III. i. I. 6. They were adduced before in II. i. IV. 6.

[508] CH. V. THE GREAT THING TO BE ATTENDED TO IS THE CULTIVATION OF PERSONAL CHARACTER. I think this is the idea which Mencius had in mind in the words given here. The common saying to which he refers was good so far as it went, but it did not go far enough. His course of thought is followed out to greater length in "The Great Learning." See the 4th par. of the Confucian Text there, and many passages of the Commentary.

[509] CH. VI. THE IMPORTANCE TO A RULER OF SECURING THE SUBMISSION AND ESTEEM OF THE GREAT HOUSES IN HIS STATE.

The ruler's "not offending the great Houses" means his not doing anything that will excite their resentment, but commanding their loyal attachment by his personal character and his administration. Choo He refers, in illustration of the sentiment, to a story about duke Hwan of Ts'e which we find in one of the works of Lĕw Hëang. The duke, we are told, came one day in hunting to the district of Mih-k'ëw, and lighted on an old man, who said, in answer to his inquiry, that he was 83. "A beautiful old age," said the duke. "Pray that I may be blessed with an equal longevity." The old man accordingly prayed, "May his lordship, my ruler, live to a very great age, despising gold and gems, and counting men his jewels!" The duke said, "Good! But the highest virtue is not found alone; good words must be repeated. Do you, Sir, pray for me a second time." The man did so, saying, "May his lordship, my ruler, not be ashamed to learn, nor dislike to ask his inferiors, have men of worth by his side, and give access to such as will admonish him!" The duke expressed his satisfaction with this prayer in nearly the same terms as before, and asked the old man to pray for him a third time. The man complied, and said, "May his lordship, my ruler, not offend against his ministers and the people!" The duke difficult; it lies in not offending against the great Houses. He whom the great Houses affect will be affected by the whole State; and he whom a whole State affects will be affected by all under heaven. When this is the case, [such an one's] virtue and teachings will spread over [all within] the four seas like the rush of water."

VII.[510] 1. Mencius said, "When right government prevails throughout the kingdom, [princes of] little virtue are submissive to those of great, and [those of] little worth to [those of] great. When bad government prevails, the small are submissive to the large, and the weak to the strong. Both these cases are [the law of] Heaven. They who accord with Heaven are preserved; they who rebel against Heaven perish.[511]

2. "Duke King of Ts'e said, 'Not to be able to command [others], and further to refuse to receive their commands, is to cut one's-self off from all intercourse with them.' His tears flowed forth, and he gave his daughter in marriage to [the prince of] Woo.[512]

3. "Now the small States take for their models the large States, but are ashamed to receive their commands;—this is like scholars being ashamed to receive the commands of their master.[513]

---

changed color at these words, and said, "I have heard that a son may offend against his father, and a minister against his ruler, but I have not heard of a ruler's offending against his minister;—this prayer is not of a piece with the two former ones. Please to change it." The old man knelt down in obeisance, and then stood up and said, "This prayer is superior to the two former ones. A son who has offended against his father may apologize through his aunts and uncles, and the father can forgive him. A minister who has offended against his ruler may apologize through his ruler's familiar attendants, and be forgiven. But when K'ëeh offended against T'ang, and Chow offended against king Woo, these were cases of rulers offending against their nobles. There were none through whom they could apologize; the offences were never forgiven, and the retribution for them continues to the present day." The duke acknowledged the truth of what the man said, and showed to him great honour.

[510] CH. VII. THE WILL OF HEAVEN IN REGARD TO THE SUBJECTION OF ONE STATE TO ANOTHER IS VARIOUSLY INDICATED, AND DEPENDS ON CERTAIN CONDITIONS; WHICH EXISTING, THE RESULT CANNOT BE AVOIDED. A PRINCE'S ONLY SECURITY FOR SAFETY AND PROSPERITY IS IN BEING BENEVOLENT.

[511] *Par.* 1. "Both these cases are [the law of] Heaven:"—Heaven, it is said, embraces here the ideas of what must be in reason, and the different powers of the contrasted States. This is true; in a virtuous age, the greatest virtue will influence the most, and in a bad age, the greatest strength will prevail. But why sink the idea of a Providential government which is implied in "Heaven"?

[512] *Par.* 2. Duke King of Ts'e has been mentioned already in I. ii. IV. 4, *et al.* The affair here referred to does not appear in the Tso Chuen, but is mentioned by Lëw Hëang and other writers. The duke, it appears, purchased peace from Hoh-leu, king of Woo as he called himself, by sending his daughter to Woo to be married to his son. Woo, corresponding to the northern part of Cheh-këang and the south of Këang-soo, was still considered a barbarous State in the time of Confucius, and the civilized States of Chow were ashamed to have dealings with it on equal terms. The princess of Ts'e mentioned here soon pined away and died, and was followed to the grave ere long by her husband, the old barbarian king showing much sympathy with her case.

[513] *Par.* 3. The smaller States followed the example of the larger in what was evil,

4. "For [a prince] who is ashamed of this, the best plan is to make king Wăn his model. Let one take king Wăn as his model and in five years, if his State be large, or in seven years, if it be small, he will be sure to give law to all under heaven.[514]

5. "It is said in the Book of Poetry,

'The descendants of [the sovereigns of] Shang
Were more in number than a hundred thousand;
But when God gave the command,
They became subject to Chow.

'They became subject to Chow.
The appointment of Heaven is not constant.
The officers of Yin, admirable and alert,
Assist at the libations in our capital.'

Confucius said, 'As [against so] benevolent [a ruler, the multitudes] could not be deemed multitudes.' If the ruler of a State love benevolence, he will have no opponent under heaven.

6. "Now-a-days, they wish to have no opponent under heaven, but [they do] not [seek to attain this] by being benevolent;—this is like trying to hold a heated substance, without having dipped it in water. It is said in the Book of Poetry,[515]

'Who can hold anything hot?
Must he not dip it [first] in water?'"

VIII.[516] 1. Mencius said, "How is it possible to speak with [princes] who are not benevolent? Their perils they count safety, their calamities they count profitable, and they delight in the things by which they are going to ruin. If it were possible to talk with them who [so] violate benevolence, how should we have such ruin of States and destruction of families?

2. "There was a boy singing,[517]

---

and yet were ashamed to submit to them.

[514] *Parr.* 4, 5. See the She, III. i. I. stt. 4,5. We are to understand that the remark of Confucius was made on reading the stanzas of the ode just referred to:—Against a benevolent prince, like king Wăn, the myriads of the adherents of the Shang dynasty ceased to be myriads. They would not act against him.

[515] *Par.* 6. See the She, III. iii. III. 5, with the remarks which I have there made in Vol. IV., of my larger Work, on the passage.

[516] CH. VIII. THAT A PRINCE IS THE AGENT OF HIS OWN RUIN BY HIS VICIOUS WAYS AND HIS REFUSING TO BE COUNSELLED.

[517] *Par.* 2. The name Ts'ang-lang is found applied to different streams. One is mentioned in the Shoo, III. i. Pt II. 8; but the one in the text was probably in Shan-tung, in the present district of Yih, department Yen-chow.

'When the water of the Ts'ang-lang is clear,
It does to wash the strings of my cap;
When the water of the Ts'ang-lang is muddy,
It does to wash my feet.'

3. "Confucius said, 'Hear what he says, my children:—when clear, to wash the cap strings; when muddy, to wash the feet.' [This different application] is brought [by the water] on itself.[518]

4. "A man must [first] despise himself, and then others will despise him. A family must [first] overthrow itself, and then others will overthrow it. A State must [first] smite itself, and then others will smite it.

5. "This is illustrated by the passage in the T'ae-kĕah, 'Calamities sent by Heaven may be avoided; but when we bring on the calamities ourselves, it is not possible to live.'"[519]

IX.[520] 1. Mencius said, "Kĕeh and Chow's losing the kingdom arose from their losing the people; and to lose the people means to lose their hearts. There is a way to get the kingdom;—get the people, and the kingdom is got. There is a way to get the people;—get their hearts, and the people are got. There is a way to get their hearts;—it is simply to collect for them what they desire, and not to lay on them what they dislike.[521]

2. "The people turn to a benevolent [rule] as water flows downwards, and as wild beasts run to the wilds.

3. "Accordingly [as] the otter aids the deep waters, driving the fish to them, and [as] the hawk aids the thickets, driving the little birds to them, [so] did Kĕeh and Chow aid T'ang and Woo, driving the people to them.

4. "If among the present rulers throughout the kingdom there were

---

[518] *Par.* 3. The boy was singing without any thought of the meaning which the sage could find in his words, and of the expansion of that meaning which our philosopher would give.

[519] *Par.* 5. See on II. i. IV. 6.

[520] CH. IX. BEING BENEVOLENT IS THE SURE WAY FOR A RULER TO RISE TO THE HEIGHT OF THE ROYAL DIGNITY; AND IS MOREOVER THE ONLY WAY TO AVOID DEATH AND RUIN.

[521] *Par.* 1. Choo He illustrates what is said here about getting the people's hearts by what we find in the Biographies of the Books of Han about Ch'aou Ts'oh, who is mentioned in the Prolegomena to the Shoo, in my larger Work, p.16, in connection with the recovery of some of the books of that classic through the scholar Fuh-săng. The tranquility of the kingdom, according to Ts'oh, depended on its government being administered in harmony with the feelings of the people. "By those feelings," said Ts'oh, "people are desirous of longevity, and the three kings cherished the people's lives and allowed no injury to happen to them. They are desirous of riches, and the three kings were generous, and subjected them to no straits. They are desirous of security, of ease, &c., and the three kings secured to them the enjoyment of these."

one who loved benevolence, all the [other] princes would aid him by driving the people to him. Although he wished not to exercise the royal sway, he could not avoid doing so.

5. "The case of [one of the] present [princes] wishing to attain to the royal sway is like the having to seek for mugwort three years old to cure a seven years' illness. If it have not been kept in store, the whole life may pass without getting it. If [the princes] do not set their minds on a benevolent [government], all their days will be in sorrow and disgrace, till they are involved in death and ruin.[522]

6. "This is illustrated by what is said in the Book of Poetry,[523]

'How can you [by your method] bring a good state of affairs about?

You [and your] advisers will sink together in ruin.'"

X.[524] 1. Mencius said, "With those who do violence to themselves it is impossible to speak. With those who throw themselves away it is impossible to do anything. To disown in his conversation propriety and righteousness is what we mean by saying of a man that he does violence to himself; that [he says], 'I am not able to dwell in benevolence and pursue the path of righteousness' is what we mean by saying of a man that he throws himself away.

2. "Benevolence is the tranquil habitation of man, and righteousness is his straight path.

3. "Alas for those who leave the tranquil dwelling empty and do not reside in it, and who neglect the straight path and do not pursue it!"

XI.[525] Mencius said, "The path [of duty] is in what is near, and [men] seek for it in what is remote. The work [of duty] is in what is easy, and [men] seek for it in what is difficult. If each man would love his parents, and show the due respect to his elders, all-under-heaven

---

[522] *Par.* 5. The down of the mugwort burnt on the skin wag and is used for purposes of cautery. The older the plant, the more valuable for this application. and the longer any disease in which it could be employed had existed, the more desirable it was to get the most effectual remedy for it. The kingdom and each State had long been suffering from cruel and oppressive government, and their cure must come from a benevolent rule long pursued and consolidated. This seems to be Mencius' idea.

[523] *Par.* 6. See the She, III. iii. III. 5. The lines immediately follow the two quoted at the end of ch. vii.

[524] CH. X. A WARNING TO THE VIOLENTLY EVIL AND THE WEAKLY EVIL. Choo He concludes his comments here with the words:—"This chapter tells us that the principles of rectitude and virtue do originally belong to human nature, while men extinguish them by their voluntary act. Profound is the caution here conveyed by the sages and worthies, and learners ought to give the most earnest heed to it."

[525] CH. XI. THE WAY OF DUTY IS NOT FAR TO SEEK; AND THE TRANQUIL PROSPERITY OF THE KINGDOM DEPENDS ON THE DISCHARGE OF THE COMMON RELATIONS OF LIFE. Compare the 12th, 13th, and several other chapters of "The Doctrine of the Mean."

good order would prevail."

XII.[526] 1. When those occupying inferior situations do not obtain the confidence of their superior, they cannot succeed in governing the people. There is a way to obtain the confidence of the superior;—if one is not trusted by his friends, he will not obtain the confidence of his superior. There is a way to being trusted by one's friends;—if one do not serve his parents so as to make them pleased, he will not be trusted by his friends. There is a way to make one's parents pleased;—if one on turning his thoughts inwards finds a want of sincerity, he will not give pleasure to his parents. There is a way to the attainment of sincerity in one's-self;—if a man do not understand what is good, he will not attain to sincerity in himself.

2. "Therefore sincerity is the way of Heaven; and to think [how] to be sincere is the way of man."

3. "Never was there one possessed of complete sincerity who did not move [others]. Never was there one without sincerity who yet was able to move others."

XIII.[527] 1. Mencius said, "Pih-e, that he might avoid Chow, was dwelling on the coast of the northern sea. When he heard of the rise of king Wăn, he roused himself and said, 'Why should I not attach myself to him? I have heard that the chief of the West knows well how to nourish the old.' T'ae-kung, that he might avoid Chow, was dwelling on the west coast of the eastern sea. When he heard of the rise of king Wăn, he roused himself and said, 'Why should I not attach myself to him? I have heard that the chief of the West knows well how to nourish the old.'[528]

---

[526] CH. XII. THE GREAT WORK OF EVERY MAN SHOULD BE TO TRY TO ATTAIN COMPLETE SINCERITY IN HIMSELF, WHICH WILL GIVE HIM A FAR-REACHING POWER OVER OTHERS. Compare the 17th and 18th paragraphs of the 20th chapter of "The Doctrine of the Mean," which are here substantially quoted. As that chapter, however, is also found in the "Family Sayings," Mencius may have had the fragmentary memorabilia of Confucius, from which that compilation was made, before him, and not the Chung Yung.

[527] CH. XIII. THE GOVERNMENT OF KING WĂN IN ITS ASPECT TOWARDS THE AGED AND HELPLESS; AND THE INFLUENCE WHICH ANY GOVERNMENT LIKE IT WOULD PRODUCE.

[528] *Par.* 1. Pih-e;—See II. i. II. 22; IX. i.; III. ii. X. 3. What is here called the northern sea must be, I think, the northern part of the gulf of Pih-chih-le. T'ae-kung is Leu Shang, a great counselor of the kings Wăn and Woo. He claimed to be descended from one of Yu's assistants in the regulation of the waters, from whom he had the surname of Kĕang; and some member of the family had been invested with the principality of Leu, so that Leu became a clan-name or second surname of his descendants. The legend goes that king Wăn first met with T'ae-kung as a fisherman on the banks of the Wei, which is not according to the account of Mencius here, which would make us suppose that he was living somewhere in the east of the present Shantung when he went over to the side of Wăn. King Wăn had been warned by an oracle that he was to meet with a powerful assistant on the day that he encountered T'ae-kung, and accordingly he said to him, "My grandfather expected you long," which led to his being

2. "These two old men were the greatest old men in the kingdom. When they attached themselves to [king Wăn] it was [like] all the fathers in the kingdom taking his side. When the fathers of the kingdom joined him, to whom could the sons go?"[529]

3. "Were any of the princes to practise the government of king Wăn, within seven years he would be sure to be giving law to all under heaven."[530]

XIV.[531] 1. Mencius said, "(K'ĕw acted as chief officer to the Head of the Ke family, whose [evil] ways he was unable to change, while he exacted from the people double the grain which they had formerly paid. Confucius said, 'He is no disciple of mine. Little children, beat the drum and assail him.'[532]

2. "Looking at the subject from this case, [we perceive that] when a ruler who was not practicing benevolent government, all [his ministers] who enriched him were disowned by Confucius;—how much more [would he have disowned] those who are vehement to fight [for their ruler]! Some contention about territory is the ground on which they fight, and they slaughter men till the fields are filled with them; or they fight for the possession of some fortified city, and slaughter men till the walls are covered with them. This is what is called 'leading land on to devour human flesh.' Death is not enough for such a crime.[533]

3. "Therefore those who are skilful to fight should suffer the highest punishment. Next to them [should be punished] those who unite the princes in leagues; and next to them, those who take in grassy

---

called T'ae-kung Wang, or "Grandfather Hope." Though Pih-e and T'ae-kung are here represented as led to king Wăn in the same way, their subsequent course and relation to the new dynasty of Chow were very different. Pih-e would not sanction the overthrow of the Shang dynasty, while T'ae-kung acted an important part in that achievement, and was rewarded with the marquisate of Ts'e. Wăn is here styled "Chief of the West," because he was appointed by the sovereign of Shang his viceroy or chief over all the States in that part of the kingdom. Wăn's government is spoken of here only in its relation to the aged, but we must consider that term as embracing other helpless classes;—see the description in I. ii. V. 3.

[529] *Par.* 2. On this par. the "Daily Explanation" says:—"Moreover these two old men were not ordinary men. Distinguished alike by age and virtue, they were the greatest old men of the kingdom. Fit to be so named, the hopes of all looked to them, and the hearts of all were bound to them. All under heaven looked up to them as fathers, and felt as their children, so that when they were moved by the government of king Wăn, and came to him from the coasts of the sea, how could the children leave their fathers and go to any other?"

[530] *Par.* 3. Compare what Confucius says of the results which he could produce if he were put in charge of the government of a State, in Ana. XIII. x., *et al.*

[531] CH. XIV. AGAINST THE MINISTERS OF THE TIME, WHO PURSUED THEIR WARLIKE AND OTHER SCHEMES, REGARDLESS OF THE LIVES AND HAPPINESS OF THE PEOPLE.

[532] *Par.* 1. For the case of K'ĕw or Yen Yĕw, see the Ana. XI. xvi. See also the last narrative of the Tso Chuen under the 11th year of duke Gae.

[533] *Par.* 2. "Leading on land to devour human flesh;" this is a striking variation of the language in I. i. IV. 4, *et al.*

wastes, and impose the cultivation of the ground [upon the people]."[534]

XV.[535] 1. Mencius said, "Of all the parts of a man's [body] there is none more excellent than the pupil of the eye. The pupil cannot [be used to] hide a man's wickedness. If within the breast [all] be correct, the pupil is bright; if within the breast [all] be not correct, the pupil is dull.

2. "Listen to a man's words, and look at the pupil of his eye;—how can a man conceal [his character]?"

XVI.[536] Mencius said, "The courteous do not insult others, and the economical do not plunder others. The ruler who treats men with insult and plunders them is only afraid that they will not prove submissive to him;—how can he be regarded as courteous or economical? How can courtesy and economy be made out of tones of the voice and a smiling manner?"

XVII.[537] 1. Shun-yu K'wăn said, "Is it the rule that males and females shall not allow their hands to touch in giving or receiving anything?" Mencius replied, "It is the rule." "If a man's sister-in-law be drowning," asked K'wăn, "shall he rescue her by the hand?" [Mencius] said, "He who would not [so] rescue his drowning sister-in-law would be a wolf. For males and females not to allow their hands to touch in giving and receiving is the [general] rule; to rescue by the hand a drowning sister-in-law is a peculiar exigency.[538]

2. [K'wăn] said, "Now the whole kingdom is drowning; and how is it that you, Master, will not rescue it?"

3. [Mencius] replied, "A drowning kingdom must be rescued by

---

[534] *Par.* 3. Here we have three classes of adventurers who were rife in Mencius' times, and who recommended themselves to the princes of the States in the ways described, pursuing the while their own ends, and regardless of the people. Some advanced themselves by their skill in war; some by their talents for intrigue, forming confederacies among the States, especially to oppose the encroachments of Ts'in; and some by their plans to make the most of the ground, turning every bit of it to account, but for the good of the ruler, not of the people.

[535] CH. XV. THE PUPIL OF THE EYE THE INDEX OF THE MIND AND HEART. This chapter is to be understood as spoken by Mencius for the use of those who thought they had only to hear men's words to judge of them. Compare Ana. II. x.

[536] CH. XVI. DEEDS, NOT WORDS OR MANNER, NECESSARY TO PROVE MENTAL QUALITIES. The first sentence is as general in the original as in the translation, but all the Chinese critics say that the statements are to be understood of the princes of Mencius' time, who made great pretensions to courtesy and economy, of which their actions proved the insincerity. But I think the propositions in the first sentence are quite general. Our philosopher proceeds to make the application of them.

[537] CH. XVII. HELP—EFFECTUAL HELP—CAN BE GIVEN TO THE WORLD ONLY IN HARMONY WITH RIGHT AND PROPRIETY.

[538] *Par.* 1. Shun-yu K'wăn was a native of Ts'e, a famous sophist, and otherwise a man of note in his day. See his biography in the 126th Book of the "Historical Records." He here tries to entrap Mencius into a confession that he did not do well in maintaining the dignity of reserve, which marked him in his intercourse with the princes. For the rule of propriety referred to, see the Le Ke, I. ii. 31.

right principles, as a drowning sister-in-law has to be rescued by the hand. Do you, Sir, wish me to rescue the kingdom with my hand?"[539]

XVIII.[540] 1. Kung-sun Ch'ow said, "Why is it that the superior man does not [himself] teach his son?"

2. Mencius replied, "The circumstances of the case forbid its being done. A teacher must inculcate what is correct. Doing this, and his lesson not being learned, he follows it up with being angry; and through thus being angry, he is offended, contrary to what should be, [with his pupil]. [At the same time, the pupil] says, 'My master inculcates on me what is correct, and he himself does not proceed in a correct path.' Thus father and son would be offended with each other, but when father and son come to be offended with each other, the case is evil.[541]

3. "The ancients exchanged sons, and one taught the son of another.[542]

4. "Between father and son there should be no reproving admonitions as to what is good. Such reproofs lead to alienation; and there is nothing more inauspicious than alienation."

XIX.[543] 1. Mencius said, "Of services which is the greatest? The service of parents is the greatest. Of charges which is the greatest? The charge of .one's self is the greatest. That those who do not fail to keep themselves are able to serve their parents is what I have heard. [But] I have never heard of any who, having failed to keep themselves, were able [notwithstanding] to serve their parents.[544]

2. "Everything [done] is a service, but the service of parents is the

---

[539] *Par.* 3. Choo He expands here:—"The drowning kingdom can be rescued only by right principles;—the case is different from that of a drowning sister-in-law who can be rescued with the hand. Now you, wishing to rescue the kingdom, would have me, in violation of right principles, seek alliance with the princes, and so begin by losing the means wherewith it might be rescued;—do you wish to make me rescue the kingdom with the hand?" I do not see the point of the last question.

[540] CH. XVIII. THE SEASON WHY A FATHER SHOULD NOT HIMSELF UNDERTAKE THE TEACHING OF HIS SON. But the assertion of Kung-sun Ch'ow is not to be taken in all its generality. Confucius taught his son, and so did other famous men their sons. Of the statement in par.3 about the custom of antiquity I have not been able to find any proof or illustration.

[541] *Par.* 2. "The circumstances of the case" here refer to that of a stupid or perverse child.

[542] *Par.* 3. The commentators all say that "the exchanging of sons" merely means that the ancients sent out their sons to be taught away from home by masters. It is difficult to see what else the expression can mean, though this is explaining away the force of the term "exchanged."

[543] CH. XIX. THE IMPORTANCE OF SERVING ONE'S PARENTS, AND HOW THE DUTY SHOULD BE PERFORMED. IN ORDER TO DISCHARGE IT WE MUST WATCH OVER OURSELVES. ILLUSTRATED IN THE CASES OF TSĂNG-TSZE AND HIS SON.

[544] *Par.* 1. By "services" we are to understand the duties of service which a man has to render to others, and by "charges," what a man has to guard and keep. The "keeping one's self" is the holding one's self aloof from all unrighteousness.

root of all others. Everything [obligatory] is a charge, but the charge of one's self is the root of all others.[545]

3. "Tsăng-tsze, in nourishing Tsăng Seih, was always sure to have spirits and flesh provided. And when they were about to be removed, he would ask respectfully to whom [what was left] should be given. If [his father] asked whether there was anything left, he was sure to say, 'There is.' After the death of Tsăng Seih, when Tsăng Yuen came to nourish Tsăng-tsze, he was sure to have spirits and flesh provided; but when the things were about to be removed, he did not ask to whom [what was left] should be given, and if [his father] asked whether there was anything left, he would answer, 'No;'—intending to bring them on again. This was what is called—'nourishing the mouth and body.' We may call Tsăng-tsze's practice—'nourishing the will.'[546]

4. "To serve one's father as Tsăng-tsze served his may [be pronounced filial piety]."[547]

XX.[548] Mencius said, "It is not enough to reprove [a ruler] on account of [his mal-employment of] men, nor to blame [errors of] government. It is only the great man who can correct what is wrong in the ruler's mind. Let the ruler be benevolent, and all [his acts] will be benevolent. Let the ruler be righteous, and all [his acts] will be righteous. Let the ruler be correct, and everything will be correct. Once rectify the ruler, and the State will be firmly settled."

XXI.[549] Mencius said, "There are cases of praise which could not have been expected, and of reproach where the parties have been seeking to be perfect."

---

[545] *Par.* 2. "The service of parents" is represented as the "root of all other services," according to the Chinese doctrine of filial piety;—see the "Classic of Filial Piety," *passim.* There is more truth in the 2nd part of the paragraph.

[546] *Par.* 3. Seih was the father of the more celebrated Tsăng-tsze, or Tsăng Sin;—see the Ana. XI. XXV. "Nourishing the will" means gratifying, carrying out, and fostering the father's wishes.

[547] On par. 4 Choo He quotes the following words from one of the brothers Ch'ing:—"To serve one's father as Tsăng Sin did his may be called the height of filial piety, and yet Mencius says only that it might be accepted as that virtue. Did he really think that there was something supererogatory in Tsăng's service?" Possibly Mencius may have been referring to Tsăng's-tsze's disclaimer of being considered a model of filial piety. See the Le Ke, XXI. ii. 14, where Tsăng-tsze says, "What the superior man calls filial piety is to anticipate the wishes and carry out the mind of one's parents, always leading them on in what is right and true. I am only one who nourishes his parents;—how can I be deemed filial?"

[548] CH. XX. A TRULY GREAT MINISTER WILL DIRECT HIS EFFORTS NOT SO MUCH TO CORRECT ERRORS IN MATTERS OF DETAIL, AS TO CORRECT HIS RULER'S CHARACTER, FROM WHICH ALL BENEFITS WILL ACCRUE TO THE STATE. The sentiment of the chapter is illustrated by an incident related of Mencius in one of the Books of Seun K'ing:—"Mencius having had three interviews with the king of Ts'e without speaking to him of any particular affair, his disciples were troubled, but the philosopher said to them, 'I must first attack his wayward mind.'"

[549] CH. XXI. PRAISE AND BLAME ARE SOMETIMES GIVEN WITHOUT ANY PROPER GROUND FOR THEM.

XXII.[550] Mencius said, "Men's being ready with their words arises simply from their not having been reproved."

XXIII.[551] Mencius said, "The evil with men is that they like to be teachers of others."

XXIV.[552] 1. The disciple Yoh-ching went in the train of Tsze-gaou to Ts'e.[553]

2. He came to see Mencius, who said to him, "Are you, Sir, also come to see me?" "Master, why do you use such words?" was the reply. "How many days have you been here?" asked [Mencius]. "I came [only] yesterday," said [the other]. "Yesterday! Then is it not with reason that I thus speak?" "My lodging-house was not arranged," urged [Yoh-ching]. "Have you heard," said [Mencius] "that a scholar's lodging-house must be arranged before he visits his master?"[554]

3. [Yoh-ching] said, "I have done wrong."

XXV.[555] Mencius, addressing the disciple Yoh-ching, said, "Your coming here in the train of Tsze-gaou was only [because of] the food and the drink [that you would so get]. I could not have thought that you, Sir, having learned the ways of the ancients, would have acted with a view to eating and drinking."

XXVI.[556] 1. Mencius said, "There are three things which are unfilial, and to have no posterity is the greatest of them.[557]

---

[550] CH. XXII. WHEN A MAN IS REPROVED FOR LIGHT SPEECH, HE DOES NOT SO READILY REPEAT THE OFFENCE. Choo He supposes that the remark here was made with some particular reference.

[551] CH. XXIII. BE NOT MANY MASTERS. The tendency here rebuked indicates, it is said, a self-sufficiency, which puts an end to self-improvement.

[552] CH. XXIV. HOW MENCIUS REPROVED YOH-CHING FOR ASSOCIATING WITH AN UNWORTHY MAN OF POSITION, AND BEING REMISS ON WAITING ON HIMSELF, HIS MASTER.

[553] *Par.* 1. Yoh-ching;—see I. ii. XVI. 2. Tsze-gaou was the designation of Wang Hwan mentioned in II. ii. VI. From that chapter we may understand that Mencius would not be pleased with one of his disciples who associated with such a person.

We must understand that Tsze-gaou had gone on a mission from Ts'e to Loo, and that Yoh-ching took the opportunity to go in his train back with him to Ts'e, pretending that he wished to see his master Mencius.

[554] *Par.* 2. Chaou K'e understands the word which I have rendered yesterday to mean—"formerly," "some days ago." It may have that meaning; but it is undoubtedly used for "yesterday," in II. ii. II. 2, and the whole par. here has more force by giving to it that meaning. We see what respectful attention to himself Mencius exacted from his followers.

[555] CH. XXV. FURTHER AND MORE DIRECT REPROOF OF YOH-CHING. The terms used here for "eating and drinking" are both contemptuous, =our application of "the loaves and fishes."

[556] CH. XXVI. SHUN'S EXTRAORDINARY WAY OF CONTRACTING MARRIAGE JUSTIFIED BY THE MOTIVE, WHICH WAS TO RAISE UP POSTERITY TO HIS PARENTS.

[557] *Par.* 1. The two other things which are unfilial are, according to Chaou K'e, 1st, by a flattering assent to encourage parents in unrighteousness, and 2nd, not to succor their poverty and old age by engaging in official service. To be without posterity is greater than those faults, because it is an offence against the whole line of ancestors, and brings the sacrifices to them to an end. In ii. XXX. 2, Mencius specifies five things which were

2. "Shun married without informing his parents because of this,—lest he should have no posterity. Superior men consider that his doing so was the same as if he had informed them."[558]

XXVII.[559] 1. Mencius said, "The richest fruit of benevolence is this,—the service of one's parents. The richest fruit of righteousness is this,—the service of one's elder brother.[560]

2. "The richest fruit of wisdom is this,—the knowing those two things and not departing from them. The richest fruit of propriety is this,—the ordering and adorning those two things. The richest fruit of music is this,—the joying in those two things. When joyed in, they grow. Growing, how can they be repressed? When they come to this state that they cannot be repressed, then unconsciously the feet begin to dance and the hands to move."[561]

XXVIII.[562] 1. Mencius said, "[Suppose the case of] all under heaven turning with great delight to an individual to submit to him. To regard all under heaven [thus] turning to him with delight but as a bundle of grass;—only Shun was capable of this. [He considered that] if [one] could not get [the hearts of] his parents he could not be considered a man, and if he could not get to an entire accord with his parents, he could not be considered a son.[563]

commonly deemed unfilial, and not one of these three is amongst them. The sentiment here is to be understood as spoken from the point of view of the superior man, and moreover as laying down the ground for the vindication of Shun.

[558] *Par.* 2. See the account of Shun's marriage at the end of the first Book of the Shoo. From that we might give a different reason for his contracting it from that which Mencius assigns. He intimates that Shun's parents were so hostile to him, that they would have forbidden his marriage, if he had told them about it.

[559] CH. XXVII. FILIAL PIETY AND FRATERNAL AFFECTION IN THEIR RELATION TO BENEVOLENCE, RIGHTEOUSNESS, WISDOM, PROPRIETY, AND MUSIC.

[560] *Par.* 1. Benevolence, righteousness, &c., are the principles of filial piety and fraternal affection,—the capabilities of them in human nature, which may have endless manifestations, but are chiefly and primarily to be seen in those two virtues.

[561] *Par.* 2. The introduction of the subject music here strikes us as strange. A commentator tries to explain it in the following way:—"Benevolence, righteousness, propriety, and wisdom are the four virtues, but Mencius here proceeds to speak of music also. and the principles of music are really a branch of propriety; and when the ordering and adorning, which belong to that, are perfect, then harmony and pleasure spring up as a matter of course. In this way we have propriety mentioned first and then music. Moreover, the fervency of benevolence, the exactness of righteousness, the clearness of knowledge, and the firmness of maintenance must all have their depth manifested in music. If this chapter had not spoken of music, we should not have seen the whole amount of achievement."

[562] CH. XXVIII. HOW SHUN VALUED FILIAL PIETY MORE THAN THE POSSESSION OF THE EMPIRE, AND EXEMPLIFIED IT TILL HE WROUGHT A GLORIOUS CHANGE IN HIS FATHER'S CHARACTER.

[563] *Par.* 1. The first sentence is to be understood as of general application, and not with reference to Shun simply. It is incomplete. The conclusion of it would be something like—"this would be accounted the greatest happiness and glory." Choo He and others Endeavour to find in the "getting to an entire accord with his parents" the bringing them to accord with what is right, so as then fully to accord with them.

2. "By Shun's completely fulfilling the duty of serving parents, Koo-sow was brought to feel delight [in what was good]. When Koo-sow was brought to feel delight [in what was good], all under heaven were transformed. When Koo-sow was brought to feel delight [in what was good], all fathers and sons under heaven were established [in their respective duties]. This may well be called great filial piety."[564]

## BOOK IV. LE LOW. PART II.

CHAPTER I.[565] 1. MENCIUS said, "Shun was born in Choo-fung, removed to Foo-hea, and died in Ming-t'ĕaou;—A man [from the country] of the wild tribes on the east.[566]

2. "King Wăn was born in K'e-chow and died in Peih-ying;—a man [from the country] of the wild tribes on the west.[567]

3. "Those regions were distant from each other more than a thousand *le*, and the age of the one [sage] was posterior to that of the other more than a thousand years. But when they got their wish and earned out [their principles] throughout the middle States, it was like uniting the two halves of a seal.[568]

4. "[When we Examine] the sages—the earlier and the later—their principles are found to be the same."

---

[564] *Par.* 2. Shun's father is known in history by the name of Koo-sow. The characters representing those sounds both denote "blind" or rather "eyeless," and K'ung Gan-kwoh says that the individual in question was so styled because of his mental blindness and opposition to all that was good.

[565] CH. 1. THE AGREEMENT OF SAGES NOT AFFECTED BY TIME OR PLACE;—SHOWN IN THE CASES OF SHUN AND KING WĂN.

[566] *Par.* 1. According to Sze-ma Ts'ĕen, Shun was a native of K'e-chow, for the dimensions of which see the note on the Shoo, III i. Pt I. 2; and all the places here mentioned are referred by him to the same province. Some, however, and especially Tsăng Tsze-koo of the Sung dynasty, find Shun's birth-place in the department of Tse-nan, Shan-tung, and this would seem to be supported by Mencius in this passage. According to Ts'ĕen, moreover, Shun died, when on a tour of inspection in the south, in the wild of Ts'ang-woo, and was buried in mount Kĕw-e, in the present district of Ling-ling, department of Yung-chow, Hoo-nan. The discussions on the point are numerous. It was Mencius' object to place Shun in the east, and his birth and life were in the country east from that of king Wăn. He can hardly have intended to say that Shun and Wăn were themselves men of the wild tribes of the east and west, though his words, literally taken, say so.

[567] *Par.* 2. K'e-chow, or the plain of Chow at the foot of mount K'e, was in the present department of Fung-ts'ĕang, Shen-se. Peih-ying is to be distinguished from Ying, the capital of the large State of Ts'oo. It was in the present district of Hĕen-ning, department Se-gan of Shen-se; and there the grave of king Wăn, or the place of it, is still pointed out.

[568] *Par.* 3. "The two halves of a seal;"—perhaps it would be as well to say "a tally," or "a token." Anciently the king delivered, as the token of investiture, one half of a tally of wood or of jade, reserving the other half in his own keeping. It was cut right through a line of characters, indicating the appointment, and the halves fitting each other when occasion required was the test of truth and identity. The formation of the character for the term shows that the tally was originally of bamboo.

II.[569] 1. When Tsze-ch'an was chief minister of the State of Ch'ing, he would convey people across the Tsin and the Wei in his carriage.[570]

2. Mencius said, "It was kind, [but showed that] he did not understand the practice of government.

3. "In the eleventh month of the year the foot-bridges should be completed, and the carriage-bridges in the twelfth month, and the people will [then] not have the trouble of wading.[571]

4. "Let a governor conduct his rule on the principles of equal justice, and he may cause people to be removed out of his path when he goes abroad; but how can he convey everybody across the rivers?[572]

5. "Thus if a governor will [try] to please everybody, he will find the days not sufficient [for his work]."

III.[573] 1. Mencius addressed himself to king Seuen of Ts'e, saying, "When a ruler regards his ministers as his hands and feet, they regard him as their belly and heart; when he regards them as his dogs and horses, they regard him as they do any ordinary man; when he regards them as the ground or as grass, they regard him as a robber and an enemy."[574]

2. The king said, "According to the rules of propriety, [a minister] should wear mourning [when he hears of the death of] a ruler whose service he had left;—how must [the ruler] have regarded him that [the minister] shall thus wear mourning for him?"[575]

---

[569] CH. II. GOOD GOVERNMENT LIES IN EQUAL MEASURES FOR THE GENERAL GOOD, AND NOT IN ACTS OF KINDNESS TO INDIVIDUALS;—ILLUSTRATED FROM THE HISTORY OF TSZE-CH'AN.

[570] *Par.* 1. Tsze-ch'an;—see on Ana. V. xv. The Tsin and Wei were two rivers of Ch'ing, having their rise in the Ma-ling hills in the present department of Ho-nan, Ho-nan province. They met at a certain point, after which the common stream seems to have borne the names of both its affluents. Mencius has reference to a conversation between Confucius and Tsze-yĕw about Tsze-ch'an, related in the fourth Book of the Kĕa Yu. The sage held that Tsze-ch'an was kind, but only as a mother who loves but does not teach her children, and in illustration of his view says that "Tsze-ch'an used the carriage in which he rode to convey over those who were wading through the water in the winter."

[571] *Par.* 3. The 11th and 12th months here correspond to the 9th and 10th of the present calendar. Mencius is referring to a rule for the repair of the bridges on the termination of the agricultural labors of the year.

[572] *Par.* 4. "Removing people from the way," when the ruler was going abroad, was also a rule of the Chow dynasty; and not only did it take effect, in the case of the ruler, but also in that of many officers and women;—see the Official Book of Chow, VII. ix.

[573] CH. III. WHAT TREATMENT RULERS GIVE TO THEIR MINISTERS WILL BE RETURNED TO THEM IN A CORRESPONDING BEHAVIOUR.

[574] *Par.* 1. "As his hands and feet;" *i.e.*, with kindness and attention. "As his belly and heart;" *i.e.*, with watchfulness and honour. "As his dogs and horses;" *i.e.*, without respect, but feeding them. "As any ordinary man" is, literally, "as a man of the State," meaning without any distinction or reverence. "As the ground or as grass;"—*i.e.* trampling on them, and cutting them off.

[575] *Par.* 2. The rule here is mentioned in the 13th Book of the E Le, or "Rules of Deportment;" but the passage is obscure. The king falls back on this rule, thinking that Mencius had expressed himself too strongly.

3. Mencius said, "The admonitions [of a minister] having been followed and his advice listened to, so that blessings have descended on the people, if for some cause he leaves [the State], the ruler sends an escort to conduct him beyond the boundaries, and also sends before him [a recommendatory notice of him] to the State to which he is proceeding. When he has been gone three years and does not return, [only] then does he take back his fields and residence. This treatment is what we call 'a thrice-repeated display of consideration.' When a ruler acts thus, mourning will be worn [on hearing of his death].[576]

4. "Now-a-days the remonstrances of a minister are not followed, and his advice is not listened to, so that no blessings descend on the people. When for any cause he leaves the State, the ruler tries to seize and hold him as a prisoner. He also pushes him to extremity in the State to which he has gone, and on the day of his departure he takes back his fields and residence. This treatment shows [the ruler] to be what we call 'a robber and an enemy;'—how can mourning be worn for 'a robber and an enemy'?"

IV.[577] Mencius said, "When inferior officers are put to death without any crime, it is [time] for the great officers to leave [the State]. When the people are slaughtered without any cause, it is [time] for the inferior officers to remove."

V.[578] Mencius said, "If the ruler be benevolent, all will be benevolent; if the ruler be righteous, all will be righteous."

VI.[579] Mencius said, "Acts of propriety which are not [really] proper, and acts of righteousness which are not [really] righteous, the great man does not do."

VII.[580] Mencius said, "Those who keep the Mean train up those who do not, and those who have ability train up those who have not, and therefore men rejoice in having fathers and elder brothers of virtue and talent. If those who keep the Mean spurn those who do not, and

---

[576] *Par.* 3. "Fields" here is to be taken in the sense of revenue or emolument. The "thrice-repeated display of consideration" refers, 1st, to the escort as a protection from danger; 2nd, to the anticipatory recommendations; and 3rd, to the long-continued emoluments.

[577] CH. IV. PROMPT ACTION IS NECESSARY AT THE RIGHT TIME. HOW OFFICERS MAY KNOW WHEN THEY SHOULD LEAVE A STATE.

[578] CH. V. THE INFLUENCE OF THE RULER'S EXAMPLE. See the 20th chapter of Part I. There we find the same statements, intended to stir up ministers to seek to correct the errors of their ruler.

[579] CH. VI. GREAT MEN MAKE NO MISTAKES IN MATTERS OF PROPRIETY AND RIGHTEOUSNESS. What is proper and right at one time, it is said, may not be so at another. Respect belongs to propriety, but it may be carried so far as to amount to flattery. These are among the instances which are given of the things mentioned in this chapter.

[580] CH. VII. IF THOSE WHO ARE MORE HIGHLY GIFTED THAN OTHERS DO NOT USE THEIR GIFTS FOR THE BENEFIT OF THOSE OTHERS, THEY ARE NOT TO BE CONSIDERED AS SUPERIOR TO THEM.

those who have ability spurn those who have not, then the space between them—those who have the virtue and talents and those who are inferior to them—will not amount to an inch."

VIII.[581] Mencius said, "When men have what they will not do, they are prepared to act in what they do do [with effect]."

IX.[582] Mencius said, "What future misery are they sure to have to endure who talk of what is not good in others!"

X.[583] Mencius said, "Chung-ne did not do extraordinary things."

XI.[584] Mencius said, "The great man does not think before hand of his words that they shall be sincere, nor of his actions that they shall be resolute;—he simply [speaks and does] what is right."

XII.[585] Mencius said, "The great man is he who does not lose his child's heart."

XIII.[586] Mencius said, "The nourishment of the living is not fit to be accounted the great thing. It is only in performing their obsequies when dead that we have what can be considered the great thing."

XIV.[587] Mencius said, "The superior man makes profound

---

[581] CH. VIII. HE WHO ESCHEWS WHAT IS WRONG CAN DO WITH BOLD DECISION WHAT IS RIGHT. In illustration of the sentiment here, Chaou K'e says, "If a man will not descend to any irregular acquisition, he will be prepared to yield even a thousand chariots," *i.e.*, a large State.

[582] CH. IX. EVIL SPEAKING IS SURE TO BRING WITH IT EVIL CONSEQUENCES. Choo He supposes that the remark here was made with some particular reference.

[583] CH. X. THAT CONFUCIUS KEPT THE MEAN. Compare with this the Doctrine of the Mean, XI. and XIII., and Ana. VII. xx., *et al.*

[584] CH. XI. WHAT IS RIGHT IS THE SUPREME PURSUIT OR THE SUPERIOR MAN. Compare Ana. IV. x.

[585] CH. XII. A MAN IS GREAT IN PROPORTION AS HE IS CHILDLIKE. Chaou K'e supposes that "the great man" is a ruler, and that the sentiment is that he treats his people as his children, and does not lose their hearts. The meaning given in the version is, no doubt, the correct one, and the saying is sure to suggest to my readers the words of our Savior,—"Except ye be converted, and become as little children, ye shall not enter into the kingdom of heaven." With Mencius "the child's heart" is the ideal moral condition of humanity. Choo He says on this chapter:—"The mind of the great man comprehends all changes of phenomena, and the mind of the child id nothing but a pure simplicity, free from all hypocrisy. Yet the great man is the great man, just as he is not led astray by external things, but keeps his original simplicity and freedom from hypocrisy. Carrying this out, he becomes omniscient and omnipotent, and reaches the extreme point of greatness." We need not suppose that Mencius would himself have expanded his thought in this way.

[586] CH. XIII. FILIAL PIETY IS MOST SURELY SEEN IN THE WAY IN WHICH THE OBSEQUIES OF PARENTS ARE PERFORMED.

Some critics suppose, and with reason probably, that the saying here was directed against the Mihist practice of burying the dead with a spare simplicity;—see III. i. V. 4. The funeral rites, it is said, are performed once for all; and if they are done wrong, the fault cannot be remedied.

[587] CH. XIV. THE VALUE OF LEARNING THOROUGHLY INWROUGHT INTO THE MIND. One may read scores of pages in the Chinese commentators, and yet not get a clear idea in his own mind of Mencius' teaching in this chapter. Most of them understand the subject studied to be man's own self, and not things external to him.

advances [in what he is learning], and by the proper course, wishing to get hold of it as in himself. Having got hold of it in himself, he abides in it quietly and firmly. Abiding in it quietly and firmly, he reposes a deep reliance on it. Reposing a deep reliance on it, he lays hold of it on the right and left, meeting with it as a fountain [from which things flow]. It is on this account that the superior man wishes to get hold of [what he is learning] in himself."

XV.[588] Mencius said, "In learning extensively and setting forth minutely [what is learned], [the object of the superior man] is to go back and set forth in brief what is essential."

XVI.[589] Mencius said, "Never has he who would by his excellence subdue men been able to subdue them. Let [a ruler seek] by his excellence to nourish men, and he will be able to subdue all under heaven. It is impossible that one should attain to the true royal sway to whom the hearts of all under heaven are not subject."

XVII.[590] Mencius said, "Words which are not true are [all] inauspicious, but those which are most truly obnoxious to the charge of being inauspicious are those which throw into the shade men of talents and virtue."

XVIII.[591] 1. The disciple Seu said, "Chung-ne often praised water, saying, 'O water! O water!' What did he find in water [to praise]?"[592]

2. Mencius replied, "How the water from a spring gushes out! It rests not day nor night. It fills up every hole, and then advances, flowing on to the four seas. Such is water having a spring! It was this which he found in it [to praise].

3. "But suppose that [the water] has no spring. In the seventh and eighth months the rain collects, and the channels in the fields are all filled, but their being dried up again may be expected in a short time. Thus it is that a superior man is ashamed of a reputation beyond the

---

[588] Ch. XV. Choo He says, and with reason apparently, that this is a continuation of the former chapter, showing that the object of the superior man, in the extensive studies which he pursues, is not vain-glory, but to get to the substance and essence of things.

[589] CH. XVI. WHEN PEOPLE'S MINDS ARE SUBJECT TO A PRINCE, THEY WILL MAKE HIM KING. HOW THEIR MINDS CAN BE MADE SO SUBJECT. The first utterance here is to me quite enigmatical. Paul's sentiment, that "scarcely for a righteous man will one die, yet peradventure for a good man some would even dare to die," occurs to the mind on reading the first and second parts; but the native commentators make the "nourishing" to have nothing to do with men's bodies.

[590] CH. XVII. THE WORDS WHICH ARE MOST INAUSPICIOUS ARE THOSE WHICH ARE INTENDED TO PREVENT THE RECOGNITION OF TALENTS AND VIRTUE. The words of this chapter may also be translated:—"There are no words really inauspicious, but those which may really be considered inauspicious," &c. The version which I have preferred is equally allowable.

[591] CH. XVIII. HOW MENCIUS EXPLAINED CONFUCIUS' FREQUENT PRAISE OF WATER, FROM THE PERMANENCE OF A SPRING-FED STREAM.

[592] *Par.* 1. See Ana. IX. xvi. for instance of the sage's praise of water.

fact [of his merits]."[593]

XIX.[594] 1. Mencius said, "That whereby man differs from the animals is but small. The mass of men cast it away, while superior men preserve it.[595]

2. "Shun clearly understood the multitude of things, and closely observed the relations of humanity. He walked along the path of benevolence and righteousness, and did not pursue [as by any effort] benevolence and righteousness."[596]

XX.[597] 1. Mencius said, "Yu hated the pleasant wine, and loved good words.[598]

2. "T'ang held fast the Mean, and employed men of talents and virtue wherever they came from.[599]

3. "King Wan looked on the people as [he would do with affectionate interest] on a man who was wounded; he looked towards the right path as [earnestly as] if he did not see it.[600]

4. "King Woo did not disregard the near, nor forget the distant.

5. "The duke of Chow desired to unite in himself [the virtues of those] kings, [the founders of the] three [dynasties], that he might display in his practice [those] four things [which they did]. If [in his practice] there was anything which did not agree with them, he looked up and thought of it, from day-time into the night; and when he was fortunate enough to master [the difficulty], he sat waiting for the morning."

---

[593] *Par.* 3. Here again the months must be reduced to the 5th and 6th,—those of the Chow year.

[594] CH. XIX. THAT THE SMALL DIFFERENCE BETWEEN MEN AND ANIMALS IS PRESERVED ONLY BY SUPERIOR MEN;—ILLUSTRATED IN SHUN.

[595] *Par.* 1. Mencius has not told us in what the small point distinguishing men from birds and beasts consists. Chaou K'e says that it is simply the interval between the knowledge of righteousness and the want of that knowledge. and this is so far correct; but this difference cannot be said to be "small." According to Choo He, men and creatures have the *le*—the intellectual and moral principles—of Heaven and earth to form their nature, and the *k'e*, or matter, of Heaven and earth to form their bodies, only men's *k'e* is more correct than that of animals, so that they are able to fill up the capacity of their nature. This seems to deny any essential difference between men and animals, what difference there is being merely corporeal and in degree.

[596] *Par.* 2. The first predicate of Shun is to me hardly intelligible; the last seems to say that benevolence and righteousness were natural to him, observed without any effort.

[597] CH. XX. THE SAME SUBJECT ILLUSTRATED IN YU, T'ANG, WĂN, WOO, AND THE DUKE OF CHOW.

[598] *Par.* 1. In the "Plans of the Warring States," it is safe that "E-teih made spirits which Yu tasted and liked, but be said, 'In after-ages there will be those who through spirits will lose their states;' so he degraded E-teih, and refused to drink the pleasant spirits." What we read in the Shoo, III iii. 6, gives some countenance to this story. For his love of good words, see the Shoo, II. ii. 21.

[599] *Par.* 2. In illustration of what is said of T'ang, commentators refer to the Shoo, IV. ii. 7, 8.

[600] *Par.* 3. For an illustration of Wăn's fostering care of the people, see the Shoo, V. xv. 9, 10, and the She, III i, VI., *et al*, tor the other characteristic.

XXI.[601] 1. Mencius said, "The traces of true royal rule were extinguished, and [the royal] odes ceased to be produced. When those odes ceased to be produced, then the Ch'un Ts'ëw was made.

2. "The Shing of Tsin, the T'aou-wuh of Ts'oo, and the Ch'un Ts'ëw of Loo were [books] of the same character.

3. "The subjects [of the Ch'un Ts'ëw] are Hwan of Ts'e and Wăn of Tsin, and its style is the historical. Confucius said, 'Its righteous decisions I ventured to make.'"

XXII.[602] 1. Mencius said, "The influence of a sovereign sage terminates in the fifth generation. The influence of one who is merely a sage does the same.[603]

2. "I could not be a disciple of Confucius himself, but I have endeavoured to cultivate my virtue by means of others [who were].[604]

XXIII.[605] Mencius said, "When it appears proper to take [a thing], and [afterwards] not proper, to take it is contrary to moderation. When it appears proper to give [a thing], and [afterwards] not proper, to give it is contrary to kindness. When it appears proper to sacrifice one's life, and [afterwards] not proper, to sacrifice it is contrary to bravery."

XXIV.[606] 1. P'ang Mung learned archery of E. When he had completely acquired all the method of E, thinking that under heaven only E was superior to himself, he slew him. Mencius said, "In this case E also was to blame. Kung-ming E [indeed] said, 'It would appear that E was not to be blamed.' but he [only] meant that the blame attaching to him was slight;—how can he be held to have been without any blame?[607]

---

[601] CH. XXI. This chapter is said to continue the subject of the two preceding, and to illustrate it by the case of Confucius. I confess that I am not able to trace the connection. See what I have said on the difficulties belonging to several of the statements in the chapter in the first Book of my Prolegomena to the Ch'un Ts'ëw.

[602] CH. XXII. MENCIUS INSINUATES THAT, THOUGH HE HAD NOT BEEN IN PERSONAL CONTACT WITH CONFUCIUS, HE SHOULD BE CONSIDERED HIS SUCCESSOR. This chapter is further said to continue the subject of the three preceding, and to illustrate it in the case of Mencius himself. I should be inclined to make the former paragraph of ch. xix. a chapter by itself, and to read the other paragraph, and chapters xx., xxi., and this one, as one chapter.

[603] *Par.* 1. Thirty years are held to cover one generation. We might suppose that the influence of "a sovereign sage" would last longer than that of one who had no distinction of authority; but Mencius is pleased to say that it lasts only the same time.

[604] *Par.* 2. What Mencius is here supposed to insinuate would seem to indicate that a space of about five generations should be placed between him and Confucius.

[605] CH. XXIII. FIRST JUDGMENTS ARE NOT ALWAYS CORRECT. IMPULSES MUST BE WEIGHED IN THE BALANCE OF REASON, AND WHAT REASON DICTATES SHOULD BE FOLLOWED.

[606] CH. XXIV. THE IMPORTANCE OF BEING CAREFUL WHOM WE MAKE FRIENDS OF. The sentiment is good, but surely Mencius might have found better illustrations of it than those which he gives.

[607] *Par.* 1. On E see the note to Ana. XIV. vi. Both Chaou K'e and Choo He strangely explain P'ang Mung as meaning *Këa chung*, E's domestics. I suspect there is an error in their texts, and that we should read Kea shin = E's "steward." He may have been

2. "The people of Ch'ing sent Tsze-choh Yu-tsze to make an incursion into Wei, which sent Yu Kung-sze to pursue him. Tsze-choh Yu-tsze said, 'To-day I feel unwell, and cannot hold my bow;—I am a dead man.' [At the same time] he asked his driver who was his pursuer; and being told that it was Yu Kung-sze, he said, 'I shall live.' The driver said, 'Yu Kung-sze is the best archer of Wei, what do you mean by saying that you shall live?' 'Yu Kung-sze,' replied he, 'learned archery from Yin Kung-t'o, who again learned it from me. Yin Kung-t'o is an upright man, and the friends of his selection must be upright [also].' When Yu Kung-sze came up, he said, 'Master, why are you not holding your bow?' [Yu-tsze] answered, 'To-day I am feeling unwell, and am unable to hold my bow.' [Kung-sze] said, 'I learned archery from Yin Kung-t'o, who again learned it from you. I cannot bear to injure you with your own science. The business of to-day, however, is my ruler's business, which I dare not neglect.' He then took an arrow and knocked off the steel against his carriage-wheel. [In this way] he discharged four of them, and turned back."[608]

XXV.[609] 1. Mencius said, "If the lady Se had been wearing a filthy head-dress, people would all have stopped their noses in passing her.[610]

2. "Though a man be wicked, yet, if he adjust his thoughts, fast, and bathe, he may sacrifice to God."[611]

XXVI.[612] 1. Mencius said, "All who speak of the natures [of

---

employed by the Han Tsuh in the note referred to, to do the deed. Kung-ming E has already been quoted by Mencius in III. i. I., and ii. III. and IX. The idea of Mencius was that E was to blame for having made a friend of such a man as P'ang Mung.

[608] *Par.* 2. In the Tso Chuen, under the 14th year of duke Sĕang, we have a narrative bearing some likeness to the account here given by Mencius, and in which Yin Kung-t'o and a Yu Kung-ch'ae (or ts'ze) figure as famous archers of Wei. Yet the differences between Tso's narrative and the text here are so great that we can hardly receive them as relating to the same passage of history.

[609] CH. XXV. BEAUTY THROUGH CERTAIN ACCESSORIES MAY BE DISGUSTING TO MEN, AND WICKEDNESS, BY HOLY ENDEAVOUR, MAY BECOME ACCEPTABLE TO GOD.

[610] *Par.* 1. The lady Se, or if we translate the terms, "the western lady," was a poor girl of Yueh, called She E, of surpassing beauty, presented by the king of Yueh to his enemy, the king of Woo, who became besottedly attached to her, and neglected all the duties of his government. She was contemporary with Confucius. If we may receive the works of Kwan-tsze, however, as genuine, there had been a celebrated beauty called "the western lady," two hundred years before that time, and the lady of Yueh chose to assume her designation.

[611] *Par.* 2. Chaou K'e and Choo He take the character which I have translated "wicked" in the sense of "ugly." It may have either signification according to the context. I cannot but suppose, however, that Mencius intended it in the sense which I have given, and that his object was to encourage men to repentance and well-doing. By the law of China it was competent only for the king to sacrifice to God, and the language of our .philosopher strikingly shows the virtue he attached to penitent purification.

[612] CH. XXVI. HOW KNOWLEDGE OUGHT TO BE PURSUED BY THE CAREFUL STUDY OF PHENOMENA. Mencius here points out correctly the path to science. The rule which he lays down is in harmony with the philosophy of Bacon; yet in China, more perhaps than in any other part of the world, the proper method has been disregarded.

things], have in fact only their phenomena [to reason from], and the value of a phenomenon is in its being natural.[613]

2. "What I hate in your wise men is their chiseling out [their conclusions]. If those wise men would act as Yu did when he conveyed away the waters, there would be nothing to dislike in their wisdom. The way in which Yu conveyed away the waters was by doing that which gave him no trouble. If your wise men would also do that which gave them no trouble, their wisdom would also be great.[614]

3. "There is heaven so high; there are the stars and zodiacal spaces so distant. If we have investigated their phenomena, we may, while sitting [in our places], ascertain the solstices for a thousand years [past]."[615]

XXVII.[616] 1. The officer Kung-hăng having in hand the funeral of his son, the master of the Right went to condole with him. When [this noble] entered the door, some motioned to him to come to them, and spoke with him, and others went to his place and spoke with him.[617]

2. Mencius did not speak with him, on which the master of the Bight was displeased, and said, "All the gentlemen have spoken with me. There is only Mencius who has not spoken with me, thereby slighting me."

3. When Mencius heard of this remark, he said, "According to the prescribed rules, in the court we must not change our places to speak with one another, and must not pass out of our own rank to bow to one another. I was wishing to observe these rules;—is it not strange that Tsze-gaou should think I was thereby slighting him?"[618]

---

[613] *Par.* 1. "Natures" is to be taken here quite generally, and not, as some commentators think, in the singular, referring to the nature of man. Possibly, Mencius may have had in view the discussions about human nature which were rife in his days; but he is speaking generally, and those discussions were only one perversion of the method on which he insists.

[614] *Par.* 2. By "chiseling" or "boring" we are to understand the violent forcing out of conclusions, instead of pursuing the inductive method. Yu's operations gave him abundance of trouble; what Mencius means to say is that they were all in harmony with the nature and circumstances of the waters, which he was laboring to reduce.

[615] *Par.* 3. Compare the language of the tat sentence of par. 9 in the 26th chapter of the Doctrine of the Mean. The solstices referred to are those of winter. Most modern commentators hold that one solstice is intended,—that from which the Chinese cycle dates its commencement, when the sun, moon, and planets are all supposed to have been in conjunction at midnight. This is not necessary.

[616] CH. XXVII. HOW MENCIUS WOULD NOT IMITATE OTHERS IN PAYING COURT TO A FAVOURITE, AND HOW HE EXCUSED HIMSELF.

[617] *Par.* 1. Many think that the death which gave occasion to what is here related was that of the officer Kung-hăng himself. The view which I have followed is more in accordance with the Chinese text. The master of the Bight was the Wang Hwan of II. ii. 6, and the Tsze-gaou of XXIV. and XXV. of the first Part of this Book. He was a man with whom our philosopher would have nothing to do.

[618] *Par.* 3. The officers were not now "in the court," but they had gone by the king's order to condole with Kung-hăng, and ought therefore to have observed the rules which regulated their positions and movements when in the court. On those rules, see the

XXVIII.[619] 1. Mencius said, "That wherein the superior man is different from other men is what he preserves in his heart;—namely, benevolence and propriety.

2. "The benevolent man loves others; the man of propriety shows respect to others.

3. "He who loves others is always loved by them, and he who respects others is always respected by them.

4. "Here is a man who treats me in a perverse and unreasonable manner;—[as] a superior man, I will turn round upon myself, [and say,] 'I must have been wanting in benevolence; I must have been devoid of propriety;—how [else] should this have happened to [me]?'

5. "Having thus examined myself, I am [specially] benevolent, and [specially] observant of propriety. If the perversity and unreasonableness of the other be still the same, [as] a superior man [I will say], 'I must have been failing to do my utmost.'

6. "I again turn round upon myself, and proceed to do my utmost. If the perversity and unreasonableness of the other be still the same, [as] a superior man, I will say, 'This is a man utterly lost indeed. Since he conducts him so, there is nothing to choose between him and a beast; why should I go to trouble myself about a beast?'

7 "Thus it is that the superior man has a life-long anxiety, but not one morning's serious trouble. As to what is matter of anxiety to him, he has it [thus]:—'Shun,' [he says,] 'was a man, and I also am a man. Shun gave an example to all under heaven, and [his conduct] was fit to be handed down to future ages, while I am nothing better than a villager.' This indeed is proper matter of anxiety to him; but in what way is he anxious? Simply that he may be like Shun. As to what would be matter of serious trouble to a superior man, there is no such thing. He does nothing which is contrary to benevolence; he does nothing which is not according to propriety. Should there be one morning's trouble, as a superior man he does not reckon it a trouble."

XXIX.[620] 1. Yu and Tseih, in an age of tranquillizing [government], thrice passed their doors without entering them. Confucius praised them.[621]

---

Official Book of Chow, XXII. iii. 1, *et al.*

[619] CH. XXVIII. HOW THE SUPERIOR MAN IS DISTINGUISHED FROM OTHERS BY THE CULTIVATION OF HIS MORAL EXCELLENCE; AND HOW IN THAT HE HAS HIS REMEDY AGAINST THE MISCONDUCT OF OTHERS TO HIM.

Mencius shows here an admirable faith in the power of goodness to produce a corresponding response in others, and in the peace which the consciousness of having acted in kindness and righteousness will produce under the most perverse treatment.

[620] CH. XXIX. HOW AN UNDERLYING PRINCIPLE WILL BE FOUND TO RECONCILE THE DIFFERENCES IN THE CONDUCT OF GREAT AND GOOD MEN OCCASIONED BY THEIR DIFFERENT CIRCUMSTANCES ILLUSTRATED IN THE CASES OF YU, TSEIH, AND YEN HWUY.

[621] *Par.* 1. See III. i. IV. 7, *et al.* The thrice passing his door was peculiar to Yu,

2. Yen-tsze, in an age of disorder, dwelt in a mean narrow lane, having his single bamboo-dish of rice, and his single gourd-cup of water. Other men could not have endured the distress, but he did not allow his joy to be affected by it. Confucius [also] praised him.[622]

3. Mencius said, "Yu, Tseih, and Yen Hwuy agreed in the principles of their conduct.

4. "Yu thought that if any one under heaven were drowned, it was as if he himself drowned him. Tseih thought that if any one under heaven suffered hunger, it was as if he himself famished him. It was on this account that they were so earnest.

5. "If Yu and Tseih, and Yen-tsze could have exchanged places, they would have done each what the other did.

6. "Here now in the same apartment with you are people fighting; and [you wish to] part them. Though you were to part them with your cap tied on over your hair unbound, your conduct would be allowable.[623]

7. "If the fighting were [only] in your village or neighborhood, and you were to go to part them with your cap [so] tied on over your hair unbound, you would be in error. Though you were to shut your door [in such a case], your conduct would be allowable."

XXX.[624] 1. The disciple Kung-too said, "Throughout the whole State, all pronounce K'wang Chang unfilial, and yet you, Master, keep company with him, and moreover treat him with politeness. I venture to ask why you do so."[625]

---

though it is here ascribed also to Tseih, or How-tseih. Their age was not one of tranquility, but the government in it was good, and they were employed to bring it to tranquility.

[622] *Par.* 2. See Ana. VI. ix.

[623] *Parr.* 6, 7. The rules anciently prescribed for dressing were very minute. Much had to be done with the hair, before the final act of putting on the cap, with the strings tied under the chin. In the case in par. 6 all these rules are neglected. The urgency of the case, and the intimacy of the individual with the parties quarrelling, justified such neglect. This was the case of Yu and Tseih in relation to their age, while that in par. 7 is supposed to illustrate Hwuy's relation to his.—But Mencius' illustrations are for the most part happier than these.

[624] CH. XXX. HOW MENCIUS EXPLAINED HIS INTERCOURSE WITH A MAN COMMONLY HELD TO BE UNFILIAL. THE CASE OF K'WANG CHANG.

[625] *Par.* 1. K'wang Chang was an officer of Ts'e, and had been employed in important military affairs. He commanded the troops of Ts'e in the operations against Yen referred to in I. ii. X., *et al.* We have no account of the particulars of his conduct which made him be regarded throughout the State as unfilial, though perhaps a hint about them may be obtained from a narrative in the "Plans of the Warring States," in the first Book relating to Ts'e. It is there said that king Wei of Ts'e appointed K'wang Chang to command an army against Ts'in, which was threatening the State. For some time reports were rife that Chang-tsze was playing the traitor, but king Wei refused to believe them, saying he was confident of the good faith of his general. At last news came of a great defeat inflicted on Ts'in, and the king, being asked what had made him bo trustful of K'wang Chang, said, "Chang-tsze's mother offended his father, and was put to death by him, and buried in a stable. When I was sending him forth on this expedition, I said that,

2. Mencius replied, "There are five things which in the common parlance of the age are said to be unfilial. The first is laziness in the use of one's four limbs, so as not to attend to the maintenance of his parents. The second is gambling and chess-playing, and being fond of spirits, so as not to attend to the maintenance of one's parents. The third is being fond of goods and money, and being selfishly attached to one's wife and children, so as not to attend to the maintenance of one's parents. The fourth is following the desires of one's ears and eyes, so as to bring one's parents to disgrace. The fifth is being fond of bravery, fighting and quarrelling, so as to endanger his parents. Is Chang-tsze guilty of any one of these things?[626]

3. "Between Chang-tsze and his father there arose disagreement, he, the son, reproving his father to urge him to what was good.[627]

4. "To urge one another by reproofs to what is good is the way of friends. But such urging between father and son is the greatest injury to the kindly feeling [that should prevail between them].

5. "Did not Chang-tsze wish to have all that belongs to [the relationships] of husband and wife, child and mother? But because he had offended his father and was not permitted to approach him, he sent away his wife and drove forth his son, and would not for all [the rest of] his life receive any cherishing attentions from them. He settled it in his mind that, if he did not act in this way, his would be the greatest of crimes. Such and nothing more is the case of Chang-tsze."[628]

XXXI.[629] 1. When Tsăng-tsze dwelt in Woo-shing, there came [a band of] plunderers from Yueh. Some one said [to him], "The plunderers are come; why not leave this?" [On this Tsăng-tsze left the city], saying [to the man in charge of his house], "Do not let any one lodge in my house, lest he break and injure the plants and shrubs about it." But when the plunderers were withdrawing [he sent word], saying, "Repair the walls and roof of my house; I will return to it;" and when

---

if he conducted it vigorously, I would on his return bury his mother elsewhere, but he said that he might have done so before, but his mother having offended his father, and his father having died without giving him any instructions on the point, he did not dare to remove the body to another grave, lest he should be dealing wrongly by his deceased father. If Chang-tsze is thus faithful to his deceased father, he will not be faithless to me." Possibly, the alienation between Chang-tsze and his father may have arisen about the latter's putting his mother to death. Whatever was the cause of it, it is evident from what Mencius says that it did not seriously compromise his character.

[626] *Par.* 2. "Gambling and chess-playing;"—see on Ana. XVII. xxii. But the chess-playing could not be the game analogous to ours, for the emperor of the Chow dynasty alluded to in the note there as its inventor belonged to the latter dynasty of that name in the 10th century of our era.

[627] *Parr.* 3, 4. Compare Part i. XVIII. 2.

[628] *Par.* 5. Readers not Chinese will think that Chang's treatment of his wife and son was more criminal than his conduct to his father.

[629] CH. XXXI. HOW MENCIUS EXPLAINED THE DIFFERENT CONDUCT OF TSĂNG-TSZE AND TSZE-SZE IN OUTWARDLY SIMILAR CIRCUMSTANCES. Compare chapter xxix.

the plunderers had retired, he returned. His disciples said, "Since our Master was treated with so much attention and respect, for him to be the first, on the arrival of the plunderers, to go away, so as to be observed by the people, and then, on their retiring, to return, seems to us to be improper." Shin-yew Hăng said [to them], "You do not understand this matter. Formerly, when [the house of us], the Shin-yew, was exposed to the outbreak of the grass-carriers, there were seventy disciples in our Master's following, and none of them took any part in the matter."[630]

2. When Tsze-sze was living in Wei, there came plunderers from Ts'e. Some one said to him, "The plunderers are Coming; why not leave this?" [But] Tsze-sze said, "If I go away, whom will the ruler have with him to guard [the city]?"[631]

3. Mencius said, "Tsăng-tsze and Tsze-sze agreed in the principle of their conduct. Tsăng-tsze was a teacher;—in the position of a father or elder brother. Tsze-sze was a minister;—in a meaner position. If they could have exchanged places, each would have done what the other did."[632]

XXXII.[633] The officer Ch'oo said [to Mencius], "The king sent a person to spy out whether you, Sir, were really different from other men." Mencius replied, "How should I be different from other men? Yaou and Shun were just the same as other men."

XXXIII.[634] 1. "A man of Ts'e had a wife and a concubine, and lived together with them in his house. When their good-man went out, he was sure to get himself well filled with spirits and flesh and then return, and on his wife's asking him with whom he had been eating and drinking, they were sure to be all men of wealth and rank. The wife

---

[630] *Par.* 1. Woo-shing was a city of Loo,—90 *le* to the south-west of the present district city of Pe, department E-chow. Tsăng-tsze had here opened a school or lecture-room hi the place, having, probably, as many suppose, been invited to do 80—to be "agnest and teacher"—by the commandant. It was thus in the south of the present Shantung province. South from it, and covering the present Kĕang-soo and part of Cheh-kĕang, were the States of Woo and Yueh, all at this time subject to Yueh. Shin-yĕw Hăng is supposed to have been a disciple of Tsăng-tsze, and a native of Woo-shing. The Shin-yĕw of whom he speaks must mean the head of his clan, or rather his House. When it was in peril, Tsăng-tsze's seventy disciples would have been abundantly able to cope with the grass-carriers. That they did not attempt to do so, showed that there was some reason for his conduct more than the objectors to it saw on the surface.

[631] *Par.* 2. Tsze-sze of course is Confucius' grandson. He was living in Wei, and sustaining office in it.

[632] *Par.* 3. We have here a striking illustration of the importance attached to tike position of a "teacher," of which I have spoken in the Prolegomena.

[633] CH. XXXII. SAGES ARE JUST LIKE OTHER MEN IN THEIR PERSONAL APPEARANCE AND ORDINARY WAYS.

Ch'oo was a minister of Ts'e. The incident mentioned probably occurred on Mencius1 first arrival in Ts'e, and before he had any interview with the king.

[634] CH. XXXIII. THE DISGRACEFUL MEANS WHICH MANY TOOK TO SEEK FOR WEALTH AND HONOURS.

informed, the concubine, saying, 'When the good-man goes out, he is sure to come back having partaken plentifully of spirits and flesh, and when I ask him with whom he has been eating and drinking, they are all men of wealth and rank. And yet no men of distinction ever come [here]. I will spy out where our good-man goes.' [Accordingly] she got up early in the morning, and privately followed the good-man to where he was going. All through the city there was nobody who stood and talked with him. At last he came to those who were sacrificing among the tombs outside the outer wall on the east, and begged what they had left. Not being satisfied, he looked round him and went to another party;—and this was the way in which he got himself satiated. His wife went home; and informed the concubine, saying, 'It was to the good-man that we looked up in hopeful contemplation, and with whom our lot is cast for life;—and these are his ways.' [On this] she and the concubine reviled their good-man, arid wept together in the middle courtyard. [In the mean time] the good-man, knowing nothing of all this, came in with a jaunty air, carrying himself proudly to them.[635]

2. "According to the view which a superior man takes of things, as to the ways by which men seek for riches, honors, gain, and advancement, there are few of their wives and concubines who might not be ashamed and weep together because of them."[636]

BOOK V. WAN CHANG.[637] PART I.

CHAPTER I.[638] 1. WAN CHANG asked [Mencius], saying, "[When] Shun went into the fields, he cried out and wept towards the pitying heavens. Why did he cry out and weep?" Mencius replied, "He was dissatisfied and full of earnest desire."[639]

---

[635] *Par.* 1. A "Mencius said" must have dropt out of the text at the beginning of this paragraph. All the commentators seem to be agreed in this. The statement that the man "lived together with his wife and concubine in the house" seems to be intended to indicate that he passed as a man of wealth, who was not engaged in trade, or any business that called him away from home. "Good-man" is equivalent to husband; so "good-man" used to be employed in Scotland.

[636] *Par.* 2 contains the moral and application of the narrative given in the former paragraph.

[637] TITLE OF THE BOOK. The Book is named from Wan Chang, who is almost the only interlocutor with Mencius in it. He has been mentioned before in III. ii. V. The tradition is that it was in company with Wan's disciples that Mencius, baffled in all his hopes of doing public service, and having retired into privacy, composed the seven Books which constitute his Works. The first Part of this Book is all occupied with discussions in vindication of Shun and other ancient worthies.

[638] CH. I. SHUN'S GREAT FILIAL PIETY;—HOW IT CARRIED HIM INTO THE FIELDS TO WEEP AND DEPLORE HIS INABILITY TO SECURE THE AFFECTION AND SYMPATHY OF HIS PARENTS, AND THAT HE NEVER CHERISHED ANY GRUDGE AGAINST THEM FOR THEIR TREATMENT OF HIM.

[639] *Par.* 1. The incident about Shun here mentioned is found in the Shoo, II. ii. 21. It is given there, however, as having occurred in the early part of his life; and this, as will

2. Wan Chang pursued, "When his parents love him, [a son] rejoices and forgets them not; and when they hate him, though they punish him, he does not allow himself to be dissatisfied. Was Shun then dissatisfied [with his parents]?" [Mencius said], "Ch'ang Seih asked Kung-ming Kaou, saying, 'As to Shun's going into the fields, I have received your instructions; but I do not understand about his weeping and crying out to the pitying heavens, and to his parents.' Kung-ming Kaou answered him, 'You do not understand that matter.' Now Kung-ming Kaou thought that the heart of a filial son [like Shun] could not be so free from sorrow [as Seih seemed to imagine he might have been]. [Shun would be saying,] 'I exert my strength to cultivate the fields, but I am thereby only discharging my duty as a son. What is there [wrong] in me that my parents do not love me?'[640]

3. "The emperor caused his own [children],—nine sons and two daughters, the various officers, oxen and sheep, storehouses and granaries, [all] to be prepared for the service of Shun amid the channeled fields. Most of the officers in the empire repaired to him. The emperor designed that he should superintend the empire along with himself, and then to transfer it to him. But because his parents were not in accord with him, he felt like a poor man who has nowhere to turn to.[641]

4. "To be an object of complacency to the officers of the empire is what men desire; but it was not sufficient to remove the sorrow of [Shun]. The possession of beauty is what men desire,—but though [Shun] had for his wives the two daughters of the emperor, it was not sufficient to remove his sorrow. Riches are what men desire, but though the empire was the rich property [of Shun], it was not enough to

---

be seen, makes it difficult, even impossible, to reconcile what we read in the Shoo about Shun with Mencius' statements in this chapter.

[640] *Par.* 2. Shun's dissatisfaction was with himself, but this is at first kept in the background, and Wan Chang either misunderstood it, and thought that his dissatisfaction was with his parents, or chose to appear to do so. On what he says about the relations of a son with his parents, see Ana. IV. xviii. Kung-ming Kaou is believed to have been a disciple of Tsăng-tsze; and Ch'ang Seih again was Kaou's disciple. The latter probably means to say that he understood Shun's going into the fields to have been that he might cultivate them in order to nourish his parents. He then quotes the words of the Shoo more fully than they are quoted in the preceding paragraph, and says he could not understand the grief which they described, his idea being the same which Wan Chang had that they must indicate that Shun was dissatisfied with his parents. "A filial son could not be so free from sorrow [as Seih seemed to imagine that Shun might have been];" that is, Seih understood that Shun did his duty in cultivating the fields for his parents, and imagined that he should then have dismissed all care from his mind as to any differences between them and him.

[641] *Par.* 3. "The emperor" is, of course, Yaou. See the Shoo, I 12, where Yaou gives his two daughters in marriage to Shun. It is stated there, however, that Shun had by that time transformed his parents and his half-brother Sĕang, and brought them to be in harmony with him. This is the chronological difficulty in the account of Shun's history in the Shoo and that given by Mencius in this chapter.

remove his sorrow. Honors are what men desire, but though [Shun] had the dignity of being the son of Heaven, it was not sufficient to remove his sorrow. The reason why his being the object of men's complacency, the possession of beauty, riches, and honors, could not remove his sorrow was because it could be removed only by his being in [entire] accord with his parents.

5. "The desire of a child is towards his father and mother. When he becomes conscious of [the attractions of] beauty, his desire is towards young and beautiful women. When he [comes to] have a wife and children, his desire is towards them. When he obtains office, his desire is towards his ruler; and if he cannot get the regard of his ruler, he burns within. [But] the man of great filial piety, all his life, has his desire towards his parents. In the great Shun I see the case of one whose desire was towards them when he was fifty years old."

II.[642] 1. Wan Chang asked [Mencius], saying, "It is said in the Book of Poetry,

> 'How do we proceed in taking a wife?
> Announcement must [first] be made to our parents.'

If [the rule] be indeed as thus expressed, no one ought to have illustrated it so well as Shun;—how was it that Shun's marriage took place without his informing [his parents]?" Mencius replied, "If he had informed them, he would not have been able to marry. That male and female dwell together is the greatest of human relations. If [Shun] had informed his parents, he must have made void this greatest of human relations, and incurred thereby their resentment. It was on this account that he did not inform them."[643]

2. Wan Chang said, "As to Shun's marrying without making announcement [to his parents], I have heard your instructions. [But] how was it that the emperor gave him his daughters as wives without informing [his parents]?" [Mencius] said, "The emperor also knew that, if he informed his parents, he could not have given him his daughters as wives."[644]

3. Wan Chang said, "His parents set Shun to repair a granary, and then removed the ladder [by which he had ascended], [after which]

---

[642] CH. II. DEFENCE OF SHUN AGAINST THE CHARGE OR MARRYING WITHOUT INFORMING HIS PARENTS, AND OF HYPOCRISY IN HIS FRIENDLY BEARING AND CONDUCT TOWARDS HIS BROTHER. DEFENCE ALSO OF YAOU FOR GIVING HIS DAUGHTERS TO SHUN, WITHOUT THE APPROVAL OF SHUN'S PARENTS.

[643] *Par.* 1. The Lines from the Book of Poetry are in the She, I. viii. VI 2; But the rule expressed in them was overruled by the higher duty to raise up posterity for one's parents;—see IV. i, XXVI.

[644] *Par.* 2. As all negotiations for the marriage of children should be between the parents on both sides, Yaou should have communicated with Shun's father; but here again the same consideration absolved Yaou from blame.

Koo-sow set fire to it. They sent him to dig a well, [from which he managed to] get out; but they, [not knowing this,] proceeded to cover it up. [His brother] Sëang said, 'Of this scheme to cover up the city-forming gentleman the merit is all mine. Let my parents have his oxen and sheep; let them have his granaries and storehouses. His shield and spear shall be mine; his lute shall be mine; his carved bow shall be mine; and I will make his two wives attend for me to my bed.' Sëang then went away and entered Shun's house, and there was Shun upon a couch with his lute. Sëang said, '[I am come] simply because I was thinking anxiously about you,' [and at the same time] he looked ashamed. Shun said to him, 'There are all my officers; do you take the management of them for me.' I do not know whether Shun was ignorant of Sëang's wishing to kill him." [Mencius] replied, "How could he be ignorant of it? But when Sëang was sorrowful, he was also sorrowful, and when Sëang was joyful, he was also joyful."[645]

4. [Wan Chang] continued, "Then was Shun one who rejoiced hypocritically?" "No," was the reply. "Formerly some one sent a present of a live fish to Tsze-ch'an of Ch'ing. Tsze-ch'an ordered his pond-keeper to feed it in the pond; but the man cooked it, and reported the execution of his commission, saying, 'When I first let it go, it looked embarrassed. In a little it seemed to be somewhat at ease, and then it swam away as if delighted.' 'It had got into its element!' said Tsze-ch'an. 'It had got into its element!' The pond-keeper went out and said, 'Who calls Tsze-ch'an wise? When I had cooked and eaten the fish, he said, "It has got into its element! It has got into its element!"' Thus a superior man may be imposed on by what seems to be as it ought to be, but it is difficult to entrap him by what is contrary to right principle. Sëang came in the way in which the love of his elder brother would have made him come, and therefore Shun truly believed him, and rejoiced at it. What hypocrisy was there?"[646]

III.[647] 1. Wan Chang said, "Sëang made it his daily business to kill

---

[645] *Par.* 3. Sëang, it is understood, was only the half-brother of Shun. On the death of Shun's mother, Koo-sow had married again, or raised a former concubine, whose son was Sëang, to the rank of his wife. The various incidents here mentioned are taken from tradition, or perhaps the Shoo was more complete in Mencius' days than it has come down to us. Sze-ma Ts'ëen tells us that Shun got through the flames by screening himself with two bamboo hats, and that he escaped from the well by a concealed passage which led from it. Sëang calls him "the city-forming gentleman." This is the most natural rendering of the terms, though it is not that of Chaou K'e. They say that wherever Shun lived three years, the people flocked to him, so as to form a *too*,—a city only inferior to the capital city of a State.

[646] *Par.* 4. If Tsze-ch'an had known that his pond-keeper had eaten the fish, would he not have punished him? The case is not in point to vindicate Shun's treatment of Sëang, of whose vile designs he was well aware. His defense of his hero against the charge of hypocrisy is ingenious, and amusing. Its fault is, as in other arguments of Mencius, that he will make his point too plain.

[647] CH. III. VINDICATION OF SHUN'S CONDUCT IN THE CASE OF HIS WICKED

Shun;—why was it that, when [the latter] was raised to be the son of Heaven, he [only] banished him?" Mencius replied, "He invested him with a State, and some have said that it was banishing him."[648]

2. Wan Chang said, "Shun banished the superintendent of Works to Yĕw-chow, sent away Hwan-tow to mount Ts'ung, slew the [prince of] San-mĕaou in San-wei, and imprisoned K'Wăn on mount Yu. When those four criminals [were thus dealt with], all under heaven submitted to him;—it was a cutting off of men who were destitute of benevolence. But Sĕang was [of all men] the most destitute of benevolence, and [Shun] invested him with the State of Pe;—of what crime had the people of Pe been guilty? Does a benevolent man really act thus? In the case of other men, he cut them off; in the case of his brother, he invested him with a State." [Mencius] replied, "A benevolent man does not lay up anger, nor cherish resentment, against his brother, but only regards him with affection and love. Regarding him with affection, he wishes him to enjoy honor; loving him, he wishes him to be rich. The investing him with Pe was to enrich and ennoble him. If while [Shun] himself was emperor, his brother had been a common man, could he have been said to regard him with affection and love?"[649]

3. [Wan Chang said,] "I venture to ask what is meant by some saying that it was a banishing [of Sĕang]." [Mencius] replied, "Sĕang could do nothing [of himself] in his State. The emperor appointed an officer to manage its government, and to pay over its revenues to him; and therefore it was said that it was a banishing of him? How [indeed] could he be allowed the means of oppressing the people there? Nevertheless, [Shun] wished to be continually seeing him, and therefore he came unceasingly to court, as is signified in that expression, 'He did not wait for the rendering of tribute, or affairs of government, to receive [the prince of] Pe.'"[650]

IV.[651] 1. Hĕen-k'ĕw Mung asked Mencius, saying, "There is the old saying,—'An officer of complete virtue cannot be employed as a minister by his ruler, nor treated as a son by his father.' Shun stood with his face to the south, and Yaou, at the head of all the feudal

---

BROTHER SĔANG;—HOW HE BOTH DISTINGUISHED HIM AND KEPT HIM UNDER RESTRAINT.

[648] *Par.* 1. We must introduce *only*, I think, to bring out Wan's idea in what he says about Shun's treatment of Sĕang.

[649] *Par.* 2. Wan here changes his ground, and proceeds to argue against Shun from what Mencius had said. See Hwan-tow and the other criminals, and Shun's dealing with them, in the Shoo, II i. 12. The old State of Pe is commonly referred to the present district of Ling-ling, department Yung-chow, Ho-nan. But if Sĕang had been placed there, he would have been too far away to meet the conditions of his intercourse with Shun in the next paragraph.

[650] *Par,* 3. We have in the conclusion a quotation by Mencius from some book that is now lost.

[651] CH. IV. VINDICATION OF A CHARGE AGAINST SHUN IN HIS RELATIONS WITH THE EMPEROR YAOU, AND WITH HIS OWN FATHER KOO-SOW.

princes, appeared in his court with his face to the north. Koo-sow also appeared at Shun's court with his face to the north; and when Shun saw him, his countenance assumed a look of distress. Confucius said, 'At this time the empire was in a perilous condition indeed! How unsettled was its state!' I do not know whether what is thus said really took place." Mencius said, "No. These are not the words of a superior man, but the sayings of an uncultivated person of the east of Ts'e. When Yaou was old, Shun took the management of affairs for him. It is said in the Canon of Yaou, 'After twenty-eight years, Fang-heun demised, and the people mourned for him as for a parent three years. All within the four seas, the eight instruments of music were stopped and hushed.' Confucius said, 'There are not two suns in the sky, nor two sovereigns over the people. [If] Shun had already been [in the position of] the son of Heaven, and had moreover led on all the feudal princes of the empire to observe the three years' mourning for Yaou, there must in that case have been two sons of Heaven.'"[652]

2. Hëen-k'ëw Mung said, "On the point of Shun's not employing Yaou as a minister, I have received your instructions. But it is said in the Book of Poetry,

> 'Under the wide heaven,
> All is the king's land;
> Within the sea-boundaries of the land,
> All are the king's servants.'

When Shun became emperor, I venture to ask how it was that Koo-sow was not one of his servants." [Mencius] replied, "That ode is not to be understood in that way;—[it speaks of] being laboriously engaged in the king's business, and not being able to nourish one's parents, [as if the subject of it] said, 'This is all the king's business, but I alone am supposed to have ability, and made to toil in it.' Therefore those who explain the odes must not insist on one term so as to do violence to a

---

[652] *Par.* 1. Hëen-k'ëw Mung was a disciple of Mencius, a man of Ts'e, but deriving his double surname from Hëen-k'ew in Loo, where, probably, his ancestors had resided. Of the first part of the saying which Mung adduces two different views are taken. That which I have followed is given by Chaou K'e. Modern commentators generally take it as meaning—"The scholar of complete virtue cannot treat his ruler as a minister nor his father as a son;" and Julien in his translation of Mencius emphatically prefers this. I am satisfied that the older interpretation is the correct one. According to the sequel of the saying, Shun appears with his face to the south, *i.e.* in the place of the emperor, and Yaou, "a scholar of complete virtue," appears before him with his face to the north, *i.e.*, in the place of homage or of a subject. So also does Shun's father. These are intended as instances contrary to the principles in the old saying; and then Confucius' words are brought in to explain how such instances came to occur, and show that they were abnormal. Mencius denies entirely the truth of the statement in the saying about Yaou, and proves it from the Shoo, II. i. 13, and an inference from words that Confucius had once used.

sentence, not on a sentence so as to do violence to the general scope. They must try with their thoughts to meet that scope, and then they will apprehend it. If we simply take single sentences, there is that in the ode called the 'Yun Han,'

> 'Of the remnant of Chow, among the black-haired people,
> There will not be half a man left.'

If it had really been as thus expressed, then not an individual of the people of Chow would have been left.[653]

3. "Of all that a filial son can attain to, there is nothing greater than his honoring his parents. Of what can be attained to in honoring one's parents, there is nothing greater than the nourishing them with the empire. To be the father of the son of Heaven is the height of honor. To be nourished with the empire is the height of nourishment. In this was verified the sentiment in the Book of Poetry,

> 'Ever thinking how to be filial,
> His filial mind was the model [which he supplied].'

4. "In the Book of History it is said, '(With respectful service he appeared before Koo-sow, looking grave and awe-struck, till Koo-sow also was transformed by his example.' This is the true case of [the scholar of complete virtue] not being treated as a son by his father."

V.[654] 1. Wan Chang said, "[It is said that] Yaou gave the empire to Shun; was it so?" Mencius replied, "No; the emperor cannot give the empire to another."

2. "Yes; but Shun possessed the empire. Who gave it to him?" "Heaven gave it to him," was the reply.[655]

---

[653] *Parr.* 2, 3, 4. The instance of Koo-sow's appearing at the court of Shun could not be so easily disposed of. Mencius, however, was not without a good answer to his disciple, and turns the instance against him satisfactorily enough. For the first quotation In par. 2, see the She, II. vi. I. 2, and for the other, III. iii. IV. 3. For that in par. 3, see the She, III i. IX. 3; and for the quotation in par. 4, see the Shoo, II ii. 21. The appearance of Shun before Koo-sow, however, which is there described, would seem to have been before the former became emperor.

[654] CH. V. HOW SHUN GOT THE EMPIRE BY THE GIFT OF HEAVEN, AND NOT OF YAOU; AND HOW THE ACTION OF HEAVEN IN SUCH A MATTER IS TO BE UNDERSTOOD. VOX POPULI VOX DEI.

[655] *Par.* 2. Is it not plain that here, and throughout the chapter, by Heaven we must understand God? Many commentators, however, understand by it *le,* "reason," or "the truth and fitness of things," excepting in the expression in par. 7, "Therefore I said that it was Heaven," where they think the term = *soo,* "the determination of fate." On this, Le P'ei-lin of the present dynasty says:—"Ts'ae Heu-chae (of the Sung dynasty) observes that by Heaven in this one place we are to understand *fate,* and in all the other places *reason* or *the fitness of things.* But this is a great error. Throughout this chapter 'Heaven' means the government of God, within which are included both reason and fate."

3. "'Heaven gave it to him;' did [Heaven] confer the appointment on him with specific injunctions?"

4. [Mencius] said, "No; Heaven does not speak. It simply showed its will by his [personal] conduct, and by [his conduct of] affairs."

5. "'It showed its will by his [personal] conduct, and by [his conduct of] affairs,'" returned the other;—"how was this?" [Mencius] said, "The emperor can present a man to Heaven, but he cannot make Heaven give that man the empire. A feudal prince can present a man to the emperor [to take his place], but he cannot make the emperor give the princedom to that man. A great officer can present a man to his prince, but he cannot cause the prince to make that man a great officer [in his own room]. Anciently Yaou presented Shun to Heaven, and Heaven accepted him; he displayed him to the people, and the people accepted him. Therefore I say, 'Heaven does not speak. It simply indicated its will by his [personal] conduct, and by [his conduct of] affairs.'"

6. [Chang] said, "I presume to ask how it was that [Yaou] presented Shun to Heaven, and Heaven accepted him, and displayed him to the people, and the people accepted him." The reply was, "He caused him to preside over the sacrifices, and all the Spirits were well pleased with them; thus it was that Heaven accepted him. He caused him to preside over the conduct of affairs, and affairs were well administered, so that all the people reposed under him;—thus it was that the people accepted him. Heaven gave [the empire] to him, and the people gave it to him. Therefore I said, 'The emperor cannot give the empire to another.'[656]

7. "Shun assisted Yaou [in the government] for twenty and eight years;—this was more than man could have done, and was from Heaven. When the three years' mourning consequent on the death of Yaou were accomplished, Shun withdrew from the son of Yaou to the south of the southern Ho. The princes of the empire, however, repairing to court, went not to the son of Yaou, but to Shun. Litigants went not to the son of Yaou, but to Shun. Singers sang not the son of Yaou, but Shun. Therefore I said that it was Heaven [that gave him the empire]. It was after this that he went to the Middle State, and occupied the seat of the son of Heaven. If he had [before these things] taken up his residence in the palace of Yaou, and applied pressure to his son, it would have been an act of usurpation, and not the gift of Heaven.[657]

---

[656] *Par.* 6. "All the Spirits" is here explained as "the Spirits of heaven, earth, the mountains, and the rivers;" *i.e.*, all spiritual Beings, real or supposed. The emperor was "the host of all the Spirits," and Shun entered, as conducting the government for Yaou, into all his duties. But how the Spirits enjoyed the sacrifices thus presided over by Shun we are not told.

[657] *Par.* 7. "The south of the southern Ho" was, I apprehend, the ancient Yu-chow, lying south from K'e-chow, and separated from it by the Ho. All the Ho might be called

8. "This view [of Shun's obtaining the empire] is in accordance with what is said in The Great Declaration,—'Heaven sees as my people see, Heaven hears as my people hear.'"[658]

VI.[659] 1. Wan Chang said, "People say, 'When [the disposal of the empire] came to Yu, his virtue was inferior [to that of Yaou and Shun], and he did not transmit it to the worthiest, but to his son;'—was it so?" Mencius replied, "No; it was not so. When Heaven gave [the empire] to the worthiest, it was given to the worthiest; when Heaven gave it to the son [of the preceding emperor], it was given to that son. Formerly Shun presented Yu to Heaven for [a period of] seventeen years; and when the three years' mourning, consequent on the death of Shun, were accomplished, Yu withdrew from the son of Yu to Yang-shing. The people of the empire followed him as, after the death of Yaou, they had not followed his son, but followed Shun. Yu presented Yih to Heaven for [a period of] seven years; and when the three years' mourning consequent on the death of Yu were accomplished, Yih withdrew from the son of Yu to the north of Mount Ke. [The princes] repairing to court, and litigants, went not to Yih, but to K'e, saying, 'He is the son of our ruler.' Singers did not sing Yih, but they sang K'e, saying, '(He is the son of our ruler.'[660]

2. "That Tan-choo was not equal [to his father], and Shun's son also not equal [to his]; that Shun assisted Yaou, and Yu assisted Shun, for a period of many years, conferring benefits on the people for a long time; that K'e was virtuous and able, and could reverently enter into and continue the ways of Yu; that Yih assisted Yu for a period of few years, conferring benefits on the people not for a long time; that the

---

southern, from where the river after flowing from the north to the south turns to the east. "Litigants" must indicate parties whose contentions the ordinary authorities had not been able to settle, and who therefore appealed to the decision of the supreme authority.

[658] *Par.* 8. See the Shoo, V. i. Pt I. 7.

[659] CH. VI. HOW THE THRONE DESCENDED FROM YU TO HIS SON, AND NOT TO HIS MINISTER YIH; AND THAT YU WAS NOT TO BE CONSIDERED ON THAT ACCOUNT AS INFERIOR IN VIRTUE TO YAOU AND SHUN. ALSO, THE CONDITIONS UNDER WHICH A CHANGE OF THE RULING FAMILY WILL TAKE PLACE, WHEN THE PRINCIPLE OF HEREDITARY SUCCESSION HAS BEEN ESTABLISHED, WITH REFERENCE TO THE CASES OF E YIN, THE DUKE OF CHOW, AND CONFUCIUS.

[660] *Par.* 1. Neither Wan Chang nor our philosopher seems to have clearly seen the thing which was to be explained in connection with Yu,—the establishment of China as a hereditary monarchy in his family. The passing of the throne from him to his son may have taken place as Mencius says; but how did it pass again from K'e to *his* son? I have spoken on this point in the Prolegomena to the Shoo. It might have been asked of Mencius why Yu presented Yih to Heaven as his successor, if his son were worthier than Yih. Yih appears in the Shoo, II. i. 22, as Shun's forester. He assisted Yu in his labors on the waters (the Shoo, II. iv. I.), and is said to have become Yu's principal minister after the death of Kaou Yaou. Yang-shing, we should judge, was the name of a city, or settlement in those early days. Many affirm, however, that it was the name of a mountain, and that it and mount Ke were near each other in the present department of Ho-nan, Ho-nan province.

length of time that Shun, Yu, and Yih [assisted in the government] was so different; and that the sons [of the emperors] were [one] a man of talents and virtue, and [the other two] inferior [to their fathers]:—all these things were from Heaven, and what could not be produced by man. That which is done without any one's [seeming] to do it is from Heaven. That which comes to pass without any one's [seeming] to bring it about is from Heaven.

3. "In the case of a private man's obtaining the empire, there must be in him virtue equal to that of Shun and Yu, and moreover there must be the presenting him to Heaven by the [preceding] emperor. It was on this [latter] account that Chung-ne did not obtain the kingdom.[661]

4. "When the throne descends by natural succession, he who is displaced by Heaven must be like Kĕeh or Chow. It was on this account that Yih, E Yin, and the duke of Chow did not obtain the kingdom.[662]

5. "E Yin assisted T'ang so that he became sovereign of the kingdom. After the demise of T'ang, T'ae-ting having died without being appointed [in his place], Wae-ping [reigned] two years, and Chung-jin four. T'ae-Kĕah [then] was turning upside down the canons and example of T'ang, and E Yin placed him in T'ung for three years. [There] he repented of his errors, was contrite, and reformed himself. In T'ung he came to dwell in benevolence and moved towards righteousness, during those three years listening to the lessons given to him by E Yin, [after which] that minister again returned [with him] to Poh.[663]

6. "The duke of Chow's not getting the kingdom was like that of Yih's not getting [the throne of] Hĕa, or E Yin's [that of] Yin.[664]

7. "Confucius said, 'T'ang and Yu resigned [the throne to the worthiest]; the founders of the Hĕa, Yin, and Chow [dynasties] transmitted it to their sons. The principle of righteousness was the same in [all the cases]."[665]

VII.[666] 1. Wan Chang asked [Mencius], saying, "People say that E Yin sought [an introduction to] T'ang by his [knowledge of]

---

[661] *Par.* 3. Confucius bad the virtue, and more, according to Mencius, than the virtue of Shun and. Yu, but no king of his time ever thought of presenting him to Heaven to succeed him on the throne. We do not know that any king knew of his existence.

[662] *Par.* 4. We have met with E Yin in Mencius before,—in II. i. II. 22, et al.; and he is spoken of more at length in the next chapter. The duke of Chow is the well-known brother of king Woo. He might have got the throne without any change of the dynasty of Chow.

[663] *Par.* 5. See the Shoo, IV., Books iv. and v.

[664] *Par.* 6. The duke of Chow's case was hardly analogous either to that of Yih or of E Yin.

[665] *Par.* 7. Where and when Confucius thus spoke, we do not know. T'ang and Yu are the dynastic designations of Yaou and Shun;—see on the titles of the first and second Parts of the Shoo.

[666] CH. VII. VINDICATION OF E YIN FROM THE CHARGE OF INTRODUCING HIMSELF TO THE SERVICE OF T'ANG BY MEANS OF HIS SKILL IN COOKING.

---

cookery;—was it so?"[667]

2. Mencius replied, "No, it was not so. E Yin was farming in the 'lands of the State of Sin, delighting in the principles of Yaou and Shun. In any matter contrary to the righteousness which they prescribed, or to the course which they enjoined, though he had been salaried with the empire, he would not have regarded it; though there had been yoked for him a thousand teams, he would not have looked at them. In any matter contrary to the righteousness which they prescribed, or to the course which they enjoined, he would not have given nor taken [even] a single straw.[668]

3. "T'ang sent persons with presents of silk to ask him to enter his service. With an air of indifference and self-satisfaction, he said, 'What can I do with these silks with which T'ang invites me? Is it not best for me to abide in these channeled fields, and therein delight myself with the principles of Yaou and Shun?'

4. "T'ang thrice sent persons thus to invite him. After this, with the change of purpose displayed in his countenance, be spoke in a different style, saying, 'Instead of abiding in the channeled fields, and therein delighting myself with the principles of Yaou and Shun, had I not better make this ruler one after the style of Yaou and Shun? had I not better make this people like the people of Yaou and Shun? had I not better in my own person see these things for myself?[669]

5. "'Heaven's plan in the production of this people is this:—that they who are first informed, should instruct those who are later in being informed, and those who first apprehend [principles] should instruct those who are slower to do so. I am the one of Heaven's people who have first apprehended; I will take these principles and instruct this people in them. If I do not instruct them, who will do so?'

6. "He thought that among all the people of the kingdom, even the private men and women, if there were any that did not enjoy such benefits as Yaou and Shun conferred, it was as if he himself pushed them into a ditch. He took upon himself the heavy charge of all under Heaven in this way, and therefore he went to T'ang, and pressed upon him the duty of attacking Hëa, and saving the people.

---

[667] *Par.* 1. E Yin has been mentioned already in II. i. II. and ii. II 10. The popular account of him (found also in Sze-ma Ts'ëen) in the time of Mencius was, that he came to Poh in the train of a princess of Sin whom T'ang was marrying, carrying with him his cooking utensils, that by his skill in "cutting and boiling," he might recommend himself to that prince.

[668] *Par.* 2. Sin was probably the same territory with what was called Kwoh during the Chow dynasty,—the present Shen Chow in Ho-nan, and not far from T'ang's seat in Poh. I have not been able to discover what were the antecedents to his farming life in Sin, nor how it was that his merits and ability became known to T'ang. He was evidently living the life of a recluse, at the time that Mencius brings him on the stage.

[669] *Parr.* 4, 5, 6. Compare II. i. II 22, and below in Part ii. I. 2, 5. "In my own person," in par. 5, must mean, I think, "by my own efforts."

7. "I have not heard of one who bent himself and at the same time made others straight;—how much less could one disgrace himself, and thereby rectify the whole kingdom? The actions of the sages have been different. Some have kept far away [from office], and others have drawn near to it; some have left [their offices], and others have not done so; that in which these different courses all meet, is simply the keeping of their persons pure.[670]

8. "I have heard that E Yin sought [an introduction to] T'ang by the principles of Yaou and Shun; I have not heard that he did so by his [knowledge of] cookery.

9. "In the 'Instructions of E,' it is said, 'Heaven, destroying [Kĕeh], commenced attacking him in the palace of Muh; we commenced in Poh.'"[671]

VIII.[672] 1. Wan Chang asked [Mencius], saying, "Some say that Confucius in Wei lived with an ulcer-[doctor], and in Ts'e with Tseih Hwan, the chief of the eunuchs; was it so?" Mencius said, "No, it was not so. Those are the inventions of men fond of [strange] things.[673]

2. "In Wei he lived in the house of Yen Ch'ow-yĕw. The wife of the officer Mei and the wife of Tsze-loo were sisters. Mei-tsze spoke to Tsze-loo, saying, 'If Confucius will lodge with me, he may get to be a high noble of Wei.' Tsze-loo reported this to Confucius, who said, 'That is as ordered [by Heaven].' Confucius advanced according to propriety, and retired according to righteousness. In regard to his obtaining [office and honor] or not obtaining them, he said 'That is as ordered.' But if he had lodged with an ulcer-[doctor] and with Tseih Hwan, the chief of the eunuchs, that would neither have been according to righteousness, nor any ordering [of Heaven].[674]

---

[670] *Par.* 7. The concluding sentiment about the common object of all sages is worded so as to show the grossness of the story about E Yin's commending himself to T'ang by his skill in cooking.

[671] *Par.* 9. See the Shoo, IV. iv. 2; but the text there differs considerably from that which Mencius gives. The meaning is that Kĕeh's atrocities in his palace at Muh led Heaven to destroy him, while E Yin, in accordance with the will of Heaven, advised T'ang in Poh to take action against him.

[672] CH. VIII. VINDICATION OF CONFUCIUS FROM THE CHARGE OF LODGING WITH UNSUITABLE PERSONS.

[673] *Par.* 1. Sze-ma Ts'ëen, in his history of Confucius, says that on the occasion when the sage made the observation in Ana. IX. xvii. that he "had never met with one who loved virtue as he loved beauty," there was a Yung K'eu in the same carriage with the marquis of Wei, and his notorious wife. That Yung K'eu was, no doubt, the ulcer-doctor of the text, and I am inclined to think that there may be some error in the formation of the characters as we read them. If there be not, we must suppose that the marquis of Wei had a parasite so named, who had been raised to his favor from the mean position of a curer of sores and ulcers. Of the same character was Tseih Hwan a favorite of one of the marquises of Ts'e, and his master of the eunuchs, in the time of the sage.

[674] *Par.* 2. Sze-ma Ts'ëen gives Yen Chuh-tsow for Yen Ch'ow-yĕw, and says he was the elder brother (or brother-in-law) of Tsze-loo. This is contrary to what Mencius says. There were two traditions, probably, on the point. On a later occasion Confucius

3. "When Confucius, being dissatisfied in Loo and Wei, [had left those States], he met with the attempt of Hwan, the master of the Horse, in Sung, to intercept and. kill him, so that he had to pass through Sung in the dress of a private man. At that time, [though] he was in circumstances of distress, he lodged in the house of Ching-tsze, the minister of works, who was [then] a minister of Chow, the marquis of Ch'in.[675]

4. "I have heard that ministers in the service of a court may be known from those to whom they are hosts, and that ministers coming from a distance may be known from those with whom they lodge. If Confucius had lodged with an ulcer-[doctor] and with Tseih Hwan, the chief of the eunuchs, how could he have been Confucius?"

IX.[676] 1. Wan Chang asked [Mencius], saying, "Some say that Pih-le He sold himself to a cattle-keeper of Ts'in for five sheep-skins, and fed his cattle for him, to seek an introduction to duke Muh of Ts'in; is this true?" Mencius said, "No, it was not so. This is the invention of some one fond of [strange] things.[677]

---

lodged in Wei with a worthy officer called Keu Pih-yuh. Mei Hëa is mentioned in the Tso Chuen under the 6th year of duke Ting, and the 25 the of duke Gae. He was a favorite with the marquis; and wished by his proposal to ingratiate himself with Confucius.

[675] *Par.* 3. "Hwan of Sung;"—see on Ana. VII. xxii. Hwan is the Hwan T'uy of that chapter. After Confucius had left Wei, he was proceeding to Ch'in, and on the way Hwan T'uy made the attempt on his life which is here alluded to. I do not know that the sage was in circumstances of distress after his arrival at the chief city of Ch'in. Mencius must refer to what he did immediately on reaching it. Ching-tsze, or "the officer Pure," was the honorary or posthumous epithet of the officer who was Confucius' host, and Chow was the name of the last marquis of Ch'in, known as duke Min. Ching-tsze, it is said, after the extinction of Ch'in, went to Sung, and there became minister of Works, and was afterwards known as such; hence he is so styled here by Mencius, when referring to an earlier period of his life.

[676] CH. IX. VINDICATION OF PIH-LE HE FROM THE CHARGE OF SELLING HIMSELF AS A STEP TOWARDS HIS ADVANCEMENT TO THE SERVICE OF DUKE MUH OF TS'IN.

[677] *Par.* 1. Pih-le He was chief minister to duke Muh of Ts'in, whose rule extended from B.C. 658 to 618. The incidents of his life will be found interestingly detailed in the 25th and some subsequent chapters of the "History of the various States," though some of them are different from the statements of Mencius about him. According to Sze-ma Ts'ëen, He, who had been a minister of Yu, after the subversion of that State by Tsin, followed its captive duke, and was sent by the marquis of Tsin, in the train of the eldest daughter of his house, to Tsin, where she was to become the wife of duke Muh. Disgusted at being reduced to such a position, he absconded on the road, and, fleeing to Ts'oo, became noted there for his skill in rearing cattle. Duke Muh heard somehow of his great capacity, and sent to Ts'oo to reclaim him as a runaway servant, offering also to pay for him five rams' skins. He was afraid to offer anything more valuable, lest he should awaken suspicions in Ts'oo that he wanted to get He on account of his ability; and on obtaining him, he at once made him his chief minister. In the "Plans of the Warring States," we have an account of Pih-le He's introduction to duke Muh, more in accordance with what Mencius said. He is there introduced as a borderer of Ts'oo, who wished to get introduced to the service of duke Muh. With this purpose he sold himself for five rams' skins to a gentleman of Ts'in, whose cattle he took care of. By and by he attracted the notice of duke Muh, who perceived his merit, and raised him to the distinction where he so abundantly repaid the duke's kindness.

2. "Pih-le He was a man of Yu. The people of Ts'in by the inducement of a *peih* of Ch'uy-keih and a team of Këuh-ch'an horses were asking liberty to march through Yu to attack Kwoh. Kung Che-k'e remonstrated [with the duke of Yu, asking him not to grant their request], but Pih-le He did not remonstrate.[678]

3. "When he knew that the duke of Yu was not to be remonstrated with, and went in consequence from that State to Ts'in, he had reached the age of seventy. If by that time he did not know that it would be a disgraceful thing to seek for an introduction to duke Muh of Ts'in by feeding cattle, could he be called wise? But not remonstrating where it was of no use to remonstrate, could he be said not to be wise? Knowing that the duke of Yu would be ruined, and leaving his State before that event, he could not be said to be not wise. As soon as he was advanced in Ts'in, he knew that duke Muh was one with whom he could have a field for action, and became chief minister to him;—could he be said to be not wise? Acting as chief minister in Ts'in, he made his ruler distinguished throughout the kingdom, and worthy to be handed down to future ages;—if he had not been a man of talents and virtue, could he have done this? As to selling himself in order to bring about the destruction of his ruler, even a villager who had a regard for himself, would not do such a thing;—and shall we say that a man of talents and virtue did it?"

## BOOK V. WAN CHANG. PART II.

CHAPTER I.[679] 1. MENCIUS said, "Pih-e would not allow his eyes to look at a bad sight, nor his ears to listen to a bad sound. He would not serve a ruler, nor employ a people, of whom he did not approve. In a time of good government he took office, and in a time of disorder he retired. He could not bear to dwell [at a court] from which lawless government proceeded, nor among lawless people. To be in the same place with an [ordinary] villager was the same in his estimation as to stand in his court robes and court cap amid mire and charcoal. In the time of Chow, he dwelt by the shores of the northern sea, waiting for the purification of the kingdom. Therefore when men [now] hear the character of Pih-e, the corrupt become pure, and the weak acquire determination.[680]

---

[678] *Par.* 2. See the history of this transaction given from Kung-yang and Kuh-lëang in the Prolegomena to Vol. V., pp. 62, 63. Pih-le He, indeed, is not mentioned there, because, I suppose, he held his peace at the time. Perhaps, "a team of Këuh-ch'an horses" should be "a team of horses from Këuh."

[679] CH. I. HOW CONFUCIUS DIFFERED FROM, AND WAS SUPERIOR TO, ALL OTHER SAGES, POSSESSING ALL SAGELY QUALITIES IN FULL MEASURE, WHICH THEY DID NOT DO;—ILLUSTRATED BY AN EXHIBITION OF CHARACTERISTICS OF PIH-E, E YIN, AND HWUY OF LËW-HËA.

[680] *Par.* 1. Compare II. i. II 22; IX. I, 3: III. ii. X. 3: IV. i. XIII 1: VI. ii. VI. 2; and

2. "E Yin said, 'Whom may I not serve as my ruler? whom may I not employ as my people?' In a time of good government he took office, and in a time of disorder he did the same. He said, 'Heaven's plan in the production of this people is this:—that they who are first informed should instruct those who are later in being informed, and they who first apprehend [principles] should instruct those who are slower to do so. I am the one of Heaven's people who have first apprehended;—I will take these principles and instruct this people in them.' He thought that among all the people of the kingdom, even the private men and women, if there were any that did not enjoy such benefits as Yaou and Shun conferred, it was as if he himself pushed them into a ditch;—so did he take on himself the heavy charge of all under heaven.[681]

3. "Hwuy of Lĕw-hĕa was not ashamed to serve an impure ruler, nor did he decline a small office. When advanced to employment, he did not keep his talents and virtue concealed, but made it a point to carry out his principles. When neglected and left out of office, he did not murmur, and when straitened by poverty, he did not grieve. When in the company of village people, he was quite at ease and could not bear to leave them. [He would say], 'You are you, and I am I. Though you stand by my side with bare arms and breast, how can you defile me?' Therefore when men [now] hear the character of Hwuy of Lĕw-hĕa, the mean become generous, and the niggardly become liberal.[682]

4. "When Confucius was leaving Ts'e he took with his hands the water from the rice which was being washed in it, and went away [with the uncooked rice]. When he was about to leave Loo, he said, 'I will go by and by;'—it was right he should leave the country of his parents in this way. When it was proper to go away quickly he did so; when it was proper to delay, he did so; when it was proper to keep in retirement, he did so; when it was proper to go into office, he did so;—this was Confucius."[683]

5. Mencius said, "Pih-e among the sages was the pure one; E Yin was the one most inclined to take office; Hwuy of Lĕw-hĕa was the accommodating one; and Confucius was the timeous one.[684]

6. "In Confucius we have what is called a complete concert. A complete concert is when the bell proclaims [the commencement of the

---

VII. i. XXII. 1; ii. XV. 1.

[681] *Par.* 2. Compare II. i. II. 22; ii. II. 10: V. i. VI. 4, 5; VII.: VI. ii. VI.2: and VII. i. XXXI. 1; ii. XXXVIII. 2.

[682] *Par.* 3. Compare II. i. IX. 2, 3: VI. ii. VI. 2: VII. i. XXVIII; ii. XV. 1.

[683] *Par.* 4. Compare II. i. II. 22. I do not know that we have in any other ancient record an account of the incident mentioned here in connection with the departure of Confucius from Ts'e.

[684] *Par.* 5. I have invented the adjective "timeous," which would be a literal translation of the original term, if it were current in our language. Its meaning is that Confucius did at every time what the circumstances of it required to be done.

music], and the [ringing] stone closes it. The metal sound commences the blended harmony [of all the instruments], and the winding up with the stone terminates that blended harmony. The commencing that harmony is the work of wisdom, and the terminating it is the work of sageness.[685]

7. "As a comparison for wisdom, we may liken it to skill, and as a comparison for sageness, we may liken it to strength,—as in the case of shooting at a mark a hundred paces distant. That you reach the mark is owing to your strength; but that you hit it is not owing to your strength."[686]

II.[687] 1. Pih-kung E asked [Mencius], "What was the arrangement of dignities and emoluments made by the House of Chow?"[688]

2. Mencius said, "The particulars of that arrangement cannot be learned, for the feudal princes, disliking them as injurious to themselves, have all made away with the records of them. Nevertheless I have learned the general outline of them.[689]

3. "THE SON OF HEAVEN was one dignity; the DUKE one; the MARQUIS one; the EARL one; and the VISCOUNT and BARON formed one, being of equal rank:—altogether making five degrees of dignity. The RULER was one dignity; the MINISTER one; the GREAT OFFICER one; the OFFICER OF THE FIRST CLASS one; the OFFICER OF THE SECOND CLASS one; and the officer of the lowest class one:—altogether making six grades.[690]

---

[685] *Par.* 6. The illustration of Confucius here is from a grand performance of music, in which all the eight kinds of musical instruments were employed. One instrument would make "a small performance;" all joined, they made "a collected great performance," = "a complete concert."

[686] *Par.* 7. The other sages had, as well as Confucius, what might be compared to "strength," but they were deficient, as compared with him, in wisdom or skill. We may compare each of them, it has been said, "to one of the seasons; but Confucius was the grand, harmonious air of heaven flowing through all the seasons."

[687] CH. II. THE ARRANGEMENT OF DIGNITIES AND EMOLUMENTS ACCORDING TO THE DYNASTY OF CHOW. Some of the statements of Mencius in this chapter are at variance with what we find on the same subjects in the "Official Book of Chow," and parts of the Le Ke. I will not, however, take any notice here of those differences, but reserve the discussion of them till I come to the examination of those other Works.

[688] *Par.* 1. Pih-kung E was a high officer of Wei, one of a family descended from duke Ch'ing of that State from B.C. 633 to 597. Various members of it appear in the Tso Chuen. Its clan-name of Pih-kung or "Northern-palace" would be taken from the residence of its founder.

[689] *Par.* 2. It is an important fact which Mencius here mentions, that before his time the feudal princes had destroyed many of the records affecting the constitution and territories of their States. The founder of the Ts'in dynasty had had predecessors and fathers in what he did in this way.

[690] *Par.* 3. The five degrees of dignity here are degrees of rank, and the six are degrees of position or official employment. The title "son of Heaven" is equally applicable to the Head of the nation, whether emperor or king, and is an emphatic designation of him as appointed by God. "Son of Heaven" is equivalent to "Heaven-sonned;" *i.e.*, dealt with by Heaven as its son, and placed in the highest station. See the

4. "To the son of Heaven there was allotted a territory of a thousand *le* square; a duke and a marquis had each a hundred *le* square; an earl, seventy *le*; a viscount and a baron, fifty *le*. The assignments altogether were of four amounts. Where the territory did not amount to fifty *le*, the holder could not himself have access to the son of Heaven. His land was attached to some one of the feudal princes, and was called a FOO-YUNG.[691]

5. "A high minister of the son of Heaven received an amount of territory equal to that of a marquis; a great officer, as much as an earl; and an officer of the first class, as much as a viscount or baron.

6. "In a great State, where the territory was a hundred *le* square, the

---

She, IV. i. [i], VIII After the study of the Shoo, the She, and the Ch'un Ts'ëw, I think it is much better to adopt the titles of the five orders of nobility in the feudal kingdoms of Europe for those which were employed for the five corresponding orders in China, when it was in the feudal State. "Duke," in Chinese *kung*, was the highest title of nobility. *Kung* gives the idea of "just, correct, without selfishness." "Marquis," in Chinese *how*, was the second. *How* gives the idea of "taking care of," and was given to the nobles dignified with it, as "guardians of the borders" of the kingdom. "Earl," in Chinese *pih*, was the third. *Pih* conveys the ideas of "elder and intelligent," "one by his intelligence and virtue capable of presiding over others." "Viscount or count," in Chinese *tsze*, was the fourth. "*Tsze*" means "a son," but as a title means "to treat as a son," giving the idea of "generally nourishing the people." "Baron," in Chinese *nan*, was the fifth. *Nan* is the common designation for "a male-child." Composed of the characters for "field" and "strength," it conveys the idea of "one adequate to office and labor." According to Mencius the viscount and the baron were considered equal in rank. All from the "son of Heaven" downwards might be styled *koun* or "ruler." Of the six grades of official position, the highest after the ruler was the minister,—in Chinese *k'ing*. *K'ing* is explained as meaning "luminous," "one who can illustrate what is good and right" At the court of Chow there were properly six *k'ing*, though sometimes nine are spoken of. The Heads of the "Six Boards" may now be considered as their successors. For a feudal State the number of *k'ing* was three, but some of them claimed to have a greater number. Their appointment required the confirmation of the king. The second official grade consisted of the "great officers," in Chinese *ta foo*. *Ta foo* may be translated by "great sustainer." The number of these was indefinite. As *ta foo*, they had no specific office, but might be employed by their rulers, as occasion required, being men of experience, recognized ability, and trustworthiness. The other grades were made up of the three orders of officers. In Chinese *sze* is explained as "one fit to be entrusted with the conduct of affairs." Its meaning is often given as = "scholar;" and it is difficult always to discriminate between the two significations. In fact a fundamental principle in the Chinese nation has ever been that for office a certain amount of literary cultivation was required.

[691] *Par.* 4. "A thousand *le* square," *i.e.*, according to some, "a thousand *le* in breadth and a thousand *le* in length, making an area of a million *le*."

On this, however, the editors of the imperial edition of the *king* under the present dynasty, say:—"Where we find the term *square*, we are not to think of an exact square, but only that, on calculation, the territory would be found equal to so many square *le*. So, in regard to the States of the various princes, we are to understand that, however their form might be varied by the hills and rivers, their area in round numbers amounted to so much." On an "attached territory," see Ana. XVI. i. 1. These States were too small to bear the expenses of appearing at the royal court, and so the names and surnames of their chiefs were presented by the greater feudal lords to whom they were attached, and in whose train they also sometimes appeared.

ruler had ten times as much income as one of his high ministers; a high minister had four times as much as a great officer; a great officer twice as much as an officer of the first class; an officer of the first class, twice as much as one of the middle; and an officer of the middle class twice as much as one of the lowest. Officers of the lowest class, and such of the common people as were employed in the public offices, had the same emolument,—as much, namely, as what they would have made by tilling the fields.[692]

7. "In a State of the next order, where the territory was seventy *le* square, the ruler had ten times as much income as one of his high ministers; a high minister, thrice as much as a great officer; a great officer, twice as much as an officer of the first class; an officer of the first class, twice as much as one of the second; and one of the second twice as much as one of the lowest. Officers of the lowest class and such of the common people as were employed in the public offices, had the same emolument,—as much, namely, as they would have made by tilling the fields.

8. "In a small State, where the territory was fifty *le* square, the ruler had ten times as much income as one of his high ministers; a high minister twice as much as a great officer; a great officer twice as much as an officer of the first class; an officer of the first class twice as much as one of the second; one of the second class twice as much as one of the lowest. Officers of the lowest class, and such of the common people as were employed in the public offices, had the same emolument,—as much, namely, as they would have made by tilling the fields.[693]

9. "As to those who tilled the fields, each head of a family received a hundred *mow*. When these were manured, the [best] husbandmen of the first class supported nine individuals, and those ranking next to them supported eight. The [best] husbandmen of the second class supported seven men, and those ranking next to them supported six; while the lowest class [only] supported five. The salaries of the common people who were employed in the public offices, were regulated according to these differences."

III.[694] 1. Wan Chang asked [Mencius], saying, "I venture to ask

---

[692] *Par.* 6. "A great State" was that of a duke or a marquis. One commentator says:—"The ruler had 32,000 *mow*, the income of which would suffice to feed 2,880 men. A minister had 3,200 *mow*, sufficient to feed 288 men. A great officer had 800 *mow*, sufficient to feed 72 men. An officer of the first class had 400 *mow*, sufficient to feed 36 men; one of the second class had 200 *mow*, sufficient to feed 18 men; and one of the lowest class had 100 *mow*, sufficient to feed from nine men to five men (see par. 9)" "The common people employed in the public offices" would be the runners or policemen, and other subordinates.

[693] *Parr.* 7, 8. "A State of the second order" was that of an earl, and "a small State" was that of a viscount or a baron.

[694] CH. III. THE PRINCIPLES OF FRIENDSHIP. FRIENDSHIP SHOULD HAVE REFERENCE TO THE VIRTUE OF THE FRIEND, AND THERE SHOULD BE NO ASSUMPTION IN

about [the principles of] friendship." Mencius replied, "Friendship does not permit of any presuming on the ground of one's age, or station, or [the circumstances of] one's relations. Friendship [with a man] is friendship with his virtue, and there cannot be any presuming [on such things].[695]

2. "The minister Măng Hĕen was [chief of] a family of a hundred chariots, and he had five friends,—Yoh-ching K'ĕw, Muh Ching, and three [others whose names] I have forgotten. With these five men Hĕen-tsze maintained a friendship, because they thought nothing about his family. If they had thought about his family, he would not have maintained his friendship with them.[696]

3. "Not only has [the chief of] a family of a hundred chariots acted thus. The same has been exemplified even in the ruler of a small State. Duke Hwuy of Pe said, "I treat Tsze-sze as my master, and Yen Pan as my friend. As to Wang Shun and Ch'ang Seih, they serve me.[697]

4. "Not only has the ruler of a small State acted thus. The same thing has been exemplified by the ruler of a large State. There was duke P'ing of Tsin with Hae T'ang:—when [T'ang] told him to come into his house, he came; when he told him to be seated, he sat; when he told him to eat, he ate. There might be only coarse rice, and soup of vegetables, but he always ate his fill, not daring to do otherwise. Here, however, [the duke] stopped, and went no farther. He did not call [T'ang] to share with him his Heavenly place, nor to administer with him his Heavenly office, nor to partake with him his Heavenly emolument. His conduct was a scholar's honoring of virtue and talent; not a king or a duke's honoring of them.[698]

5. "Shun went up and had an interview with the emperor, and the emperor lodged him as his son-in-law in the second palace. He also partook of Shun's hospitality. He was host and guest alternately. This

---

IT ON THE GROUND OF ONE'S SUPERIORITY IN YEARS, SOCIAL POSITION, OR RELATIONAL ADVANTAGES.

[695] *Par.* 1. It is a fine idea of the Chinese that only virtue should be the bond of friendship, and the object of friendship should be the support and increase of one's virtue.

[696] *Par.* 2. Măng Hĕen was the same who is mentioned in "the Great Learning," Comm. X. 22, *q. v.* Yoh-ching K'ĕw would be an ancestor of Yoh-ching, one of our philosopher's disciples, mentioned in L ii. XVI., *et al.* It appears from a passage in the "Narratives of the States," IV. ix. 5, that the fact of Măng Hĕen's having five friends was well known.

[697] *Par.* 3. Pe,—see on Ana. VI. vii. Pe was the city of the Ke-sun family in Loo. Mencius is probably speaking of it when it had fallen under the power of Ts'oo, and had been erected by it into the chief city of a small State dependent on itself. Tsze-sze was the grandson of Confucius Yen Pan is understood to have been the son of Yen Hwuy, Confucius' favorite disciple. Of Wang Shun nothing is known. Ch'ang Seih,—see Pt i. I. 2.

[698] *Par.* 4. Duke P'ing (hon. title, = "the Pacificator") was Pĕw, marquis of Tsin from B.C. 554 to 529. Hae T'ang was a worthy of his State.

was the emperor maintaining friendship with a common man.[699]

6. "Respect shown by inferiors to superiors is called giving to the noble the observance due to rank. Respect shown by superiors to inferiors is called giving honor to virtue and talents. The principle of righteousness is the same in both cases."[700]

IV.[701] 1. Wan Chang asked [Mencius], saying, "I venture to ask what [sentiment of the] mind is expressed in the gifts of courteous intercourse." Mencius replied, "[The sentiment of] respect."[702]

2. "Why is it," pursued the other, "that to decline a gift decidedly is accounted disrespectful?" The answer was, "When one of honorable rank presents a gift, to say [in the mind], 'Was the way in which he got this righteous or not? I must know this before I receive it,'—this is counted disrespectful, and therefore gifts are not declined."

3. [Wan Chang] went on, "Let me ask this:—If one do not in so many express words decline the gift, but having declined it in his heart, saying, 'He took it from the people, and it is not righteous,' if he then assign some other reason for not receiving it, is not this a proper course?" Mencius said, "When the donor offers it on the ground of reason, and his manner of doing so is according to propriety, in such a case Confucius would have received it."[703]

4. Wan Chang said, "Here now is one who stops [and robs] people outside the city gates;—he offers his gift on a ground of reason, and presents it in accordance with propriety;—would the reception of the gift so acquired by robbery be proper?" [Mencius] said, "It would not be proper. In the 'Announcement to the Prince of K'ang' it is said, 'Where men kill others, or violently assault them, to take their property, being reckless and fearless of death, they are abhorred by all the people;'—these are to be put to death without waiting to give them any

---

[699] *Par.* 5. Here we have the highest style of friendship, where the object of the friendship was called to share in the heavenly place, &c. But was not this introducing an element which does not belong to the idea of friendship?

[700] *Par.* 6. The meaning of "righteousness" here is what is "right in the propriety of things."

[701] CH. IV. HOW MENCIUS DEFENDED THE ACCEPTING PRESENTS FROM THE PRINCES WHO WERE THE OPPRESSORS OF THE PEOPLE, AND MIGHT BE REPRESENTED AS ROBBERS OF THEM. Wan chang does not speak expressly of Mencius' own practice, but no doubt he had it in mind; and never was our philosopher more closely pressed by any of his disciples on what was a stumbling-block to them,—his living so freely on the presents of the kings and princes of his day, while yet he refused to take office under any of them.

[702] *Par.* 1. The subject about which the disciple asks here is not presents of friendship, but the gifts offered by superiors to scholars not in office, and the acceptance of them by these.

[703] *Par.* 3. Mencius does not seem to meet fairly the question proposed by Wan Chang. We might have expected him to say that the scholar to whom the gift was offered should decline it, boldly stating the reason why he did so. This, I think, would have been more in accordance with the boldness of his own character. His diverting the conversation to the subject of Confucius was merely an ingenious ruse.

lesson [or warning]. Yin received [this rule] from Hea, and Chow received it from Yin; it cannot be questioned, and to the present day is clearly acknowledged. How can [the gift of a robber] be received?"[704]

5. [Wan Chang] continued, "The princes of the present day take from their people, as if they were [so many] robbers. But if they put a good face of propriety on their gifts, then the superior man receives them;—I venture to ask how you explain this?" [Mencius] replied, "Do you think that if a true king were to arise, he would collect all the princes of the present day, and put them to death? Or would he admonish them, and then, when they did not change [their ways], put them to death? To say that [every one] who takes what does not properly belong to him is a robber is pushing a point of resemblance to the utmost, and insisting on the most refined idea of righteousness. When Confucius took office in Loo, the people struggled together for the game taken in hunting, and he also did the same. If that struggling for the captured game was allowable, how much more may the gifts [of the princes] be received!"[705]

6. [Chang] urged, "Then, when Confucius took office, was it not with the object that his principles should be carried into practice?" "It was with that object," was the reply. [The other said,] "If the practice of his principles was his business, what had he to do with that struggling for the captured game?" [Mencius] answered, "Confucius first rectified the vessels of sacrifice according to the registers, and [enacted] that being so rectified they should not be supplied with food gathered from every quarter." "But why did he not leave [the State]?" said [Chang]. [Mencius] replied, "He would first make a trial [of carrying his principles into practice]. When this trial was sufficient [to show] they could be practiced, and they were still not practiced [on a larger scale], he would then go away. Thus it was that he never completed a residence [in any State] of three years.[706]

7. "Confucius took office when he saw that the practice [of his principles] was possible; when the reception accorded to him was proper; and when he was supported by the State. In his relations with the minister Ke Hwan, he took office because he saw that the practice

---

[704] *Par.* 4. On the case proposed by Wan Chang Mencius could only give the reply which he does. For the quotation from the Shoo, see that Work, V. ix. 15.

[705] *Par.* 5. The answer given here by Mencius to the application made by Wan Chang of the above case has in it a great deal of ingenuity. We may admit it on the ground of expediency; but a man of his character and pretensions should have been more chary of receiving gifts from the princes of his time than he was. The practice in hunting which Confucius sanctioned is not well understood. The view which I have followed in the translation is that given by Chaou K'e.

[706] *Par.* 6. The practice in hunting which is alluded to had something to do with the offering of sacrifices, and Confucius, by the measures which he took, wished to obviate the necessity for using any flesh so obtained in sacrifice, so that the practice might thus die of itself, and fall into disuse.

[of his principles] was possible. With the duke Ling of Wei he took office, because the reception accorded to him was proper. With duke Hëaou of Wei he took office, because he was maintained by the State."[707]

V.[708] 1. Mencius said, "Office should not be [sought] on account of poverty, but there are times [when it may be sought] on that account. A wife should not be taken for the sake of being attended to by her, but there are times [when marriage may be entered on] with that view.[709]

2. "He who takes office because of his poverty must decline an honorable situation, and occupy a poor one; he must decline riches and prefer a poor [sufficiency].

3. "What [office] will be in harmony with this declining an honorable situation and occupying a low one, with this declining riches and preferring a poor sufficiency? [Such an one] as that of being a gate-warder, or beating the watchman's stick.[710]

4. "Confucius was once keeper of stores, and he [then] said, 'My accounts must all be correct; that is all I have to think about.' He was once in charge of the [ducal] lands, and he [then] said, 'The oxen and sheep must be large, and fat, and superior. That is all I have to think about.'[711]

5. "When one is in a low station, to speak of high matters is a crime. To stand in the court of his prince, and his principles not be carried into practice, is a disgrace."[712]

---

[707] *Par.* 7. The text says that Confucius took service with Ke Hwan, and not with duke Ting, because the duke and his government were under the control of that nobleman. I do not know that the sage ever held office in Wei, though Mencius here says so. When he first went to that State, its marquis was he who is here called "duke Ling," and whose incumbency extended from B.C. 533 to 492. Ling allotted to Confucius the salary which he had had in Loo. When he went to it the second time, the State was probably held by duke Ling's son Cheh, whom his father had expelled. He was, we may suppose, called Hëaou ("The Filial") by his partisans after his death, but we have no "duke Hëaou" in the Annals of Wei. He would offer liberal support to Confucius in order to get on his side the influence of his character and name.

[708] CH. V. THAT OFFICE MAY SOMETIMES BE TAKEN ON ACCOUNT OF POVERTY, BUT ONLY UNDER CERTAIN SPECIFIED CONDITIONS.

[709] *Par.* 1. The proper reason for taking office is said to be the carrying out of principles,—the truth and the right, and the proper reason for marrying is the begetting of children, or rather of a son, to continue one's line, and not allow the sacrifices to one's ancestors to be discontinued.

[710] *Par.* 3. Chaou K'e thinks that only one office is here specified,—that of a gate-warder. It seems better to understand two offices; that of a warder, one who "embraces the gate," *i.e.*, does not leave it, and that of a watchman, one "who beats his stick or rattle."

[711] *Par.* 4. What Mencius calls here "keeper of stores" appears in Sze-ma Ts'ëen as "an officer of the Ke family." Mencius' authority in such a case is to be followed. This was the first office which Confucius held, when he was young and poor. Ts'ëen also gives a different name for the second office, but apparently having the same meaning.

[712] *Par.* 5. This is to the effect that he who takes office because of his poverty, should not be as in a higher position where he would have to speak of high matters, and

VI.[713] 1. Wan Chang said, "What is the reason that an officer [unemployed] does not look to a prince for his maintenance?" Mencius answered, "He does not presume [to do so]. When one prince loses his State, and then throws himself on another for his maintenance, this is in accordance with propriety. But for [such an] officer to look to any of the princes for his maintenance is contrary to propriety."[714]

2. Wan Chang said, "If the prince sends him a present of grain, will he receive it?" "He will receive it," was the answer. "What is the principle of right in his receiving it?" [Mencius] said, "Such is the relation between a ruler and his people that as a matter of course he should help them in their necessities."[715]

3. "What is the reason that [an officer unemployed] will [thus] accept relief, but will not accept a [stated] bounty?" asked [Chang], and [Mencius] said, "He does not presume [to do the latter]." "Allow me to ask," urged the other, "why he does not presume to do so." The reply was, "[Even] the warder of a gate and the beater of a watchman's rattle have their regular duties for which they can take their support from their superiors; but he who without any regular office receives his superior's bounty must be deemed wanting in humility."[716]

4. [Chang again] said, "When a ruler sends a present [to an officer unemployed], he accepts it;—I do not know whether this present may be constantly repeated." [Mencius] answered, "There was the way of duke Muh towards Tsze-sze:—He sent frequent inquiries after his health, and made frequent presents of cooked meat. Tsze-sze was displeased, and at last, having motioned to the messenger to go outside the great door, he bowed his head to the ground with his face to the north, then put his hands twice to the ground, and declined the present, saying, 'From this time forth I shall know that the ruler supports me as a dog or a horse.' And from this time an inferior officer was not sent with the present. When [a ruler] professes to be pleased with a man of talents and virtue, and can neither raise him to office nor support him [in the proper way], can ho be said to be [really] pleased with his

---

that he who is in a high office and a frequenter of the court should make it his business to be carrying out his principles.

[713] CH. VI. HOW A SCHOLAR UNEMPLOYED SHOULD NOT BECOME A DEPENDENT BY ACCEPTING PAY WITHOUT OFFICE, WHILE YET A PRINCE MAY SEND HIM REPEATED GIFTS, PROVIDED HE DO SO IN THE PROPER MANNER. There is, no doubt, here, as in chapter iv., a reference to Mencius' habit of receiving gifts, and yet keeping himself aloof, from the princes.

[714] *Par.* 1. In the Le Ke, IX. i. 13, it is said that a prince should not employ another prince, a refugee with him, as a minister, but it is only from Mencius here, so far as I am aware, that we know that a prince, driven from his own territory, would find maintenance in another State, according to a sort of law.

[715] *Par.* 2. This is making the case very simple.

[716] *Par.* 3. "Must be deemed wanting in humility" is given by Julien as "*oensetur expers reverentiæ.*" The idea is that such a scholar puts himself in the position of one who has a regular office, and does not recognize his own unofficial position.

talents and virtue?"[717]

5. [Chang] said, "I venture to ask how the ruler of a State, when he wishes to support a superior man, must proceed that he may be said to do so [in the proper way]." [Mencius] answered, "The present will [at first] be offered as by the ruler's commission, and [the superior man] will receive it, twice putting his hands to the ground, and then his head to the ground. After this, the store-keeper will continue to send grain, and the master of the kitchen to send meat, presenting it without any mention of the ruler's commission. Tsze-sze considered that the meat from the [ruler's] caldron, giving him the trouble of constantly doing obeisance, was not the way to support a superior man.[718]

6. "There was the way of Yaou with Shun:—He caused his nine sons to serve him, and gave him his two daughters as wives; he caused the various officers, oxen and sheep, storehouses and granaries, [all] to be prepared to support Shun amid the channeled fields; and then he raised him to the most exalted station. Hence we have the expression—'The honoring of virtue and talents proper to a king or a duke.'"[719]

VII.[720] 1. Wan Chang said, "I venture to ask what is the principle of right in not going to see the princes." Mencius replied, "[A scholar unemployed], residing in the city, is called 'a minister of the market-place and well;' one residing in the country is called 'a minister of the grass and plants.' In both cases he is a common man, and it is a rule of propriety that common men who have not presented the introductory present, and so become ministers [of the court], should not presume to have interviews with any of the princes."[721]

---

[717] *Par.* 4. On the duke Muh and Tsze-sze, see II. ii. XI. 3. See also ch. iii. 3. The modes of salutation in ancient times are thus described:—"The ancients sat on their mats on the ground. When one raised up his body erect, resting on the knees, that was a long kneeling. When the head was bowed down to the hands, that was a *pae* or bow with the hands; when the hands were put to the ground, that was a *pae* or bow; when the head was put to the earth, that was a bowing with the head to the ground." Tsze-sze is here described as making first the third or profoundest obeisance, and then twice bowing with his hands to the ground. "An inferior officer" here denotes one of a mean order employed to convey messages.

[718] *Par.* 5. The method of obeisance or acknowledgment described here is, it will be seen, the reverse of that employed by Tsze-sze in the preceding paragraph. This method indicated, it is said, the acceptance of the gift, while the other indicated its refusal.

[719] *Par.* 6. See Pt i. I. 3, et at.

[720] CH. VII. WHY A SCHOLAR NOT IN OFFICE SHOULD DECLINE TO GO TO SEE ANY OF THE PRINCES, WHEN CALLED BY THEM. Wan Chang evidently had his master, and the way in which he kept himself aloof from the princes, in his mind here, though he does not say so. Our philosopher's practice in this respect was matter of surprise and of frequent inquiry to his disciples. See III. ii. I., *et al.*

[721] *Par.* 1. Every one may be called a minister (*shin*), as being a subject, and bound to serve the ruler. This is the meaning of the term in the first two instances of its occurrence in this paragraph. In the other instance it denotes those who are ministers holding office. On the "introductory present," see III. ii. III.

2. Wan Chang said, "If a common man be called to perform any service, he goes and performs it. When a ruler wishes to see a scholar, and calls him, how is it that he does not go?" "To go and perform the service is right; to go and see the ruler would not be right."

3. "And" [added Mencius] "on what account is it that the prince wishes to see [the scholar]?" "Because of his extensive information," was the reply, "or because of his talents and virtue." "If because of his extensive information," said [Mencius], "even the son of Heaven does not call [one thus fit to be] a teacher, and how much less may one of the princes do so! If because of his talents and virtue, I have not heard of any one's wishing to see a person with these qualities, and calling him to his presence.[722]

4. "During the frequent interviews of duke Muh with Tsze-sze, he [once] said, 'Anciently in States of a thousand chariots, their rulers, with all their resources, have been on terms of friendship with scholars;—what do you think of such cases?' Tsze-sze was displeased and said, 'The ancients had a saying that, "[The scholar] should be served;" how should they have said merely that "He should be made a friend of?" Did not the displeasure of Tsze-sze say [in effect], 'So far as station is concerned, you are ruler, and I am a subject; how should I presume to be on terms of friendship with my ruler? But in respect of virtue, you ought to make me your master; how can you be on terms of friendship with me?' [Thus], when a ruler of a thousand chariots sought to be on terms of friendship with a scholar, he could not obtain his wish, and how much less might he [presume to] call him [to his presence]!

5. "Duke King of Ts'e [once] when he was hunting, called the forester to him with a flag. [The forester] refused to come, and the duke was going to kill him. [With reference to this incident, Confucius said,] 'The resolute officer does not forget [that his end may be] in a ditch or in a stream; the bold officer does not forget that he may lose his head.' What was it [in the forester] that Confucius [thus] approved? He approved his not going when summoned by an article which was not appropriate to him."[723]

6. [Chang] said, "I venture to ask with what a forester should be called." "With a fur cap," was the reply. "A common man should be called with a plain banner; a scholar [who has taken office], with a flag having dragons embroidered on it; and a great officer, with one having feathers suspended from the top of the staff.

7. "When a forester is called with the article appropriate to the calling of a great officer, he would die rather than presume to go. When

---

[722] *Par.* 3. Here and throughout this chapter we see in a striking manner how Mencius magnified his position as a scholar and teacher.

[723] *Par.* 5. See III. ii. I. 2.

a common man is called with the article for the calling of a scholar [in office], how should he presume to go? How much more may we expect a man of talents and virtue to refuse to go, when he is called in a way unbecoming his character!

8. "To wish to see a man of talents and virtue, and not take the way to bring it about, is like calling him to enter and shutting the door against him. Now righteousness is the way, and propriety is the door, but it is only the superior man who can follow this way, and go out and in by this door. It is said in the Book of Poetry:—[724]

'The way to Chow was like a whetstone
And straight as an arrow.
[So] the officers trod it,
And the common people looked on it.'"

9. Wan Chang said, "When Confucius received his ruler's message calling him [to his presence], he went without waiting for his carriage to be yoked; did Confucius then do wrong?" [Mencius] replied, "Confucius was in office, and had its appropriate duties devolving on him; and moreover he was called on the ground of his office."[725]

VIII.[726] 1. Mencius said to Wan Chang, "The scholar whose excellence is most distinguished in a village will thereon make friends of the [other] excellent scholars of the village. The scholar whose excellence is most distinguished in a State will thereon make friends of the [other] excellent scholars of the State. The scholar whose excellence is most distinguished in the kingdom will thereon make friends of the [other] excellent scholars of the kingdom.[727]

2. "When [a scholar] finds that his friendship with the excellent scholars of the kingdom is not sufficient [to satisfy him], he will ascend

---

[724] *Par.* 8. See the She, II. v. IX. 1. Righteousness is the way which all men ought to be found in, and propriety the door by which they should enter it. Many, however, forsake the way, and try to enter by other doors. But not so with the superior man; and therefore rulers in dealing with him should be specially observant of righteousness and propriety. This seems to be the undercurrent of thought in this paragraph. and so it seems, as indicated in the words of the ode quoted, it once was in the best days of the Chow. The way to Chow was as it is here described, because the ways of the kings of Chow had been fashioned according to righteousness and propriety.

[725] *Par.* 9. See Ana. X. xiii. 4.

[726] CH. VIII. HOW FRIENDSHIP WILL FIND ITS CONGENIAL ASSOCIATIONS ACCORDING TO THE CONDITIONS OF PLACE AND TIME, AND WE MAY MAKE OUR FRIENDS OF THE GREAT AND GOOD OF ANTIQUITY BY STUDYING THEIR POEMS AND OTHER BOOKS, AND HISTORY.

[727] *Par.* 1. The eminence of the most excellent scholars specified attracts others to them, and they have thus the opportunity of learning and adding to their own excellence, which no inflation arising from their own superiority prevents them from doing. It is a pity that the Chinese mind should be so unwilling to admit that excellence may be found out of China.

to consider the men of antiquity. He will repeat their poems, and read their books; and as he does not know whether they were as men all that was approvable, he will consider their history. This is to ascend and make friends [of the men of antiquity]."[728]

IX.[729] 1. King Seuen of Ts'e asked about high ministers. Mencius said, "Which high ministers is your Majesty asking about?" "Are there differences among them?" said the king. "Yes," was the reply; "there are high ministers who are noble, and relatives of the ruler, and there are those who are of a different surname from him." "Allow me to ask," said the king, "about the high ministers who are noble, and relatives of the ruler." [Mencius] answered, "If the ruler have great faults, they ought to remonstrate with him; and if he do not listen to them, when they have done so again and again, they ought to appoint another in his place."[730]

2. The king looked moved, and changed countenance.[731]

3. [Mencius] said, "Let not your Majesty think [what I say] strange. You asked me, and I did not dare to reply but correctly."

4. The king's countenance became composed, and he begged to ask about the high ministers who were of a different surname from the ruler. [Mencius] said, "When the ruler has faults, they ought to remonstrate with him; and if he do not listen to them when they have done so again and again, they ought to leave [the State]."

---

[728] *Par.* 2. It is certainly a discriminating study of the worthies of antiquity which Mencius here recommends.

[729] CH. IX. THE DUTIES OF MINISTERS TO THEIR RULER, ACCORDING AS THEY ARE OF THE SAME SURNAME WITH HIM, OR A DIFFERENT, THAT IS, ACCORDING AS THEY ARE RELATED TO HIM OR NOT.

[730] *Par.* 1. By "great faults" is meant such as endangered the State, or at least the safety of the ruling House. It seems to be intimated that of other and lesser faults these ministers would not take any notice. In par. 4 all the ruler's faults, small or great, come under the notice and criticism of his other ministers.

[731] *Parr.* 2, 3. It was not surprising that king Seuen should be annoyed and surprised at the words of Mencius. They certainly afford a striking instance of the boldness of our philosopher's thinking, and of the decided manner in which he gave expression to his sentiments. All the members of the family of which the ruler is the Head may be said to have an interest in the throne, but to suggest to them that it may become their duty to displace the actual occupant of it and substitute another of their number in his place, may open the way to confusion and disaster.

## BOOK VI. KAOU-TSZE.[732] PART I.

CHAPTER I.[733] 1. KAOU-TSZE said, "[Man's] nature is like a willow tree, and righteousness is like a cup or a bowl. The fashioning benevolence and righteousness out of man's nature is like making cups and bowls from a willow tree."

2. Mencius replied, "Can you, in accordance with the nature of the willow tree, make cups and bowls from it? You will do violence and injury to the tree before you can make cups and bowls from it. If you will do violence and injury to the willow tree in order to make cups and bowls, will you also do violence and injury to a man, to fashion benevolence and righteousness [from him]? Your words, alas! would certainly with all men occasion calamity to benevolence and righteousness."[734]

II.[735] 1. Kaou-tsze said, "[Man's] nature is like water whirling round [in a corner]. Open a passage for it on the east, and it will flow to

---

[732] TITLE OF THIS BOOK. Kaou-tsze, *i.e.* Mr. Kaou, or the scholar Kaou, who appears in the first and other chapters questioning Mencius, gives his name to the Book. He is probably the same who is referred to by our philosopher in II. Part I. ii. 2. Chaou K'e tells us that his name was Puh-hae, seeming to identify him with Haou-săng Puh-hae of VII. Pt II. xxv. He adds that Kaou, while a student under Mencius, gave himself also to the examination of the doctrines of the heresiarch Mih (III. Pt I. v., Pt II. ix. 9); and from a passage in Mih's writings this is not unlikely, but the name of Kaou appears there as Shing.

Kaou appears from this Book to have been much perplexed respecting the real character of human nature in its relations to good and evil, which is the subject mainly discussed throughout it; and it is to the view of human nature as here developed that Mencius is chiefly indebted for his place among the sages of his country. "The Book," says the Relish and Root of the four Books, "treats first of the *nature*; then of the *heart*; and then of *instruction*: the whole being analogous to the lessons in the doctrine of the Mean. The second Part continues to treat of the same subject, and a resemblance will generally be found between the views of the parties there combated and those of the scholar Kaou."

[733] CH. I. THAT BENEVOLENCE AND RIGHTEOUSNESS ARE NO UNNATURAL AND FORCED PRODUCTS OF HUMAN NATURE. Choo He says that there underlies the words of Kaou here the view of human nature afterwards insisted on by the philosopher Seun (see the *prolegomena*), that human nature is evil. But Kaou might have disallowed such an induction from his words. Seun maintained that human nature was positively evil, and that any good in it was an artificial product Kaou perhaps would have contended that it was like a *tabula rasa*, on which either good or evil might be made to appear.

[734] *Par.* 2. "In accordance with the nature of the willow tree;" *i.e.*, leaving its nature untouched, doing no violence to it. "Will you also do violence and injury to a man?"—*i.e.* to a man's nature, to humanity.

[735] CH. II. THAT MAN'S NATURE IS NOT INDIFFERENT TO GOOD AND EVIL. ITS PROPER TENDENCY IS TO GOOD. Here, it seems to me, Kaou more clearly explains what he meant in the last chapter. Choo He says, however, that his idea here was akin to that of Yang Hëung, a writer about the beginning of our era. Yang held that good and evil were mixed in the nature of man, and that the passion-nature was like a horse drawing the man, according as it moved, either to good or to evil. Kaou, however, appears to have differed from him in thinking that there was neither good nor evil in the nature itself.

the east; open a passage for it on the west, and it will flow to the west. Man's nature is indifferent to good and evil, just as water is indifferent to the east and west."[736]

2. Mencius replied, "Water indeed will flow indifferently to the east or west, but will it flow indifferently up or down? The [tendency of] man's nature to goodness is like the [tendency of] water to flow downwards. There are none but have [this tendency to] goodness, [just as] water flows downwards.[737]

3. "Now by striking water, and causing it to leap up, you may make it go over your forehead; and by damming and leading it, you may make it go up a hill; but are [such movements according to] the nature of water. It is the force applied which causes them. In the case of a man's being made to do what is not good, his nature is dealt with in this way."

III.[738] 1. Kaou-tsze said, "[The phenomena of] life is what I call nature."

2. Mencius replied, "Do you say that life is nature just as you say that white is white?" "Yes," was the reply. [Mencius asked again], "Is the whiteness of a white feather like the whiteness of white snow, and the whiteness of white snow like that of white jade?" "Yes," returned [the other].

3. Mencius retorted, "Very well. Is the nature of a dog like the nature of an ox, and the nature of an ox like the nature of a man?"

IV.[739] 1. Kaou-tsze said, "[To delight in] food and in sexual pleasure is nature. Benevolence is from within, and not from without;

---

[736] *Par.* 1. The phrase which I have translated—"water whirling round" is explained in the dictionaries as "water flowing rapidly," "water flowing quickly over sand;" and hence Julian renders it by *"rapide fluens aqua."* So also Williams. Chaou K'e, followed by Choo He, gives the meaning which I have adopted.

[737] *Parr.* 2, 3. Choo He says:—"This chapter tells us that the nature is properly good, so that if we accord with it, we shall do nothing but what is good; and that it is properly without evil, so that we must violate it before we do what is evil. It shows that the nature is not properly without a decided character so that it may do good or evil indifferently."

[738] CH. III. THE NATURE IS NOT TO BE CONFOUNDED WITH THE PHENOMENA OF LIFE. Choo He says that "by life is intended that whereby men and animals perceive and move," and he adds that Kaou's sentiment was analogous to that of the Buddhists, who made "doing and moving" to be the nature. We must understand, I think, by *life* here the phenomena of the life of sensation, and Kaou's idea led to the ridiculous conclusion that wherever there were those phenomena the nature of the subjects is the same. We find it difficult to place ourselves in sympathy with him in this conversation, and also to follow Mencius in passing from the second paragraph to the third. His questions in the former refer to the qualities of inanimate things, and then he jumps to others about the nature of animals and of man.

[739] CH. IV. THAT THE DISCRIMINATION OF WHAT IS RIGHT, AS WELL AS THE FEELING OF LOVE OR BENEVOLENCE, IS INTERNAL, AND NOT MERELY DETERMINED BY WHAT IS EXTERNAL TO US.

righteousness is from without and not from within."[740]

2. Mencius said, "What is the ground of your saying that benevolence is from within, and righteousness from without?" [The other] replied, "There is a man older than I, and I give honor to his age;—it is not that there is in me a principle of reverence for age. It is just as when there is a white man, and I consider him white;—according as he is so externally to me. It is on this account that I say [of righteousness] that it is from without."

3. [Mencius] said, "There is no difference to us between the whiteness of a white horse, and the whiteness of a white man, but I do not know that there is no difference between the regard with which we acknowledge the age of an old horse, and that with which we acknowledge the age of a man older [than ourselves]? And what is it which we call righteousness? The fact of a man's being older [than we]? or the fact of our giving honor to his age"

4. [Kaou] said, "There is my younger brother; I love him. But the younger brother of a man of Ts'in I do not love; that is, it is [the relationship to] myself which occasions my complacency, and therefore I say that benevolence is from within. I give the honor due to age to an old man of Ts'oo, and to an old man of my own [kindred]; that is, it is the age which occasions the complacency, and therefore I say that righteousness is from without."[741]

5. [Mencius] answered him, "Our enjoyment of meat broiled by a man of Ts'in does not differ from our enjoyment of meat broiled by [one of] our [own kindred]. Thus [what you insist on] takes place also in the case of [such] things; but is our enjoyment of broiled meat also from without?"[742]

V.[743] 1. Mr. Măng Ke asked the disciple Kung-too, saying, "On what ground is it said that righteousness is from within?"[744]

---

[740] *Par.* 1. The first remark of Kaou here would seem to be intended to explain his statement in the preceding chapter that "life was nature." Then he seems to give in to the view of Mencius that benevolence proceeds from a principle within us, just as we are moved by an internal feeling to food and sexual pleasure, but he still contends that it is not so in the exercise of righteousness;—by which term Chinese writers mean, "the conduct proper in reference to men and things without us, and the showing it to them." This meaning of "righteousness" is put out by Mencius at the close of the third paragraph.

[741] *Par.* 4. "A man of Ts'in," "a man of Ts'oo;"—*i.e.*, people indifferent to me, strangers to me.

[742] *Par.* 5. Mencius silences his opponent by showing that the difficulty which he alleged in regard to righteousness would attach also to the enjoyment of food, which he had himself allowed, at the outset of the conversation, to be internal, from the inward constitution of our nature.

[743] CH. V. THE SAME SUBJECT:—A DIFFICULTY OBVIATED IN THE WAY OF THE CONCLUSION THAT THE DISCRIMINATION OF WHAT IS RIGHT IS FROM WITHIN.

[744] *Par.* 1. Măng Ke was, probably, a younger brother of Măng Chung, who appears in II. Pt II. ii. 3 in close attendance on Mencius. He had heard the previous conversation with Kaou, or heard of it; and feeling some doubts on the subject, he applied to the disciple Kung-too.

2. [Kung-too] replied, "It is the acting out of our feeling of respect, and therefore it is said to be from within."

3. [The other] said, "[In the case of] a villager one year older than your elder brother, to which of them will you show the [greater] respect?" "To my brother," was the reply. "But for which would you pour out spirits first?" [Kung-too] said, "For the villager." [Măng Ke then argued], "Your feeling of respect rests on the one, but your reverence for age is rendered to the other; [righteousness] is certainly determined by what is without, and not by internal feeling."[745]

4. The disciple Kung-too was unable to reply, and reported [the conversation] to Mencius, who said, "[You should ask him], 'Which do you respect more, your uncle, or your younger brother?' He will reply, 'My uncle.' [Ask him again], 'If your younger brother be personating a deceased ancestor, to whom will you show respect more,—[to him or to your uncle]?' He will say, 'To my younger brother.' [You can go on], 'But where is the [greater] respect due, as you said, to your uncle?' He will say, '[I show it to my younger brother,] because he is in the position [of the deceased ancestor]' And then you must say, 'Because he is in that position;—and so ordinarily my respect is given to my elder brother, but a momentary respect is given to the villager.'"[746]

5. When Ke-tsze heard this, he observed, "When respect is due to my uncle, I give it to him; and when respect is due to my younger brother, I give it to him. The thing is certainly determined by what is without us, and does not come from within." Kung-too replied, "In winter we drink things warm, but in summer we drink things cold; but is then our eating and drinking determined by what is external to us?"[747]

VI.[748] 1. The disciple Kung-too said, "Kaou-tsze says, '[Man's] nature is neither good nor bad.'[749]

2. "Some say, '[Man's] nature may be made to do good, and it may be made to do evil; and accordingly, under Wăn and Woo, the people loved what was good, and under Yĕw and Le they loved what was

---

[745] *Par.* 3. "For whom would you pour out spirits first?"—*i.e.*, at a feast. Courtesy then required that the honour should be given to a stranger; but Măng Ke does not consider this, but maintains that the manifestation of respect varied with the individual, and was therefore not from within.

[746] *Par.* 4. "Personating a deceased ancestor;"—see the Prolegomena to Vol. IV. of my larger Work, pp. 135, 136, on the strange custom under the Chow dynasty of personating a deceased ancestor at a sacrificial feast by one of the descendants of the family.

[747] *Par.* 5. Kung-too here beats down the caviling of Măng Ke as Mencius did that of Kaou in the conclusion of last chapter.

[748] CH. VI. VARIOUS VIEWS OF HUMAN NATURE, AND MENCIUS' VINDICATION OF HIS OWN DOCTRINE, THAT IT IS GOOD.

[749] *Par.* 1. Choo He says that this view had been revived near his own times by the famous Soo Tung-po, and by Hoo Woo-fung, a son of the more celebrated Hoo Wăn-ting.

cruel.'[750]

3. "Some say, 'The nature of some is good, and the nature of others is bad. Hence it was that under such a ruler as Yaou, there yet appeared Sëang; that with such a father as Koo-sow, there yet appeared Shun; and that, with Chow for their ruler and the son of their elder brother besides, there yet appeared K'e, the viscount of Wei, and prince Pe-kan.'[751]

4. "And now you say, 'The nature is good.' Then are all those wrong?"

5. Mencius replied, "From the feelings proper to it, [we see] that it is constituted for the doing of what is good. This is what I mean in saying that [the nature] is good.[752]

6. "If [men] do what is not good, the guilt cannot be imputed to their natural powers.

7. "The feeling of compassionate distress belongs to all men; so does that of shame and dislike; and that of modesty and respect; and that of approving and disapproving. The feeling of compassion and distress is the principle of benevolence; the feeling of shame and dislike is the principle of righteousness; the feeling of modesty and respect is the principle of propriety; and the feeling of approving and disapproving is the principle of knowledge. Benevolence, righteousness, propriety, and knowledge are not fused into us from without; they naturally belong to us, and [a different view] is simply from want of reflection. Hence it is said, 'Seek, and you will find them; neglect, and you will lose them.' [Men differ from one another in regard to them]; some as much again as others, some five times as much, and some to an incalculable amount; it is because they cannot fully carry out their [natural] endowments.[753]

8. "It is said in the Book of Poetry,

'Heaven in giving birth to the multitudes of the people,
To every faculty and relationship annexed its law:
The people possess this normal nature,
And they [consequently] love its normal virtue.'

---

[750] *Par.* 2. Kaou had also given this view,—in the second chapter. Wăn and Woo are the famous founders of the Chow dynasty; Yĕw and Le were two of their successors whose character and course damaged the dynasty not a little.

[751] *Par.* 3. This view was afterwards advocated, with an addition to it, by Han Yu of the T'ang dynasty;—see his essay in the *prolegomena.* Sëang was the wicked brother of Shun;—for him and Koo-sow see V. Pt I. ii., *et al.* For Chow (or Show) of the Shang dynasty and his relatives, see on the Analects XVIII. i., and on the Book of History, Pt IV. xi.

[752] *Parr.* 5, 6. These paragraphs are important for the correct understanding of our philosopher's views.

[753] *Par.* 7. See II. Pt I. vi. 4, 5.

Confucius said, 'The maker of this ode knew indeed the constitution [of our nature].' We may thus see that to every faculty and. relationship there must belong its law, and that since the people possess this normal nature, they therefore love its normal virtue."[754]

VII.[755] 1. Mencius said, "In good years the children of the people are most of them good, and in bad years they are most of them evil. It is not owing to their natural endowments conferred by Heaven, that they are thus different. It is owing to the circumstances in which they allow their minds to be ensnared and devoured that they appear so [as in the latter case].[756]

2. "There now is barley.—Let the seed be sown and covered up; the ground being the same, and the time of sowing also the same, it grows luxuriantly, and when the full time is come, it is all found to be ripe. Although there may be inequalities [of produce], that is owing to [the difference of] the soil as rich or poor, to the [unequal] nourishment afforded by rain and dew, and to the different ways in which man has performed his business.

3. "Thus all things which are the same in kind are like to one another;—why should we doubt in regard to man, as if he were a solitary exception to this? The sage and we are the same in kind.

4. "In accordance with this, Lung-tsze said, 'If a man make hempen sandals, without knowing [the size of people's] feet, yet I know that he will not make them like baskets' Sandals are like one another, because all men's feet are like one other.[757]

5. "So with the mouth and flavors;—all mouths have the same relishes. Yih Ya [simply] appreciated before me what my mouth relishes. Suppose that his mouth, in its relish for flavors, were of a different nature from [the mouths of] other men, in the same way as dogs and horses are not of the same kind with us, how should all men be found following Yih Ya in their relishes? In the matter of tastes, the whole kingdom models itself after Yih Ya; that is, the mouths, of all men are like one another.[758]

---

[754] *Par.* 8. See the Book of Poetry, Bk III. Pt III. vi. 1, and' my commentary there.

[755] CH. VII. THE PHENOMENA OF GOOD AND EVIL IN MEN'S CHARACTER AND CONDUCT ARE TO BE EXPLAINED FROM THE DIFFERENT CIRCUMSTANCES ACTING ON THEM. ALL MEN, SAGES AND OTHERS, ARE THE SAME IN MIND, AND IT FOLLOWS THAT THE NATURE OF OTHER MEN IS GOOD, LIKE THAT OF THE SAGES.

[756] *Par.* 1. The idea seems to be that in good years, the supply of food and clothes being sufficient, the young escape temptations to robbery and other wickedness. Mencius elsewhere puts forth powerfully the truth that adversity is often a school of superior virtue. The general sentiment enunciated here, that a competence is favorable to virtue, must be admitted, and it has the warrant of Confucius in Ana. XIII. ix.

[757] *Par.* 4. Of Mr. Lung, who is here quoted, nothing is known. Mencius purposely quotes his saying on an ordinary matter as being well known, and serving to illustrate the point in hand.

[758] *Par.* 5. Yih Ya was the cook of the famous duke Hwan of Ts'e (B.C. 684-642), otherwise a worthless man, but great in his art.

6. "So it is with the ear also. In the matter of sounds, the whole kingdom models itself after the music-master Kwang; that is, the ears of all men are like one another.[759]

7. "And so it is also with the eye. In the case of Tsze-too, there is no one under heaven but would recognize that he was beautiful. Any one who did not recognize the beauty of Tsze-too would [be said to] have no eyes.[760]

8. "Therefore [I] say,—[Men's] mouths agree in having the same relishes; their ears agree in enjoying the same sounds; their eyes agree in recognizing the same beauty:—shall their minds alone be without that which they similarly approve? What is it then of which their minds similarly approve? It is the principles [of things], and the [consequent determinations of] righteousness. The sages only apprehended before me that which I and other men agree in approving. Therefore the principles [of things] and [the determinations of] righteousness are agreeable to my mind just as [the flesh] of grass and grain-fed [animals] is agreeable to my mouth."

VIII.[761] 1. Mencius said, "The trees of Něw hill were once beautiful. Being situated, however, in the suburbs of [the capital of] a large State, they were hewn down with axes and bills; and could they retain their beauty? Still through the growth from the vegetative life day and night, and the nourishing influence of the rain and dew, they were not without buds and sprouts springing out. But then came the cattle and goats, and browsed upon them. To these things is owing the bare and stript appearance [of the hill]; and when people see this, they think it was never finely wooded. But is this the nature of the hill?[762]

2. "And so even of what properly belongs to man; shall it be said that the mind [of any man] was without benevolence and righteousness. The way in which a man loses the proper goodness of his mind is like the way in which [those] trees were denuded by axes and bills. Hewn down day after day, can it retain its excellence? But there is some growth of its life day and night, and in the [calm] air of the morning, just between night and day, the mind feels in a degree those desires and aversions which are proper to humanity; but the feeling is not strong; and then it is fettered and destroyed by what the man does during the day. This fettering takes place again and again; the restorative influence of the night is not sufficient to preserve [the proper goodness];.and

---

[759] *Par.* 6. Of the music-master Kwang see on IV. Pt I. i. 1.

[760] *Par.* 7. Tsze-too was the designation of Kung-sun Oh, a scion of the house of Ch'ing about B.C. 700, distinguished for his beauty. See an account of his villainy and death in the 7th chapter of the "History of the several States." See also in the Tso Chuen under the 11th year of duke Yin, and the 16th year of duke Chwang.

[761] CH. VIII. HOW IT IS THAT THE NATURE, PROPERLY GOOD, COMES TO APPEAR AS IF IT WERE NOT SO;—FROM NOT RECEIVING ITS PROPER NOURISHMENT.

[762] *Par.* 1. Něw hill, *i.e.* Ox hill, was a mountain not far from the capital of Ts'e. It is 10 *le* south of the present district city of Lin-tsze, department of Ts'ing-chow.

when this proves insufficient for that purpose, the [nature] becomes not much different from [that of] the irrational animals; and when people see this, they think that it never had those endowments [which I assert]. But does this condition represent the feelings proper to humanity?

3. "Therefore if it receive its proper nourishment, there is nothing which will not grow; if it lose its proper nourishment, there is nothing which will not decay away.

4. "Confucius said, 'Hold it fast, and it remains with you; let it go, and you lose it. Its out-going and in-coming cannot be defined as to time and place.' It was the mental nature of which this was said.[763]

IX.[764] 1. Mencius said, "It is not to be wondered at that the king is not wise![765]

2. "Suppose the case of the most easily growing thing in the world;—if you let it have one day's genial heat, and then expose it for ten days to cold, it will not be able to grow. It is but seldom that I have an audience [of the king], and when I retire, there come [all] those who act upon him like the cold. Though I succeed in bringing out some buds of goodness, of what avail is it?[766]

3. "Now chess-playing is an art, though a small one; but without his whole mind being given, and his will bent to it, a man cannot succeed in it. Chess Ts'ĕw is the best chess-player in all the kingdom. Suppose that he is teaching two men to play;—the one gives all his mind to the game, and bends to it all his will, doing nothing but listen to Chess Ts'ĕw; the other, though he [seems to] be listening to him, has his whole mind running on a swan which he thinks is approaching, and wishes to bend his bow, adjust the arrow to the string, and shoot it. Though the latter is learning along with the former, his progress is not equal to his. Is it because his intelligence is not equal? Not so."[767]

---

[763] *Par.* 4. This is a saying of Confucius for which we are indebted to Mencius. Choo He thus expands the paragraph:—"Confucius said of the mind, '*If you hold it fast, it is here; if you let it go, it is lost and gone; so indeterminate in regard to time is its outgoing and incoming, and also in regard to place.*' Mencius quoted his words to illustrate the unfathomableness of the mind as spiritual and intelligent, how easy it is to have it or to lose it, and how difficult to preserve and keep it so that it should not be left unnourished for a moment. Learners ought constantly to be using their strength to insure the pureness of its spirit and the settledness of its passion-nature, as in the calm of the morning between day and night; then will the proper mind always be preserved, and everywhere and in all circumstances its manifestations will be those of benevolence and righteousness."

[764] CH. IX. ILLUSTRATING THE PRECEDING CHAPTER.—HOW THE KING OF TS'E'S WANT OF WISDOM WAS OWING TO HIS NEGLECT OF MENCIUS' INSTRUCTIONS AND TO BAD ASSOCIATIONS.

[765] *Par.* 1. The king is understood to have been Seuen of Ts'e;—see L Pt L vii., *et al.*

[766] *Par.* 2. The last sentence may also be taken, with Choo He, as meaning—"Though there may be [some] sprouts of goodness in him, what can I do?"

[767] *Par.* 3. "Chess Ts'ĕw;"—Ts'ĕw was the man's name, and he was called Chess Ts'ĕw from his skill at the game.

X.[768] 1. Mencius said, "I like fish, and I also like bears' paws. If I cannot get both together, I will let the fish go, and take the bears' paws. So I like life, and I also like righteousness. If I cannot keep the two together, I will let life go, and choose righteousness.[769]

2. "I like life indeed, but there is that which I like more than life; and therefore I will not seek to hold it by any improper ways. I dislike death indeed, but there is that which I dislike more than death, and therefore there are occasions when I will not avoid calamity [that may occasion death].

3. "If among the things which man likes there were nothing which he liked more than life, why should he not use all means by which he could preserve it? If among the things which man dislikes there were nothing which he disliked more than death, why should he not do everything by which he could avoid calamity [that might occasion it].

4. "[But as man is], there are cases when by a certain course men might preserve life, and yet they do not employ it; and when by certain things they might avoid calamity [that will occasion death], and yet they will not do them.

5. "Therefore men have that which they like more than life, and that which they dislike more than death. They are not men of talents and virtue only who have this mental nature. All men have it;—what belongs to such men is simply that they are able not to lose it.[770]

6. "Here are a small basket of rice and a basin of soup;—and the case is one where the getting them will preserve life, and the want of them will be death. If they are offered to him in an insulting tone, [even] a tramper on the road will not receive them, or if you first tread upon them, [even] a beggar will not stoop to take them.[771]

---

[768] CH. X. THAT IT IS PROPER TO MAN'S NATURE TO LOVE RIGHTEOUSNESS MORE THAN LIFE; AND HOW IT IS THAT MANY ACT AS IF IT WERE NOT SO.

[769] *Par.* 1. "Bears paws," *lit.*, palms, have been a delicacy in China from the earliest times. They require a long time to cook them thoroughly. In B.C. 425, the king Ch'ing of Ts'oo, being besieged in his palace, requested that he might have a dish of bears' palms before he was put to death,—hoping that help would come while they were being cooked.

[770] *Par.* 5. Up to this point our philosopher has been bringing out his great point,—that all men have the good heart, which he clinches by the cases in the two paragraphs that follow, which are very well conceived and expressed.

[771] *Parr.* 6-8. The reader will remember that it was with 10,000 *chung* that the king of Ts'e tried to bribe Mencius to remain in his country;—see II. Pt II. x. "What can the 10,000 *chung* really add to him?" is literally, in Chinese—"What do the 10,000 *chung* add to *me*?" The meaning is better brought out in English by changing the person from the first to the third; but there is in the Chinese idiom also the lofty, and true, idea—that a man's personality is something independent, of, and higher than, all external advantages. The same peculiarity of Chinese idiom appears in the conclusion of the paragraph. "Is it not that the poor and needy of his acquaintance may be helped by him?" is, literally, "Is it not that the poor and needy may get *me*? *i.e.*, may get my help?" On this a Chinese writer says, "The thinking of the poor would seem to show a kindly feeling, but the true nature of it appears in the—'*may get me.*' The idea is not one of benevolence, but of selfishness."

7. "[And yet] a man will accept of ten thousand *chung*, without any question as to the propriety and righteousness of his doing so. What can the ten thousand *chung* really add to him? [When he takes them], is it not that he may get beautiful mansions? or that he may secure the services of wives and concubines? or that the poor and needy of his acquaintance may be helped by him?

8. "In the former case, the [offered bounty] was not received, though it would have saved from death, and now the man takes [the emolument] for the sake of beautiful mansions. [The bounty] that would have saved from death was not received, and [the emolument] is taken to get the services of wives and concubines. [The bounty] that would have saved from death was not received, and [the emolument] is taken that one's poor and needy acquaintances may be helped by him. Was it not possible then to decline [the emolument] in these instances? This is a case of what is called—losing the proper nature of one's mind."

XI.[772] 1. Mencius said, "Benevolence is [the proper quality of] man's mind, and righteousness is man's [proper] path.[773]

2. "How lamentable is it to neglect this path and not pursue it, to lose this mind and not know to seek it [again],

3. "When men's fowls and dogs are lost, they know to seek them [again]; but they lose their mind, and do not know to seek it [again].

4. "The object of learning is nothing else but to seek for the lost mind."[774]

XII.[775] 1. Mencius said, "Here is a man whose fourth finger is bent, and cannot be stretched out straight. It is not painful, nor does it incommode his business; but if there were any one who could make it straight, he would not think it far to go all the way from Ts'in to Ts'oo [to find him]; —because his finger is not like those of other people.[776]

---

[772] CH. XI. HOW MEN, HAVING LOST THE PROPER QUALITIES OF THEIR NATURE, SHOULD SEEK TO RECOVER THEM.

[773] *Par.* 1. "Benevolence is man's mind (or heart)," *i.e.*, it is the proper and universal characteristic of man's nature, what, as the commentators often say, "all men have." "Benevolence" would seem here to include all the moral qualities of humanity; but it is followed by the Mencian specification of "righteousness." Compare our philosopher's yet more remarkable saying in VII. Pt II. xvi., that "Benevolence is man."

[774] *Par.* 4. "The object of learning" is, literally, "The way of learning and asking," "the way" meaning *the proper course*, that which is to be pursued. Mencius would seem to be guarding himself against being supposed to teach that man need not go beyond himself to secure his renovation. To illustrate his "learning and asking" we are referred to Confucius' words in the Doctrine of the Mean, XX. 19, and those of Tsze-hëa in Ana. XIX. vi.—It will be noted that the Chinese sages always end with the recovery of the old heart, and that the Christian idea of "a new heart" is unknown to them.

[775] CH. XII. HOW MEN ARE SENSIBLE OF BODILY DEFECTS, HOWEVER SLIGHT, BUT ARE NOT SENSIBLE OF MENTAL OR MORAL DEFECTS.

[776] *Par.* 1. The thumb is called by the Chinese "the great finger;" next to it is "the eating finger;" then "the leading finger;" then "the fourth or nameless finger;" and last, "the little finger." The fourth is called "nameless," as being of less use than the others.

2. "When a man's finger is not like other people's, he knows to feel dissatisfied; but when his mind is not like other people's, he does not know to feel dissatisfied. This is what is called—ignorance of the relative [importance of things]."

XIII.[777] Mencius said, "Anybody who wishes to cultivate a *t'ung* tree, or a *tsze*, which may be grasped with the two hands, [perhaps] with one, knows by what means to nourish it; but in the case of their own persons men do not know by what means to nourish them. Is it to be supposed that their regard for their own persons is inferior to their regard for a *t'ung* or a *tsze*? Their want of reflection is extreme."

XIV.[778] 1. Mencius said, "Men love every part of their persons; and as they love every part, so they [should] nourish every part. There is not an inch of skin which they do not love, and so there is not an inch of skin which they will not nourish. For examining whether his [way of nourishing] be good or not, what other rule is there but simply this, that a man determine, [by reflecting] on himself, where it should be applied?[779]

2. "Some parts of the body are noble, and some ignoble; some great, and some small. The great must not be injured for the small, nor the noble for the ignoble. He who nourishes the little belonging to him is a small man; he who nourishes the great is a great man.[780]

3. "Here is a plantation-keeper, who neglects his woo and *këa*, and nourishes his small jujube trees;—he is a poor plantation-keeper.[781]

4. "He who nourishes one of his fingers, neglecting his shoulders and back, without knowing that he is doing so, is a man [who

The capital of Ts'in was in the present department of Fung-ts'ëang, Shen-se, and that of Ts'oo in King-chow, Hoo-pih.

[777] CH. XIII. MEN'S EXTREME WANT OF THOUGHT IN REGARD TO THE CULTIVATION OF THEMSELVES.

The *t'ung* here is probably the *bignonia*. The wood of it was good for making lutes. The *tsze* also yields a valuable wood, and is spoken of as "the king of all trees."

[778] CH. XIV. THE ATTENTION GIVEN BY MEN TO THE NOURISHMENT OF THE DIFFERENT PARTS OF THEIR NATURE MUST BE REGULATED BY THE RELATIVE IMPORTANCE OF THOSE PARTS, WHICH EVERY MAN CAN DETERMINE FOR HIMSELF BY REFLECTION.

[779] *Par.* 1. The concluding part of this par. is rather difficult to translate, but the meaning is plain:—A man is to determine, by reflection on his constitution, what parts are more important, and should have the greater attention paid to them. It will be seen that there underlies the argument of Mencius in this chapter the important point that the human constitution is a system, certain parts of which should be kept subordinate to others.

[780] *Par.* 2. "The great must not be injured for the small";—it is implied that to neglect the greater and nobler parts of the constitution, is really to injure them. They are badly treated, not receiving the attention they deserve; and the language implies that positive injury is done to them.

[781] *Par.* 3. The "plantation-keeper" was an officer under the Chow dynasty, who had the superintendence of the sovereign's plantations and orchards. The *woo* was the *woo-t'ung*, the *dryandra condifolia* of Thunberg. The *këa* was also a valuable tree; some identify it with the *tsze* of last chapter.

resembles] a hurried wolf.[782]

5. "A man who [only] eats and drinks is counted mean by others; because he nourishes what is little to the neglect of what is great.

6. "If a man, [fond of] eating and drinking, do [yet] not fail [in nourishing what in him is great], how should his mouth and belly be accounted as no more than an inch of skin?"[783]

XV.[784] 1. The disciple Kung-too asked, saying, "All are equally men, but some are great men, and others are little men; how is this?" Mencius replied, "Those who follow that part of themselves which is great are great men; those who follow that part which is little are little men."

2. Kung-too pursued, "All are equally men; but some follow that part of themselves which is great, and some that which is little; how is this?" Mencius said, "The ears and the eyes have it not in their office to think, and are [liable to be] obscured by things [affecting them]; and when one thing comes into contact with another, it simply leads it away. But it is in the office of the mind to think. By thinking, it gets [the right view of things]; when neglecting to think, it fails to do this. These—[the senses and the mind]—are what Heaven has given to us. Let a man first stand in [the supremacy of] the greater [and nobler] part of his constitution, and the smaller part will not be able to take it from him. It is simply this which makes the great man."

XVI.[785] 1. Mencius said, "There is a nobility of Heaven, and there is a nobility of man. Benevolence, righteousness, self-consecration, and fidelity, with unwearied joy in the goodness [of these virtues],—these constitute the nobility of Heaven. To be a duke, a minister, or a great officer,—this constitutes the nobility of man.[786]

---

[782] *Par.* 4. The illustrations here are not so happy. Chaou K'e, indeed, introduces the idea of the parts mentioned being diseased so that the "nourishing" is equivalent to trying to heal; but this does not appear in the text. The wolf, it is said, is very wary, and has a quick sight to discern danger; but when chased, he is unable to exercise this faculty, hence "a hurried wolf" is the image of a man pursuing his course heedlessly.

[783] *Par.* 6. The meaning here is—that the parts considered small and ignoble may have, and should have, their share of attention, if the more important parts are first cared for as they ought to be. While Mencius argued that the appetites and passions should be kept in subjection, he would give no countenance to the practice of asceticism.

[784] CH. XV. THAT SOME ARE GREAT MEN, LORDS OF REASON; AND SOME ARE LITTLE MEN, SLAVES OF SENSE.

Kung-too might have gone on to inquire:—"All are equally men; but some stand fast in the nobler part of their constitution, and others allow its supremacy to be snatched away by the inferior part:—how is this?" Mencius would have tried to carry the difficulty a step farther back, and after all have left it where it originally was. His saying that the nature of man is good can be reconciled with the teaching of Christianity; but his views of human nature as a whole are open to the three objections which I have stated in the note to the 21st chapter of the *Doctrine of the Mean.*

[785] CH. XVI. THERE IS A NOBILITY THAT IS OF HEAVEN, AND A NOBILITY THAT IS OF MAN; AND THE NEGLECT OF THE FORMER LEADS TO THE LOSS OF THE LATTER.

[786] *Par.* 1. On the "nobility of man," and its classes, see V. Pt II. ii. What I have

2. "The men of antiquity cultivated their nobility of Heaven, and the nobility of man came in its train.[787]

3. "The men of the present day cultivate their nobility of Heaven in order to seek for the nobility of man, and when they have obtained this, they throw away the other; their delusion is extreme. The issue is simply this, that they must lose [that nobility of man] as well."[788]

XVII.[789] 1. Mencius said, "To desire to be what is considered honorable is the common mind of men. And all men have what is [truly] honorable in themselves; only they do not think of it.

2. "The honor which man confers is not the truly good honor. Those to whom Chaou-măng gave honorable rank he could make mean again.[790]

3. "It is said in the Book of Poetry

'You have made us to drink to the full of your spirits;
You have satiated us with your kindness;

meaning that [the guests] were filled with benevolence and righteousness, and therefore did not wish for the fat meat and fine millet of men. When a good reputation and far-reaching praise fall to [a man's] person, he does not desire the elegant embroidered garments of men."[791]

---

translated "self-consecration" and "fidelity" are taken as devotion in mind and act to "benevolence and righteousness" and the "joy in goodness" is also the goodness of those virtues.

[787] *Par.* 2. We have here merely the laudation *temporis acti.*

[788] *Par.* 3. On "their delusion is extreme" it is said:—"When the nobility of Heaven is cultivated in order to seek for the nobility of man, at the very time it is cultivated, there is a previous mind to throw it away;—showing the existence of delusion. Then when the nobility of man has been got, to throw away the nobility of Heaven exhibits conduct after the attainment not equal even to that in the time of search, so that the delusion is extreme." Several commentators observe that facts may be referred to, apparently inconsistent with what is said in the last sentence of this paragraph, and then go on to say that the preservation of the nobility of man, in the case supposed, is only a lucky accident, and that, the issue ought always to be as Mencius affirms. Yes; but all moral teachings must be imperfect where the thoughts are bounded by what is seen and temporal.

[789] CH. XVII. THE TRUE HONOUR WHICH MEN SHOULD DESIRE. A sequel to the preceding chapter. "Nobility" is the material dignity, and "honour" is the estimation which springs from it.

[790] *Par.* 2. The "really good honour" is that which springs from the nobility of Heaven, and of which human power cannot deprive its possessor. The Chaou family was one of the principal houses of the State of Tsin, and four of its chiefs had had the title of Măng, or "the chief," combined with their surname. They were a sort of "king-making Warwicks," and figure largely in the narratives of Tso K'ëw-ming.

[791] *Par.* 3. See the Book of Poetry, Part III. ii. Ode III. st. 1. The Ode is one responsive from the uncles and cousins of the reigning king of Chow for the kindness he had shown and the honour he had done to them at a sacrificial feast. Mencius' use of the lines is a mere accommodation of them.

XVIII.[792] 1. Mencius said, "Benevolence subdues its opposite just as water subdues fire. Those, however, who now-a-days practise benevolence [do it] as if with a cup of water they could save a whole wagon-load of faggots which was on fire, and when the flames were not extinguished were to say that water cannot subdue fire. Such a course, moreover, is the greatest aid to what is not benevolent.[793]

2. "The final issue will simply be this, the loss [of that small amount of benevolence]."

XIX.[794] Mencius said, "Of all seeds the best are the five kinds of grain, but if they are not ripe, they are not equal to the *t'e* or the *pae*. So the value of benevolence lies simply in its being brought to maturity."

XX.[795] 1. Mencius said, "E, in teaching men to shoot, made it a rule to draw the bow to the full, and his pupils were required to do the same.[796]

2. "A master-workman, in teaching others, must use the compass and square, and his pupils must do the same."

---

[792] CH. XVIII. IN ORDER TO ACCOMPLISH WHAT IT IS ADAPTED TO DO, BENEVOLENCE MUST BE PRACTISED VIGOROUSLY AND FULLY. SO ONLY, INDEED, CAN IT BE PRESERVED. Compare with this chapter Mencius' conversation with king Hwuy of Lëang in I. Pt I. iii., and also his saying in VI. Pt II. i. 6.

[793] *Par.* 1. Chaou K'e takes the conclusion of this paragraph as meaning—"This moreover is equivalent to the course of those who are the greatest practicers of what is not benevolent." But both the sentiment and construction are in this way made more difficult.

[794] CH. XIX. BENEVOLENCE MUST BE MATURED. The sentiment here is akin to that of the former chapter, and is perhaps rather unguardedly expressed.

For "the five kinds of grain" see on III. Pt I. iv. 8. The *t'e* and *pae* are two plants closely resembling each other. "They are a kind of spurious grain, yielding a small seed like rice or millet. They are to be found at all times, in wet situations and dry, and, when crushed and roasted, may satisfy the hunger in a time of famine."

[795] CH. XX. LEARNING MUST NOT BE BY HALVES, BUT BY THE FULL USE OF THE RULES APPROPRIATE TO WHAT IS LEARNED. Compare with this chapter what Mencius says in IV. Pt I. i. and ii.

[796] *Par.* 1. For E see on IV. Pt II. xxiv. 1. On this chapter Choo He says:—"This chapter shows that affairs must be proceeded with according to their laws, and then they can be accomplished. But if a master neglect these, he cannot teach; and if a pupil neglect them, he cannot learn. In small arts it is so;—how much more with the principles of the sages!"

## BOOK VI. KAOU-TSZE. PART II.

CHAPTER I.[797] 1. A MAN of Jin asked the disciple Uh-loo, saying, "Is [an observance of] the rules of propriety [in regard to eating] or the eating the more important?" The answer was, "[The observance of] the rules of propriety is the more important."[798]

2. "Is [the gratifying] the appetite of sex or [the doing so only] according to the rules of propriety the more important?"

3. The answer [again] was, "[The observance of] the rules of propriety [in the matter] is the more important;" [and then the man] said, "If the consequence of eating [only] according to the rules of propriety will be death from starvation, while by disregarding those rules one can get food, must he still observe them [in such a case]? If, according to the rule that he shall go in person to meet his bride, a man cannot get married, while by disregarding the rule he can get married, must he still hold to the rule [in such a case]?"

4. Uh-loo was unable to reply [to these questions], and next day he went to Tsow and told them to Mencius, who said, "What difficulty is there in answering these inquiries?

5. "If you do not bring them together at the bottom, but only at their tops, a piece of wood an inch square may be made to be higher than the pointed ridge of a high building.

6. "'Metal is heavier than feathers;'—but does that saying have reference to a single clasp of metal and a wagon-load of feathers?

7. "If you take a case where the eating is all-important, and the observing the rules of propriety is of little importance, and compare them together, why merely say that the eating is the more important? [So,] taking the case where the gratifying the appetite of sex is all-important, and the observing the rules of propriety is of little importance, why merely say that the gratifying the appetite is the more important?[799]

---

[797] CH. I. TO OBSERVE THE RULES OF PROPRIETY IN OUR CONDUCT IS A MOST IMPORTANT PRINCIPLE, AND WHERE THEY MAY BE DISREGARDED. THE EXCEPTION WILL BE FOUND TO PROVE THE RULE. EXTREME CASES MUST NOT BE PRESSED SO AS TO INVALIDATE THE PRINCIPLE.

[798] *Par.* 1. Jin was a small earldom, referred to the present Tse-ning Chow, in Yen chow department, Shan-tung. The distance between the city of Jin and Mencius' native city of Tsow was only between 30 and 40 miles. Uh-loo, by name Lëen, a native of Tsin, was a disciple of Mencius, and is said by some to have written on the doctrines of "the old P'ăng" and Laou-tsze. The man of Jin's questions are not to be understood of propriety in the abstract, but of the rules of propriety understood to regulate the other things which he mentioned.

[799] *Par.* 7. See in V. Pt I. ii. 1 how Mencius disposes of the charge against Shun for marrying without the knowledge of his parents,—an offence against the rules of propriety greater than that which the man of Jin bad supposed. That case and even those adduced here came under the category of that necessity which has no law.

8. "Go and answer him thus: 'If by twisting round your elder brother's arm, and snatching from him what he is eating, you can get food for yourself, while, if you do not do so, you cannot get such food, will you so twist round his arm? And if by getting over your neighbor's wall, and dragging away his virgin daughter, you can get a wife for yourself, while if you do not do so, you cannot get such wife, will you so drag her away?'"

II.[800] 1. Kĕaou of Ts'aou asked, saying, "[It is said,] 'All men may be Yaous and Shuns;'—is it so?" Mencius said, "It is."[801]

2. [Kĕaou went on], "I have heard that king Wăn was ten cubits high, and T'ang nine. Now I am nine cubits and four inches in height; but I can do nothing but eat my millet. What am I to do to realize that saying?"[802]

3. The reply was, "What has the thing to do with this,—[the question of size]? It all lies simply in acting as such. Here is a man whose strength was not equal to lift a duckling or a chicken,—he was [then] a man of no strength. [But] to-day he says, 'I can lift three thousand catties;' he is [now] a man of strength. And so, he who can lift the weight which Woo Hwoh lifted is just another Woo Hwoh. Why should a man make a want of ability the subject of his grief? It is only that he will not do the thing.[803]

4. "To walk slowly, keeping behind his elders, is to perform the part of a younger. To walk rapidly, going before his elders, is to violate the duty of a younger. But is walking slowly what any man cannot do? it is [only] what he does not do. The course of Yaou and Shun was simply that of filial piety and fraternal duty.[804]

---

[800] CH. II. ALL MAY BECOME YAOUS AND SHUNS, AND TO DO SO THEY HAVE ONLY SINCERELY TO CULTIVATE YAOU AND SHUN'S PRINCIPLES AND WAYS. IT IS THE MIND WHICH IS THE MEASURE OF THE MAN. HOW MENCIUS DEALT WITH AN APPLICANT IN WHOM HE HAD NOT CONFIDENCE.

[801] *Par.* 1. Ts'aou had been an earldom, held by descendants of one of king Wăn's sons; but it had been extinguished and absorbed by Sung before the end of the Ch'un Ts'ĕw period,—a considerable time before Mencius. The descendants of its earls had probably adopted the name of their ancient patrimony as their surname; and the Kĕaou of the text was, we may suppose, one of them.

[802] *Par.* 2. As to the heights mentioned here, see on Ana. VIII vi. The ancient cubit was only, it is said, .74 of the present, so that Wăn's 10 cubits become reduced to 7.4, and T'ang's 9 to 6.66 of the present standard; but these estimates must still be too high. Kĕaou was evidently pluming himself on his dimensions.

[803] *Par.* 3. "It all lies simply in acting as such;"—compare the way in which Mencius puts the question of physical and moral ability in I. Pt I. vii. 10, 11. Woo Hwoh was a man noted for his strength. Sze-ma Ts'ĕen and others mention him in connection with king Woo of Ts'in (B.C. 309-306).

[804] *Par.* 4. In illustration of this paragraph, Choo He quotes two other commentators,—Ch'in Yang, or Ch'in Tsin-che (about the beginning of the 11th century), who says:—"Filial piety and fraternal duty, of which men have an intuitive knowledge, and for which they have an inborn ability, are the natural out-goings of the nature. Yaou and Shun exhibited the perfection of the human relations; but yet they

5. "Do you wear the clothes of Yaou, repeat the words of Yaou, and do the actions of Yaou, and you will just be a Yaou. And if you wear the clothes of Kĕeh, repeat the words of Kĕeh, and do the actions of Kĕeh, you will just be a Kĕeh."[805]

6. [Kĕaou] said, "When I have an audience of the ruler of Tsow, I can ask him to let me have a house to lodge in. I wish to remain here, and receive instruction at your gate."[806]

7. [Mencius] replied, "The way [of truth] is like a great road; it is not difficult to know it. The evil is only that men will not seek for it. Do you go home, and seek it, and you will have abundance of teachers."

III.[807] 1. Kung-sun Ch'ow asked, saying, "Kaou-tsze says that the *Sëaou pwan* is the ode of a small man;—[is it so?]" Mencius replied, "Why does he say so?" and [the disciple] said, "Because of the murmuring [which it expresses].[808]

2. [Mencius] answered, "How stupid is that old Kaou in dealing with the ode! There is a man here, and a native of Yueh bends his bow to shoot him, while I will talk smilingly, and advise him [not to do so];—for no other reason but that he is not related to me. [But] if my own elder brother be bending his bow to shoot the man, then I will advise him [not to do so], weeping and crying the while;—for no other reason but that he is related to me. The dissatisfaction expressed in the *Sëaou pwan* is the working of relative affection; and that affection shows benevolence. Stupid indeed is that old Kaou's criticism of the

---

simply acted in accordance with this nature. How could they add a hair's point to it?" and Yang She or Yang Chung-teih (A.D. 1053-1099), who says:—"The way of Yaou and Shun was great, but what made it so was now the rapidity and now the slowness of their walking and stopping, and not things that were very high and difficult to practice. This is what may be present to the common people in their daily usages, but they do not know it."

[805] *Par.* 5. The meaning is simply—Imitate the men, doing as they did, and you will be such as they.

[806] *Par.* 6. There is an indication here that Kĕaou was presuming on his nobility, and vaunting his influence with the ruler of Tsow. Moreover, his wish to secure a lodging before he became a pupil in Mencius' school is held to show that he was devoid of genuine earnestness. On these grounds Mencius would give him no encouragement, yet there are important truths and a valuable lesson in the words of the next paragraph, with which he sent him away.

[807] CH. III. MENCIUS' EXPLANATION OF THE ODES SËAOU PWAN AND K'AE FUNG. COMPLAINTS AGAINST A PARENT ARE NOT NECESSARILY UNFILIAL.

[808] *Par.* 1. Who the Kaou-tsze, mentioned here, was, must be left in doubt From Mencius calling him "that old Kaou," it would seem plain that he could not be the individual of the same surname who appears in IL Part II. xii. 2, and was, we may suppose, a disciple of our philosopher.

For the Sëaou pwan see the Book of Poetry, Part II. vii. Ode III. That Ode is commonly, though not by Chaou K'e, accepted as having been written by E-k'ĕw, the son and heir-apparent of king Yĕw (B.C. 780-770), or by the prince's master. Led away by the arts of a mistress, the king degraded E-k'ĕw and his mother, and the Ode expresses the sorrow and dissatisfaction which the son could not but feel in such circumstances.

ode!"[809]

3. [Ch'ow then] said, "How is it that there is no murmuring in the *K'ae fung*?"[810]

4. [Mencius] replied, "The parent's fault referred to in the *K'ae fung* was small, while that referred to in the *Sëaou pwan* was great. Where the parent's fault was great, not to have murmured at it would have increased the alienation [between father and son]. Where the parent's fault was small, to have murmured at it would have been [like water which frets and foams about a rock that stands in its channel], unable to suffer the interruption to its course. To increase the want of natural affection would have been unfilial; to have refused to suffer such an interruption [to the flow of natural affection] would also have been unfilial.[811]

5. "Confucius said, 'Shun was indeed perfectly filial! Even when fifty, he was fall of longing desire for [the affection of] his parents.'"[812]

IV.[813] 1. Sung K'ăng being on his way to Ts'oo, Mencius met him in Shih-k'ëw.[814]

2. "Where are you going, respected Sir?" said [Mencius].[815]

3. [K'ăng] replied, "I have heard that Ts'in and Ts'oo are fighting together, and I am going to see the king of Ts'oo, and advise him to cease hostilities. If he should not be pleased with my advice, I will go and see the king of Ts'in, and advise him in the same way. Of the two kings I shall [surely] find that I can succeed with one of them."[816]

---

[809] *Par.* 2. This is Mencius' vindication of the dissatisfaction and even indignation expressed in the Sëaou pwan. The first shooter well appears as a man of Yueh, a barbarous country in the south, in whom the beholder could have no interest.

[810] *Par.* 3. For the K'ae fung see the Book of Poetry, Part I. iii. Ode VII. That Ode is supposed to be the production of seven sons in the State of Wei, whose widowed mother could not live quietly and chastely at home; but they take all the blame for her conduct to themselves, and express no dissatisfaction with her.

[811] *Par.* 4. We must think there was room for dissatisfaction in both cases. Mencius' justification of the K'ae fung is an instance in point to show how filial piety in China often dominates other feelings, though he would seem to intimate that, where great public interests are in question, it should be kept in check.

[812] *Par.* 5. See V. Pt I. i.

[813] CH. IV. MENCIUS' WARNING TO SUNG K'ĂNG ON THE ERROR AND DANGER OF COUNSELLING THE PRINCES TO ABSTAIN FROM WAR ON THE GROUND OF ITS UNPROFITABLENESS, THE PROPER GROUND BEING THAT OF BENEVOLENCE AND RIGHTEOUSNESS. Compare especially I. Pt I. i., where we have the key-note to much of our philosopher's teaching.

[814] *Par.* 1. Sung K'ăng, or K'ăng of Sung, was one of the travelling scholars of the times, who made it their business to go from State to State to counsel the princes. He was, it is said, a disciple of Mih Teih. Shih-k'ëw was in Sung, but where does not seem to be ascertained.

[815] *Par.* 2. "Respected Sir," is literally "elder born." It would seem that Mencius and K'ang must have had some previous acquaintance. Our philosopher must have been travelling at this time in Sung. The hostilities which had called forth K'ăng on his mission have been referred to the year B.C. 311.

[816] *Par.* 3. Does not Mencius himself in the conclusion bring in the idea of

4. [Mencius] said, "I will not presume to ask the particulars, but I should like to hear the scope [of your plan]. What course will you take in advising them?" "I will tell them," was the reply, "the unprofitableness [of their strife]." "Your aim, Sir," rejoined [Mencius], "is great, but your argument is not good.

5. "If you, respected Sir, starting from the point of profit, offer your counsels to the kings of Ts'in and Ts'oo, and they, being pleased with the consideration of profit, should stop the movements of their armies, then all belonging to those armies will rejoice in the cessation [of war], and find their pleasure in [the pursuit of] profit. Ministers will serve their rulers for the profit of which they cherish the thought; sons will serve their fathers, and younger brothers will serve their elder brothers, from the same consideration; and the issue will be that, abandoning benevolence and righteousness, ruler and minister, father and son, elder brother and younger, will carry on their intercourse with this thought of profit cherished in their breasts. But never has there been such a state [of society] without ruin being the result of it.

6. "If you, Sir, starting from the ground of benevolence and righteousness, offer your counsels to the kings of Ts'in and Ts'oo, and they, being pleased with benevolence and righteousness, should stop the movements of their armies, then all belonging to those armies will rejoice in the cessation [of war], and find their pleasure in benevolence and righteousness. Ministers will serve their rulers from-the benevolence and righteousness of which they cherish the thought. Sons will serve their fathers, and younger brothers will serve their elder brothers, from the same;—and the issue will be that, abandoning [the thought of] profit, ruler and minister, father and son, elder brother and younger, will carry on their intercourse with benevolence and righteousness cherished in their breasts. But never has there been such a state [of society] without the result of it being the attainment of true Royal sway. Why must you speak of profit?"

V.[817] 1. When Mencius was residing in Tsow, the younger brother of [the ruler of] Jin, who was guardian of the State at the time, sent him a gift of [some] pieces of silk, which he received, without [going] to give thanks for it. When he was staying for a time in P'ing-luh, Ch'oo, who was prime-minister [of Ts'e], sent him [likewise] a gift of silks, which he received, without [going] to give thanks for it.[818]

2. Subsequently, when he went from Tsow to Jin, he visited the

---

profitableness, when he says that the course which he recommended would raise the kinglet who followed it to the true royal sway?

[817] CH. V. HOW MENCIUS REGULATED HIMSELF IN DIFFERENTLY ACKNOWLEDGING DIFFERENT FAVOURS WHICH HE RECEIVED.

[818] *Par.* 1. Jin,—see on ch. i. P'ing-luh,—see on II. Pt II. iv. 1. The ruler of Jin must have gone abroad on some State duty or service, leaving his brother guardian of the State for the time.

younger brother of the ruler, but when he went from P'ing-luh to [the capital of] Ts'e, he did not visit the minister Ch'oo. The disciple Uh-loo was glad, and said, "I have got an opportunity [to obtain some information]

3. He asked accordingly, "Master, when you went to Jin, you visited the ruler's younger brother. Bat when you went to [the capital of] Ts'e, you did not visit the minister Ch'oo; was it because he is [only] the minister?"

4. [Mencius] replied, "No. It is said in the Book of History, 'In offerings, there are many ceremonial observances. If the observances are not equal to the articles, it may be said that there is no offering, there being no service of the will in the offering.'[819]

5. "[This is] because the things [so presented] do not constitute an offering."[820]

6. Uh-loo was pleased; and when some one asked him [what Mencius meant], he said, "The younger brother [of the ruler of Jin] could not go to Tsow, but the minister Ch'oo could have gone to P'ing-luh."[821]

VI.[822] 1. Shun-yu 'wăn, said, "He who makes the fame and real service his first object acts from a regard to others; he who makes them only secondary objects acts from a regard to himself. You, Master, were ranked among the three high ministers of the kingdom, and before your fame and services had reached either to the ruler or the people, you went away. Is this indeed the way of the benevolent?"[823]

2. Mencius replied, "There was Pih-e;—he abode in an inferior position, and would not with his virtue and talents serve a degenerate ruler. There was E Yin;—he five times went to T'ang, and five times went to Kĕeh. There was Hwuy of Lĕw-hĕa;—he did not disdain to serve a vile ruler, nor did he decline a small office. The courses pursued by those three worthies were different, but their aim was one. And what

---

[819] *Par.* 4. See the Book of History, V. xiii. 12.

[820] *Par.* 5. This is Mencius' explanation of the passage which he had quoted.

[821] *Par.* 6. Uh-loo now understood the reasons of Mencius' different conduct. By his guardianship the prince of Jin was prevented from leaving the State to go to Tsow; but the minister of Ts'e could have gone to P'ing-luh which was in that State.

[822] CH. VI. HOW MENCIUS REPLIED TO THE INSINUATIONS OF SHUN-YU K'WĂN, WHO CONDEMNED HIM FOR LEAVING OFFICE IN TS'E WITHOUT HAVING ACCOMPLISHED ANYTHING.

[823] *Par.* 1. For Shun-yu K'wăn see on IV. Pt I. xvii. He there appears, as here, captiously questioning our philosopher. "Acts from a regard to others;"—*i.e.*, such a man's motive is to benefit others. "Acts from a regard to himself;"—*i.e.*, such a man is bent on the personal cultivation of himself. "The three high ministers" were those of Instruction, of War, and of Works. The kings of Chow had six high ministers; but though the princes of Ts'e and other States had usurped the title of king, it would appear that their organization of offices had not been fully completed. Some say that in these kingdoms the high ministers were distinguished into three classes,—upper, middle, and lower, without the special designations used in Chow.

was their one aim? We must answer—benevolence. And so it is simply after this that superior men strive;—why must they [all] pursue the same [course]?"[824]

3. [K'wăn] pursued, "In the time of duke Muh of Loo, the government was in the hands of Kung-e, while Tsze-lĕw and Tsze-sze were ministers. [And yet] the dismemberment of Loo increased exceedingly. Such was the case,—a specimen of how your men of talents and virtue are of no use to a State!"[825]

4. [Mencius] replied, "[The duke of] Yu did not use Pih-le He, and [thereby] lost his State; duke Muh of Ts'in used him, and became chief of all the princes. The consequence of not employing men of talents and virtue is ruin;—how can it end in dismemberment [merely]?"[826]

5. [K'wăn] urged [again], "Formerly, when Wang Paou dwelt on the K'e, the people on the west of the Ho became skilful at singing in his abrupt manner. When Mĕen K'eu dwelt in Kaou-t'ang, the people in the west of Ts'e became skilful at singing in his prolonged manner. The wives of Hwa Chow and K'e Lĕang bewailed their husbands so skillfully that they changed the manners of the State. When there is [the gift] within, it is sure to manifest itself without. I have never seen the man who could do the deeds [of a worthy] and did not realize the work of one. Therefore there are [now] no men of talents and virtue; if there were, I should know them."[827]

6. [Mencius] replied, "When Confucius was minister of crime in Loo, [the ruler] came not to follow [his counsels]. Soon after there was the [solstitial] sacrifice, and when a part of the flesh there presented did not come to him, he went away [even] without taking off his cap of ceremony. Those who did not know him supposed that [he went away] because the flesh [did not come to him]. Those who knew him [somewhat] supposed that it was because of the neglect of the [usual]

---

[824] *Par.* 2. For Pih-e, E Yin, and Hwuy of Lĕw-hĕa, see II. Pt I. ii. ix.: IV. Pt I. xiii.: V. Pt II. i.; *et al.*

[825] *Par.* 3. K'wăn here advances in his condemnation of Mencius. He had charged him with having left his office before he had accomplished anything, but here he insinuates that though he had remained in office, he would not have done anything. Tsze-lĕw is the same with the Sĕeh Lĕw of II Pt II. xi., which paragraph should be compared with this. Kung-e, called Hĕw, was prime-minister of Loo,—a man of merit and principle. The facts of duke Muh's history by no means justify what K'wăn alleges here as to the dismemberment of Loo in his time.

[826] *Par.* 4. For Pih-le He see V. Pt I. 9.

[827] *Par.* 5. Of the men here all belonged to Ts'e, except Wang Paou, who was of Wei, in which was the river K'e. Of him and Men K'eu little is known. The bravery of K'e Lĕang and Hwa Chow is much celebrated, and also the virtue of K'e Lĕang's wife, with the way in which she and the wife of Hwa Chow bewailed their husbands. See a narrative in the Tso Chuen, under the 23rd year of duke Sĕang; the Le Ke, II. Pt II. iii. 1; *et al* In the citation of these instances, K'wăn's object was to insinuate that Mencius was a pretender, because, wherever there was ability, it was sure to come out, and to prove itself by its fruits.

ceremony. The truth was that Confucius wished to go on occasion of
some small offence, and did not wish to go without an apparent cause.
All men cannot be expected to understand the conduct of a superior
man."[828]

VII.[829] 1. Mencius said, "The five presidents of the princes were
sinners against the three kings. The princes of the present day are
sinners against the five presidents. The great officers of the present day
are sinners against the princes of the present day.[830]

2. "When the son of Heaven visited the princes, it was called 'A
tour of inspection.' When the princes attended at his court, it was called
'A report of office.' In the spring they examined the plowing, and
supplied any deficiency [of seed]; in the autumn they examined the
reaping, and assisted where there was a deficiency [of yield]. When
[the son of Heaven] entered the boundaries [of a State], if [new] ground
was being reclaimed, and the old fields were well cultivated; if the old
were nourished, and honor shown to men of talents and virtue; and if
men of distinguished ability were placed in office:—then [the ruler]
was rewarded,—rewarded with [an addition to his] territory. [On the
other hand], if on his entering a State, the ground was found left wild or
overrun with weeds; if the old were neglected, and no attention paid to
men of talents and virtue; and if hard tax-gatherers were placed in
office:—then [the ruler] was reprimanded. If [a prince] once omitted
his attendance at court, he was punished by degradation of rank; if he
did so a second time, he was deprived of a portion of his territory; and
if he did so a third time, the royal armies [were set in motion], and he
was removed [from his government]. Thus the son of Heaven
commanded the punishment, but did not himself inflict it, while the
various feudal princes inflicted the punishment, but did not command
it. The five presidents, [however,] dragged the princes of the States to
attack other princes, and therefore I say that they were sinners against

---

[828] *Par.* 6. Mencius shields himself by the example of Confucius, implying that he
was beyond the knowledge of a sophist like K'wăn. See the Life of Confucius in Vol. I.

[829] CH. VII. THE PROGRESS AND MANNER OF DEGENERACY FROM THE THREE
KINGS TO THE FIVE PRESIDENTS OF THE PRINCES. AND FROM THE FIVE PRESIDENTS OF
THE PRINCES TO THE PRINCES AND OFFICERS OF MENCIUS' TIME.

[830] *Par.* 1. "The three kings" are the founders of the three dynasties of Hĕa, Shang,
and Chow. "The five presidents of the princes" were Hwan of Ts'e (B.C. 683-642), Wăn
of Tsin (634-627), Sĕang of Sung, (649-636); Muh of Tsin (658-620); and Chwang of
Ts'oo (612-590). These professed to take the lead and direction of the various States, and
exercised really royal functions throughout the kingdom, while yet there was a profession
of loyal attachment to the house of Chow. There are two enumerations of the "five
presidents;"—one called "the presidents of the three dynasties," and one called "the
presidents of the Ch'un Ts'ĕw period:"—only Hwan of Ts'e and Wăn of Tsin are
common to the two. But Mencius is speaking, probably, only of those included in the
second enumeration; and though there is some difference of opinion in regard to the
individuals in the list, the names I have given were, I think, those he had in his mind.
"Were sinners against;"—*i.e.* violated their principles and ways.

the three kings.[831]

3. "Of the five presidents duke Hwan was the most distinguished. At the assembly of the princes in K'wei-k'ĕw, they bound the victim, and placed the writing [of the covenant] upon it, but did not [slay it], and smear their mouths with its blood. The first article in the covenant was:—'Slay the unfilial; do not change the son who has been appointed heir; do not exalt a concubine to the rank of wife.' The second was:—'Give honor to the worthy, and cherish the talented,—to give distinction to the virtuous.' The third was:—'Reverence the old, and be kind to the young; be not forgetful of visitors and travelers.' The fourth was :—'Let not offices be hereditary, nor let officers be pluralists; in the selection of officers let the object be to get the proper men; let not [a ruler] take it on himself to put a great officer to death.' The fifth was:—'Follow no crooked policy in making embankments; do not restrict the sale of grain; do not grant any investiture without [first] informing [the king, and getting his sanction].' It was [then] said, 'All we who have united in this covenant shall hereafter maintain amicable relations.' The princes of the present day all violate those five prohibitions, and therefore I say that they are sinners against the five presidents.[832]

4. "The crime of him who connives at and aids the wickedness of his ruler is small, but the crime of him who anticipates and excites that wickedness is great. The great officers of the present day all are guilty of this latter crime, and I say that they are sinners against the princes."

VIII.[833] 1. [The ruler of] Loo wanted to employ Shin-tsze in the command of an army.[834]

---

[831] *Par.* 2. See I. Pt II. iv. 5. This par. exhibits the principles and ways of "the three kings," and concludes by showing how "the five presidents" violated them.

[832] *Par.* 3. Duke Hwan brought the princes of the States together many times, but no occasion perhaps was greater than the assembly at K'wei-k'ĕw (probably in the present district of K'aou-shing, department K'wei-fung), in B.C. 650. Mencius, no doubt, selected this because he had a full account of it, which enabled him to exhibit it as a specimen of the principles and ways of the presidents of the States. The object in assembling the prince was to get them to form a covenant with conditions required by the existing state of things in the kingdom. The usual practice at those meetings was first to dig a square pit over which the victim was slain. Its left ear was then cut off, and placed in a vessel ornamented with pearls, and the blood was received in a vessel of jade. Holding these vessels the president of the assembly read out the articles of the covenant, with his face to the north, announcing them to the Spirits of the sun and moon, the mountains and rivers. After this he and all the others smeared the corners of their mouths with the blood, placed the victim in the pit, with the articles of the covenant upon it, and then covered it up.

[833] CH. VIII. MENCIUS' OPPOSITION TO THE WARLIKE AMBITION OF THE MARQUIS OF LOO:—A CONVERSATION WITH THE GENERAL SHIN KUH-LE.

[834] *Par.* 1. We do not have much information about the Shin who appears here. According to Sze-ma Ts'ĕen there was, in Mencius' time, a Shin Taou, a native of Chaou, and a writer of the Taouist sect it is supposed that he had also studied the art of war, and that duke P'ing of Loo now wished to take advantage of his skill. In par. 4, Shin appears to call himself by the name of Kuh-le—which is against his being this Shin Taou.

2. Mencius said [to Shin], "To employ an uninstructed people [in war] is what is called—destroying the people. A destroyer of the people was not tolerated in the age of Yaou and Shun.[835]

3. "Though by a single battle you should vanquish Ts'e, and so get possession of Nan-yang, the thing ought not to be done."[836]

4. Shin changed countenance, was displeased, and said, "This is what I, Kuh-le, do not understand."[837]

5. [Mencius] said, "I will lay the case plainly before you. The territory of the son of Heaven is a thousand *le* square;—without a thousand *le*, he would not have enough for his entertainment of the princes. The territory of a prince [of the highest rank] is a hundred *le* square;—without a hundred *le*, he would not have enough wherewith to observe the statutes kept in his ancestral temple.

6. "When the duke of Chow was invested with [the marquisate of] Loo, it was a hundred *le* square. The territory was indeed enough, but it was limited to a hundred *le*. When T'ae-kung was invested with [the marquisate of] Ts'e, it was also a hundred *le* square;—sufficient indeed, but limited to that amount.[838]

7. "Now Loo is five times a hundred *le* square. If a true king were to arise, whether do you think that Loo would be diminished or increased by him?

8. "If it were merely taking from one [State] to give to another, a benevolent person would not do it; how much less would he do so, when the thing has to be sought by the slaughter of men!

9. "The way in which a superior man serves his ruler is simply an earnest endeavour to lead him in the right path, and to direct his mind to benevolence."

IX.[839] 1. Mencius said, "Those who now-a-days serve their rulers,

---

Some there-fore say that he had studied under a Mihist professor of the time, who was called K'in Kuh-le, and that we should translate in par. 4—"This is what [even] Kuh-le does not understand." But Kuh-le there must be Shin's own name. We must leave the question of who he was undetermined. The title of "army-commander" which appears here had come into use in the Ch'un Ts'ĕw period.

[835] *Par.* 2. Compare what Confucius says in Ana. XIII. xxix. and xxx.

[836] *Par.* 3. Nan-yang was a tract of country south of mount T'ae, which originally belonged to Loo, but had been taken and appropriated by Ts'e, Duke P'ing of Loo now wanted to take advantage of the difficulties of Ts'e to regain the territory.—The fact of Nan-yang's having originally been Loo territory certainly made it a bad text for Mencius to give his lecture to Shin-tsze on it.

[837] *Par.* 4. The statutes kept in the ancestral temple would prescribe all things relating to the public sacrifices, the interviews of the ruler of Loo with other princes, and other public matters, the expense of which required a territory of 100 *le* square to defray them.

[838] *Par.* 6. "Tae-kung;"—see on IV. Pt I xiii.

[839] CH. IX. MENCIUS CONDEMNS THE MINISTERS OF HIS TIME FOR PANDERING TO, AND EVEN ENCOURAGING, THEIR RULERS' THIRST FOR WEALTH AND POWER. This chapter probably owes its place here to its being a sort of sequel to the last paragraph of the preceding one.

say, 'We can for our ruler enlarge the limits of the cultivated ground, and fill his treasuries and arsenals.' Such men are now-a-days called 'Good ministers,' but anciently they were called 'Robbers of the people.' If a ruler is not following the [right] path, nor has his mind bent on benevolence, to seek to enrich him is to enrich a Kĕeh."[840]

2. "[Or they will say], 'We can for our ruler make engagements with our allied States, so that our battles must be successful.' Such men are now-a-days called 'Good ministers,' but anciently they were called 'Robbers of the people.' If a ruler is not following the [right] path, nor has his mind bent on benevolence, to seek to make him stronger in battle is to help a Kĕeh.

3. "Although a [ruler], by the path of the present day, and with no change of its practices, were to have all under heaven given to him, he could not keep it for a single morning."[841]

X.[842] 1. Pih Kwei said, "I want to take [for the government] only a twentieth [of the produce]; what do you say to it?"[843]

2. Mencius replied, "Your way, Sir, would be that of the Mih.[844]

3. "In a State of ten thousand families, would it do to have [only] one potter?" "No," said the other; "the vessels would not be enow for use."

4. [Mencius] went on, "In Mih [all] the five kinds of grain are not grown;—it only produces the millet. There are no fortified cities with their walled suburbs, no great edifices, no ancestral temples, no ceremonies of sacrifice; there are no feudal princes requiring gifts of silk and entertainments; there is no system of officers with their various subordinates. On this account a tax of one twentieth of the produce is [there] sufficient.

5. "But now, [as] we live in the middle States, how can such a state of things be thought of, which would do away with the relationships of

---

[840] *Par.* 1. "We can enlarge the territory of the cultivated ground;"—compare IV. Pt I. xiv. 3. The territory would be enlarged at the expense of the people, taking their commons from them, and making them labor upon them for the ruler. Chaou K'e takes the phrase as meaning the appropriation of small States;—which is not so good.

[841] *Par.* 4. See IV. Pt I. xiv. 2.

[842] CH. X. AN ORDERED STATE CAN ONLY SUBSIST WITH A PROPER SYSTEM OF TAXATION; AND THAT WHICH ORIGINATED WITH YAOU AND SHUN IS THE PROPER ONE FOR CHINA.

[843] *Par.* 1. Pih Kwei (as appears from next chapter, named Tan) is generally supposed to have been a man of Chow, ascetic in his own habits and fond of innovations. Such is the account of him given by Sze-ma Ts'een; but there are difficulties in the way of our supposing Ts'een's Pih Kwei to be the same as the person who appears here.

[844] *Par.* 2. The Mih were one of the wild tribes lying on the north of the middle States,—the China of Mencius' time. The name does not occur in the Ch'un Ts'ëw, nor in the Tso Chuen. Its territory, lying far north, would be unfit for most of the kinds of grain. The people would be for the most part nomads, and very inferior in civilization to those of the States of China, though Mencius perhaps rather exaggerates the extent of their barbarism.

men, and have no officers of superior rank?

6. "A State cannot be made to subsist with but few potters; how much less can it be so without men of a superior rank to others!

7. "If we wish to make the taxation lighter than the system of Yaou and Shun, we shall have a great Mih and a small Mih. If we wish to make it heavier, we shall have the great Kĕeh and the small Kĕeh."[845]

XI.[846] 1. Pih Kwei said, "My management of the waters is superior to that of Yu."

2. Mencius said, "You are wrong, Sir. Yu's regulation of the waters was according to the laws of water.

3. "He therefore made the four seas their receptacle, while you now, Sir, make the neighbouring States their receptacle.

4. "When waters flow out of their natural channels, we have what is called an inundation. Inundating waters form a vast [waste] of water, and are what a benevolent man detests. You are wrong, my good Sir."

XII.[847] Mencius said, "If a superior man have not confidence [in his views], how shall he take a firm hold [of things]?"

XIII.[848] 1. [The ruler of] Loo wishing to commit the administration of his government to the disciple Yoh-ching, Mencius said, "When I heard of it, I was so glad that I could not sleep."[849]

2. Kung-sun Ch'ow said, "Is Yoh-ching a man of vigour?" "No." "Is he wise in council?" "No." "Is he a man of much information?" "No."[850]

3. "What then made you so glad 'that you could not sleep?"

4. "He is a man who loves what is good," was the reply.[851]

5. "Is the love of what is good sufficient?"

6. [Mencius] replied, "The love of what is good is more than a sufficient qualification for the government of the whole kingdom; how much more is it so for the State of Loo!

---

[845] *Par.* 7. Under the system of taxation proposed by Pih Kwei, China would become a copy of the Mih; under a heavier system than that of Yaou and Shun, it would be brought to its state under the tyrant Kĕeh.

[846] CH. XI. PIH KWEI'S PRESUMPTUOUS IDEA THAT HE COULD REGULATE INUNDATIONS OF THE RIVERS BETTER THAN YU HAD DONE.

There must have been some partial inundations at this time, and Pih Kwei had been called in to remedy them. This he had done in an unsatisfactory way, benefiting one State at the expense of others.

[847] CH. XII. FAITH IN PRINCIPLES IS NECESSARY TO FIRMNESS IN ACTION.

[848] CH. XIII. OF WHAT IMPORTANCE IT IS TO A MINISTER—TO GOVERNMENT—TO LOVE WHAT IS GOOD.

[849] *Par.* 1. Yoh-ching,—see I. Pt II xvi.; *et al.*

[850] *Par,* 2. The three gifts mentioned here were those generally considered most important to government, and Kung-sun Ch'ow, knowing Yoh-ching to be deficient in them, shaped his questions accordingly.

[851] *Par.* 4. On this it is said:—"In the administration of government, the most excellent quality is without prejudice and dispassionately to receive what is good. Now Yoh-ching in his heart sincerely loved all good words and good actions."

7. "If [a minister] love what is good, then all within the four seas will think a thousand *le* but a small distance to come and lay [their thoughts about] what is good before him.

8. "If he do not love what is good, men will say, 'How self-conceited he looks! [He is saying], "I know it."' The language and looks of that self-conceit will repel men to more than the distance of a thousand *le*. When good men stop more than a thousand *le* off, calumniators, flatterers, and sycophants will make their appearance. When [a minister] lives with calumniators, flatterers, and sycophants about him, though he may wish the State to be well governed, is it possible for it to be so?"

XIV.[852] 1. The disciple Ch'in said, "What were the principles on which superior men of old took office?" Mencius said, "There were three cases in which they accepted office, and three in which they left it.[853]

2. "If received with the utmost respect and all courteous observances, and they could say [to themselves] that [the ruler] would carry their words into practice, then they went to him [and took office]. [Afterwards], though there might be no remission of the courteous observances, if their words were not carried into practice, they left him.[854]

3. "The second case was that in which, though [the ruler] could not [be expected] at once to carry their words into practice, yet being received by him with the utmost respect and all courteous observances, they went to him [and took office]. [But afterwards], if there was a remission of the courteous observances, they left him.

4. "The last case was that of [the superior man] who had nothing to eat either morning or evening, and was so famished that he could not move out of his door. If the ruler, on hearing of his state, said, 'I must fail of the great point,—that of carrying his principles into practice, and moreover I cannot follow his words, but I am ashamed to allow him to starve in my country,' and so assisted him, the help might be accepted in such a case, but not beyond what was sufficient to avert death."

XV.[855] 1. Mencius said, "Shun rose [to the empire] from among the channeled fields. Foo Yueh was called to office from the midst of his [building] frames and [earth-] beaters; Kaou Kih from his fish and salt;

---

[852] CH. XIV. THE GROUNDS ON WHICH WORTHIES OF OLD TOOK OFFICE OR LEFT IT.

[853] *Par.* 1. "The disciple Ch'in" here was the Ch'in Ts'in of II. Pt II. iii.

[854] *Parr.* 2-4. Compare V. Pt II. iv. 7. There Confucius appears as having taken office on all the grounds mentioned here. In this chapter our philosopher enters more into the grounds why the office once undertaken should again be abandoned;—if in the third case we can speak of office having been taken.

[855] CH. XV. TRIALS AND HARDSHIPS THE WAY IN WHICH HEAVEN PREPARES MEN FOR GREAT SERVICES. ILLUSTRATED BY THE CASES OF SEVERAL EMINENT WORTHIES OF FORMER TIMES.

Kwan E-woo from the hands of the officer in charge of him; Sun Shuh-gaou from [his hiding by] the sea-shore; and Pih-le He from the market-place.[856]

2. "Thus, when Heaven is about to confer a great office on any one, it first exercises his mind with suffering, and his sinews and bones with toil; it exposes his body to hunger, and subjects him to extreme poverty; and it confounds his undertakings. In all these ways it stimulates his mind, hardens his nature, and supplies his incompetencies.

3. "Men constantly err, but are afterwards able to reform. They are distressed in mind, and perplexed in thought, and then they arise to vigorous endeavour. When things have been evidenced in men's looks, and set forth in their words, then they understand them.[857]

4. "If a ruler have not about his court families attached to the laws and able officers, and if abroad there are no hostile States or other external calamities, the State will generally come to ruin.[858]

5. "From such things we see how life springs from sorrow and calamity, and death from ease and pleasure."

---

[856] *Par.* 1. The rise of Shun is well known;—see the 1st part of the Book of History. Foo Yueh,—see the Book of History, Part IV. viii., where it is related that king Kaou-tsung, having dreamt that "God gave him a good assistant," caused a picture of the man he had seen in his dream to be made, and search made for him through the kingdom, when he was found dwelling in the wilderness of Foo-yen. Sze-ma Ts'ëen says that the surname of the man was given in the dream as Foo, and his name as Yueh, which the king interpreted as meaning, that he would be a "tutor" (*foo*) to himself, and a "blessing" (*yueh*) to the people. Kaou Kih is mentioned in II. Pt I. i. 8, as an able assistant of the last king of Yin. In the disorders and misgovernment of that king Kaou Kih had retired to obscurity, and was discovered by the lord of Chow in the guise of a seller of fish and salt, and induced to take office under the king, with whom Kih continued faithful to the last.

Kwan E-woo was the chief minister of duke Hwan of Ts'e;—see II Pt I. i.; *et al.* He was carried from Loo to Ts'e in a cage, Hwan having demanded his surrender that he might have the pleasure of putting him to death; but he met him outside the city and raised him to the greatest distinction. Shuh-sun Gaou was chief minister to king Chwang of Ts'oo, one of the five presidents of the States. He appears in the narratives of the Tso Chuen (see Book VII. xi.; *et al.*) as Wei Gae-lëeh. He belonged to one of the principal families of Ts'oo; but being at one time treated with neglect by the king, be had retired into obscurity, and lived somewhere (it must have been out of Ts'oo) on the sea-coast. The events of his life at this time, however, are all but lost to history. Afterwards, he did good service to the State. Sun-shuh must have been his designation originally, and Gaou was the name of an office in Ts'oo,—probably the sound of its appellation in the original language of the country. Pih-le He,—see V. Pt I. ix.

[857] *Par.* 3. This par. is intended to show that the same thing may in a manner be predicated of ordinary men. The concluding part seems to say that though most men are not quick of apprehension, yet when things are brought clearly before them, they can lay hold of them.

[858] *Par.* 4. The same thing is true of a State. "Families attached to the laws" will not readily submit to the infraction of those laws without remonstrating, and their feelings will find a voice in the "able counselors." This will stimulate the ruler's mind; and foreign danger will make him careful, and rouse him to exertion.

XVI.[859] Mencius said, "There are many arts in teaching. I refuse, as inconsistent with my character, to teach a man, but I am only thereby still teaching him."

## BOOK VII. TSIN SIN.[860] PART I.

CHAPTER I.[861] 1. MENCIUS said, "He who has exhaustively studied all his mental constitution knows his nature. Knowing his nature, he knows Heaven.[862]

2. "To preserve one's mental constitution, and nourish one's nature, is the way to serve Heaven.[863]

3. "When neither [the thought] of premature death nor [that] of long life causes a man any double-mindedness, but he waits in the cultivation of himself for whichever issue,—this is the way in which he establishes his [Heaven-] ordained being."[864]

---

[859] CH. XVI. THAT A REFUSAL TO TEACH MAY BE TEACHING.
There is a sufficient example of what Mencius states here in the second chapter.

[860] TITLE OF THIS BOOK. Like the previous Books, this is named from the commencing words—*Tsin Sin*, "The exhausting of all the mental constitution." It contains many more chapters than any of the others,—brief, enigmatical sentences for the most part, conveying Mencius' views on human nature. It is more abstruse also, and the student will have much difficulty in satisfying himself that he has hit the exact meaning of our philosopher. The author of "The Root and Relish of the four Books" says:—"This Book was made by Mencius in his old age. Its style is terse, and its meaning deep, and we cannot discover an order of subjects in its chapters. He had completed the previous chapters, and this grew up under his *stylus*, as his mind was affected, and he was prompted to give expression to his thoughts. The first chapter, however, may be regarded as a compendium of the whole."

[861] CH. I. BY THE KNOWLEDGE OF OURSELVES WE COME TO THE KNOWLEDGE OF HEAVEN, AND HEAVEN IS SERVED BY OUR OBEYING OUR NATURE.

[862] *Par.* 1. "To exhaust our mental constitution" is, I conceive, to make one's-self acquainted with *all* his mental constitution, having arrested his consciousness, and ascertained what it is. This of course gives a man the knowledge of his nature; and as he is the creature of Heaven, its attributes must be corresponding. I can get no other meaning from this paragraph. Choo He, however, and all his school, say that there is no work or labor in "exhausting the mental constitution;"—that it is "the extension to the utmost of knowledge" of the 1st chapter of "The Great Learning;" and that all the labor is in "knowing the nature," which is "the investigation of things" of that chapter. On this view we should translate, "He who completely develops his mental constitution has known (come to know) his nature;" but this is a forced construction of the text.

[863] *Par.* 2. The "preservation" is the holding fast that which we have from Heaven, and the "nourishing" is the acting in accordance therewith, so that the "serving Heaven" is just the being and doing what It has intimated in our constitution to be its will concerning us.

[864] *Par.* 3. Man's "[Heaven-]ordained being" is his nature according to the opening words of "The Doctrine of the Mean;"—"What Heaven has conferred is called THE NATURE." "Establishing" this means "keeping entire what Heaven has conferred upon us, and not injuring it by any doing of our own."
It may be well to give the remarks of Chaou K'e on this chapter. On the 1st par. he says:—"To the nature there belong the principles of benevolence, righteousness, propriety, and knowledge. The mind is designed to regulate them. When the mind is

II.[865] 1. Mencius said, "There is an appointment for everything. A man should submissively receive what is correctly ascribed thereto.[866]

2. "Therefore, he who knows what is [Heaven's] appointment will not stand beneath a dangerous wall.

3. "Death sustained in the fulfillment of one's proper course may correctly be ascribed to the appointment [of Heaven].

4. "Death under handcuffs and fetters cannot correctly be so ascribed."[867]

III. 1. Mencius said, "When we get by our seeking, and lose by our neglecting, in that case seeking is of use to getting;—the things sought are those which are in ourselves.[868]

---

correct, a man can put it all forth in thinking of doing good, and then he may be said to know his nature. When he knows his nature, then he knows how the way of Heaven considers as excellent what is good."

On the 2nd par. he says:—"When one is able to preserve his mind and nourish his correct [nature], he may be called a man of perfect virtue. The way of Heaven loves life, and the perfect man also loves life. The way of Heaven is without partiality, and only approves of the virtuous. [Thus] the acting [of the perfect man] agrees with Heaven, and therefore it is said, 'This is the way by which he serves Heaven.'"

On the 3rd par. he says:—"'Double' means two. The perfect man in his conduct is guided by one rule simply. Although he sees that some who have gone before him have been short-lived, and some long-lived, he never has two minds or changes his way. Let life be short like that of Yen Yuen, or long like that of the duke of Shaou, he refers both eases equally to the appointment of Heaven, and cultivates and rectifies his own person to wait for that. It is in this way that he establishes the root of [Heaven's] appointments."

The differences between these interpretations and those of Choo He may well lead the foreign student to put forth his strength on the study of the text more than on the commentaries.

[865] CH. II. MAN'S DUTY AS AFFECTED BY THE DECREES OR APPOINTMENTS OF HEAVEN. WHAT MAY BE CORRECTLY ASCRIBED TO THOSE, AND WHAT NOT. Choo He says this is a continuation of the last chapter, developing the meaning of its concluding paragraph. There is a connection between the chapters, but Heaven's decree or appointment is here taken more widely, as extending not only to man's nature, but to all the events that befall him.

[866] *Par.* 1. "A man should submissively receive what may be correctly ascribed to appointment" is, literally, "a man should submissively receive the correct appointment." The correct appointment is that which is directly from the will of Heaven; and no consequence flowing from evil or careless conduct is to be understood as being so.

[867] *Par.* 4. The handcuffs or fetters are understood to be those of an evildoer.—There is important truth underlying this chapter. Compare with it various passages in the 1st Epistle of Peter.

[868] CH. III. VIRTUE IS SURE TO BE FOUND BY SEEKING IT, BUT RICHES AND OTHER EXTERNAL THINGS NOT.

The general sentiment of this chapter is good, but truth is sacrificed to the point of the antithesis, when it is said in the second case that seeking is of *no* use to getting. The things "in ourselves" are the virtues of benevolence, righteousness, propriety, and knowledge,—the endowments proper of our nature. Those "without ourselves" are riches and dignities. The "proper course" to seek them is that ascribed to Confucius,—"Advancing according to propriety, and retiring according to righteousness;" but yet they are not at our command and control. Chaou K'e appropriately quotes in reference to them the words of the sage in Ana. VII. xi., "as the search may not be successful, I will follow after that which I love."

2. "When the seeking is according to the proper course, and the getting is [only] as appointed, in that case the seeking is of no use to getting;—the things sought are without ourselves."

IV.[869] 1. Mencius said, "All things are already complete in us.[870]

2. "There is no greater delight than to be conscious of sincerity on self-examination.[871]

3. "If one acts with a vigorous effort at the law of reciprocity, nothing, when he seeks for [the realization of] perfect virtue, can be closer than his approximation to it."[872]

V.[873] Mencius said, "They do the thing, without clearly knowing [its propriety]; they practise the doing, without discriminating [the reason of it]; they [thus] pursue the path all their life, without knowing its nature:—this is the case of multitudes."

VI.[874] Mencius said, "A man should not be without shame. When a man is ashamed of having been without shame, he will [afterwards] not have [occasion for] shame."

VII.[875] 1. Mencius said, "The sense of shame is to a man of great importance.

2. "Those who form contrivances and versatile schemes distinguished for their artfulness do not allow their sense of shame to come into action.[876]

3. "When one differs from other men in not having this sense of shame, what will he have in common with them?"[877]

---

[869] CH. IV. MAN IS FITTED FOR AND HAPPY IN DOING GOOD, AND MAY BECOME PERFECT THEREIN.

[870] *Par.* 1. This brief saying is quite mystical. The "all things" are taken as "the radical nature of the reasons of things," and then the things must be further restricted to the relations of society and the duties belonging to them. If we extend them farther, we only get perplexed.

[871] *Par.* 2. The "sincerity" is that so largely treated of in the Doctrine of the Mean.

[872] *Par.* 3. For "the law of reciprocity" see Ana. XV. xxiii. To have complete sincerity, it is said, would be perfect virtue. Where there is something wanting in this, the way is to act vigorously on the law of reciprocity.

[873] CH. V. MANY MAY ACT RIGHTLY WITHOUT KNOWING WHY THEY DO SO. A LESSON FOR THE PHILOSOPHER'S PUPILS.

It would be easier to understand such chapters as this, if we had before us the conversation or discussion out of which they grew, and of which they contain Mencius' own condensed summary.

[874] CH. VI. THE VALUE OF THE FEELING OF SHAME. A wise and deep utterance.

[875] CH. VII. THE IMPORTANCE OF THE FEELING OF SHAME, AND THE CONSEQUENCE OF BEING WITHOUT IT. The former chapter, it is said, was by way of exhortation; and this is by way of warning.

[876] *Par.* 2. In this Mencius may have been aiming at the wandering scholars of his time, who were full of plots and schemes to unite and disunite the various kinglets. Chaou K'e supposes that the inventors of destructive engines for purposes of war are intended. It is implied that if those parties had the sense of shame, they would not form such plots nor make such engines.

[877] *Par.* 3. Choo He gives another view of this par., as also admissible;—"If a man be not ashamed of not being like other men, how will he be able to be like them?" This is

VIII.[878] Mencius said, "The able and virtuous monarchs of antiquity loved what was good and forgot [their own] power. And shall an exception be made of the able and virtuous scholars of antiquity—that they did not act in a similar way? They delighted in their own principles, and forgot the power [of princes]. Therefore, if kings and dukes did not cherish the utmost respect [for them] and observe all forms of ceremony, they were not permitted to see them frequently. If they found it not in their power to see them frequently, how much less could they get to employ them as ministers!"

IX.[879] 1. Mencius said, to Sung Kow-tsëen, "Are you fond, Sir, of travelling [to the different courts]? I will tell you about [such] travelling.[880]

2. "If any [of the princes] acknowledge you [and follow your counsels], look perfectly satisfied. If no one do so, still do the same."

3. [The other] asked, "What must I do that I may always wear this look of perfect satisfaction?" "Honor virtue," was the reply, "and delight in righteousness; and so you may [always] appear to be perfectly satisfied.

4. "So it is that a scholar, though he may be poor, does not let go his righteousness, and, though prosperous, does not leave [his own] path.

5. "Poor and not letting go his righteousness;—it is thus that the scholar holds possession of himself. Prosperous, and not leaving [his own] path;—it is thus that the expectations of the people [from him] are not disappointed.[881]

6. "When the men of antiquity realized their wishes, benefits accrued [from them] to the people. When they did not realize their wishes, they cultivated their personal character, and became illustrious in the world. When poor, they attended to the improvement of themselves in solitude; when advanced to dignity, they promoted the improvement of all under heaven as well."

---

Chaou K'e's view generalized.

[878] CH. VIII. HOW THE ANCIENT SCHOLARS MAINTAINED THEIR DIGNITY AND RESERVE, AND HOW THE ANCIENT KINGS APPRECIATED THEM.

Mencius had, no doubt, in mind in these remarks to indicate his own character and course, and to condemn the wandering scholars of his time.

[879] CH. IX. HOW AN ADVISER OF THE PRINCES MIGHT ALWAYS APPEAR PERFECTLY SATISFIED;—ILLUSTRATED BY THE EXAMPLE OF THE SCHOLARS OF ANTIQUITY.

[880] *Par.* 1. Nothing is known of Sung Kow-tsëen beyond what appears here. He was, we may assume, like Sung K'ăng (VI. Pt II. iv.) one of the adventurers who travelled about tendering their advice to the different princes.

[881] *Par.* 5. "Holds possession of himself;"—Chaou K'e expounds:—"Holds possession of his proper nature." Rather it is—holds possession of himself as described in par. 3, "honoring virtue, and delighting in righteousness." Choo He says:—"This chapter shows how the scholar, attaching weight to what is internal, and holding what is external light, will approve himself good in all places and circumstances."

X.[882] Mencius said, "The mass of men wait for a king Wăn, and then receive a rousing impulse. Scholars distinguished from the mass, even without a king Wăn, rouse themselves."

XI.[883] Mencius said, "Add to a man [the wealth of] the families of Han and Wei, and, if he [still] look upon himself without being elated, he is far beyond [the mass of] men."

XII.[884] Mencius said, "Let the people be employed in the way which is intended to secure their ease, and, though they be toiled, they will not murmur. Let them be put to death in the way which is intended to preserve their lives, and, though they die, they will not murmur."

XIII.[885] 1. Mencius said, "Under a president of the States, the people look brisk and cheerful; under a true king they have an air of deep contentment.[886]

2. "Though he slay them, they do not murmur; when he benefits them, they do not think of his merit. From day to day they make progress towards what is good, without knowing who makes them do so.[887]

3. "Wherever the superior man passes through, transformation follows; wherever he abides, his influence is of a spiritual nature. It flows abroad, above, and beneath like that of heaven and earth. How can it be said that he mends [society] but in a small way?"[888]

---

[882] CH. X. HOW SUPERIOR PEOPLE GET THEIR INSPIRATION TO GOOD IN THEMSELVES.

"The mass of men" is literally "all men;" *i.e.*, ordinary people.

[883] CH. XI. NOT TO BE ELATED BY GREAT RICHES IS A PROOF OF REAL SUPERIORITY.

The word "add," especially the Chinese term here so rendered, implies that the person here spoken of is already wealthy. Han and Wei were two of the six great families of the State of Tsin,—of whom some account is given on I. Pt I. i. 1.

[884] CH. XII. WHEN A RULER'S AIM IS EVIDENTLY THE PEOPLE'S GOOD, THEY WILL NOT MURMUR AT HIS HARSHEST MEASURES.

The first part is explained rightly of toils in agriculture, road-making, bridge-making, &c.; and the second is supposed to refer to the administration of justice, but I should prefer thinking that Mencius had the idea of a just war before him. Compare Ana. XX. ii. 2.

[885] CH. XIII. THE INFLUENCE EXERTED BY A TRUE SOVEREIGN AND HIS RULE. THE DIFFERENT AND INFERIOR INFLUENCE OF A PRESIDENT OF THE STATES.

[886] *Par.* 1. "Brisk and cheerful;"—but the permanence of this cannot be looked for. In illustration of the condition and appearance of the people under a true sovereign, commentators generally quote a tradition of their state under Yaou, when, "entire harmony reigned under heaven, and the lives of the people passed easily away." Then the old men struck the clods, and sang:—

"We rise at sunrise,
We rest at sunset,
Dig wells and drink,
Till our fields and eat;—
What is the strength of the emperor to us?"

[887] *Par.* 2. There is the same difficulty in interpreting the first clause here of the administration of justice, which I have adverted to in the note on ch. xii.

[888] *Par.* 3. "The superior man" has the highest meaning of which the phrase is

XIV.[889] 1. Mencius said, "Kindly words do not enter into men so deeply as a reputation for kindness.[890]

2. "Good government does not lay hold of the people so much as good instructions.[891]

3. "Good government is feared by the people, [but] good instructions are loved by them. Good government gets the people's wealth, [but] good instructions get their hearts."[892]

XV.[893] 1. Mencius said, "The ability possessed by men without having been acquired by learning is their intuitive ability, and the knowledge possessed by them without the exercise of thought is their intuitive knowledge.[894]

2. "Children carried in the arms all know to love their parents; and when they are grown [a little], they all know to respect their elder brothers.

3. "Filial affection for parents is benevolence; respect for elders is righteousness. There is no other [cause for these feelings] they belong to all under heaven."[895]

XVI.[896] Mencius said, "When Shun was living amidst the deep retired mountains, dwelling with the trees and rocks, and wandering

---

susceptible, and = a sage, and even a sage on the throne. In the influence of Shun in the time of his obscurity, when the ploughmen yielded the furrow among themselves, and the potters made their vessels all sound, we have an example, it is said, of a sage's transforming influence wherever he passed through, or resided for a time. In what would have been the influence of Confucius, had he been in the position of a ruler, as described in Ana. XIX. xxv. 4, we have, it is said, an example of the spiritual nature of a sage, wherever he abides. A "spiritual" influence is one which is wonderful and mysterious, great but not palpable, like the plastic energy of nature,—the growth and transformations constantly going on under heaven and earth. These last terms show that a pantheistic view of the universe had come, at times at least, to supersede the idea of the operation of a personal God.

[889] CH. XIV. THE VALUE TO A RULER OF A GOOD REPUTATION AND OF MORAL INFLUENCES.

[890] *Par.* 1. Kindly words are but brief, and on an occasion. A reputation for kindness is the growth of time and of many evidences.

[891] *Par.* 2. "Good government" refers to the various enactments of law, affecting the external condition of the people "Good instructions" are the lessons of duty, which should be impressed in connection with these.—Commentators, to make out a connection between this par. and the former, say that the "good reputation" has grown out of the good government.

[892] *Par.* 3. Compare Ana. II. iii.

[893] CH. XV. BENEVOLENCE AND RIGHTEOUSNESS PROVED BY THE CASE OF CHILDREN TO BE NATURAL TO MAN, AND PARTS OF HIS CONSTITUTION.

[894] *Par.* 1. The phrases translated "intuitive ability," "intuitive knowledge" have also the idea of *goodness* in them.

[895] *Par.* 3. The latter half of this paragraph is by no means clear, or easily translated. I have given Choo He's view of it. Chaou K'e says:—"Those who wish to do good have nothing else to do but to extend these ways of children to all under heaven."

[896] CH. XVI. HOW WHAT SHUN WAS DISCOVERED ITSELF IN HIS GREATEST OBSCURITY.

Shun's emotion of mind was as here pictured.

with the deer and swine, the difference between him and the rude inhabitants of those remote hills was very small. But when he heard a single good word, or saw a single good action, he was like the Kĕang or the Ho, bursting its banks, and grandly flowing out in an irresistible flood."

XVII.[897] Mencius said, "Let a man not do what [his sense of righteousness tells him] not to do, and let him not desire what [the same sense tells him] not to desire:—to act thus is all that he has to do."

XVIII.[898] 1. Mencius said, "When men are possessed of intelligent virtue and prudence in the management of affairs, it generally arises from their having been in distress.

2. "They are the friendless minister and the despised concubine's son who keep their hearts under a sense of peril, and use deep precautions against calamity. They become in consequence distinguished for their intelligence."

XIX.[899] 1. Mencius said, "There are persons who serve the ruler;—they serve the ruler, that is, for the sake of his countenance and favor.[900]

2. There are ministers who seek the safety of the altars;—they find their pleasure in securing that tranquility.[901]

3. "There are those who are the people of Heaven;—[judging that], if they were in office, they could carry out [their principles] all under heaven, they proceed [so] to carry them out.[902]

4. "There are those who are great men;—they rectify themselves, and [all] things are rectified."[903]

XX.[904] 1. Mencius said, "The superior man has three things in which he delights, and to be sovereign over all under heaven is not one of them.

2. "That his father and mother are both alive, and that his brothers afford no cause [for distress of mind];—this is his first delight.

---

[897] CH. XVII. MAN'S WHOLE DUTY IS TO OBEY THE LAW IN HIMSELF.

It would not be easy to make this utterance intelligible without supplement. Chaou interprets and supplies thus: "Do not make a man do what you yourself do not do," &o.

[898] CH. XVIII. THE BENEFITS OF TROUBLE AND AFFLICTION;—ILLUSTRATED. Compare VI. Pt II. xv.

[899] CH. XIX. FOUR DIFFERENT CLASSES OF MINISTERS:—THE MERCENARY; THE LOYAL; THE UNSELFISH AND FAR-REACHING; THE TRULY GREAT.

[900] *Par.* 1. Mencius speaks of this class as only "persons,"—in contempt.

[901] *Par.* 2. Compare Pt II. xiv.

[902] *Par.* 3. Compare V. Pt I. vii. 5, though some contend that "the people of Heaven" has a wider meaning there than here. The phrase here denotes men who are contented with their position in obscurity, and would continue all their life in it, but are prepared at the same time to go forth to public duty, when they see the call.

[903] *Par.* 4. The "[all] things," must be understood first of the ruler and people.

[904] CH. XX. THE THREE THINGS WHICH THE SUPERIOR MAN DELIGHTS IN. ROYAL SWAY IS NOT ONE OF THEM.

A very fine chapter.

3. "That, when looking up, he has no occasion for shame before Heaven, and, below, he has no occasion to blush before men;—this is his second delight.

4. "That he gets hold of the individuals of the most superior abilities in the kingdom, and teaches and nourishes them;—this is his third delight.

5. "The superior man has three things in which he delights, and to be sovereign over all under heaven is not one of them."

XXI.[905] 1. Mencius said, "Wide territory and a numerous people are desired by the superior man, but what he delights in is not here.[906]

2. "To stand in the centre of the kingdom and give tranquility to the people within the four seas is an occasion of delight to the superior man; but [the highest element of] what belongs to him by his nature is not here.[907]

3. "What belongs to the superior man by his nature cannot be increased by the largeness of his sphere of action, nor diminished by his being in poverty and retirement;—for this reason, that it is determinately apportioned to him [by Heaven].[908]

4. "What belong to the superior man are—benevolence, righteousness, propriety, and knowledge, rooted in his heart. Their growth and manifestation are a mild harmony appearing in the countenance, a rich fullness in the back, and the character imparted to the four limbs. The four limbs understand [their several motions] without being told."[909]

XXII.[910] 1. Mencius said, "Pih-e, that he might avoid [the tyrant] Chow, was dwelling on the coast of the northern sea. When he heard of the rise of king Wăn , he roused himself and said, 'Why should I not attach myself to him? I have heard that the chief of the West knows well how to nourish the old' T'ae-kung, that he might avoid Chow, was

---

[905] CH. XXI. MAN'S NATURE THE MOST IMPORTANT THING TO HIM, AND THE SOURCE OF HIS GREATEST ENJOYMENT. ITS CONSTITUENTS AND THEIR MANIFESTATION. This also is a fine chapter, but it is not so intelligible as the last. There is a mistiness about the two last paragraphs.

[906] *Par.* 1. This describes the condition of the lord of a large State, who has many opportunities of doing good. Why he should not delight in it, as much as the subject of the next paragraph in his condition, I do not see.

[907] *Par.* 2. The subject of this par. is a true king, and why he should delight in his condition contrary to the dictum in par. 1 of last chapter, I do not see. "What belongs to his nature" would appear to be here as much as in the manifestations of it mentioned in par. 4.

[908] *Par.* 3. Does Mencius mean to say that the nature, being given from Heaven complete, cannot, where it is cherished, be added to or improved from without by any course of its possessor? What he seems to assert would need to be more clearly defined.

[909] *Par.* 4. Here our philosopher is more magniloquent than precise. The last sentence means that the limbs are instantaneously obedient to the will.

[910] CH. XXII. THE GOVERNMENT OF KING WĂN, BY WHICH HE SHOWED THAT HE KNEW WELL HOW TO SUPPORT THE OLD.

dwelling on the coast of the eastern sea. When he heard of the rise of king Wăn, he roused himself, and said, 'Why should I not attach myself to him? I have heard that the chief of the West knows well how to nourish the old.' If in the kingdom there were [now] a prince who knew well how to nourish the old, benevolent men would consider that he was the proper object for them to gather to.[911]

2. "Around the homestead with its five *mow*, the space at the foot of the walls was planted with mulberry trees, with which the [farmer's] wife nourished silkworms, and thus the old were able to have silk to wear. When the five brood-hens and the two brood-sows [of each family] were kept to their [breeding] seasons, the old were able to have flesh to eat. The husbandmen cultivated their fields of a hundred *mow*, and their families of eight mouths were secured against want.[912]

3. "The expression, 'The chief of the West knows well how to nourish the old,' referred to his regulations about the fields and dwellings, his teaching [the farmers] to plant [the mulberry tree], and nourish [those animals]; his instructing their wives and children, so that they should nourish their aged. At fifty warmth cannot be maintained without silks; and at seventy flesh is necessary to satisfy the appetite. [The aged], not kept warm, nor well supplied with food, are said to be 'starved and famished,' but among the people of king Wăn there were no aged in that condition.—This was the meaning of that expression."[913]

XXIII.[914] 1. Mencius said, "Let it be seen to that their fields of grain and flax are well cultivated, and make the taxes on them light:—so the people may be made rich.

2. "Let [the people] use their resources of food seasonably and expend them [only] on the prescribed ceremonies:—so they will be more than can be consumed.[915]

3. "The people cannot live without water and fire; yet, if you knock at a man's door in the dusk of the evening, and ask for water and fire, there is no one who will not give them, such is the great abundance of them. A sage would govern the kingdom so as to cause pulse and millet to be as abundant as fire and water. When pulse and millet are as abundant as fire and water, how shall there be among the people any

---

[911] *Par.* 1. See IV. Pt I. xiii. 1.

[912] *Par.* 2. This par. is to be translated historically, as it describes king Wăn's government. See I. Pt I. iii. 4; *et al.* Mencius has not mentioned before the number of brood hens and sows required to be kept by each family.

[913] *Par.* 3. By "fields" we are to understand the allotments of 100 *mow*, find by "dwellings," the homesteads, each with its five *mow*.

[914] CH. XXIII. THE FIRST CARE OF A GOVERNMENT, TO PROMOTE THE VIRTUE OF THE PEOPLE, SHOULD BE TO MAKE THEM WELL OFF; AND HOW THIS IS TO BE DONE.

[915] *Par.* 2. "Seasonably;"—see I. Pt I. iii. 3, 4. The "prescribed ceremonies" would be the occasions of capping, marriage, funerals, &c., excepting on which a strict economy was to be observed.

that are not virtuous?"[916]

XXIV.[917] 1. Mencius said, "Confucius ascended the eastern hill, and Loo appeared to him small. He ascended the T'ae mountain, and all beneath the heavens appeared to him small. So, he who has contemplated the sea finds it difficult to think anything of other waters; and he who has been a student in the gate of the sage finds it difficult to think anything of the words of others.[918]

2. "There is an art in the contemplation of water;—it is necessary to contemplate its swelling waves. When the sun or the moon is at its brightest, its light admitted [even] through an orifice is sure to illuminate.[919]

3. "Flowing water is a thing which does not proceed till it has filled the hollows [in its course]. The student who has set his mind on the doctrines [of the sage] does not come to the understanding of them but by completing one lesson after another."[920]

XXV.[921] 1. Mencius said, "He who rises at cock-crow, and addresses himself earnestly to the practice of what is good, is a disciple of Shun.[922]

2. "He who rises at cock-crow, and addresses himself earnestly to

---

[916] *Par.* 3. With the concluding sentiment compare VI. Pt I. vii. 1; *et al.*

[917] CH. XXIV. THE DOCTRINES OF THE SAGE, THOUGH GREAT, HAVE THEIR RADICAL PRINCIPLES, AND THE STUDENT CAN GET A KNOWLEDGE OF THEM ONLY BY A GRADUAL PROCESS.

[918] *Par.* 1. The higher one is, the smaller does what is beneath him appear to be: the more familiar we are with what is great, the more difficult do we find it to appreciate what is small. This appears to be the lesson in this paragraph, which is aptly compared to the *allusive* stanzas and odes in the Book of Poetry; the whole being designed to impress the mind with the greatness of the doctrines of the sage,—of Confucius, by way of eminence. There is a difficulty in identifying what is here called "the eastern hill." Some will have it to be a small hill, called Fang, in the present district of K'ëuh-fow, at the foot of which Confucius' parents were buried; others, the Mung hill (Ana. XVI. i. 4), in the district of Pe, department E-chow. Mount T'ae was the chief of the five great mountains of China. It lay on the extreme east of Ts'e,—in the present department of T'ae-gan, and about two miles from the city of that name. A place is shown on the mountain, barely half way to its summit, as the point to which Confucius ascended; v but there is a temple to him, now sadly dilapidated, near the summit itself. Confucius, no doubt, would go to the very top of it.

[919] *Par.* 2. The lesson here seems to be that the very greatness of the sage's doctrines must lead us to think of their elementary principles. Who can look at the foaming waves, and suppose that they are fortuitous and sourceless? The full-orbed sun or moon is so bright that we can hardly look at it, but its light evidences itself even through the smallest orifice. This par. is compared to the *metaphorical* stanzas and odes in the Book of Poetry.

[920] *Par.* 3. This par. is the practical application of the chapter. "Flowing water;"—see IV. Pt II. xviii. 2. "The student" is, literally, "the superior man,"—meaning such a man bent on learning the doctrines of the sage.

[921] CH. XXV. THE DIFFERENT RESULTS OF THE THOUGHT OF GOODNESS AND THE THOUGHT OF GAIN.

[922] *Par.* 1. "A disciple of Shun;"—*i.e.*, although such a man may not himself attain to be a sage, he is treading in the steps of one.

the pursuit of gain, is a disciple of Chih.[923]

3. "If you want to know what separated Shun from Chih it was nothing but this,—the interval between [the thought of] gain and [the thought of] goodness."

XXVI.[924] 1. Mencius said, "The principle of Yang-tsze was—'Each one for himself.' Though by plucking out one hair he might have benefited all under heaven, he would not have done it.[925]

2. "Mih-tsze loves all equally. If, by rubbing [bare all his body] from the crown to the heel, he could have benefited all under heaven, he would have done it.[926]

3. "Tsze-moh holds a medium [between these], and by holding that medium he is nearer the right. But by holding it without leaving room for the exigency of circumstances, it becomes like their holding their one point.[927]

4. "What I dislike in that holding one point is the injury it does to the way [of right principle]. It takes up one point and disregards a hundred others."[928]

XXVII.[929] 1. Mencius said, "The hungry think any food sweet, and the thirsty think the same of any drink; and thus they do not know the right [taste] of what they eat and drink. The hunger and thirst, [in fact,] injure [their palate]. And is it only the mouth and belly that are injured by hunger and thirst? Men's minds are also injured by them.[930]

2. "If a man can prevent the injurious evils of hunger and thirst from doing any injury to his mind, there need be no anxiety about his not being up with other men."[931]

---

[923] *Par.* 2. "Chih;"—see III. Pt II. x. 3.

[924] CH. XXVI. THE ERRORS OF YANG-TSZE, MIH-TSZE, AND TSZE-MOH. OBSTINATE ADHERENCE TO A PRINCIPLE, IRRESPECTIVE OF ALL OPPOSING CONSIDERATIONS, IS VERY PERILOUS.

[925] *Par.* 1. Yang-tsze is the Yang Choo of III. ii. ix. 3;—see what I have said on him in the *prolegomena.* One of the paragraphs there, exhibiting his sayings and views, contains the words here used to describe his principle by Mencius. It was, no doubt, current among scholars.

[926] *Par.* 2. Mih-tsze has appeared already in III. Pt I. v. 1, and Pt II. ix.;—see also the account of him and of his principle in the *prolegomena.*

[927] *Par.* 3. Tsze-moh is said to have belonged to Loo, but nothing more is known of him. What his principle was cannot therefore be defined. It could not have been that developed in the "Doctrine of the Mean;" what he held must have been something intermediate between the selfishness of Yang and the transcendentalism of Mih. What Mencius meant by "the exigency of circumstances" will be understood by a reference to IV. Pt I. xvii.

[928] *Par.* 4. The orthodox way of the scholars of China is to do what is right with reference to the whole circumstances of every case and time. See Mencius' defense of it in VI. Pt II. 1.

[929] CH. XXVII. THE IMPORTANCE OF NOT ALLOWING THE MIND TO BE INJURED BY POVERTY AND A MEAN CONDITION.

[930] *Par.* 1. With reference to the mind, hunger and thirst stand for poverty and a mean condition.

[931] *Par.* 2. "Other men" here are not the wealthy and honorable, but sages and

XXVIII.[932] Mencius said, "Hwuy of Lĕw-hĕa would not for the three highest offices at the royal court have changed his guiding plan of life."

XXIX.[933] Mencius said, "A man with definite aims to be accomplished may be compared to one digging a well. To dig the well to a depth of seventy-two cubits, [and stop] without reaching the spring, is after all throwing away the well."

XXX.[934] 1. Mencius said, "[Benevolence and righteousness] were natural to Yaou and Shun. T'ang and Woo made them their own. The five presidents of the States feigned them.[935]

2. "Having borrowed them long and not .returned them, how could it be known that they did not own them?"[936]

XXXI.[937] 1. Kung-sun Ch'ow said, "E Yin said, 'I cannot be near so disobedient a person,' and therewith he banished T'ae-kĕah to T'ung. The people were much pleased. When T'ae-kĕah became virtuous, he then brought him back; and the people were much pleased.[938]

2. "When worthies are ministers, and their rulers are not virtuous, may they indeed banish them in this way?"

3. Mencius replied, "If they have the mind of E Yin, they may. If they have not the mind, it would be usurpation."[939]

XXXII.[940] Kung-sun Ch'ow said, "It is said in the Book of Poetry,

---

worthies. Such a man is on the way to become one of them.

[932] CH. XXVIII. HWUY OF LĔW-HĔA'S STEADFAST ADHERENCE TO HIS PLAN OF LIFE.

On Hwuy of Lĕw-hĕa see II. Pt I. ix. 2, 3; *et al.* In V. Pt I. i. 5, a certain mildness, or accommodating of himself to others, is mentioned as Hwuy's characteristic, but Mencius takes care here that that should not be confounded with vacillating weakness. For the "three *kung*," or highest ministers at the royal court, see the Book of History, V. xx. 5.

[933] CH. XXIX. THAT LABOUR ONLY IS TO BE PRIZED WHICH ACCOMPLISHES ITS OBJECT.

Compare Ana. IX xviii; and VL Pt I. xix. The commentators mostly suppose that Mencius had the prosecution of learning in view; but the application of his words may be very wide.

[934] CH. XXX. THE DIFFERENCE OF THE CHARACTERS DISPLAYED BY YAOU AND SHUN, BY T'ANG AND WOO, AND BY THE FIVE PRESIDENTS OF THE STATES, AS NATURAL, ACQUIRED, AND FEIGNED.

[935] *Par.* 1. Mencius is speaking of the attributes displayed by the parties mentioned in their several rules. "The five presidents of the States;"—see VI. Pt II. vii.

[936] *Par.* 2. Some would interpret this par.:—"Having feigned them long, and not returned [to the right], how could they know that they did not [really] have them?"

[937] CH. XXXI. THE END MAY JUSTIFY THE MEANS IN DEALING WITH A BAD RULER, BUT THE PRINCIPLE IS NOT TO BE EASILY APPLIED.

[938] *Par.* 1. E Yin and his dealing with T'ae-kĕah;—see V. Pt I. vi. 5, and the Book of History, IV. v. Pt I. 9.

[939] *Par.* 3. The mind of E Yin was entirely loyal, and his aim was only the public good.—Compare for the general sentiment what Mencius says in V. Pt II. ix., and II. Pt II viii. 2.

[940] CH. XXXII. THE SERVICES WHICH A SUPERIOR MAN RENDERS TO A STATE

'He would not eat the bread of idleness!'

How is it that we see superior men eating without plowing?" Mencius replied, "When a superior man resides in any State, let its ruler employ his counsels, and he comes to tranquility, wealth, honor, and glory. Let the young in it follow his instructions, and they become filial, obedient to their elders, true-hearted, and faithful. What greater example can there be than this of not eating the bread of idleness?"

XXXIII.[941] 1. The king's son, Tëen, asked, saying, "What is the business of the [unemployed] scholar?"[942]

2. Mencius replied, "To exalt his aim."

3. "What do you mean by exalting the aim?" asked [the other]. The answer was, "[Setting it] simply on benevolence and righteousness. [The scholar thinks] how to put a single innocent person to death is contrary to benevolence; how to take what one has not [a right to] is contrary to righteousness; that one's dwelling-place should be benevolence, and one's path righteousness. When benevolence is the dwelling-place [of the mind], and righteousness the path [of the life], the business of the great man is complete."[943]

XXXIV.[944] Mencius said, "Supposing that the kingdom of Ts'e were offered, contrary to righteousness, to Chung-tsze, he would not receive it; and all men believe in him [as a man of the highest worth]. But this is [only] the righteousness which declines a small basket of rice and a dish of soup. A man can have no greater [crimes] than to

---

ENTITLE HIM, WITHOUT DOING OFFICIAL DUTY, TO SUPPORT.

We have here an instance of the insinuation repeatedly made by disciples of Mencius, that it was wrong in him to be supported by the princes, while he would not take office under them. Compare III Pt I. iv.; Pt II. iv.: *et al.* On the nature of Mencius' defense of his practice, see what I have said in the sketch of his Life and Character in the Prolegomena.

The Ode quoted from is the 8th of Book IX. Pt I.

[941] CH. XXXIII. HOW A SCHOLAR SHOULD PREPARE HIMSELF FOR THE DUTIES TO WHICH HE ASPIRES.

[942] *Par.* 1. Tëen was, probably, a son of king Seuen of Ts'e. In the time of the Warring State, the number of wandering scholars, seeking to be employed, had greatly increased. They were no favorites with Mencius, but he here answers the prince according to his ideal of the scholar.

[943] *Par.* 3. On benevolence as man's dwelling-place, and righteousness as man's path, see VI. Pt I. xi. We can hardly understand "the great man" here as in xix. 4. There it denotes sages, the highest style of man; here, the individuals in the various grades of official employment, with an implication, perhaps, that such a scholar was, fit for the highest office.

[944] CH. XXXIV. HOW MEN JUDGE WRONGLY OF CHARACTER, OVERLOOKING, IN THEIR ADMIRATION OF ONE ECCENTRIC EXCELLENCE, GREAT FAILURES AND DEFICIENCIES.

Chung-tsze, or Mr. Chung, is the Ch'in Chung of III. Pt II x., which chapter should be read in connection with this. On declining a small basket of rice, &c., see VI. Pt I. x. 6.

disown his parents and relatives, and [the relations of] ruler and minister, superiors and inferiors. How can it be allowed to give a man credit for the great [excellences] because he possesses a small one."

XXXV.[945] 1. T'aou Ying asked, saying, "Shun being emperor, and Kaou Yaou chief minister of justice, if Koo-sow had murdered a man, what would have been done in the case?"[946]

2. Mencius said, "[Kaou Yaou] would simply have apprehended him."[947]

3. "But would not Shun have forbidden such a thing?"

4. "Indeed," was the reply, "how could Shun have forbidden it? [The other] had received [the law] from a proper source."[948]

5. "In that case what would Shun have done?"[949]

6. [Mencius] said, "Shun would have regarded abandoning all under heaven as throwing away a worn-out sandal. He would privately have taken [his father] on his back, and withdrawn into concealment, living somewhere on the seaboard. There he would have been all his life, cheerful and happy, forgetting the empire."

XXXVI.[950] 1. Mencius, going from Fan to [the capital of] Ts'e, saw the sons of the king of Ts'e at a distance, and said with a sigh, "One's position alters the air, [just as] the nurture alters the body. Great is [the influence of] position! Are not [we] all men's sons."[951]

2. Mencius said, "The residences, the carriages and horses, and the dress of kings' sons, are mostly the same as those of other men. That the king's sons look so is occasioned by their position,—how much more should [a peculiar air distinguish] him whose position is in the wide house of the whole world![952]

3. "When the ruler of Loo went to Sung, he called out at the Tëeh-chih gate, the warder of which said, 'This is not our ruler, but how like

[945] CH. XXXV. WHAT SHUN AND HIS MINISTER OF JUSTICE WOULD HAVE DONE IF SHUN'S FATHER HAD COMMITTED A MURDER.

[946] *Par.* 1. T'aou Ying, it is supposed, was a disciple of Mencius. We hardly know anything more of him than what appears here. See Kaou Yaou's appointment to be minister of Justice in the Book of History, II. i. 20.

[947] *Par.* 2. He would have apprehended Koo-sow, and dealt with him according to his crime.

[948] *Par.* 4. The "proper source" from which Kaou Yaou had received the law, and especially that of death for the murderer, was Heaven. See Kaou Yaou's "Counsels" in the Book of History, II. iii.

[949] *Par.* 5. This is Mencius' view of what Shun would have done according to the Chinese idea of the relation of father and son.

[950] CH. XXXVI. HOW ONE'S ELEVATED SOCIAL POSITION AFFECTS HIS AIR, AND MUCH MORE MAY A SCHOLAR'S POSITION BE EXPECTED TO DO SO.

[951] *Par.* 1. Fan was at this time a city of Ts'e, and still gives its name to a district of Puh Chow, in the department of Tung-ch'ang. Chaou K'e says that it was an appanage of the king's sons by his concubines. We cannot tell, however, whether it was in Fan, or after his arrival at the capital, that Mencius saw the king's son or sons. The last sentence may also be understood—"Are not they—the king's sons—all men's sons?"

[952] *Par.* 2. "The wide house of the world:"—see III. Pt II. ii. 3.

is his voice to our ruler's!' This was occasioned by nothing but the correspondence of their positions."[953]

XXXVII.[954] 1. Mencius said, "To feed [a scholar] and not love him is to treat him as a pig; to love him and not respect him is to keep him as a domestic animal.

2. "Honoring and respecting are what should exist before any offering of gifts.

3. "If there be honoring and respecting without [that] reality of them, a superior man cannot be retained by such empty [demonstrations]"

XXXVIII.[955] Mencius said, "The bodily organs and the manifestations of sense belong to the heaven-conferred nature. But a man must be a sage, and then he may satisfy [the design of] his bodily organization."

XXXIX.[956] 1. King Seuen of Ts'e wanted to shorten the period of mourning. Kung-sun Ch'ow said, "To have a whole year's mourning is better than doing away with it altogether."[957]

2. Mencius said, "That is just as if there were one twisting round the arm of his elder brother, and you were merely to say to him, 'Gently, gently, if you please.' Your only course should be to teach him filial piety and fraternal duty."

3. [At that time] the mother of one of the king's sons had died, and his tutor asked for him that he might be allowed some months' mourning. Kung-sun Ch'ow said, "What do you say to this?"[958]

4. "This is a case," was the reply, "where the party wishes to complete the whole period, but finds it impossible to do so; the addition of a single day is better than not mourning at all. I spoke of the case where there was no hindrance and the thing was not done."

---

[953] *Par.* 3. The Tëeh-chih was the gate of the capital of Sung on the east.

[954] CH. XXXVII. THAT HE BE REALLY RESPECTED SHOULD BE ESSENTIAL TO A SCHOLAR'S REMAINING IN THE SERVICE OF A PRINCE.

This utterance was, no doubt, drawn forth by the conduct of the wandering scholars of Mencius' time, who were glad to be at a court for what they could get. There is admonition in it also to the kinglets and princes, who thought it enough, in order to get help from men who might be really scholars, to support them.

[955] CH. XXXVIII. ONLY BY A SAGE ARE THE BODILY ORGANS AND THE SENSES USED ACCORDING TO THEIR DESIGN.

Mencius' meaning is that, besides his body and his senses, man has his mind, with the principles of benevolence, righteousness, propriety, and knowledge; and the mind ought to rule the body. This is the will of Heaven.

[956] CH. XXXIX. REPROOF OF KUNG-SUN CH'OW FOR SEEMING TO ASSENT TO THE PROPOSAL TO SHORTEN THE PERIOD OF MOURNING. Compare Ana. XVII. xxi.

[957] *Par.* 1. The mourning here referred to was that of three years for a parent; but perhaps the king wanted to shorten the period in other cases as well.

[958] *Par.* 3. The "king's son" here, it is supposed, was a son by a concubine, and he was prevented by the jealous or other opposition of the queen proper from completing the full period of mourning. We cannot say whether this was the case or not. Other explanations of it have been devised; but it is not worth while to discuss them.

XL.[959] 1. Mencius said, "There are five ways by which the superior man teaches.[960]

2. "There are some on whom his transforming influence comes like seasonable rain.[961]

3. "There are some whose virtue he perfects, and some to whose talents he gives their development.[962]

4. "There are some whose inquiries he answers.[963]

5. "There are some who privately make themselves good, and correct themselves [from his example and recorded lessons].[964]

6. "These five are the ways by which the superior man teaches."

XLI.[965] 1. Kung-sun Ch'ow said, "Lofty are your doctrines and admirable, but [to learn them] may well be likened to ascending the heavens;—they seem to be unattainable. Why not [adapt them] so as to make those [learners] consider them nearly within their reach, and so daily exert themselves?"

2. Mencius said, "A great artificer does not, for the sake of a stupid workman, alter or do away with the marking-line. E did not, for the sake of a stupid archer, change his rule for drawing the bow to the full.[966]

3. "The superior man draws the bow to the full, but does not discharge the arrow;—in a way, [however,] which makes the thing leap [before the learner]. [So] does he stand in the middle of the right path;—those who are able follow him."[967]

---

[959] CH. XL. FIVE WAYS IN WHICH THE TEACHING OF THE SUPERIOR MAN IS EFFECTED.

[960] *Par.* 1. The wish of the superior man in all cases is one and the same,—to teach. His methods are modified, however, by the different characters of men. Five methods are specified here, and VI. Pt I. xvi. gives us another.

[961] *Par.* 2. This class only want the influence of the superior man, as plants need the rain and dew. So was it, it is said, with Confucius and his disciples Yen Hwuy and Tsăng-tsze.

[962] *Par.* 3. So was it with Confucius and the virtuous Jen K'ëw and Min Tsze-k'ëen, with the talented Tsze-loo and Tsze-kung.

[963] *Par.* 4. So was it with Confucius and Fan-ch'e (Ana. II. v.: *et al.*), with Mencius and Wan Chang.

[964] *Par.* 5. So was it with Confucius and Ch'in K'ang (Ana. XVI. xiii.), with Mencius and E Che (III. Pt I. v.). The best example of the case, however, is that of the influence of Confucius on our philosopher (IV. Pt II. xxii.).

[965] CH. XLI. THE TEACHER OF TRUTH MUST NOT LOWER HIS DOCTRINES TO ADAPT THEM TO THE CAPACITY OF HIS LEARNERS:—A LESSON TO KUNG-SUN CH'OW.

[966] *Par.* 2. E;—see IV. Pt II. xxiv.: *et al.*

[967] *Par.* 3. "In a way, however, which makes the thing leap before the learner;"—the phrase, "leaping-like," which requires to be so much supplemented, is difficult. It belongs, I think, to the superior man in all the action which is represented. No man can be taught how to hit; that is every man's own act. But he is taught to shoot, and that in so lively a manner, that the hitting also is, as it were, set forth before him. So with the teacher and learner of truth. As the learner tries to do as he is taught, he will be found laying hold of what seemed unapproachable.

XLII.[968] 1. Mencius said, "When right ways prevail throughout the kingdom, one's principles appear with one's person. When right ways disappear from the kingdom, one's person must vanish along with one's principles.

2. "I have not heard of one's principles being dependent for their manifestation on other men."

XLIII.[969] 1. The disciple Kung-too said, "When Kăng of T'ăng appeared at your gate, it seemed proper that a polite consideration should be shown to him, and yet you did not answer him;—why was that?"[970]

2. Mencius replied, "I do not answer him who questions me presuming on his ability, nor him who presumes on his talents and virtue, nor him who presumes on his age, nor him who presumes on services performed to me, nor him who presumes on old acquaintance:—I answer in none of these cases. And Kăng of T'ăng was chargeable with two of them."[971]

XLIV.[972] 1. Mencius said, "He who stops short where stopping is not proper will stop short in everything. He who behaves shabbily to those whom he ought to treat well will behave shabbily to all.

2. "He who advances with precipitation will retire with speed."

XLV.[973] Mencius said, "In regard to the [inferior] creatures, the superior man is loving, but does not show benevolence. In regard to people generally, he exercises benevolence but is not affectionate. He is affectionate to his parents, and exercises benevolence to people generally. He exercises benevolence to people generally, and is loving to [inferior] creatures."

---

[968] CH. XLII. ONE MUST LIVE OR DIE WITH HIS PRINCIPLES, ACTING FROM HIMSELF, NOT WITH REGARD TO OTHER MEN.

A man must direct his course from his own conviction of what is right, appearing in office when it is befitting, disappearing in obscurity, when to be in office would be inconsistent with his principles.

[969] CH. XLIII. DIFFERENT CLASSES WHOM MENCIUS WOULD NOT RECEIVE INTO HIS SCHOOL. HOW HE REQUIRED THE SIMPLE PURSUIT OF TRUTH IN THOSE WHOM HE TAUGHT. Compare VI. Pt II. ii.

[970] *Par.* 1. Kăng of T'ăng was, it is said, a younger brother of the ruler of T'ăng. His rank made Kung-too suppose that more than ordinary respect should have been shown to him, and yet it was one of those things, no doubt, which made Mencius jealously watch his spirit.

[971] *Par.* 2. The two things on which Kăng presumed were, it is supposed, his rank and his talents and virtue.

[972] CH. XLIV. WHERE VIRTUES ARE WANTING, DECENCIES CANNOT BE EXPECTED. PRECIPITATE ADVANCES ARE FOLLOWED BY SPEEDY RETREATS.

[973] CH. XLV. THE DIFFERENT SPHERES OF KINDNESS OR LOVINGNESS, OF BENEVOLENCE, AND OF AFFECTION.

Compare the language of Confucius on the graduated scale of regard and behavior to different classes of men in the Doctrine of the Mean, XX. 12. The utterance here was directed, most probably, against the Mihist doctrine of loving all equally.

XLVI.[974] 1. Mencius said, "The wise embrace all knowledge, but they are most earnest about what they ought to be most concerned about. The benevolent embrace all in their love, but to be earnest in cultivating an affection for the worthy is what most concerns them. [Even] the knowledge of Yaou and Shun did not extend to everything, but they were earnest about what first concerned them. The benevolence of Yaou and Shun did not show itself in [acts of] love to every man, but they were earnest in cultivating an affection for the worthy.[975]

2. "Not to be able to keep the three years' mourning, and to be very particular about that of three months, or that of five months; to eat immoderately and swill down the drink, and [at the same time] to inquire about [the precept] not to tear off the flesh with the teeth;—such things illustrate what I say about not knowing what is most to be attended to."[976]

## BOOK VII. TSIN SIN. PART II.

CHAPTER I.[977] 1. MENCIUS said, "Opposite indeed of benevolent was king Hwuy of Lĕang! The benevolent begin with what they [most] love, and proceed to what they do not [so naturally] love. Those who are not benevolent, beginning with what they do not [so naturally] love, proceed to what they [most] love."[978]

2. Kung-sun Ch'ow said, "What do you mean?" [Mencius replied], "King Hwuy of Lĕang, for the matter of territory, tore and destroyed his people by employing them in fighting. Having sustained a great defeat, he wished to fight again; and, fearing lest the people should not be able to get the victory, he urged his son, a youth, whom he loved, [to take the command,] and sacrificed him with them. This is what I

---

[974] CH. XLVI. ON KNOWING AND PURSUING WHAT IS MOST IMPORTANT TO BE KNOWN AND PURSUED:—ILLUSTRATED BY THE CASES OF YAOU AND SHUN, AND BY OPPOSITE INSTANCES.

[975] *Par.* 1. See the conversation of Confucius with Fan Ch'e in Ana. XII. xxii., where the principles enunciated here by Mencius are implied. The first two parts of the Book of History may also be referred to. In them we have Yaou and Shun looking out for the best men whom they could be friendly with and employ, and attending to the things which in their time and circumstances were most required for the well-being of the empire.

[976] *Par.* 2. The illustrations here are of men neglecting what is important, and concerned about what is trivial in comparison. For the references to customs at meals, see the Le Ke, I. Pt I. iii. 54-59. To tear off the roasted meat from a bone with the teeth was but a small matter compared with such an exhibition of gluttony as the other clauses speak of.

[977] CH. I. THE OPPOSITE WAYS OF THE BENEVOLENT AND THOSE WHO ARE NOT BENEVOLENT AN EMPHATIC CONDEMNATION OF KING HWUY OF LĔANG.

[978] *Par.* 1. King Hwuy of Lĕang;—see on I. Pt I. i. 1. See the gradation of loving regards in the benevolent in Pt I. xlv. With what is said of those who are not benevolent, we may compare Pt I. xliv.

call—beginning with what they do not [so naturally] love, and proceeding to what they [most] love."[979]

II.[980] 1. Mencius said, "In the 'spring and Autumn' there are no righteous wars. Instances indeed there are of one war better than another.[981]

2. "'Punitive expeditions' are when the supreme authority smites its subjects. Hostile States conduct no punitive expeditions against one another."[982]

III.[983] 1. Mencius said, "It would be better to be without the Book of History than to give entire credit to it.[984]

2. "In the 'Successful Completion of the War' I select two or three passages only, [and repose entire credit in them].[985]

3. "The benevolent man has no enemy under heaven. When [the prince] the most benevolent was attacking him who was the most the opposite, how could the blood have flowed till it floated the pestles of the mortars?"[986]

IV.[987] 1. Mencius said, "There are some who say, 'We are skilful at

---

[979] *Par.* 2. "He tore and lacerated his people;"—the characters suggest the idea of the king's dealing with his people as rice is dealt with when it is boiled to a pulpy mass. "He sacrificed his son;"—see I. Pt I. v. 1.

[980] CH. II. HOW ALL THE FIGHTINGS IN THE CH'UN TS'ĔW WERE UNRIGHTEOUS:—A WARNING TO THE WARRING STATES OF MENCIUS' TIME.

[981] *Par.* 1. "The Spring and Autumn;"—see t lie 5th volume of my larger work, "The Ch'un Ts'ĕw, with the Tso Chuen." "Wars;"—the term, according to the phraseology of the Spring and Autumn, should be translated "battles;" but Mencius meant, I believe, to indicate by it all the operations of war mentioned in the Classic of Confucius. We have there 23 battles or fightings, 213 attacks or smitings, with a multitude of "incursions," "sieges," "carryings away," "surprises," &c.

[982] *Par.* 2. "Punitive," or perhaps, from the composition of the Chinese term, I should say corrective, "expeditions" were competent only to the king, who might carry them out in his own person, or entrust them to one of the princes, or to a combination of them. and some of the presidents of the States in the Ch'un Ts'ĕw period might in a measure plead his delegation for their proceedings. Compare what Mencius says in VI Pt II vii. 2.

[983] CH. III. WITH WHAT ABATEMENT OF FAITH IN IT MENCIUS READ THE BOOK OF HISTORY.

[984] *Par.* 1. The utterance here seems at first sight of it in Chinese to mean—"It would be better to have no books, than to put entire credit in them;" but the reference in par. 2 shows that Mencius had in mind "the Book" *par excellence*,—the Book of History.

[985] *Par.* 2. See the Book of History, V. iii. The par. referred to-in the next par. here, about the bloodshed, is the 9th. "Passages" is literally "tablets," referring to the slips of wood or bamboo, on which the characters were pricked out with a *stylus*.

[986] *Par.* 3. The slaughter here described was made by the forces of the tyrant Chow turning against one another, and not by the troops of "the most benevolent" king Woo. The amount of it is probably exaggerated; but something of the kind is easily conceivable.

Some writers think that Mencius expressed himself so strongly, foreseeing what precedents for their abnormal courses might in future time be sought in the Book of History by rebels and oppressors. Compare our philosopher's rule for the interpretation of the Book of Poetry in V. Pt I. iv. 2.

[987] CH. IV. COUNSEL INTENDED FOR RULERS,—THAT THEY SHOULD NOT ALLOW

marshalling troops; we are skilful at conducting battles.' They are great criminals.[988]

2. "If the ruler of a State love benevolence, he will have no adversary under heaven.[989]

3. "When [T'ang] was conducting his punitive expeditions in the south, the rude tribes on the north murmured. When he was doing so in the east, the rude tribes on the west murmured Their cry was,—'Why does he make us last?'[990]

4. "When king Woo attacked Yin, he had [only] three hundred chariots of war, and three thousand guards.[991]

5. "The king said, 'Do not fear. Let me give you repose. I am no enemy to the people.'[On this] they bowed their heads to the ground, like the horns [of animals] falling off.[992]

6. "The phrase 'punitive expedition' has in it the meaning of correction. Each [State] wishing to have itself corrected, what need is there for fighting?"[993]

V.[994] Mencius said, "Cabinet-makers, builders, wheelwrights, and carriage-builders can give to a man the compass and square, but they cannot make him skilful [in the use of them]."

VI.[995] Mencius said, "Shun ate [his] parched grain, and partook of [his] coarse herbs, as if he were to be doing so all his life. When he became emperor, and had the embroidered robes to wear, [his] lute to play on, and [Yaou's] two daughters to wait on him, he was as if those things belonged to him as a matter of course."

VII.[996] Mencius said, "From this time forth I know the heavy

---

THEMSELVES TO BE DECEIVED BY MEN WHO WOULD ADVISE THEM TO WAR. GRAND SUCCESS IS TO BE OBTAINED BY BENEVOLENCE.

[988] *Par.* 1. Compare IV. Pt I. xiv., and VI. Pt II. ix.

[989] *Par.* 2. See the saying at the beginning of par. 3 of the preceding chapter.

[990] *Par.* 3. See I. Pt II. xi. 2: *et al.*

[991] *Par.* 4. In the Preface to the Book of History, par. 3, it is said that on the occasion referred to here Woo had 300 war chariots, and 300 guards. Much has been written on the difference between the two statements, but it is needless to enter here on the matter. Mencius wants to show that Woo's forces were very small as compared with those of his opponent;—and so, no doubt, they were.

[992] *Par.*5 See the Book of History, V. i. Pt II. 9; but the text of that Classic is hardly recognizable in Mencius' version of it, and the meaning of Woo's words in the two Works is different. I do not know how to account for the different texts.

[993] *Par.* 6. See the note on par. 2 of chapter ii.

[994] CH. V. REAL ATTAINMENTS MUST BE MADE BY THE LEARNER FOR HIMSELF.

For the general sentiment compare Pt I. xli. The same names of workers in wood, &c., occur in III. Pt II. iv.

[995] CH. VI. THE EQUANIMITY OF SHUN IN POVERTY AND AS EMPEROR.

[996] CH. VII. THE THOUGHT OR ITS CONSEQUENCES SHOULD MAKE MEN CAREFUL OF THEIR CONDUCT:—ILLUSTRATED BY THE RESULT OF KILLING THE NEAR RELATIVES OF ANOTHER.

This remark was made, probably, as observed by Choo He, with reference to some particular case which had come under Mencius' observation. It was a maxim of Chinese society, sanctioned by Confucius, that "a man should not live under the same heaven with

consequences of killing a man's near relations. When a man kills another's father, that other will kill his father; when a man kills another's elder brother, that other will kill his elder brother. So he does not himself indeed do the act, but there is only a [small] interval [between him and it]"

VIII.[997] 1. Mencius said, "Anciently, the establishment of frontier-gates was to guard against violence.[998]

2. "Now-a-days, it is to exercise violence."[999]

IX.[1000] Mencius said, "If a man do not himself walk in the right way, it will not be walked in [even] by his wife and children. If he order others but not according to the right way, he will not be able to get the obedience [even] of his wife and children."

X.[1001] Mencius said, "A bad year cannot prove the cause of death to him whose [stores of] what is needful are complete; an age of corruption cannot throw him into disorder whose [equipment of] virtue is complete."

XI.[1002] Mencius said, "A man who loves fame may be able to decline a kingdom of a thousand chariots; but if he be not [really] the man [to do such a thing], it will appear in his countenance in the matter of a small basket of rice, or a dish of soup."

XII.[1003] 1. Mencius said, "If the benevolent and worthy be not confided in, a State will become empty and void.[1004]

2. "Without the rules of propriety and distinctions of what is right, high and low will be thrown into confusion.

3. "Without the various business of government, there will not be

---

the slayer of his father, nor in the same State with the slayer of his elder brother."

[997] CH. VIII. THE BENEVOLENCE OF ANCIENT RULE AND THE SELFISHNESS OF MODERN SEEN IN THE REGULATIONS ABOUT THE FRONTIER-GATES.

[998] *Par.* 1. Anciently the object contemplated by these gates was to prevent the ingress or egress of parties dangerous to the State.

[999] *Par.* 2. In Mencius' time they were maintained chiefly for the collection of duties.—Compare II. Pt I. v. 3.

[1000] CH. IX. HOW A MAN'S INFLUENCE DEPENDS ON HIS OWN EXAMPLE AND PROCEDURE.

His wife and children are the most amenable to a man's example and orders, but unless he is all right in his example and procedure, they will not be or do what is right;—how much less other men! On the latter part compare Ana. XIII. xiii.

[1001] CH. X. CORRUPT TIMES ARE PROVIDED AGAINST BY ESTABLISHED VIRTUE. Compare the Doctrine of the Mean, XX. 16.

[1002] CH. XI. A MAN'S TRUE DISPOSITION WILL APPEAR IN SMALL MATTERS, WHEN A LOVE OF FAME MAY HAVE ENABLED HIM TO DO GREAT THINGS.

Choo He says on this:—"A man is seen not so much in things that require an effort as in things which he thinks little of. By bearing this in mind when we observe him, we can see what he really rests in." Chaou K'e, on the contrary, takes the utterance superficially, as an approval of the love of fame.

[1003] CH. XII. THREE THINGS ARE ESSENTIAL TO THE WELL-BEING OF A STATE:—THE RIGHT MEN; THE RULES OF PROPRIETY; AND WISE ADMINISTRATION.

[1004] *Par.* 1. This condition not obtaining, such men will leave the State, and then it will become as if no men were in it.

resources sufficient for the expenditure."[1005]

XIII.[1006] Mencius said, "There are instances of individuals without benevolence who have got possession of a [single] State, but there is no instance of the whole kingdom's being got by one without benevolence."

XIV.[1007] 1. Mencius said, "The people are the most important element [in a country]; the Spirits of the land and grain are the next; the ruler is the lightest.[1008]

2. "Therefore to gain the peasantry is the way to become the son of Heaven; to gain the son of Heaven is the way to become the prince of a State; to gain the prince of a State is the way to become a great officer.[1009]

3. "When the prince of a State endangers the altars of the Spirits of the land and grain, he is changed and another appointed [in his place].[1010]

4. "When the sacrificial victims have been perfect, the millet in its vessels all pure, and the sacrifices offered at their proper seasons, if there yet ensue drought or inundations, then the altars of the Spirits of the land and grain are changed, and others appointed."[1011]

XV.[1012] Mencius said, "A sage is the teacher of a hundred

---

[1005] *Par.* 3. The various business of government refers to all the sources of revenue and their administration.

[1006] CH. XIII. ONLY BY THE BENEVOLENT CAN THE KINGDOM BE GOT.

A commentator observes:—"From the dynasty of Ts'in downwards, there have been cases when the empire was got by men without benevolence; but it has been lost again in such instances after one or two reigns."

[1007] CH. XIV. THE DIFFERENT CONSTITUENTS OF A COUNTRY IN RESPECT OF THEIR IMPORTANCE;—THE RULER, THE TUTELARY SPIRITS, AND THE PEOPLE.

[1008] *Par.* 1. Translated into our modes of thinking, the three elements in a nation would be,—the ruler, the established religion, and the people. It is not easy to determine the exact force of the terms by which the second element is described;—whether we are to understand merely the altars to the tutelary Spirits, or those Spirits themselves. Choo He takes the former view; other commentators maintain the latter;—and with them I am inclined to agree. Of course when the presiding Spirits were changed, the place and form of their altars might also be changed.

[1009] *Par.* 2. This shows that the people are the most important constituent in a country. "The peasantry" is here equivalent to "the people," the land being the source of the maintenance of all classes, and the original constitution of the Chinese nation as a whole, as well as of every State, being based on recognition of this. Even the highest authority therefore came from the people.

[1010] *Par.* 3. This shows that the tutelary Spirits of a State were of more importance than its ruler.

[1011] *Par.* 4. This shows that the people were still more important than the tutelary Spirits. They were appointed and worshipped for the good of the people; the people did not exist for them.—No chapter in his Works shows the boldness of Mencius' thinking more than this.

[1012] CH. XV. THAT PIH-E AND HWUY OF LÊW-HÊA WERE SAGES IS PROVED BY THE PERMANENCE OF THEIR INFLUENCE.

Compare V. Pt II. i., and the references there given. I do not think that Mencius intended *sages* here to be understood in the highest sense of the name. Confucius is "the generations;—this is true of Pih-e and Hwuy of Lĕw-hĕa. Therefore when men [now] hear the character of Pih-e, the corrupt become pure, and the weak acquire determination. When they hear the character of Hwuy of Lĕw-hĕa, the mean become generous, and the niggardly become liberal. [Those two] made themselves distinguished a hundred generations back, and, a hundred generations after them, those who hear of them are all aroused [in this manner]. Could such effects be produced by them if they had not been sages? And how much more did they affect those who were in contiguity with them and warned by them!"

XVI.[1013] Mencius said, "By benevolence is meant [the distinguishing characteristic of] man. When it is embodied in man's conduct, we have what we call the path [of duty]."

XVII.[1014] Mencius said, "When Confucius was about to leave Loo, he said, 'I will go by and by;'—it was right that he should leave the State of his parents in this way. When he was leaving Ts'e, he took with his hands the water from the rice which was being washed in it, and went away [With the rice uncooked];—it was right he should leave another State in this way."

XVIII.[1015] Mencius said, "The reason why the superior man was reduced to straits between Ch'in and Ts'ae was because none of the rulers or of their ministers communicated with him."

XIX.[1016] 1. Mih K'e said, "Greatly am I without anything to depend on from the mouths [of men]."[1017]

2. Mencius replied, "There is no harm in that. Scholars suffer more than others from the mouths of people.

3. It is said in the Book of Poetry,

'My anxious heart is full of trouble;
I am hated by the herd of mean people.'

---

teacher of ten thousand generations."

[1013] CH. XVI. THE PRINCIPLE OF BENEVOLENCE IN MAN'S NATURE, AND IN HIS CONDUCT.

Compare VI. Pt I. xi. 1. See also the Doctrine of the Mean, XX. 5.

[1014] CH. XVII. THE DIFFERENT WAYS IN WHICH CONFUCIUS LEFT LOO AND TS'E. See V. Pt II. i. 4.

[1015] CH. XVIII. THE REASON OF CONFUCIUS BEING IN STRAITS BETWEEN CH'IN AND TS'AE.

See Ana. XI. ii., which puts it beyond doubt that by "the superior man" here we are to understand Confucius. So to designate him, however, is not after the usual style of our philosopher.

[1016] CH. XIX. MENCIUS COMFORTS ONE MIH K'E UNDER CALUMNY BY THE REFLECTION THAT DISTINGUISHED MEN WERE MORE ESPECIALLY EXPOSED TO SUCH A THING.

[1017] *Par.* 1. Mih K'e was, it is supposed, a scholar of the time. He was smarting, we must assume, under some calumny when he had this conversation with Mencius.

[Such was the case of] Confucius. And again,

> 'Though he could not prevent the rage [of his foes],
> He did not let fall his own fame.'

[Such was the case of] king Wăn."[1018]

XX.[1019] Mencius said, "[Anciently], men of virtue and talents by means of their own enlightenment made others enlightened. Now-a-days, [those who would be deemed such, seek] by means of their own darkness to make others enlightened."

XXI.[1020] Mencius said to Kaou-tsze, "There are the narrow foot-paths along the hills;—if suddenly they be used, they become roads, and if in a short space they are [again] disused, the wild grass fills them up. Now the wild grass is filling up your mind, Sir."

XXII.[1021] 1. Kaou-tsze said, "The music of Yu was better than that of king Wăn."

2. Mencius asked, "On what ground do you say so?" and the other replied, "Because the knob of [Yu's] bells is nearly worn through."

3. Mencius rejoined, "How can that be a sufficient proof? Have the ruts at a city-gate been made [merely] by the two horsed carriage?"

XXIII.[1022] 1. There was a famine in Ts'e, and, Ch'in Tsin said [to

---

[1018] *Par.* 3. See the Book of Poetry, Pt I. iii., Ode I. 4, and Pt III. i. Ode III. 8. It is difficult to see why Mencius should apply the former passage to Confucius, and the latter to king Wăn.

[1019] CH. XX. How of Old Men of Worth Led on Men by their Example, While in Mencius' Time it was Tried by Rulers to Urge Men Contrary to their Example.

Of old laws and example went together in the ruling class; in Mencius' time there remained the laws, but the example was all bad.

[1020] CH. XXI. That the Cultivation of the Mind Should Not be Intermitted.

Kaou-tsze,—see on VI. Pt II. iii. 1. The individual here would seem to be the same as the one in II. Pt II. xii. 2. Chaou K'e says that after studying with Mencius for some time, and before he fully understood his principles, he went off and addicted himself to some other teacher, so that what our philosopher here says to him was with reference to this course and its consequences.

[1021] CH. XXII. Refutation of an Absurd Remark of Kaou-Tsze About Yu's Music Being Better Than That of King Wăn.

What Kaou insisted on as the basis of his assertion was only the effect of time or long use. As Yu was long anterior to king Wăn, those of his bells which remained were necessarily more worn than the more recent ones, but this did not imply any superiority of the music which they made. At the entrance to a gate the road contracts, and all the carriages which had been distributed over its breadth are obliged to run in the same ruts, which hence are deeper there than elsewhere. How much more must this be the case when in the case supposed we have to think of the two-horsed carriages of the Hëa dynasty, followed by the three-horsed ones of the Shang, and those by the four-horsed of the Chow!

[1022] CH. XXIII. How Mencius Knew Where to Stop and Maintain His Own

Mencius], "The people are all thinking that you, Master, will again obtain for them the opening of [the granary of] T'ang, but I apprehend you will not do so a second time."[1023]

2. [Mencius] replied, "To do so would be to act like Fung Foo. There was a man of that name in Tsin, distinguished for his skill in seizing tigers. He afterwards became a scholar of reputation, and going once into the wild country, he found a crowd in pursuit of a tiger. The tiger took refuge in a corner of a hill, where no one dared to attack him; but when the people descried Fung Foo, they ran and met him. He [immediately] bared his arms, and descended from his carriage. The multitude were pleased with him, but those who were scholars laughed at him."[1024]

XXIV.[1025] 1. Mencius said, "For the mouth to desire tastes, the eye colors, the ear sounds, the nose odors, and the four limbs ease and rest;—these things are natural. But there is the appointment [of Heaven in connation with them]; and the superior man does not say [in his pursuit of them], 'It is my nature'.[1026]

2. "[The exercise of] love between father and son, [the observance of] righteousness between ruler and minister, the rules of ceremony between guest and host, [the display of] knowledge in [recognizing] the able and virtuous, and the [fulfilling the whole] heavenly course by the sage:—these are appointed [by Heaven and may be realized in different degrees]. But there is [an adaptation of our] nature [for them], and the superior man does not say [in reference to them], 'There is a [limiting] appointment [of Heaven].'"[1027]

---

DIGNITY IN HIS INTERCOURSE WITH THE PRINCES.

[1023] *Par.* 1. Ch'in Tsin,—see II. Pt. II. iii.; *et al.* At T'ang, the name of which is still preserved in the village of Kan-t'ang, district of Tseih-mih, department Lae-chow, Shantung, the rulers of Ts'e, it would appear, kept grain in store, and on some previous occurrence of famine, Mencius had advised the king to open the granary and give out its contents. In the mean time, however, he had not found the king willing to obey his higher counsels, and intended to leave the State. He considered that his work in Ts'e was done, and that it would be inconsistent with his character to make such an application as he had done before.—I must believe also that the famine at this time was not very severe.

[1024] *Par.* 2. It did not belong to Fung Foo, now an officer and scholar, to be fighting with tigers and playing the part of a bravo.

[1025] CH. XXIV. THE SUPERIOR MAN SUBJECTS THE GRATIFICATION OF HIS NATURAL APPETITES TO THE WILL OF HEAVEN, AND PURSUES THE DOING OF GOOD WITHOUT THINKING THAT THE AMOUNT WHICH HE CAN DO MAY BE LIMITED BY THAT WILL.

[1026] *Par.* 1. Every appetite naturally desires its unlimited gratification, but a limited amount or an entire denial of such gratification may be the will of Heaven; and the superior man submits to that will. He holds that the appetites belong to the part of his constitution which is less noble;—see VI. Pt I. xiv.

[1027] *Par.* 2. Underneath this paragraph there lies the Mercian doctrine of human nature as formed for the practice of what is good.—Choo He says well on the whole:—"I have heard it observed by my master that the things mentioned in both of these paragraphs are in the constitution of our nature, and are limited also by the appointment of Heaven. Mankind, however, consider that the former five are more especially natural,

XXV.[1028] 1. Haou-Săng Puh-hae asked, saying, "What sort of man is Yoh-ching?" Mencius replied, "He is a good man, a real man."[1029]

2. "What do you mean by 'A good man?' What do you mean by 'A real man?'"

3. The reply was, "A man who commands our liking is what is called *good*.[1030]

4. "He whose [goodness] is part of himself is what is called *a real man*.

5. "He whose [goodness] is accumulated in full measure is what is called a *beautiful man*.

6. "He whose completed [goodness] is brightly displayed is what is called *a great man*.

7. "When this great man exercises a transforming influence, he is what is called *a sage*.

8. "When the sage is beyond our knowledge, he is what is called *a spirit-man*.[1031]

9. "Yoh-ching is between the [first] two characters, and below the [last] four."

XXVI.[1032] 1. Mencius said, "Those who are fleeing from [the errors of] Mih naturally turn to Yang, and those who are fleeing from [the errors of] Yang naturally turn to orthodoxy. When they so turn, they should at once and simply be received.[1033]

---

and, though they may be prevented from obtaining them, still desire them; and that the latter five are indeed appointed by Heaven, but if the fulfillment of them does not come to them readily, they do not go on to pat forth their strength to attain to it. On this account Mencius shows what is most important in each case, that he may induce a broader way of thinking in regard to the latter class, and repress the way of thinking in regard to the former."

[1028] CH. XXV. THE CHARACTER OF YOH-CHING. DIFFERENT DEGREES OF ATTAINMENT IN CHARACTER.

[1029] *Par.* 1. Chaou K'e says that Haou-săng Puh-hae was a man of Ts'e. Nothing is known of him. Yoh-ching,—see I. Pt II. xvi., *et al.*, especially VI. Pt II. xiv.

[1030] *Par.* 3. It is assumed here that the general verdict of mankind will be on the side of goodness. Hence when a man is *desirable*, and commands universal liking, he must be a *good* man.

[1031] *Par.* 8. Compare with this what is said in the Doctrine of the Mean, ch. xxiv., that "the individual possessed of complete sincerity is like a Spirit." It is said that the expression in the text is stronger than that there, but the two are substantially to the same effect. Ch'ing-tsze says here, "Sage and beyond our knowledge denotes the utmost profundity of sage-hood, what is unfathomable by men. We are not to suppose that above the sage there is another style of man,—the spirit-man." Some would indeed say here—"the divine man," but that is a rendering of the Chinese term which it never admits of; and yet in applying to man the term appropriate to Him whose way is in the sea and His judgments a great deep, Chinese writers are guilty of blasphemy in the sense of derogating from the prerogatives of God.

[1032] CH. XXVI. RECOVERED HERETICS SHOULD BE RECEIVED WITHOUT CASTING THEIR OLD ERRORS IN THEIR TEETH.

[1033] *Par.* 1. Many of the commentators protest against its being supposed from the words of Mencius that he thought worse of the errors of Mih than he did of those of

2. "Those who now-a-days dispute with [those who had been] Yangists and Mihists, do so as if they had been pursuing a stray pig, the leg of which, after they have got it to enter the pen, they proceed to tie."[1034]

XXVII.[1035] Mencius said, "There are the exactions of hempen cloth and silken thread, of grain, and of personal service. The wise ruler requires but one of these [at once], deferring the other two. If he require two of them [at once], then the people die of hunger. If he require the three [at once], then fathers and sons are separated."

XXVIII.[1036] Mencius said, "The precious things of the prince of a State are three;—the territory, the people, and the business of the government. If a prince value as most precious pearls and gems, calamity is sure to befall him."

XXIX.[1037] P'wan-shing Kwoh having obtained an official situation in Ts'e, Mencius said, "He is a dead man,—P'wan-shing Kwoh!" P'wan-shing Kwoh having been put to death, the disciples asked, saying, "How did you know, Master, that he would be put to death?" Mencius replied, "He was a man who had a little ability, but he had not learned the great principles of the superior man. He was just qualified to bring death upon himself, but for nothing more."

XXX.[1038] 1. When Mencius went to Tăng, he was lodged in the upper palace. A sandal in the process of making had been placed there in a window, and when the keeper of the place [came to] look for it, he could not find it.

---

Yang. It is certainly not easy to understand the process of conversion as indicated by our philosopher. We must rank Yang as far more astray than Mih. "Turn to orthodoxy" is, literally, "turn to the learned." "The learned" in Chinese phrase is equivalent to our "the orthodox." The name is still claimed by the followers of Confucius in opposition to the Taouists and Buddhists.

[1034] *Par.* 2. Not the orthodox of China only have dealt with recovered heretics in the way that Mencius condemns.

[1035] CH. XXVII. THE JUST EXACTIONS OF THE GOVERNMENT SHOULD BE MADE DISCRIMINATINGLY AND CONSIDERATELY.

The tax of cloth and silk was due in summer, that of grain after harvest, and personal service,—in war, building, road-making, &C., in winter, when it would not interfere with the labors of husbandry. The government ought to require them at their proper seasons, and only one at a time.

[1036] CH. XXVIII. THE PRECIOUS THINGS OF THE PRINCE OF A STATE, AND THE DANGER OF HIS OVERLOOKING THEM FOR OTHER THINGS.

[1037] CH. XXIX. A LITTLE ABILITY, WITHOUT A KNOWLEDGE OF GREAT PRINCIPLES, MAY BE A PERILOUS THING:—ILLUSTRATED BY THE CASE OF P'WAN-SHING KWOH.

Compare Confucius' prediction of the death of Tsze-loo;—Ana. XI xii. Nothing is known of the P'wan-shing Kwoh here, though Chaou K'e says that he had wished to be a disciple of Mencius, but had soon gone away, not understanding what he heard.

[1038] CH. XXX. AN AWKWARD DISAPPEARANCE OF A SANDAL FROM MENCIUS' LODGING. HIS READINESS TO RECEIVE LEARNERS WITHOUT INQUIRING INTO THEIR PAST HISTORY.

T'ăng,—see on I. Pt II. xiii. "The upper palace" was the name, probably, of a palace in the capital of T'ăng, appropriated to the lodging of honorable visitors.

2. [On this], some one asked [Mencius] about the matter, saying, "Is it thus that your followers pilfer?" "Do you think, Sir," was the reply, "that they came here for the purpose of pilfering the sandal?" The man said, "I apprehend not. But you, Master, having arranged to give lessons, do not go back to inquire into the past, and you do not reject those who come to you. If they come with the mind [to learn], you at once receive them without any more ado."

XXXI.[1039] 1. Mencius said, "All men have some things which they cannot bear [to see];—extend that feeling to what they can bear, and the result will be benevolence. All men have some things which they will not do;—extend that feeling to the things which they do, and righteousness will be the result.[1040]

2. "If a man can give full development to the feeling which makes him shrink from injuring others, his benevolence will be more than can be put into practice. If he can give full development to the feeling which refuses to dig through or jump over [a wall, for a bad purpose], his righteousness will be more than can be put into practice.

3. "If a man can give full development to the real feeling [of dislike] with which he receives [the salutation of] 'Thou,' 'Thou' he will act righteously in all places and circumstances.[1041]

4. "When a scholar speaks what he ought not to speak, by his speaking seeking to gain some end, and when he does not speak what he ought to speak, by his silence seeking to gain the same end;—both these cases are of a piece with digging through or jumping over a wall."

XXXII.[1042] 1. Mencius said, "Words which are plain and simple, while their scope is far-reaching, are good words. Principles which, as held, are compendious, while their application is extensive, are good principles. The words of the superior man do not go below the girdle, but [great] principles are contained in them.[1043]

---

[1039] CH. XXXI. A MAN HAS ONLY TO GIVE DEVELOPMENT TO THE PRINCIPLES OF GOOD WHICH ARE NATURAL TO HIM AND SHOW THEMSELVES IN SOME THINGS, TO BE ENTIRELY GOOD AND CORRECT.

[1040] *Par.* 1. Compare II. Pt I. vi.; *et al.* The sentiment of this chapter is continually insisted on by Mencius; but it supposes that man has much more power over himself than he really has.

[1041] *Par.* 3. "Thou," "Thou," is a style of address greatly at variance with Chinese notions of propriety. It can only be used with the very young and the very mean. However it may be submitted to occasionally, there is a real feeling of dislike to it; and if a man be as careful to avoid all other things which would make him be looked down upon, or liberties be taken with him, he will everywhere quit himself as a righteous man.

[1042] CH. XXXII. THE WAY TO ARRIVE AT WHAT IS REMOTE IS TO ATTEND TO WHAT IS NEAR. WHAT ARE GOOD WORDS AND GOOD PRINCIPLES. WHEREIN MEN ERR IN DEALING WITH THEMSELVES AND OTHERS.

[1043] *Par.* 1. "Do not go below the girdle,"—see the Book of Rites, I. Pt II ch. iii. 14, where we have the rule for looking at the sovereign, the eyes not going above his collar nor below his girdle. Generally, the ancient rule was—not to look at a person below the girdle, so that all above might be considered as plain and near, beneath the eyes. Chaou K'e says merely that "words not below the girdle are from near the heart."

2. "The principle which the superior man holds is that of personal cultivation, but all under heaven is thereby tranquillized.[1044]

3. "The disease of men is this:—that they neglect their own fields and go to weed the fields of others, and that what they require from others is great, while what they lay upon themselves is light."

XXXIII.[1045] 1. Mencius said, "Yaou and Shun were what they were by nature; T'ang and Woo were so by returning to [their natural virtues].[1046]

2. "When all the movements in the countenance and every turn [of the body], are exactly according to propriety, that shows the greatest degree of complete virtue. Weeping for the dead [should be] the expression of [real] sorrow, and not as the [proper affection] of the living. The regular path of virtue [is to be pursued] without any bend, from no view to emolument. Words should be in themselves sincere, not with a desire to make one's conduct [appear to be] correct.[1047]

3. "The superior man obeys the law [of right], and waits simply for what is appointed."[1048]

XXXIV.[1049] 1. Mencius said, "Those who give counsel to great men should despise them, and not look at their pomp and display.[1050]

2. "Halls several times eight cubits high, with beams projecting at the eaves several cubits;—these, if I could realize my wishes, I would not have. Food spread before me over ten cubits square, and attendant girls to the number of several hundred;—these, if I could realize my wishes, I would not have. Pleasure and drinking, and the dash of hunting, with a thousand chariots following after me;—these, if I could realize my wishes, I would not have. What they esteem are what I would have nothing to do with; what I esteem are the rules of the ancients.—Why should I stand in awe of them?"[1051]

XXXV.[1052] Mencius said, "For nourishing the mind there is

---

[1044] *Par.* 2. This is the explanation of good principles,—compendious, but of extensive application. It is a good summary of the teaching of "The Great Learning."

[1045] CH. XXXIII. THE VIRTUE OF THE HIGHEST SAGES, AND HOW OTHER MEN MAY TRY TO FOLLOW IT.

[1046] *Par.* 1. Compare Pt I. xxx.

[1047] *Par.* 2. Here is the highest virtue, where everything is done right, with no motive beyond the doing so. If the dead be mourned for as the tribute due to them from the living, a depraving element has been admitted into the grief.

[1048] *Par.* 3. Here is a virtue equally correct as the above, but from an intellectual constraint.

[1049] CH. XXXIV. HE WHO UNDERTAKES TO COUNSEL THE GREAT SHOULD IN HIS TASTES AND PRINCIPLES BE FAR ABOVE THEM.

[1050] *Par.* 1. The "great men" here are merely the socially great. Mencius had special reference to the princes and nobles of his time, dignified by their position, but with no corresponding moral qualities.

[1051] *Par.* 2. This is a good description of Mencius' own tastes and principles, but it is somewhat magniloquent.

[1052] CH. XXXV. THE REGULATION OF THE DESIRES IS ESSENTIAL TO THE HEALTHY MORAL NOURISHMENT OF THE MIND.

The Works of Mencius.

nothing better than to make the desires few. Here is a man whose desires are few:—there may be some [right qualities] not kept in his heart, but they will be few. Here is a man whose desires are many;—there may be some [right qualities] kept in his heart, but they will be few."

XXXVI.[1053] 1. Mencius said, Tsăng Seih was fond of sheep-dates, and [his son] Tsăng-tsze could not bear to eat them."[1054]

2. Kung-sun Ch'ow asked, saying, "Which is better,—minced meat and roasted meat, or sheep-dates?" Mencius said, "Mince and roast-meat to be sure!" Kung-sun Ch'ow went on, "Then why did Tsăng-tsze eat mince and roast-meat, while he would not eat sheep-dates?" "For mince and roast-meat," was the reply, "there is a common liking, while that for sheep-dates was peculiar. We avoid the name, but do not avoid the surname. The surname is common, but the name is peculiar."[1055]

XXXVII.[1056] 1. Wan Chang asked, saying, "Confucius, when he was in Ch'in, said, 'Why not return? The scholars of my school are ardent and hasty. They advance and seize [their object], but do not forget their early ways.' When Confucius was in Ch'in, why did he think of the ambitious scholars of Loo?"[1057]

2. Mencius replied, "Confucius, not getting men who would pursue the due medium, felt that he must take the ardent and cautiously-decided. The ardent would advance and seize [their object]; the cautiously-decided would keep themselves from certain things. It is not to be thought that Confucius did not wish for men pursuing the due medium, but being unable to assure himself of finding such, he therefore thought of the next class."[1058]

3. "I venture to ask," [said Ch'ow,] "what sort of men they were who could be called 'the ardent?'"

4. "Such," was the reply, "as K'in Chang, Tsăng Seih, and Muh

---

A truly valuable utterance.

[1053] CH. XXXVI. THE FILIAL FEELING OF TSĂNG-TSZE SEEN IN HIS NOT EATING SHEEP'S DATES.

[1054] Par. 1. Tsăng Seih and Tsăng-tsze,—see IV. Pt I. xix. The "sheep's date" was, probably, the fruit of the *zizyphus jujuba*.

[1055] Par. 2. Seih's liking for the sheep's dates was peculiar, so that the sight of them brought him vividly back to his son, who therefore could not bear to eat such dates. There are many rules for avoiding the names of parents, ancestors, rulers, &c.;—see the Book of Rites, I. Pt I. Ch. v. 15-20; *et al*. This is peculiar, probably, to the Chinese, to avoid calling a son by the name of the father.

[1056] CH. XXXVII. THE CHARACTER OF MANY OF CONFUCIUS' DISCIPLES. THE SAGE HAS ONE OBJECT,—TO GET MEN TO PURSUE THE PERFECT PATH. HE HATES ALL MERE SEMBLANCES, AND ESPECIALLY THOSE WHO ARE CONSIDERED BY THE MULTITUDE GOOD, CAREFUL MEN, WHO YET HAVE NO HIGH AIM OR AMBITION.

[1057] Par. 1. See Ana. V. xxi.; though the text there is considerably different from what we find here. Perhaps Kung-sun Ch'ow quoted loosely from memory.

[1058] Par. 2. Most of Mencius' reply here is taken from the words of Confucius in Ana. XIII. xxi.

P'ei were those whom Confucius styled 'the ardent.'"[1059]

5. "Why are they styled 'the ardent?'"

6. [Mencius] said, "Their aim led them to talk magniloquently, saying, 'The ancients! The ancients!' But their actions, compared with [their words], did not come up to them.

7. "When he found that neither could he get those who were [thus] ardent, he wished to get scholars who would consider anything impure as beneath them, and to communicate [his instructions] to them. These were the cautiously-decided,—a class next to the other."

8. [Chang pursued his questioning], "Confucius said, 'They are only the good careful people of the villages at whom I feel no indignation when they pass my door without entering my house. Your good careful people of the villages are the thieves of virtue.' What sort of people were they who could be styled 'the good careful people of the villages?'"[1060]

9. [Mencius replied], "They say [of the ardent], 'Why are they so magniloquent? Their words have not respect to their actions, nor their actions to their words, and then they say, "The ancients! The ancients!" [And] why do these—[the cautiously-decided]—act so peculiarly, and carry themselves so cold and distant? Born in this age, we should be of this age;—to be [deemed] good is all that is needed.' Eunuch-like flattering their generation,—such are your good careful men of the villages."[1061]

10. Wan Chang said, "Their whole village styles those men good and careful. In all their conduct they are so. Why was it that Confucius considered them to be the thieves of virtue?"

11. [Mencius] replied, "If you would blame them, you find nothing to allege. If you would criticize them, you have nothing to criticize. They agree with the current customs; they are at one with an impure age. Their principles have a semblance of right-heartedness and truth; their conduct has a semblance of disinterestedness and purity. All men are pleased with them, and they think themselves right, so that it is impossible to proceed with them to the principles of Yaou and Shun. On this account they are called 'the thieves of virtue.'

12. "Confucius said, 'I hate a semblance which is not the reality. I hate the *yĕw*-weed, lest it be confounded with the growing corn. I hate glib-tonguedness, lest it be confounded with righteousness. I hate sharpness of tongue, lest it be confounded with sincerity. I hate the notes of Ch'ing, lest they be confounded with [true] music. I hate the reddish-blue, lest it be confounded with vermilion. I hate your good

---

[1059] *Par.* 4. K'in Chang was the Laou mentioned in Ana. IX. vi. 4. Tsăng Seih is the same who appears in the preceding chapter. Of Muh P'ei nothing is known.

[1060] *Par.* 8. The first part of the saying here attributed to Confucius is not found in the Analects. For the second see XVII. xiii.

[1061] *Parr.* 9 to 12 contain a good description of the parties in hand.

careful men of the villages, lest they be confounded with the [truly] virtuous'.[1062]

13. "The superior man would simply bring back the unchanging standard [of truth and duty]. That being rectified, the masses of the people are roused [to virtue]. When they are so aroused, forthwith perversities and glossed wickedness disappear."

XXXVIII.[1063] 1. Mencius said, "From Yaou and Shun down to T'ang were five hundred years and more. As to Yu and Kaou Yaou, they saw [those earliest sages], and [so] knew [their doctrines], while T'ang heard those doctrines [as transmitted], and [so] knew them.[1064]

2. "From T'ang to king Wăn were five hundred years and more. As to E Yin and Lae Choo, they saw [T'ang], and [so] knew [his doctrines], while king Wăn heard them [as transmitted], and so knew them.[1065]

3. "From king Wăn to Confucius were five hundred years and more. As to T'ae-kung Wang and San E-săng, they saw [Wăn], and [so] knew his doctrines, while Confucius heard them [as transmitted], and [so] knew them.[1066]

4. "From Confucius to now there are [only] a hundred years and [somewhat] more;—so far from being remote is the distance from the sage in point of time, and so very near at hand was the sage's residence. In these circumstances, is there no one [to transmit his doctrines]? Yea, is there no one [to do so]?"[1067]

## THE END

---

[1062] *Par.* 12. These sayings of Confucius are only found here. Such a string of them is not in the sage's style. The notes of Ch'ing,—see Ana. XV. x. 6.

[1063] CH. XXXVIII. ON THE TRANSMISSION OF THE LINE OF DOCTRINE FROM YAOU TO CONFUCIUS. SAGES MAY BE EXPECTED TO ARISE AT INTERVALS OF ABOUT FIVE HUNDRED YEARS. MENCIUS MIGHT HIMSELF CLAIM TO BE A TRANSMITTER OF CONFUCIUS' DOCTRINES.

[1064] *Par.* 1. According to the received chronology, from the commencement of Yaou's reign to T'ang were more than 550 years. Mencius uses a round number.

[1065] *Par.* 2. From T'ang to king Wăn were more than 600 years. Lae Choo was, perhaps, Chung-hwuy, T'ang's minister;—see the Book of History, IV. ii.

[1066] *Par.* 3. San E-săng or San-e Săng was an able minister of king Wăn; but little more is known of him.

[1067] *Par.* 4. The concluding two sentences wonderfully vex commentators; but all agree that Mencius somehow takes on himself the duty and responsibility of handing down the doctrines of Confucius.—Compare what he says in II Pt II xiii.; III. Pt II. x.; *et al.*